Nathan Söderblom

His Life and Work

'In the choir of the church the Archbishop in his magnificent cope, holding high the venerable crozier, blessing a new church. I saw that spiritual face of his. I saw nothing but this spirit-filled expression. Thus I wished to try to paint him.' Emanuel Vigeland interpreting his painting, now in the Vasa Castle, Uppsala.

Nathan Söderblom

His Life and Work

BY

BENGT SUNDKLER

LUTTERWORTH PRESS

LONDON

First published 1968

Edited with the aid of grants from

Konung Gustaf VI Adolfs 70-årsfond
för svensk kultur
Statens Humanistiska forskningsråd
Carl-Bertel Nathhorsts vetenskapliga och
allmännyttiga stiftelser

SBN 7188 1573 4

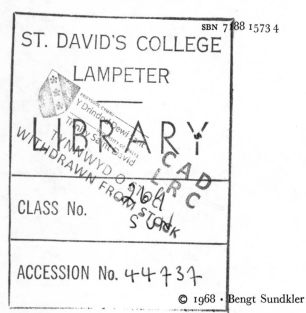
Printed in Sweden by
Almqvist & Wiksells Boktryckeri AB
Uppsala 1968

Contents

List of illustrations

Foreword

Nathan Söderblom, 1866–1931, Archbishop of Uppsala, was one of the pioneers of the ecumenical movement; it is as innovator in this field that we attempt to interpret him in this book. The Life and Work Conference, at Stockholm, 1925, was a result of his vision and work for the unity of the Church.

Yet, Söderblom has been strangely forgotten by the historians. In his native country, Sweden, there was after his death, inevitably, a crop of books and articles about him; but later, some of the Swedes seem to have neglected their great Archbishop. For anyone to undertake to write a Life of Nathan Söderblom seems to evoke a feeling of incredulity: the task is enormous in terms of sheer weight and extent of the work involved. There is also another more subtle warning for anyone so bold as to rush into a job of this kind. You cannot write about Söderblom, we were told, for was he not 'East–West–North and Söderblom'? If you state one thing about him, another, possibly contradictory assertion would prove to be just as relevant. We believe this scepticism to be misplaced in this case and hope that this book will, to some extent, show that there was in Söderblom a much greater unity, consistence and consequence than that for which he is generally given credit.

We have emphasized the genesis and first development of his role as an ecumenical leader; even to the extent of going on one point into a certain amount of detail: the years 1919–1920, under the title 'Finding the Way'. For here, it can be claimed, are the beginnings, the embryo of what became later the ecumenical movement in its modern form.

There are signs which seem to promise that in to-day's new climate of ecumenical relationships, Söderblom's visions and initiatives will be understood anew. Some of the most constructive ecumenical initiatives of recent years, related to the World Council of Churches and to the Vatican, have an affinity to Söderblom's contribution.

It is well-known that Söderblom was the pioneer of 'Life and

Work' in ecumenical history. What is less known, perhaps, is that Söderblom pursued something of a Faith and Order movement of his own, based on Uppsala and on the claims of a Swedish succession, and with an ecclesiological programme which he called 'Evangelical Catholicity'. We have devoted a section of the book to this aspect, under the title 'Uppsala and Catholicity': it is mainly concerned with initiatives and events in the brief and crowded period 1920–1923.

In the three brief chapters dealing with the period prior to 1914, the emphasis is on the preparation for the international task. The concept 'horizon' in this section has not only obvious geographical connotations, but is meant to convey other dimensions as well.

It is hoped that this book for an international public will be followed by a two volume Life of Söderblom in Swedish where we propose to give a much more adequate interpretation of Söderblom's life and work prior to 1914 than has been possible in this context. In the projected Swedish work one would hope to assess his role as a bridge-builder between church and culture in Swedish society, and also to make a more thorough study of the development of his theological concepts.

The great majority of the quotations from Söderblom are, of course my translations from a Swedish, German or French original text, rendered as faithfully as possible. In the course of writing the book I have more than once found myself regretting that in an English book it is out of the question to render some of the quotations in the Swedish original. For Söderblom's Swedish was rich and strong; pithy, with a fondness for the archaic word. I am aware that only too often has it been beyond my linguistic capacity to give an adequate equivalent of the original. Söderblom's own English is of course reproduced as he used it.

I have not personally taken the initiative for this book, but was commissioned to do so. In August 1965, at Uppsala, I was asked by Dr. W. A. Visser't Hooft and Archbishop G. Hultgren to write a Life of Söderblom. Söderblom had always fascinated me. I had also been fortunate enough to have had an interview with Archbishop Söderblom. In March, 1931, at twenty-one, as I was leaving for a year's study in his beloved France, I was called to the Archbishop's House in Uppsala and had half an hour with him; I am therefore one of those who have been under the direct influence of the magic of his personality. Not only that; in those last few weeks of his life, (he died on July 12, 1931) he found time to dictate long letters to that Swedish student in Strasbourg and Paris, planning his future, as he had done for thousands of others, more worthy of his exertions and expectations.

The Söderblom image in the literature is to a large extent determined by the Swedish book published a few months after his death by Söderblom's most brilliant student, Tor Andræ. He focussed interest almost exclusively on Söderblom's youth and his years in Paris.

An authoritative study on Söderblom's ecumenical activity in the period 1914–1918 was published in Swedish, by Dean Nils Karlström, 1947, who had had the unique opportunity of serving as Söderblom's personal secretary for five years. Söderblom's theology of Revelation and Mysticism was studied by Dr. F. Holmström, 1937, and his view of the World religions by Dr. J. M. van Veen, 1940, in Dutch and by Professor E. Ehnmark, 1949, in Swedish. A study of Söderblom as preacher was made in Swedish by Dr. S. Estborn, 1947. A valuable study in French is N. Söderblom, prophète de l'œcuménisme (1948), by Jean Hoffmann.

In 1966, Professor Siegmund-Schultze, now of Soest, Westphalia, published a commented edition of Söderblom's and his own correspondence.

Three volumes of Reminiscences of Söderblom, *Hågkomster och livsintryck*, by Swedes and non-Swedes, were published by the Lindblad publishing house in the years after 1931; and there is the important *Nathan Söderblom In Memoriam 1931*. To these should be added the two volumes of Söderblom's *Sommarminnen*, edited posthumously by his wife Anna Söderblom.

But it is only now that we are in a position to base a study of Söderblom on primary sources in their whole extension. Söderblom was meticulous in preserving his correspondence; in fact he saved and filed every piece of evidence, every scrap of paper. Mrs. Anna Söderblom who survived him by twenty-four years, gave every day of those years to the collection and ordering of her late husband's papers. These are now in the care of the Uppsala University Library. The Nathan Söderblom collection contains:

1. Some 40,000 letters to and from Nathan Söderblom.
2. Seventy big files on special subjects.
3. 150 large and small notebooks, with autobiographical notes, referred to here as diaries;
4. Extensive files of paper-clippings.

5. Eighteen big boxes containing papers relative to the Ecumenical Conference 1925 and its pre-history: this can contain anything on the subject from 1914–1931.

There are also Family letters from Nathan Söderblom to Anna Söderblom and their children. These are under seal. I have been allowed some limited use of these. Ambassador Staffan Söderblom and Mr. Jon-Olof Söderblom have kindly undertaken to make extracts for me from the family papers, referring to certain conferences and travels in 1908, 1911, 1912, 1919–20, 1926–27. I thank Mr. Jon-Olof Söderblom for making these extracts.

In connexion with my research I have interviewed a large number of people who knew Söderblom well: members of his family; relatives of the family's close friends; his old students; and the older generations of pastors in the Uppsala archdiocese; a certain number of Söderblom's co-workers in the ecumenical movement.

Two friends have helped me particularly. Docent Carl Fredrik Hallencreutz read the entire manuscript and gave invaluable criticism both for the structure and the detail of the book. Father Hugh, S.S.F., revised the English of my manuscript. To the contribution made by these two friends I wish to apply the words by Bishop Wordsworth of Salisbury, in thanking Söderblom, in 1910, for his help with a book by Wordsworth, on the National Church of Sweden 'I think it extraordinarily kind of you to take so much trouble to make my work as intelligent as it ought to be.' In this connexion I also thank Dr. Sigfrid Estborn, Dr and Mrs. Byron Swanson, and Dr. Staffan Runestam, the latter a grand-son of Söderblom. I also thank librarians and archivists at the Uppsala University Library and other Swedish and foreign libraries who so generously gave of their time.

Misses Sally-Ann Godden and Patricia Simpson worked on the English of the manuscript. Proofs have been read by Archbishop G. Hultgren, Docent T. Furberg, Mrs. Eva Riad, Dr. S. Runestam, Mr. J. O. Söderblom. I thank them for their help.

Uppsala, Whitsun 1968

Bengt Sundkler.

The Student

At Trönö, Hälsingland, one can still to-day see Jonas Söderblom's Old Testament in Hebrew. It is a solid old volume, edited by Joh. Simonis, Magdeburg, 1712. In the margin there are notes in Latin and Swedish, to certain verses, inscribed by Jonas Söderblom.

The copy has obviously been well-worn; Jonas Söderblom knew his Hebrew particularly well and read his portion of it daily. As he chose the name 'Jonathan' for his son's baptism he was deeply aware of the meaning of the name. Their boy was, indeed, a Gift of God. He seemed healthy and strong and had been spared while their first child, also a boy, born a year earlier had died when only nine months old and was now buried near the north wall of the Church.

Jonathan received two other names in his baptism, Lars Olof. These were saints' names, but also symbols of families and of nations. Lars or Laurentius was the mother's family's Danish name. Olof had been a boy's name in Jonas Söderblom's family at Orsta, Söderala for centuries: The name Jon Olsson had alternated with Olof Jonsson, generation after generation until Jonas, himself the first scholar in that long tradition of Hälsingland yeomen, chose for himself the name of Söderblom. The name Olof suggested the history of his own family as far as one could trace it. They had lived on the same farm at Orsta at least since the sixteenth century. It was thought that in the hillside were the graves of the forefathers from the Iron Age. Jonas Söderblom was rooted in the soil of Hälsingland.

But Pietism shook him and shaped him, as it shaped and formed that whole province of Hälsingland. There was a whole generation of like-minded young curates of the Church in Hälsingland at this time, who whatever the learned and probably rationalistic Archbishop in Uppsala said, were determined to know nothing but Jesus Christ and him crucified. They preached the New Birth, insisted on temperance and took a special interest both in Foreign Mis-

sions and in the emigration movement to America. Jonas Söderblom took the Pietistic concerns very seriously indeed. Pietism shook
him to the core. He found himself in a crisis, and he was driven into
a life of penance and asceticism which threatened to break the
strength of soul and body. He came close to the border line of a
disorder of the mind.[1] A colleague in the ministry helped him to leave
behind 'the threat of the law' and to accept and trust the forgiveness
of sins. He had moved, he felt, from a legalistic to an Evangelical
attitude towards Lutheran Pietism. He hastened along the stony
roads and grassy paths of his parish, his shoes in a sling on his
back, the quicker to move and also, no doubt, in order to save the
expense of shoe-mending.

He was thirty-nine when he married Sophia Blume, then twenty-
three. Jonas had been posted for a while to Hudiksvall, the central
town of Hälsingland: his message caught the attention of some of
the young and there was now in the little town something similar
to that which had happened in the rural parishes: a local revival.
Sophia had just lost her beloved mother, in July 1861. She was
sad and melancholic and eagerly accepted the assurance which the
Pietistic message seemed to bring. The pastor fell in love with her.

As she confided this to her widowed father, she found no understanding. Dr. Laurentius R. Blume was a Dane. In 1834 at the
early age of twenty-four he had qualified as a doctor in Copenhagen. The same year there was a cholera epidemic in Western
Sweden, and an appeal from Gothenburg resulted in four Danish
doctors, including L. R. Blume, going to Sweden; in 1836 he became
a Swedish citizen. In 1854 he was moved to Hudiksvall. As a Danish
doctor of that time he had little patience with Pietists, let alone
the North Swedish brand. He was not impressed by Jonas Söderblom: a fanatic, who was so mean that his wife would 'work herself
to death', was his unfeeling diagnosis of the case.[2]

He knew that his daughter came of good stock. The Blumes were
from Ribe in Denmark. Doctor Blume's father was a district judge
in Roskilde. His wife was Johanne Koefoed, thus bearing a well-
known name in the history of Danish culture; her grandfather M.
Munch had been the mayor of Copenhagen and further back there
was a Bishop of Oslo as one of the forefathers and therefore in
Nathan Söderblom's pedigree.

---

[1] Anna Söderblom, *På livets trottoir*, (1948), p. 85.
[2] L. Blume, *Släkten Blume*, (1961), p. 16.

Dr. Blume had three sons and three daughters with Johanne Koefoed. There was obviously a streak of adventure, of the pull of the high seas, in the family, for the three sons became sailors and sea-captains and one of the daughters, Sophia's sister, married another sea-captain of Norwegian descent, Abrahamsen who did very well for himself as a ship-owner in Stockholm. Later on, as a student in Uppsala, Nathan Söderblom regularly visited this uncle of his. The eldest of Dr. Blume's sons, Niels, was one of many Scandinavians who emigrated to America, in 1863, just in time to be enlisted in the Northern army in the Civil war, where he advanced to Captain in the United States Army. In 1873 he became harbour master at the Mare Island Fleet station, San Francisco. He was a faithful letter writer, particularly to his sister Sophia, and she, and somewhat later her son Nathan, corresponded regularly with Captain Niels Blume in San Francisco. The bonds became particularly strong as in 1889 Svante Söderblom, Nathan Söderblom's younger brother, who did not find High School at Hudiksvall to his taste, emigrated to America. His uncle Niels received him and helped him along, and Svante married a cousin, Niels' daughter.

We have anticipated later events: Sophia Blume married her pastor in 1863. The following year they moved to Trönö. Here their second son, Nathan Söderblom, was born on January 15, 1866.

Trönö was a beautiful part of picturesque Hälsingland. The province was dominated by the Ljusnan river, the Dellen lakes, the deep forests and the Baltic coastline. From the manse on the hill one could see a stream flowing through the valley. On each side lay fine farm houses, for the yeomen of Hälsingland formed a self-relying élite. On the banks of the stream were seven little saw-mills, started by some of the enterprising farmers. These were the result of the new timber activity in the province, under the stimulus of the Hudiksvall Steam–Sawing Mill Company of London at about that time, but which soon ceased.

Looking back on his childhood at Trönö, Archbishop Söderblom would describe the valley as a church: The winding stream and the road were the aisle. The villages on each side on the edge of the wood, were pews; the Grindberget terrace was 'the altar in the east, as it should'. The sighing of the wind in the forest in the west the young boy imagined to be the organ.

Nathan was soon at home in the church, a fine twelfth-century structure, surrounded by a medieval wall. Here and in Hälsingtuna as in the family's native Söderala, Nathan came in touch with twelfth-century churches of great and simple beauty; these early impressions were to condition his appreciation of tradition and continuity. The sound of the bells in the Trönö belfry sanctified the hours of the day and the rhythm of the week: the belfry was medieval in the style of the Nordic staff-churches. Seated in the pastor's family's pew in the Church at Trönö he looked attentive as his father preached his serious, pleading sermons; he also took in all that was to be seen in the packed church. At the back there were two galleries and in the top gallery young boys, who were not always quiet. Some of the medieval sculptures and figures fascinated him; but he tried not to see the picture on the right of the choir window with the dragon's open jaw and the bodies of men falling, and falling, into it. In preference he would study the little votive ship suspended from the roof in the choir. Imagination could take him on that ship along the river passing into the Baltic, and further still. The organist played the last hymn and the pastor's wife took her children by the hand to the members of the congregation outside the porch. 'Almost the strongest memory from my childhood's Church, the Archbishop would recall, 'was the sunny warmth outside the porch, as the congregation filed out and greeted us in their friendly way'.[3]

Back home, in the manse, there were horses and cattle to attend to, for the curate received a considerable part of his keep from the parish farm. During the winter, there was skiing on the breath-taking slopes down to the frozen stream. And in the evenings, by the light of the fire, Mother played the piano and Nathan would sit under the instrument, the more to take in that glorious volume of sound. She would accompany herself and her husband as they sang together from 'Tunes of Zion' or the 'Songs of Ahnfelt', expressions of Pietism's longing to the Heavenly City and Home.

Mother and father were Nathan's first teachers. 'I have in my life had many teachers, but none better than she', said the Archbishop about his mother. 'Therefore, even to-day I know the names of all four Balearic islands. Father's teaching was more eager than methodical. His concern that I would not learn Latin began when I was five and earned me some undigested Latin vocables.'

At nine, Nathan began school in Hudiksvall, a town of some 4,000 inhabitants at that time. On the first day his father took him to

---

[3] Anna Söderblom, op. cit., p. 96.

the school and another young boy heard Söderblom Sr. remarking: 'No, I am not nervous about Nathan. He will manage very well; he has an excellent head on his shoulders.'[4] Pastor Söderblom, now vicar at Bjuråker, some twenty-five miles from Hudiksvall, arranged a house for his three children in town. From a fisherman he bought a house near the town church, and a woman from Trönö was the housekeeper. Supplies of bread and potatoes, some butter and occasionally meat, came from the vicar's farm. There was one cow for milking; Nathan wrote in one of his very first letters. 'The cow eats well—and I believe she is going to thrive but she is a little restless, although we have borrowed for her a little bell from Westin's so that she will feel more at ease.' The cow caused some concern. Nathan wrote to his father asking him to send some mash. This had the intended results: 'Beloved parents. Immanuel. Thank you for the letter ... The cow milks somewhat better because of the mash and the milk also tastes a little better than before.' The daily yield rose from one pottle to two pottles with the result that the neighbours 'Mrs. Jungnell and Aunt Hulda' asked for that extra bounty. 'This I could not refuse them', Nathan stated as a matter of course.

Fourteen of Nathan's letters from the first two years are extant. They are addressed to: 'My beloved Parents. Immanuel!' *or* 'My beloved Parents. Grace and Peace.' They show a young boy with commonsense and practical ability; the eldest in the group of brothers and sisters, very much in charge of the others.

Occasionally there was in the letters a word of impatience in that Northern outpost of the world that the summer never arrived. On April 28, 1876 he wrote to say that he had had to stay inside for he had chaps on his hands; but he had put on glycerin a few times and was sure this would help. On another occasion: 'the palate is better now. It is not diphteria but we are skinless in the palate and on the tip of the tongue.' Outside, in the town there were the social tensions of a class society, expressed among the young in streetfights between the relatively privileged school-boys, *'piltarne'* and the others from 'East of town', called *'schaschasare'*.

His thoughts were with the parents: 'How are you? Do not work too hard so that you fall ill; rest ye sometimes, then it will be easier and more fun to work. As from time to time your thoughts fly to your children in town, let them not rest there with anxiety, but please believe that we try to steer everything for the best'.

---

[4] H. Palmgren, 'Det skulle kunna skrivas ...,' In *Idun* (Stockholm), July 26, 1931.

The whole scene in that household was from a time many decades before any Welfare–Sweden was even conceivable. This was Poverty–Sweden, a country which barely had scraped through a disastrous crop-failure in the late 1860's. Also in Hälsingland, emigration to America became the solution of the economic crisis, and Pietist pastors, such as L. Esbjörn, went with the groups to that other country. There was also constant letter contacts between the Pietists in Hälsingland and their relatives in Illinois, Kansas and Minnesota.

The Hudiksvall harbour saw many of them leave the province and the country. The harbour was one of Hudiksvall's great attractions, also to Nathan Söderblom. There were sailing ships bound for Stockholm and Helsinki, Riga and Southampton. Söderblom wrote later, 'The ships and their captains and men awakened in us our imagination and our longing for adventure.' He knew of ships through his maternal uncles. 'The barks which filled the harbour were surrounded by a poetry which made every contact highly appreciated.' In these years at Hudiksvall he learned a lot about ships; Nathan Söderblom never forgot that he was also a Blume and *therefore* a sailor like his uncles. This interest stood him in good stead when later he became a seaman's pastor at Calais and Dunkirk and, as Archbishop, Chairman *ex-officio* of the Church Board for work among seamen.

When Nathan was fifteen, in 1881, he was confirmed by his father. Confirmation in the Swedish Church at that time, as now, was always taken by the local clergy and not by the bishop and was preceded by a thorough grounding in Luther's Catechism. Jonas Söderblom's course for his son was different but no less thorough: it was a condensed course in Christian Doctrine, as understood by Jonas Söderblom. There is extant a neat little notebook in Nathan's hand after the father's dictation. One can hear the eager Pietist vicar proclaiming his message.

'Without Christ, God is a consuming fire; in Christ, our reconciled Father ... When do we become too strong for God? When we hold up His word and promises to Him to say: Do You remember these? Then I am blessed ... Again, when does God become too strong for us? When He can make us be still to His calling grace so that through self-scrutiny we recognize our guilt and spiritual death and therefore, unconditionally, must obey His gracious calling and in all our unworthiness beg and hope for and accept the unmerited grace of salvation in Christ.'

There was a Puritan streak of ascesis in the father and in his confirmation teaching. Nathan wrote after his dictation: 'Fast is to nourish the spiritual life so that our desires can be checked. Fast is the food of the soul and the tinder of devotion.[5] The spark fires easier in dry than in wet wood. The fasting body is the drywood etc'. He was also given what the father regarded as useful apologetic arguments on Baptism. 'Do children need to be baptized? Yes, for they are by nature the children of wrath. Are they fit for baptism? Yes, for they believe.' About the manner of baptism, Nathan made notes on the difference between the two Greek prepositions *Apo* and *Ek;* in Jesus' case he rose *Apo,* from the water, and this, according to Jonas Söderblom, in order to show the form in which baptism was to take place.[6]

Later in life, the professor and Archbishop, engaged in interchurch conversations on the ministry and sacraments, was to insist on the quality of the teaching for confirmation in the Swedish Church; he must have thought then of the months under his father's care.

In his home, Nathan could not but notice a disturbing and widening distance between the parents. Dr. Blume, his mother's father, had found Jonas Söderblom a fanatic, and he had his reasons. The mother's light, humorous and poetic disposition was not allowed much elbow room in the gloomy manse, particularly as the children had left for school. An increasing deafness tended to isolate her. At Norrala she withdrew to her room and lived to herself, a placid matrona, reading and re-reading the letters from her children, particularly from Nathan, occasionally making in her diary an anguished note about the husband's harshness.

And he? Well, he had his Pietistic message to proclaim. Relentlessly he drove himself and all around him. Ambitious on behalf of his children, he was never fully satisfied even with Nathan's

---

[5] Jonas Söderblom used the archaic Swedish noun *'tunder'*, *'andaktens tunder'*. To my knowledge it was never used by any other pastor, at least not in a confirmation class! This was another point where Jonas and Nathan were of one mind: They loved the provincial archaic words. When the Archbishop made his visitations to Hälsingland, he liked to sport verbal remnants of his Söderala dialect.

[6] Whether Söderblom tried these arguments out on his good friend in the school, Nathaniel Andersson–Schmidt we do not know: they were neighbours in the little town of Hudiksvall. Nathaniel's parents were Baptists. Schmidt emigrated to the United States where he, having turned Unitarian in religion, became Professor of History of Religion at the Cornell University. Söderblom and Schmidt kept up the friendship throughout life.

brilliant results in school. Yet, Nathan was his pride, and there was unmistakably an affinity between the two. This increased and was deepened over the years, until his father's death and, as Nathan Söderblom would claim, beyond death. What was it that to this extent bound Nathan to his father, apart from general filial considerations?

Was it perhaps, something particular in that eager voice, in those shining, pleading eyes? Despite all unfeeling waywardness and mannerisms of the old man, Nathan recognized that which to him became the sign and secret of religion: the spark of the Spirit. Driving himself through fasting and overwork, Jonas would say, 'Hungry dogs chase the better'. This was uncouth, and Sophia, née Blume, said so; this was the Hälsinge hunter and peasant in him from times immemorial, in those forests and glades, at lake-side and on the river's banks. Nathan recognized in this something fine and noble. He half discovered it as he took down those notes in the Confirmation class: 'the tinder of devotion'—was that not something which connected Jonas Söderblom with that flame of religion, beyond and, indeed, long before Pietism: the *scintilla* of the soul?

Nathan Söderblom was very much aware of the mysterious ways and irrational laws of heredity. He attempted to understand them in the great and in the near-greats whom he studied; in Luther, and in W. Rudin, one of his Uppsala professors. He must have meditated on his own share of heredity from those two clans of Söderala, Hälsingland and Ribe, Denmark when he wrote:

Innumerable generations are behind the child in whose embryo the wonderful treasure lies dormant. Dangerous heritages, good heritages, weak heritages, subdivided in a thousand different ways, have produced diverse results in his forefathers. A combination and a mutual influence takes place from the natural gifts of his father and mother respectively, but also from earlier heritages. ... Then the gift of genius bursts forth apparently as suddenly and unexpectedly as those phenomena which De Vries has called mutation. ... We shall never be able to analyse perfectly the causes and elements of creative genius. We shall never be able to predict it. The human eye cannot penetrate the sequence of causes and effects. Our Christian faith and our constructive outlook on life and history know something more. They know that God works in the complicated course of generations, and that the right man is there to do his work, when he is wanted.[7]

---

[7] Söderblom, *The Living God* (1932), p. 354–355. Cf. also Bengt Hildebrand, *Ärkebishop Nathan Söderbloms härstamning*, in *Personhist. tidskrift* 1931, p. 153; L. Blume, *Släkten Blume* (1961); — Anna Söderblom, Nathan Söderblom's fader, in *På Livets Trottoir*, 1 (1948), p. 71; — Nathan Söderblom, Letters to his parents.

The last four years at Hudiksvall Söderblom spent in the 'Gymnasium', concluded with matriculation in 1883. He received a thorough classical education and of modern languages: German, French and Swedish. English was only an optional in the last two years. He excelled in Scripture and Church History.

Looked at from a wider point of view it was not a foregone conclusion that he should follow in his father's footsteps for the choice of his career. The father's own preference for theology, coming from peasant stock, expressed a more general trend. But in the second generation, the range of choice tended to be more varied. Jonas Söderblom's successor as curate at Trönö, Thörnell, had two sons of whom one became an officer, later Commander-in-Cief of the Swedish Armed Forces; the second, Professor of Latin (who was to help Archbishop Söderblom with the finishing touches to his two letters to the Vatican!) In Nathan Söderblom's case he never seems to have hesitated. To his father's great satisfaction, he decided, as now he went on to the University at Uppsala, to study theology with a view to become, as his father before him, a priest in the Swedish Church.

'The driest period in world history': this was Söderblom's view of the 1880's and the Uppsala of that time. At least this was how it appeared to him as he looked back on the decade from the more interesting view-point of the following years when imagination and poetry had come into their own again. The 1880's were a tough time: 'The grey seriousness led to a denial of the Spirit and of God.'[8]

Uppsala in 1883, the year Nathan Söderblom arrived, was a little town of 17,000 inhabitants; with its thirteenth century red-brick Cathedral in the centre, and the Archbishop's house and the University next to it; the Vasa Castle on the hill; heavy old stone houses in the centre of town, and new wooden two-storey buildings in the Luthagen sector. The town was fifty miles away from Stockholm by rail, introduced in 1861. From Uppsala one could reach the capital in two hours. The university, founded in 1477, now had 1700 students, with a staff of some fifty full professors, of whom eight were in the Theological Faculty. Uppsala was the see of the Archbishop of the Church of Sweden. Archbishop A. N. Sundberg ruled his diocese and the church. As Archbishop he was expected to be an authoritarian and one must say this for him that he lived up to these expectations, not least, with regard to revivalist movements in his own

---

[8] Söderblom, *Svenskars fromhet,* II (1941), p. 128.

church or to the Augustana brethren in the United States. Sometimes he could be less than forthcoming. When in September 1889 an English visitor, by name of Randall Davidson, [then] Dean of Windsor, asked for an interview, Sundberg whose knowledge of English was limited replied:

'When I sended my last letter to you, Reverend Sir, I believed that I would be at home 10th September, but I fear now that I probably will become an unsteady traveller during the whole month. Best therefore to leave all hope of our meeting. . . .[9]

In the Cathedral one could hear Dean Torén preaching his Evangelical sermons, or Professor Sundelin whose message Söderblom liked, all the more as he took a great personal interest in the field of study which Sundelin represented: Church History. In his letters Söderblom often reported that he had listened to the Methodist preacher, F. Åhgren, whose message and presentation attracted him. Söderblom often preferred to walk to country churches near Uppsala, particularly Uppsala-Näs, to hear Professor W. Rudin, a meditative preacher with a message stamped by prayer and the concern for the inner life.

Not all Uppsala students at that time studied; there were so many other things to do in 'the town of eternal youth'. Söderblom was a real student;he worked hard and resolutely, and spent a decade at it, 1883–1892. J. Schumpeter, who of course had personal reasons of his own to glorify the years between twenty and thirty, referred to 'the sacred fertile third decade' in a scholar's life. The Austrian's formula also fits this Swedish case. Söderblom not only laid the foundation of an unusually solid classical and theological education, but also cultivated that charisma of communication which, in the new milieu of the University, he must have discovered as being to a unique extent his very own.

Söderblom took three years over his B.A., with honours in Greek and with very good results in Hebrew, Arabic and in Latin; to this he added Nordic languages, Philosophy and a smattering of Geology. (According to the rules at that time Arts students had to add one Science subject to their degree). After his B.A. degree, in September 1886, he turned to Theology, and this at a time when there were exceptionally few recruits for theological study at Uppsala. The great majority of Swedish priests at this time took a minor degree,

---

[9] G. K. A. Bell, *Randall Davidson* (1952[3]), p. 156.

called 'Dimission'. Söderblom decided to try for the Candidatus Theologiae; in the years 1883–93 there were at Uppsala some 475 who passed the former and 50 only the latter examination.

Söderblom could now build on the splendid linguistic foundation which he had acquired. His was a rare knowledge of New Testament Greek. As a matter of course he always had his Nestle edition at his elbow. In 1922 on a journey in Germany he mislaid his beloved copy of Nestle, given him by that other ecclesiastical scholar, Dr. Ryle (of Winchester and Westminster). His diary on that occasion had an anguished cry of sadness at the parting of a very dear friend. As to further studies in Hebrew his first move after having joined the Theological Faculty was to take part in a special seminar in the unvocalized text of Talmud led by Professor Almkvist and Rabbi Klein, the latter from now on one of Söderblom's close friends. The members of the seminar were all university dons, and Söderblom at twenty was definitely the Benjamin of the group.

For some time he considered specializing in the Old Testament and always tried to keep effectively in touch with the latest developments of Old and New Testament research. His life-long friendship with S. A. Fries, beginning about 1889, was helpful, for Fries was passionately interested in editions and pseudoepigrapha, and their correspondence has many a reference to these intricate matters.

At about the same time began Söderblom's contacts with Dr. F. Fehr, Pastor Primarius in Stockholm: Old Testament and Talmud scholar; the propounder of Ritschlian theology in Sweden; brilliant preacher and teacher. Fehr's example and personality stimulated Söderblom's efforts in the field of Biblical research. We emphasize this interest of Söderblom's in Bible research, as we later shall make the point that Söderblom was not so much the *Religionsgeschichtler* who happened to make certain excursions into the field of Christian theology, but rather the Bible scholar and Church historian who also studied the history of the religions.

In the Theological Association at the University, Söderblom had opportunities of discussing the new learning of Wellhausen and the other moderns. He did not accept this new theology without struggle and anxiety. When he read later of Luther's *Angst*, the Reformer's *angustiae et terrores conscientiae*, he recognized these words as an adequate description of his own state of mind, 'when the theory of the truth of Christianity wavered and fell to pieces'. He could not understand later generations who without qualms seemed to come to terms with ready-made solutions. 'For a sacred weightiness rested

on these questions of the character and history of the Bible.'[1] In the
end, the discoveries and conclusions of the Wellhausen school appeared to him as a great liberation and he said so to his own joy
and to the consternation of others. In the last resort, his theological
study became and remained a personal concern to him.

In April 1888, he wrote in his diary.

I am studying Exegesis. ... Never forget that behind all revelation
there is the one, eternal divine reality. Look for that, as [your] goal,
not the expositions thereof. Do not focus on the books of the Bible, for
remember they are only the means. As you read Isaiah, or Daniel, or
Genesis; do not ask: What kind of God was Isaiah's God? but rather:
What did Isaiah know of the one, eternal Divine Reality—God.'

Together with S. A. Fries he shared an admiration for the scholar's
exact knowledge and the specialist's command of his particular field.
Yet, even at that time he was aware of the dangers of the specialist's
ivory tower. In a speech in 1892 he warned the freshmen of that
year of limitations of the mere specialist.

The specialists, i.e. those who are content with life's small, external, limited
goals, have their dens but the Son of man hath no place where to rest
his head. This I interpret as the mind which does not limit its horizon
to the little, easily attained goals in life but which looks ... for the vision
of a true and noble mankind.'[2]

It was a widening of the horizons he wanted, for himself and the
Church. Reading Pfleiderer's Philosophy of Religion, he was struck
by the danger of too narrow a view in theology. He celebrated his
twenty-sixth birthday by making this note in his diary:

I am surprised as I see what epigones we are. Our range of vision is
infinitely more narrow than at the beginning of the century. Already in
Schleiermacher and Herder all these thoughts emerge which we [now] call
new and which must find a place for themselves in our time.'[3]

Church history and the history of Christian Doctrine were his
great interests at the beginning of the 1890's. Ritschl, Harnack, Kaftan, Pfleiderer: any book or article produced by these great German
scholars was immediately bought, read and discussed by Söderblom
and Fries: resulting in review articles or in a lecture in the Theo-

---

[1] Söderblom, *Svenskars fromhet*, 2, p. 140.
[2] Söderblom, Diary 1892, p. 100, September 29, 1892.
[3] Ibid., January 15, 1892.

logical Association or in the more intimate circle of four or five friends, where Söderblom, Fries and N. J. Göransson discussed theology, literature and current affairs.

With this interest in theological matters Söderblom passed his Candidatus Theologiae examination in December 1892 with distinction. It is worthy of note that he had earned his highest credits in the two most exacting subjects at this time, Old Testament and Church History. His contacts with the great Uppsala historian Harald Hjärne stimulated his interest in History. He now prepared a series of books on Luther and the Reformation, but also on the Early Church. When, three years later, the Church history chair in Uppsala became vacant, Söderblom, writing from Paris discussed with himself and with Fries whether he should apply for the post and devote himself to Church History.

In the meantime, however, he had decided to follow another line of study and research.

The Eighth Orientalist Congress, held at Stockholm (and Oslo) in 1889 had greatly stimulated interest in the study of Oriental and Asian religions and languages. Here Max Müller, C. de Harlez, J. Darmesteter and other great European scholars, together with turbaned Parsees and Indians appeared on the Swedish scene; some of Söderblom's close friends lectured there, such as K. Fries and G. Klein. Surprisingly Söderblom himself does not seem to have been a delegate; he may have been thought to be too young. After the event he wrote to his home of the interesting talks he had had with some of the Swedish delegates and of their experience.[4]

An article by J. H. Moulton in *The Thinker*, 1892, on Persian religion caught his eye. He discussed it with his friend, professor J. A. Ekman, who held the chair with the somewhat mysterious name 'Theological Prenotions and Theological Encyclopedia'. They decided that Söderblom should specialize in Persian religion and prepare a doctoral thesis in that field. He knew the real reason why he did this. He wrote from Uppsala to his friend N. J. Göransson.

'I am in Iran, Persia, just getting my bearings. It may appear as somewhat queer from an economic point of view to choose for a doctoral thesis a new area, when I am already well versed in e.g. History of Christian Doctrine. But left to my own devices, I may all the same be useful. I regard it as a happy complement to use that assurance and joy of the

---

[4] Cf. K. U. Nylander, *Orientalistkongressen*, (1890) and Söderblom, The Living God (1932), p. 167.

scholar which Ritschl has given me in pointing to our [own] prophet as the greatest, to Christ the Unique, in order to study the other God-revealers who have given to others their particular solutions of the problems of religion. If thus I could arrive at a concrete presentation of the history of religion, I would have reached my proudest goal. Dreams, you will say, Göran; happy dreams, I say.'[5]

Rapid in his movements, he had the ambition to conclude his Avesta study in a year or so and made preparations to this end. It proved to be a much more exacting and time-consuming exercise, but he had laid a good foundation in learning the fundamentals of Avesta's Persian from K. V. Zettersteen, later professor of Semitic languages at the Uppsala University. At the Sorbonne he was going to receive more stimulation for this study.

To Söderblom the Student Missionary Association in Uppsala constituted a bridge between the Pietistic Hälsingland from which he came and the wide world to which he turned. Jonas Söderblom and with him his whole generation of young pastors in Hälsingland were 'mission-friends'. The greatest among them, (later Bishop) Lars Landgren, incumbent in Delsbo, even wrote an impressive history of Protestant missions, in two solid volumes. As soon as the Uppsala Student Missionary Association was founded in 1884, Söderblom became a member.

The eighteen-eighties were an exciting and creative decade in the history of the Student Missionary Movement. It was in 1888 that the watchword of the Student Volunteer Movement was formulated, 'the evangelization of the world in this generation'. The American movement, under John R. Mott and Robert Wilder and others, inspired corresponding movements in other parts of the world. The Uppsala Association proved to be dynamic and had an ambitious programme. To Söderblom personally this group was important from three points of view. Firstly it gave him a thorough knowledge of missionary problems and contacts with corresponding movements in America and on the Continent. Secondly, it was to him a hearth of Christian fellowship, where Pietistic warmth was combined with the concern for a wider intellectual horizon. Here he also met with a religious challenge the solution of which he was to find in his conversion in 1890. Thirdly, it was not least because of his missionary concern and interest that he turned to that study which was

---

[5] Söderblom, February 18, 1893, to N. J. Göransson.

to be his special calling in the world of learning, the history of religions and, as we shall show presently, it was with the fundamental question of Christian missions that he undertook this study.

The Uppsala Association included some very remarkable young men. Natanael Beskow, poet, artist and social reformer, wrote mission hymns, published in the little collection of mission songs which the Association produced. One of these was the splendid *'Ack, saliga dag'*: 'Oh, Jubilee day of the world's expectation when earth is God's Kingdom of blessed accord.' Forty years later, through *Communio,* this was to be known as 'the Stockholm hymn', a clarion call of the ecumenical movement. H. Danell, later Söderblom's colleague as professor and as bishop, E. Folke, later missionary in China, E. Heuman, later bishop in South India, belonged to the group. Karl Fries was one of the leaders in the association. He represented a type of Student leader that impressed Söderblom particularly: scholar in Semitic languages and highly proficient in a number of modern languages; extrovert, enterprising, with a wide international horizon. In this group Söderblom also had the opportunity of meeting a number of Scandinavian and international missionaries. In 1888, the Association made an ambitious move. Its own Missions review under the name of *Meddelanden* was launched. Fries suggested Söderblom's name as editor; he accepted and held the post for five years.

One cannot but be impressed by this publication. It was the only one of its kind in Sweden and in Scandinavia, and comprised some articles of real excellence. Söderblom himself published his very first article here in 1888, on St. Ansgar, the first, French, missionary to Sweden. Söderblom had also the satisfaction of publishing in Meddelanden, an article by his father, on Mission interest in Hälsingland and on Nisima of Japan, by a Miss Anna Forsell, whom we shall meet presently.

The task as editor of *Meddelanden* was one he obviously liked. Sometimes it was unavoidable that readers might take exception to some article. This happened in 1890 when H. W. Tottie, [then] Secretary to the Church of Sweden Mission, had written an article which in part was less than generous to the Fosterlandsstiftelsen's Mission, suggesting that the appearance on the Swedish scene of this latter mission pointed to the divided state of missions in Sweden. A correspondent objected violently to some passages in the article and informed the Editor that he wanted to withdraw his subscription.

Söderblom's answer is extant, a four page draft in lead pencil. It is a study in persuasion, already showing some of the diplomatic tact which was to characterize the ecumenical Archbishop.

It cannot but cause deep sorrow if I and the Executive of the Student Missionary Association through some lack of consideration on our part have deprived our Association of the joy of counting you among our friends. In so far as the attitude of *Meddelanden* in this matter has given cause for some painful misunderstanding, I pray you kindly to make allowance for it.

Söderblom was to experience, that theological study could be what P. T. Forsyth once called 'one of the dangerous industries'. In 1888 and 1889 he studied the New Testament and was confronted with the new theories about the synoptic gospels. This was very different from the Bible teaching of Pietistic Hälsingland. Some of these modern theories on the Bible shook him, but not excessively. The young student soon felt that he had his own contribution to give to this problem. In the Theological Association, in November 1889, he tried to show that the authors of the synoptic Gospels were dependent on one another and the oldest Apostolic writing was an Aramaic version of what became St. Matthew's Gospel. He had also, at last, passed his examination in the New Testament for Professor Myrberg, a Swedish representative of J. T. Beck's theology. The tricky point in that connexion was to get the professor in a mood to give the oral exam. Söderblom had hoped to have this done with by April–May 1889, but the professor pleaded over-work, and that he could not attend to Söderblom or any other student until after the summer holidays. It was not until October that he was prepared to receive Söderblom, now for a four hours trial. Söderblom reported on the performance to his home.

It was an elementary and superficial exam, and add to that [the professor's] oddities. On the Epistle to the Hebrews, he asked what in the Old Testament corresponded to Christ's high priestly office. I mentioned prayer, high priestly prayer. Yes, that is correct; but [more precisely], it corresponds to the incense-offering. But, what about the burnt-offering and the sin-offering? I replied, that is Christ sacrificing himself. 'No, no, it was not so. The sin-offering which our Saviour offered as High Priest is the sins of men which are taken away, and the burnt-offering are those people who allow themselves to be sanctified.' Whoever can invent anything like that? Is that not queer, dear Father? But apart from this he was kind and friendly. ...

In the following letter Söderblom wrote on Myrberg.
'His lack of orthodoxy I would not criticize, but what makes one

fed up is the superficial and uninterested way in which he set about to explore one's knowledge.'

But there was a deeper dissatisfaction in his heart. He wrote in his diary, August 15, 1889, while still on holiday in his parent's home:

This is a dismal time. I am longing and looking for something, and more than ever I feel my own emptiness. I discover how all my work tastes of my own limitation and emptiness. Oh, that I had that richness which could fill my poor heart. I feel I do not possess the right sense of sin and guilt. It is rather an empty longing and yearning for some kind of contents, something which could fill my personality. But ... so far as I have this longing this hungry yearning, I own at least something ... Rom. 8:26, 'Then the Spirit itself maketh intercession for us with groanings which cannot be uttered'. Yesterday I was looking for a friend. He was away. Then I experienced what is written here [in Rom. 8]. Sighs came through without words. But dare I believe, that I may taste it?

Later he was to explain that he persevered in this condition of longing and expectation 'for weeks and months'; this refers to the autumn 1889. The decisive crisis and change came in the following Christmas holiday, 1889–90 in his parents' home at Norrala.

This crisis in Söderblom's life has been studied by the writers on Söderblom. Tor Andræ's analysis has been widely accepted as decisive. Andræ concluded that the conflict was double, religious and scientific.[6] Intellectual doubt and the scruples of the conscience were the background for his conversion. While this is of course true, it now seems that we must add another aspect.

The conflict was, in fact, even more complicated than that. There were three factors, three relationships involved: to those already mentioned must be added Söderblom's relation to his father. In one of his diaries hitherto not available, there is a passage of special importance. Sometime in January 1890, Söderblom wrote:

I had feared for this holiday. Earlier there had been clashes between Father and myself. I feared once again to loose something of the veneration for my dear self-sacrificing father and to be lacking in respect for him. And yet this Christmas turned out to be one of the sweetest and happiest. Mother sickly and weak. Svante [Söderblom's brother] in San Francisco. Yet it was felt in the mutual love and in the fact that God healed the storms and the wounds which had afflicted our family, [so as] to give it a good issue, so unexpectedly good; as I now write (January 24) it was felt and is now felt such a full and sweet happiness that I have a pre-

---

[6] Tor Andræ, *Nathan Söderblom* (1931) p. 107.

sentiment that it cannot last long. ... Mother, who has *suffered* as immensely as you? May God give richly to you, unspeakably beloved Mother,
for what you have suffered and struggled; my father thinks and expects
only too highly on my behalf. I can never live up to all his expectation.
He lives for us. Never a thought of [his] own comfort. Always only of us.
Let me as recompense for his sacrificing toil be a good man if not a great
man.

After having written these words about his father, Jonas Söderblom, he now turned to an interpretation of his religious conversion. A neighbour to the manse, a farmer's wife, gave him a copy
in Swedish of a book by W. P. Mackay, *Grace and Faith*. A few
words on St. John 3 in that book were of particular help: on Moses
lifting up the serpent in the wilderness as the type of how the Son
of Man must be lifted up. 'He suddenly understood that the Cross
... had achieved something. It introduced a new epoch. Here is my
Saviour. I must believe. Thanks to my God for this faith I have
not given to myself.'

Somewhat later, at Uppsala, reading a review in *Theologische
Literaturzeitung,* he felt he was given a new understanding also of
the intellectual problem with which he was faced through modern
Bible criticism. 'Suddenly, not as lightning but as the clear light of
the day' he saw that revelation consisted not in words or books.
'But God has acted with men in a holy history. The room widened
and became so light, so light. Assurance was founded not on a book
or on many books, but on what God had done in history and on the
person and work of Jesus Christ', interpreted to men by a later,
fallible, yet immensely valuable tradition. The whole thing seemed
as if a revelation, a liberation, and as if he was brought on to a solid
foundation.

We believe that in this case the typical Pietistic conversion story
should be read together with the account of the overcoming of the
conflict with his father. The conversion while understood by Söderblom as a return to the Heavenly Father, was just as much a reconciliation with his earthly father. It may well be argued which of
these came first. It is quite possible, although this can only be a
conjecture, that the reconciliation with Jonas Söderblom signified
the opening of the sluicegates, and the Pietistic conversion at the
reading of Mackay's tract followed.

We suggest that, on a deep level of the personality, his religious
conversion was a 'role-acceptance', a 'role-taking' of the role of the
Pietist father. The Schjelderups pointed out that Luther represents

the type of what they called 'father-religion' (as compared with 'mother-religion' and 'self-religion'). Söderblom clearly represents this type of father-religion.

He was far from willing to kow-tow to Jonas Söderblom. When the neurotic father would criticize him, Nathan would answer back quite firmly.[7] But there had been established between them, about Christmas 1889, a new relationship; and the new role-taking indicated here was strengthened in Nathan Söderblom as he went abroad to America and to Paris. There are passages which have tempted us to recognize father-substitutes in Moody at New Haven 1890 and Auguste Sabatier (who had once been a farmer's pastor in the Cevennes!) in Paris in the late eighteen-nineties.

His close fellowship with his father before and after Jonas Söderblom's death is a point to which we shall have to return. Some three years later, in 1893, Söderblom was to have another decisive spiritual experience. After having taken a Sunday morning service near Uppsala he had a direct experience of God's holiness. The sense of this was so overwhelming and overpowering that he could not remain standing. [He experienced this as] 'the cross; the miracle of God's holiness. Since then he has not been able in spite of everything to doubt in God.'[8]

In its broadest terms, the conversion was the Uppsala student's expression of identification with the piety of Hälsingland rather than with Pietism; it also made him ready, later on, for a sense of real affinity and brotherhood with those who placed special emphasis on the second birth. While being reticent in references to his experience, he knew that he had himself been there.[9]

---

[7] There is an important letter from Nathan Söderblom to 'My dear Father'. It is undated, but must have been written either before or just after Christmas 1889. The father had criticised him for 1: modern spelling 2: his adventurous and profligate plans to visit America. Nathan answers that he wishes to follow his father's will in everything. 'But if there is going to be anything to me, I must try to think for myself'. Later he adds: 'wherever I look, I see that on so many counts I have to ask Daddy for forgiveness, forgiveness because I fail to be a good son before God and men.'

[8] [Holmström], *Sv. Teol. Kvartalskrift*, 1935, p. 339. On this occasion he was 'with a friend', identified as Anna Söderblom, cf. S. Estborn, op. cit., p. 25 and interview with Estborn.

[9] T. Andræ, *Nathan Söderblom*, p. 107; F. Holmström, *Svensk Teol. Kvartalskrift*, (11) 1935, p. 321 with references to the passages in Söderblom's own writings dealing with his conversion. S. Estborn, *Under Guds grepp*, p. 24; H. Sundén, *Religionen och rollerna*, (1959) p. 51. H. and K. Schjelderup, *Ueber drei Haupttypen der religiösen Erlebnisformen*, 1932. Söderblom, Letters and Diaries.

Uppsala seemed far away from Hälsingland but Söderblom very faithfully kept in touch with the home province. He subscribed to the Hudiksvall weekly newspaper and at least once a week he wrote to his home, as a rule on Sunday afternoons. Until 1893, he was in fact registered in the Norrala parish; only in that year did he make the official move to the parish of Uppsala. As was the case with other country students, the student club or 'Nation', in his case Gästrike-Hälsinge, became a point of orientation; it was the extended hand of the home, reaching to the University. His friends in the first years were old Hudiksvall students, two of them prominent law students, including Herman Palmgren, who were going to reach the high ranks in the Swedish civil service.

After his B.A. in 1886, he felt free to take on such posts of responsibility as the members of the 'Nation' (with a total of some sixty-five members in 1890) would entrust to him. The Gästrike-Hälsinge Nation had moved into their new house in 1880, thereby acquiring considerable prestige. Söderblom climbed the ladder in the little world of the 'Nation': He became member of the Debating Society in 1886. (Some of the themes discussed in this society were: 'Does conscience afford sufficient guidance to moral action?' 'Ought the state to give full freedom of religion to its subjects and does the Swedish state do so?' 'Have we the right to regard Christianity as the highest possible religion?');[1] and member of the committee on 'Self-help' (which seems mainly to have spent its time on squabbles about the paragraphs of its constitution). In 1890–91, for two years, he was the Librarian of his Nation and the following year 'First Curator,' the highest post in the Nation. As a parallel to these club activities he cultivated his musical interests. He devoted a great deal of time to the study of harmonics and practised piano and organ assiduously and with gusto. Conductor of the Nation's own little choir 1886–1889, he joined the 'General' Choir of the Uppsala students to become elected, in 1890, as a member of the exclusive, internationally renowned 'O.D.', the Servants of Orpheus: as an Archbishop he was to become one of the most famous 'Great-Uncles' of all times in the O.D.

Music drew him to Eric Gustaf Geijer, poet, musician, historian, philosopher (d. 1847). His study of Geijer was of great importance for Söderblom's personal development. He could not but feel a certain affinity with Geijer and his joyful message of 'being at home

---

[1] *Gästrike–Hälsinge Nation 1811–1911*, (1911), p. 109.

in existence'. Geijer was the authority of the Swedish philosophy of personality. 'The personality is the greatest thing in history!' He emphasized what he called, 'the process of renewal—*förnyelseprocessen*—in history'. He insisted on the uniqueness of each personality, while related to the organic whole of a people. From this, Söderblom derived his appreciation of the uniqueness of provincial or national culture and language.

Through these activities he became known in wider circles of students concerns and in February 1892 was elected Vice President of the Uppsala Students Corps, 'as the most suitable representative of the Conservatives in the Student body', as he intimated to his parents. In September 1892, this was followed by his election to the important task of President of the Uppsala Students Corps. At the same time he was editor of the review of the Student Missions Association, and chairman of the local group of the YMCA; he was kept busy.

Something else happened to him. Suddenly, as it seemed, he emerged as a speaker of a unique quality. Herman Palmgren, Söderblom's friend, who for eight years shared their little two room flat in Uppsala wrote after Söderblom's death: 'Later in life [Söderblom] was lauded as a brilliant speaker, not to say a genius as a speaker. Therefore it is remarkable that during my student time, I never heard him give a speech. Later, as he was elected Curator of his Nation, his previously unknown rhetorical talent blossomed and he gave festival speeches the like of which one could not imagine.'[2] How to explain this seemingly sudden bursting into blossom about 1890? The performances in the little world of the 'Nation' gave him much of the self-assurance he needed. There was also the liberation following upon the complicated crisis about New Year 1890.

His first speeches in the Hälsinge Nation gave him a chance to try the wings of oratory to unwonted flights. In his diary he noted on one occasion that at a Nation's dinner he addressed the Rector of the University together with two foreign guests, one from America, the other from Japan. He also made careful observations on the performance of other speakers and entered these in his diary for his own benefit. He noted how the Vice-Chancellor of the Uppsala University in one short response used the word *'förhållande'* (relationship) no less than seventeen times: this taught him the virtue of variation in his own speeches.

---

[2] H. Palmgren, interview, in *Idun* (Stockholm), 1931, July 26.

He could now allow himself to combine in a striking phrase his rich intellectual associations to the different worlds of learning and experience with which he had come into contact. This, for instance, in a famous speech of his on Charles XII, November 30, 1892: 'Why do we celebrate the memory of Charles XII? Why—in order not to allow narrow mediocrity to limit our horizon. Rather, we should dare great things and expect great things for that for which we feel it worth-while to live.'[3] This was Charles XII and William Carey (the date was 1892!), meeting for once, and once only, in the mind of that young Swedish student who felt he had horizons to reach for and worlds to conquer.

All this was only the prelude to that climax where Söderblom conducted and excelled, in the celebrations of the Third Centenary of the Uppsala Assembly. This was in remembrance of the Church Assembly of 1593 which gave the stamp to the Swedish Reformation and also to the national unity of the Swedish Realm: 'Now is Sweden become one man and we have all one Lord and one God.' For the celebrations in Uppsala, the Church, the University—'the daughter of the Swedish Church', in the words of the Vice-Chancellor at that time—and the Student body, joined together for a great national manifestation. It lasted three days: the Church's day, the University's day and the day of the Student corps.

Söderblom, together with Archbishop Sundberg and Professor Fries, Vice-Chancellor of the University, held the central role throughout the three days. On the first day, with King Oscar and a medley of princes from Scandinavia and Germany present, Söderblom addressed in turn, the King and the German princes (in German). For the benefit of the foreign guests, perhaps, the speaker on this festive occasion referred to the Swedish King as 'the Summus episcopus of our Evangelical Church:' the one and only time, to our knowledge, that Söderblom made that claim, to which later, in the interest of the freedom of the Church, he was always to object. But this was student oratory and it went down well. It was a great success and Grand Duke of Saxony, Karl Alexander, insisted that he bestow upon the young student the 'Order of the White Falcon': only the tempered considerations of the Swedish hosts could make the high personage desist from his enthusiastic resolve.[4]

On the third day, that of the Student corps, Söderblom had the

---

[3] In Sophia Söderblom's Notes, there are references to her son's notes for his address, November 30, 1892.

[4] T. Andræ, *Nathan Söderblom*, p. 157.

task to address the Members of the Swedish Riksdag. He emphasized that while in 1593 most of those in charge were in clerical garb, what they did was to provide the solution for the burning question of their time. Söderblom had succeeded in persuading his friend and teacher professor Harald Hjärne to lecture in the University. This was on 'Renaissance and Reformation'. In a manner which Söderblom was never to forget, Hjärne combined the world-historical role of Gustavus Adolphus with the Uppsala meeting; two months later Söderblom himself speaking in the University Hall on Gustavus Adolphus made this same emphasis but with an anticipation of Sweden's future role which possibly was a personal declaration:

'To the North, the gaze of hope is turned once again. Is the North again to give a watchword; will the world in the next century behold a new and higher Gustavus-Adolphus-epoch? Whatever happens, it cannot be without the renewal of religion.'[5]

The Uppsala Tercentenary in 1893 was a great personal breakthrough for Söderblom. Suddenly, the young student became known as one of the great orators in the country. He might disappear to France, but those who had heard would not forget him. Neither did Söderblom himself forget, not altogether. His wife recognized something of this when commenting thirty years later on a speech he gave, in another country, the United States: 'The Archbishop replied and spoke as any old President of the Uppsala Student Corps loves to speak on November 6' [Gustavus Adolphus' day].[6] In the preparation for his own consecration in 1914, Söderblom mentioned to his consecrator, Bishop G. Billing, how his 'student's heart' yearned for a combination of Gustavus Adolphus and the Church ceremony;[7] he remembered those great weeks in 1893. As Archbishop he was to insist that his great ecumenical meeting be held, not in Geneva or Amsterdam, *or* Stockholm, but in Uppsala: There were many serious reasons for this, of course. But it cannot be altogether excluded that one subsidiary consideration was the memory of those glorious days of youth.

As President of the Uppsala Students Söderblom had interesting duties. He did however not neglect his personal contacts. The most important of these remains to be emphasized. In the autumn, 1891,

---

[5] Söderblom, *Svenska Kyrkans Kropp och själ* (1916), p. 109. C. G. Eckerberg, *Till minne af jubelåret 1893!* (1894). N. Karlström, *op. cit.* p. 168.

[6] Anna Söderblom, *En Amerikabok* (1925) p. 165.

[7] Söderblom, May 25, 1914 to G. Billing.

at a student party in Uppsala, Cand. theol. Nathan Söderblom, for the first time met Anna Forsell. She was twenty-one; he was twenty-six. She had begun her university studies at Uppsala that autumn; one among only twenty women students in the university (with a total of 1700 students). Her father was a sea-captain who had sailed the seven seas. The parents' spiritual guides, while members of the Swedish Church, were Emerson and Theodore Parker and they loved to speak English between themselves as they discussed these authorities. Anna was confirmed by Dr. Fehr, and the Liberal understanding of religion which this gave her she retained faithfully, even vigorously until her dying day.

On November 30, 1892 they were engaged. That was the day when the young speaker in one and the same sentence combined Charles XII and William Carey. Mother Sophia Söderblom, sitting at her desk in her isolation at Norrala was Nathan's confidante. The understanding mother noted in her diary: 'In his noble addresses that university term [autumn 1892] he felt he was speaking to [Anna]'. Indeed, so he was, but an interesting task would be to try to understand to what extent *all* that Nathan Söderblom was saying, also later in life, was in fact related to her as listener, censor and judge. She knew he was a genius and one of the elect; therefore she felt she could have very high demands.

It was the Student Christian Movement and the Y.M.C.A. which made possible Söderblom's visit to the United States in 1890. In the autumn of 1889 a young American Y.M.C.A. secretary J. B. Reynolds, who had spent a year on post-graduate theological work in Berlin and Paris, came to Uppsala. Karl Fries welcomed him there. Reynolds could invite a Swedish student to attend the Student Christian meeting at New Haven in June 1890, and Fries with his rare understanding for the potentialities of the young, saw to it that Söderblom got this opportunity.

It was Söderblom's first trip abroad, in fact, until then he had never been South of Stockholm (not quite 50 miles from Uppsala) or North of Sundsvall. Yet this statement needs some qualification. During his second visit to America in 1923, he wrote: 'USA, our nearest neighbour according to the map of the heart and of imagination, not the usual geography.' But that map had been drawn already in his early youth.

The emigration from Sweden, including Hälsingland, to Minnesota and Kansas was one of the great sociological facts of Swedish life

in the 1880's. America was not far away; it was more of an extension of Sweden. We recall that his maternal uncle, Niels, had settled
in San Francisco in 1863, and Nathan's brother Svante had left
Sweden in order to join his uncle in 1889. There was regular correspondence between San Francisco and the manse at Norrala. In
his letters from Uppsala to his home, Söderblom would occasionally
write: 'Let us see now if some English spirit gets into me some afternoon so that I scrawl down a few lines to America.'[8] Sometimes when
his mother complained of ailments or of disharmony in the home,
Nathan would write to her: 'But Mother, don't cry so loud that they
can hear it in America.'

Söderblom spent about two months in the United States. Reynolds invited him to stay in his parents' home, and this contact
proved to be of great importance for Söderblom's ecumenical experience. William T. Reynolds was the pastor of the North Haven Congregational Church in North Haven, Connecticut. Söderblom was
deeply impressed by the culture and refinement that he found in
the parsonage. Reynolds had built his own home—a large and
beautiful red brick building. In its sheltered setting, facing a side of
the Green, near the Congregational Church, this is still one of the
finest in the community. Both Reynolds and his son James were
graduates of Yale College and Yale Divinity School. The son, however, chose not to enter the ministry but to serve instead in social
and political areas, eventually gaining considerable fame as a special
adviser to both President Theodore Roosevelt (as a member of his
'kitchen cabinet') and President William Howard Taft. Mrs Reynolds welcomed Söderblom with generosity as 'my Swedish boy'. The
daughter Annie, a graduate of Wellesley College, was serving as a
high official in the YWCA at the time of Söderblom's visit, and
eventually became World General Secretary of the organization.

At this time, Mrs Reynold's sister, Mrs Elizabeth Campbell, wife
of a well-to-do newspaper editor (Norwich *Bulletin*) stayed with the
family. She taught Söderblom English. He met in her a highly cultured, 'a superior woman'. The meeting with her made Söderblom
conclude that the cultured American woman is possibly 'the greatest, most original and progressive of what America has to offer'.
Mrs Campbell and the remarkable Reynolds family represented
something new to him. In his home country he had met the Swedish
equivalent of these Congregationalists. Not always were they, at this

---

[8] Söderblom, September 19, 1886 to his parents.

time, particularly noted for their cultural achievement and outlook. The atmosphere of that happy home impressed him and played its part in his future development.

On his first day in New Haven Söderblom took part in a conference on denominational newspapers. The debate was introduced by a Congregationalist with a remarkable breadth of vision, Dr. Newman Smyth. 'Denominations are as essential to the Kingdom of God as the individual states are to the United States. Differences are unavoidable, but one should try to establish as positive and helpful mutual relationships between them as that between the forty-four individual states in the nation as a whole. When denominational newspapers go against this rule, they commit a sin. We should think not in terms of the Congregational Church, or the Episcopal Church, but of one Catholic Church organization.'

Söderblom and Newman Smyth—this was a very remarkable constellation indeed. The young Swedish student followed the speaker's argument and took down as best he could, notes in both English and Swedish. The lecturer himself was saying things that went far beyond anything that a good Congregationalist should have said at this time: here was the first glimpse of what eighteen years later was to be Dr. Newman Smyth's important book *Passing Protestantism and Coming Catholicism*. Söderblom noted in his diary that Mrs Reynolds did not like the man, while he and Mrs Campbell made a point of thanking him very warmly. Söderblom was impressed and inspired by this meeting. He quoted Newman Smyth: 'If the denominational newspapers serve to increase denominationalism, they should be removed.' Söderblom added his '*Good*' to this quotation. Then he went on, still writing in lead pencil, formulating a prayer which welled up from his heart. 'Lord, give me humility and wisdom to serve the great cause of the unity of Thy Church.' Was that enough? No, in that Congregationalist manse Söderblom felt that he needed to modify his understanding of what was meant by unity. So, above the line, he added an adjective. Thus the prayer reads:

Lord, give me humility and wisdom to serve the great cause of the f r e e unity of Thy Church.[9]

The Student conference at Northfield, was for Söderblom dominated by such personalities as Moody, Sankey, J. R. Mott, Wilder. In Moody he met a simple Pietistic peasant who very easily could

---

[9] Söderblom, Diary 1890.

have fitted into the Revival situation in Hälsingland. He had a generous attitude to other churches. In fact Söderblom never knew what Church he himself represented. Moody abhorred, Söderblom noted, proselytism and sectarianism. For 'God has created a blessed unity. Woe to the one who first breaks it.'[1]

Söderblom could renew his acquaintance with a young French student who had visited Uppsala in 1888, Wilfred Monod, 'a tired young man' who spoke at the Conference of the need of missionaries for France. Participating in a Conference of this kind, Söderblom summed up his experience. 'Who could escape experiencing the *universalism* of Christ's Kingdom and at the same time the width of Christian responsibility?[2]

This was the note which he would strike, when in the following year, 1891, he took part in an international YMCA Conference at Amsterdam with some 1500 delegates. 'How glorious it is that Christianity is international,' he wrote. 'Here we are from almost all countries of the world, each with his own peculiarity. But the differences need not separate us, no, rather they contribute towards making the whole richer and stronger'[3]—an attitude which much later, was to condition the archbishop as he developed his programme of Evangelical Catholicity.

The vision he had seen at North Haven he was determined to translate 'in the direction of practical Christianity', as he said, when taking part in 1892 in the Nordic Students Christian Conference at Horten, Norway. He was now himself one of the conference speakers, on 'A student's spiritual struggles and crises'. In this Scandinavian setting he showed how to come to terms with modern Bible criticism: 'Many feel that Christianity has lost something if St. Matthew did not write the first Gospel or Moses was not the author of the Pentateuch. ... Thus one binds one's faith to accidental things. ... Christ himself is the only authority and only through him the others [authorities] in so far as they belong to Him.' He spoke in Swedish to Nordic students. As he did so, the Danes and the Norwegians, expecting a Swede to express himself in unbearably solemn terms, were surprised by this Swede: 'to him, also we in Norway and Denmark felt immediately related.'[4] This was understandable, for Söderblom the Swede had much of a Danish Blume in him.

---

[1] Söderblom, in *Sommarminnen*, 1941, p. 96.
[2] Ibid., p. 102.
[3] T. Andræ, *Nathan Söderblom*, p. 95.
[4] Professor Lyder Brun, of Oslo, in *Hågkomster XIV*, p. 35.

Pastor and Scholar

'Such intentions always prove to be illusions', wise old Archbishop Sundberg said, knowingly. In an audience with King Oscar II, in autumn 1893 with a view to inviting the King to the Jubilee Festival at Uppsala, Söderblom met Dr. H. W. Tottie who happened to mention that the Swedish–Norwegian congregation in Paris was without a pastor. The idea of becoming a pastor in Paris fascinated Söderblom. He paid a visit to Archbishop Sundberg and told him he was interested in the Paris job. Sundberg tried to dissuade him: the salary was insufficient, and Söderblom had an academic future before him. Söderblom retorted that in accordance with the Swedish Church Law of 1686, he hoped to be able to study in his spare time. This was the kind of intention which Sundberg felt would prove to be fallacious. But Söderblom decided to try. April 29, 1894, Nathan Söderblom and Anna Forsell were married, by Dr. Fehr, and together they went to Paris and their new task.[1]

It consisted in fact of two jobs. The Swedish pastor in Paris also acted as chaplain to Swedish seamen in Calais and was expected to work in Calais during the summer. Söderblom liked it that way. From his home Söderblom was used to scarcity and an ascetic way of life: the little house in Calais gave him every opportunity for that kind of existence. This did not matter for it gave him interesting contacts with Swedish seamen and timberworkers. There were also slack weeks in the little harbour, and then Söderblom had his chance to add pages to his scholarly work.

The Paris congregation consisted of Norwegians and Swedes: a few civil servants at the legation; some business-men (timber and iron): a few artists, mostly artisans, workers and domestic servants; all told some 350 souls, chiefly in the Montmartre.[2] The bourgeois Swed-

---

[1] Söderblom, *Sommarminnen* (1941), p. 118 f.

[2] Archbishop Sundberg's cautious view about the Swedish pastor's financial position in Paris was derived from an investigation he had undertaken. In a memorandum to the Swedish Minister for Foreign Affairs December 30, 1892, Sundberg stated that three quarters of the Paris congregation, then consisting

ish Church Council had decided that their pastor must live near Parc Monceau, an arrangement which led to much extra travel for the conscientious young pastor.

Here Söderblom was to work for seven years. Only in August 1896 was he officially constituted as vicar (Kyrkoherde) of the congregation. His flock lived scattered over the capital and the congregation was a floating one, since the majority consisted of short-term workers (men and women) in Paris of whose existence and movements it was often very difficult to keep track. This was a constant problem also for the weekly worship in the little Swedish church at Boulevard Ornano.

All the more gratifying it was that Söderblom managed to establish a sense of unity and of a Scandinavian family. The choir which Söderblom organized helped towards this result. The weekly receptions in the little 'bird's nest' of the vicar's flat, at Rue Maleville, helped to integrate the group. Special church services, as some Lent services, were held in the Pastor's home. Lent, Easter, Whitsun, Christmas, the great festivals and seasons of the Church's year particularly interested the young pastor. 'I still long for the great Church festivals as much as when I was a child', he wrote to his parents on April 18, 1897.

Special occasions were the royal visits. King Oscar of Sweden took an interest in the Church, and liked to discuss theology (and theologians!) with the young pastor. After his visit in April 1899 Söderblom reported to his parents: 'The King sang loudly and followed the service very attentively. During the sermon he nodded assent many times and once he said, somewhat too loudly to the Envoy seated next to him: 'That was superb.' Another significant contact was that with a rich Swedish engineer at San Remo, by the name of Alfred Nobel. He had searching religious discussions with the young pastor and Söderblom was called to preach at the memorial service in San Remo, 1897.

To his flock of foreigners in the Metropolis, simple men and women, old and young, and brilliant but sometimes complicated artists, Söderblom was above all a pastor.

The group of Scandinavian artists particulary interested Nathan

---

of some 250 members, were poor domestic servants. He had a suggestion for assisting Paris which must have interested Söderblom greatly. The yearly surplus of some 11,000 Sw. kr. from Swedish property in Constantinople should according to Sundberg be used for the Swedish congregation in the French capital. Copy of Sundberg's memorandum, in Archives of the Uppsala Chapter.

and Anna Söderblom. Neither before or after had Paris seen such a brilliant galaxy of Nordic artists as in the eighteen-nineties, that *fin de siècle,* which was a beginning, the period when impressionism and expressionism emerged in the studios of the Montmartre.[3] The sculptors C. Eldh and C. Milles, Chr. Eriksson and Sörensen–Ringi, the painters Edelfeldt from Finland, F. Tavlow from Norway and from Sweden C. Larsson, and above all A. Zorn; and the musicians H. Alfvén and Sven Kjellström (the latter not only accomplished musician *but* from Hälsingland).

With some of these artists Söderblom was to be very closely connected. When later they turned up in the professor's house at Staby or in the Archbishop's House, they were as a matter of course, long-standing and beloved members of the family. The fellowship with them increased and refined his esthetic sensibility. Later as he meditated on that theme to which he liked to return, 'genius as interpreter of God's creation', he thought of Zorn's studio at Boulevard Clichy and Milles atelier in rue de la Grande Chaumière. He had witnessed there, encouraging and enraptured, the birth of ideas and visions and had shared fun and sorrows with these men in the precious formative years of their apprenticeship.

While these contacts meant much to Söderblom, it was not without importance to some of these painters and sculptors that they met in the Swedish Church a pastor who could share something of their deepest aspirations and boldest dreams. There was established between them a fellowship which lasted throughout life.

Milles wrote to Söderblom on his appointment as archbishop. He referred to 'a man whom I have always admired. I really [hope] that you will come fully to your right and flourish. At least you have now nobody else above you than the King and above him that power of nature called God or the sun or whatever we may say.'[4]

One of Söderblom's experiences in the first years in Paris was never forgotten. It may be that it determined some of his fundamental theological views at this time. A young Swedish artist had committed suicide. The little group of friends together with the pastor walked slowly behind the coffin through the endless streets, to a cemetery. What, in *fact,* could he tell these men, on that occasion, at that grave?

---

[3] G. Brandell, *Vid seklets källor,* (1961) p. 7.
[4] Carl Milles, January 23, 1915, to N. Söderblom.

There were the solemn words of the church's ritual to be read, and hymns to be sung, and there was the helpful human fellowship and solidarity. Was there anything more to it than that?

Then, there were those few, confident notes welling up from his heart, a jubilant conviction, in Händel's: *'I know that my Redeemer liveth.'* This became his message, or the channel of his message. He

had heard those notes in Stockholm in 1888. He also remembered his visit to London 1895, when together with a group of Swedish singers he had stood in the choir of Westminster Abbey below Jenny Lind's memorial plaque, 'the greatest memory of Swedish song'. Round the portrait those words were chiselled in English: 'I know ... that my Redeemer liveth.' And above Jenny Lind's portrait: a picture of father Händel himself'. In front of him lie note pages: 'Now I discovered the two first notes of the Resurrection aria in Messiah, these two notes which pronounce the firm and clear assurance of faith that the Lord and Master lives.'

Later, an old Jew, 'W.', regularly came to the worship in the Swedish church. Born in Bessarabia he had in Berlin once seen a notice that Händel's Messiah was to be performed. The name Messiah attracted him, and eventually he became a Christian. He liked to listen to the services led by the young Swedish pastor. He told Söderblom in his broken German: 'There are so many learned doctors, that is good; but to be a good pastor, that is better.' And now the old man with his hoarse, cracked voice began to sing Händel's aria in E major: 'I know that my Redeemer liveth. ...'[5] "Hardly could I have listened more devoutly", Söderblom recalled, "if it had been Jenny Lind singing"'.[6]

There were doubts about the Swedish pastor's faith at this time. Jonas Söderblom, his father, in Norrala enquired nervously and rumours came through from Sweden that he was not as orthodox, as some would like. It was true that he was *in via,* that he was on his way to a personal, to a more existential understanding of the faith. He wrote to his parents: 'It is not enough to make of Christ

---

[5] Söderblom, February 14, 1900 to S. A. Fries. Söderblom adds that Fries and he were one in the conviction that they must combine scholarship and faith.

[6] Söderblom, 'En aria av Händel, Tvenne minnen', in *Tal och Skrifter,* 5, p. 78.

the best of all men, and our example. This produces moral goodness, the highest. And this we must seek. But it is not religion, and it
cannot satisfy the soul. For that, Jesus must be unto us a Saviour, so
that through him we may receive God's grace and forgiveness. That
is my standpoint. I am not a real "Ritschlian"![7]

It was that interpretation of Händel's, that had given him conviction about the victory of Christ. On an existential level of religious
experience, the music of Händel and, of course, of Bach, expressed
the conviction of his heart. But he now needed new intellectual
tools, new categories to interpret that religious, or mystical, dimension. Where to find them? Dear old Ritschl certainly did not provide that kind of thing. But the theologians of Paris could point
to some of them.

The young pastor was *in via*. When he wrote to his father and
to Samuel Fries. 'I am not a real Ritschlian'.[8] 'I am not a Liberal',[9]
was he simply trying to tell his father that he would, after all, trudge
in his Pietistic footsteps? Hardly. But at least this much he knew,
that he was looking for something which seemed to him more essential than those moralistic precepts of Albert Ritschl, and his more or
less 'elliptic' theology. He was groping for something deeper, a secret, *the* secret perhaps.

He could hear its note in Emile Boutroux' lectures on Pascal during the winter months 1896–1897. The hall was filled with worship
(*andakt*): 'All intensive religious life is mysticism', Boutroux said
in his brief, clipped sentences, 'and mysticism is the matrix of life
whence religions renew themselves, when threatened by scholasticism
and by formalism'.[1] Söderblom went back, as so often, to his Old
Testament. A little pamphlet by the Basel scholar Bernhard Duhm
shed new light. *Das Geheimnis in der Religion,* was the title, and
this altogether remarkable little lecture of Duhm's had a real impact
on him.[2] We emphasize the role of Old Testament scholarship here.

Then he met Auguste Sabatier and his thought. We know the
exact date and day of this impact upon him. In his diary for March
19, 1895 Söderblom wrote: 'During the reading of Sabatier's book
on St. Paul I became attentive to the importance in religion of the

---

[7] Söderblom undated letter 1897 to his parents. In Sophia Söderblom's papers.
[8] N. Söderblom to his parents, undated in Sophia Söderblom's papers, 1896 or
1897.
[9] Söderblom, February 24, 1896 to S. A. Fries. Uppsala.
[1] Söderblom, *Religionsproblemet* (1910). p. 159.
[2] *Tal och Skrifter,* 6, p. 223.

mystical fellowship with God. He underlines the importance of the innermost, the heart, that life of feelings [which is] least attainable to reason.' This 'attentiveness' which he discovered in himself, was that anything else than finding in Sabatier and Duhm an echo of what he had already begun to discover for himself and which was now corroborated for him by the experience and thought of others? Yet in Sabatier he met one of those who influenced him most; Auguste Sabatier, with his experience of the frontier situation of Strasbourg prior to 1871; his literary and esthetic activity and journalistic contribution to *Le Temps, Journal de Genève* and *Revue Chrétienne;* Sabatier, the orator and preacher (we shall return to this theme); Sabatier, the author writing in lucid French; and finally, Sabatier, Söderblom's personal friend.

There appeared that book which meant more to him than most books he ever read: Sabatier's *Esquisse d'une Philosophie de la Religion,* Paris 1897. Sabatier was looking for that secret, 'the enigma of our life'.[3] In a language of compelling beauty, the French Protestant theologian, 'the greatest since Calvin' (Ménégoz) said that religion was 'the prayer of the heart', directed to *'un Dieu intérieur',* or even, 'un Dieu tout intérieur'. Conceived by 'Protestant Christianity', this idea had made possible that liberation of personality which had allowed man to 'come of age'.[4]

Sabatier's fundamental contribution was his interpretation of the symbolic nature of theological statements. The functions of symbols was to express the invisible and the spiritual through the visible and material. The symbol was a living organism, with a body and a soul, a spirit and a body.[5] Symbolism would permit to combine, Sabatier maintained, veneration for traditional symbols *and* the independence of the spirit; with this understanding, tradition would become not a yoke, but a support.[6] Theology was by Sabatier expressed in psychological terms. Psychologically, Sabatier claimed, religious inspiration was not different from poetic inspiration; and he went on to say: 'It offers no doubt the same mystery. Religious inspiration is nothing but the organic penetration of man by God, but by a totally interior God.'[7]

This was a discovery to Söderblom, and the years of Paris, so pro-

---

[3] A. Sabatier, *Esquisse,* p. 100.
[4] Ibid. p. 248.
[5] Ibid. 390 pp.
[6] Ibid. p. 410.
[7] Ibid. p. 99–100.

fitable also from other points of view, were dominated by this discovery. It has been 'received like rain by a thirsting soil', Söderblom
wrote in his review.[8] One of his Swedish contemporaries, Docent J.
A. Eklund, had written a somewhat critical review of Sabatier's
book. Söderblom took him up on this and in this connexion explained what Sabatier's theology meant to him:

'In my experience firm ground can be reached only by making
the bold leap. To him who becomes dizzy at the sight [of the abyss
to be crossed], it looks forbidding. He who after the leap stands on
terra firma will never, as long as love and life are in him, cease to
point others, in the same spiritual need, to the footing he has
gained.'[9]

He felt he had to resort to these Kierkegaardian terms in order
to convey to himself what he had found. Sabatier's *symbolo-fideism,*
the learned name for Sabatier's theological school of thought, helped
him to emphasize the religious and mystical dimension. Religion
had for too long been treated as of secondary importance as compared with morals; this was now to be changed.[1]

Sabatier had a liberating influence on Söderblom. His book inspired him in the conceptualization of some of his great thoughts
and themes: prayer, religion, ecclesiology. However, we shall have
to weigh with some care this influence. A case in point is the antinomy 'body-soul' in Söderblom's ecclesiology. We have already
touched on its role in Sabatier's book where it is an expression of
Sabatier's unmistakably spiritualistic tendency. In 1915, Söderblom
was to publish a book called *The Body and the Soul of the Swedish
Church,* and there are connexions between Sabatier's concepts and
the new archbishop's book. Yet, we must be aware of the fact that
in his book *The Religion of Revelation,* 1903, Söderblom was to
warn against a dichotomy 'spirit-body'.[2]

Neither can it be forgotten that the body-soul concept in the
Church does appear in Luther, in one of his anti-Roman moods:
'We find two churches and distinguish between them. The first ...
a spiritual, inward Christianity, the second . . . a bodily, external
Christianity'.[3] Söderblom may well have derived his own concept
from Luther himself, but Sabatier's influence helped to place in

[8] Söderblom in [S. A. Fries ed.], *Religiösa och kyrkliga frågor* (33) 1897, p. 257.
[9] Söderblom February 28, 1898 to J. A. Eklund, Uppsala.
[1] Söderblom's review, in *Religiösa och kyrkliga frågor,* 33, p. 266.
[2] Op. cit., p. 36.
[3] W. A. VI, 296, 30 f, cf. EA. XXVII: 86–139.

relief this spiritualistic emphasis in the Reformer. Besides, it was Sabatier's Lutheran colleague, E. Ménégoz, who particularly encouraged his Luther research. This helped him to emphasize *fiducia,* trust, as a central concept; this had also consequences for his ecclesiology, as it was related to what Söderblom termed Luther's universality.[4]

All this illustrates that while recognizing a certain influence by Sabatier on Söderblom, we have at the same time to exercise caution in the understanding of this influence. Söderblom himself had of course thought of this problem of influence. In speaking at this very time of another relationship in modern Church history he did, perhaps, give away the key, or clue, to the question of his own indebtedness to his admired French teacher.

This was in his lecture of 1899 on Schleiermacher's Reden. He quoted Claus Harms, the German Lutheran critic of eighteenth century rationalism, as saying about Schleiermacher's book: 'I received from that book a push towards an eternal movement.' Then Harms went on, 'More I did not receive from Schleiermacher; but *this I did receive from him,* and next to God I thank him for it.'[5]

Söderblom, ever prepared to learn from others, ever aware of influences on his own thought, was, in quoting Harms, really speaking about himself and the extent of the liberating influence which Sabatier's thought had on him. It was not a matter of Söderblom simply 'borrowing' or 'taking over' certain ideas of Sabatier's.[6] Rather, there was a certain preparedness in Söderblom himself, in his total personality and thought at this time, which made him turn to Sabatier for what he wanted and felt that he needed.

Archbishop Sundberg had expressed his doubts whether it would be possible to do much in the way of study and research parallel to the busy work as a pastor to the Swedish–Norwegian congregation in Paris and the sailors in Calais. Söderblom was to disprove

---

[4] cf. H. Fuglsang-Damgaard, *Pariserskolens Teologi,* p. 218 ff and Karlström, op. cit., p. 176.

[5] Harms' expression was, in its turn, a quotation from Jung–Stilling on Herder's influence on him. Söderblom, *Betydelsen af Schleiermacher's Reden* (1899), p. 24. He goes on to speak of Sabatier in the following page in this lecture on Schleiermacher. Ibid., p. 25.

[6] He wrote to S. A. Fries on Sabatier (April 17, 1901): 'He was an incomparable teacher and friend. Mark you, I have to thank him for [the appointment to] Uppsala. Without him /the doctoral thesis/ *La vie future* would never have been published, at least never in French'.

these doubts. Before he left Uppsala he had taken up the study of the religion of Iran and the Persian language. Paris provided him with an excellent opportunity to deepen this interest. Meillet was his teacher in Persian—a generation later Söderblom was to have the satisfaction of welcoming his teacher as an Olaus Petri lecturer at Uppsala University.

Söderblom felt that apart from the Paris experts in his field of research he also needed to consult authorities in the Low Countries. In 1895 he visited professor de Harlez in Louvain, and was greatly encouraged by the Belgian scholar's interest in his research work. In the autumn of 1898, Söderblom went to Holland where he visited the two authorities in the field of Religionsgeschichte, C. P. Tiele in Leiden and Chantepie de la Saussaye, in Amsterdam. The meeting with Tiele was important, for Söderblom was to become the editor of Tiele's famous *Compendium* in Religionsgeschichte; this contact between the two devotees of their study was an occasion which later Söderblom often liked to recall. Tiele could also tell him of his experience as a Gifford Lecturer in Edinburgh in 1896 and 1898, and Söderblom was later to prepare a Swedish edition of these lectures. There cannot be much doubt that Söderblom felt particularly drawn to Chantepie's position: 'this fine, sharp, irony-loving observer: a rich nature who to me is more sympathetic than the pure sciences.' Chantepie visited Stockholm for the Religious Studies Congress in 1897 (to which we shall return) and in this connexion declared where he stood in matters of the Christian faith. He told the Congress that he was 'convinced of the insufficiency of natural religion and of the dynamic power of historical Christianity; man could not live by general ideas but only by the assured experience that God to-day personally helps and saves him'.[7] Chantepie took Söderblom to church on Sunday morning: 'All sang, Chantepie included, although he not in tune', Söderblom noted in his Diary.[8] What Chantepie thus may have lacked in musical sense, he made up in personal consideration for, and interest in, the young Swedish scholar.

Söderblom prepared a study of guardian angels in Mazda belief, 1899, which resulted in the title of 'élève diplomé' at the Ecole des Hautes Etudes. With energy and concentration he carried on with his main study La vie future d'après le mazdéisme (1901): an impressive doctoral thesis of 450 pages. It was Sabatier who had en-

---

[7] S. A. Fries, *Religionsvetenskapliga Kongressen i Stockholm 1897*, p. 64 f.
[8] Söderblom, Diary 1898, September.

couraged him to defend the thesis for the doctorate. As Söderblom wrote his manuscript in his own language, Sabatier insisted that the book appear in French.

This is a learned and solid study, based on first-hand knowledge of ancient Persian. It deals with Persian ideas of heaven and hell and eternal life and of the destruction and reconstruction of the world as an eschatological event. These studies receive more general relevance because of comparisons over a wide field of the history of religions: Egyptian, Greek, Roman, Indo-Germanic and above all Semitic.

But the whole volume is, from one point of view, only a preparation for the final section of the book, some forty pages, devoted to the question of Eternal Life in Christianity. In conscious opposition to the general tendency of Biblical research at this time, Söderblom here, in accordance with S. A. Fries, maintained that the background of these ideas is, not Hellenistic, but Jewish. He also maintained the central role of Jesus' 'self-consciousness'. The book is concluded with a study in Luther's ideas on Eternal Life.

This thesis deepened Söderblom's interest in the problems of eschatology which were to be of importance for his interpretation of the Christian idea of revelation.

Söderblom's defence of his academic thesis, January 24, 1901 was a unique event: he was the only foreigner to have won the title of Doctor of Theology at the Protestant Faculty of the Sorbonne. As the faculty was soon to be separated from the Sorbonne, Söderblom was to be not only the first but also the last foreigner to win this degree. There were three opponents with whom the Swede had to contend, Albert Réville, A. Lods and Léon Marillier. There could be no doubt as to the result. It confirmed the author's central position in his science.

Tiele in Leiden, particularly, encouraged Söderblom. When Tiele's chair fell vacant in 1901, Söderblom's name was placed on a short list of three. This list showed that Scandinavians were well to the fore: the first was a Norwegian, Brede Kristensen, who succeeded Tiele, the second a Dane, Edvard Lehmann, with Söderblom following closely behind. But Söderblom was soon to get his chair, in his own Uppsala.

Sweden was far away from France in those days. All the same Söderblom kept up his correspondence with his friend S. A. Fries in Stockholm. The exchange of thoughts and ideas between the two young Swedish pastors and theologians, each of them hardly thirty years at the time, is of a quality which must be emphasized here. It shows a surprising intellectual awareness and excellence: the only parallel about this time, that comes to mind, is that between Troeltsch and the Webers.

Every learned article in *Theologische Literaturzeitung* or *Revue de l'Histoire des Religions* and similar publications, every new book or pronouncement by Harnack, Herrmann or Bernhard Weiss in Germany, Bernhard Duhm in Basel or Sabatier and the Révilles in Paris, let alone the Swedes, were immediately seized upon with insatiable intellectual appetite by Fries in Stockholm and Söderblom in Paris and there and then, torn to shreds or held up to enthusiastic gaze and awe of admiration.

But they were not satisfied with a role of mere onlookers. Soon they were prepared to take a bold initiative. The reaction to the 'World Parliament of Religions' in Chicago gave the opportunity. In connexion with the World Exhibition in Chicago, 1893, there was held a world congress of religions, with a distinctly syncretistic programme. Fries in 1895 published a critical book on the congress.

In Stockholm a Swedenborgian pastor, A. Björk (himself under fire from the majority of his own society) made a move in connexion with the Stockholm Exhibition of 1897 to arrange a 'Scandinavian Chicago', a similar Congress of Religions although limited to Scandinavian delegates.

Fries challenged this plan: he was afraid that a conference of this kind might become 'an excercise field for colporteurs, bragging pastors and fanatic sectarians', and pleaded with Söderblom in Paris to suggest what could be done.[9] Söderblom proposed a countermove: a series of lectures or addresses on religious subjects.[1] Fries now formed the idea of a scholarly Congress of Religious study, not limited to Scandinavia, but with prominent lecturers from the Continent.[2] Söderblom was entrusted with finding French lecturers for the Conference and he had the personal triumph of persuading August Sabatier to come. Sabatier's contribution together with the fact that Max Müller himself, of Oxford, and Chantepie de la Saussaye, of Amsterdam, had consented to attend, was an indication of the level of this Conference, arranged with amazing boldness by Fries and Söderblom.

---

[9] S. A. Fries, February 20, 1896 to Söderblom.
[1] Söderblom, February, 1896 to S. A. Fries.
[2] S. A. Fries, May 23 or 2, 1896 to Söderblom.

Söderblom felt that their congress was going to be a success. He wrote to Fries: 'It is a great undertaking. Sweden begins to fall into line. And then, forward march![3]

Stockholm 1897 did not become, what Björk had hoped, a Scandinavian Chicago. There were a few Chicago men represented there, to be sure. Björk was one, and the famous Max Müller another. The latter was prevented by illness from attending the Congress, but his lecture was read for him in Swedish by Björk, who no doubt emphasized the praise bestowed by Müller on Chicago: 'No ecumenical Council could be compared to it if one considers what *oikoumene* was at that time and what it is now.'[4] A new religion is what we really need,' he went on; 'although that religion will probably prove to be the oldest in the whole world.'[5]

On the other hand, Chantepie de la Saussaye wrote to S. A. Fries prior to the Conference: 'I take for granted that you know something of my standpoint. I am no Chicago man, but take my stand more to the right. Therefore I sympathize with a Congress which tends to emphasize the religious practical-Christian side more than the general standpoint of Chicago.'[6] Chantepie's lecture at Stockholm was an attempt at a Christian interpretation of the religions.

The Congress of Religionswissenschaft, August 31–September 4, 1897, meeting in the Swedish House of Nobility, was presided over by Bishop von Schéele of Visby. The Bishop underlined that true followers of Christ had to meet representatives of other religions with respect and indeed must work for a comparison of the various religions. He could have no doubt, he said, that Christianity had not only a relative but the absolute right to establish the criterion for this comparison. In one of the discussions on the relationship between religion and ethics, Söderblom, the young pastor from Paris gave his testimony: the answer was quite simply: 'Jesus Christ.'[7]

With his experience and inspiration from the Evangelical–Social movement in Germany, Söderblom chose to speak at Stockholm on Religion and Social Development. He there came close to the theme in Benjamin Kidd's *Social Evolution,* a book to which he specifically referred in the final printed text of his lecture.

He quoted Marx' 'Kapital', Friedrich Naumann's ideas, and the

---

[3] Söderblom undated, 1897, to S. A. Fries. Uppsala.

[4] *Religionsvetenskapliga Kongressen i Stockholm 1897*, p. 45.

[5] Ibid. p. 47.

[6] Chantepie de la Saussaye, July 6, 1897 to S. A. Fries, Uppsala.

[7] *Religionsv. kongressen 1897*, p. 483.

British Christian social reformers. Even a prominent Swedish Churchman was referred to as an authority for social reform. Archbishop Sundberg had had his misgivings about the Stockholm conference. All the more Söderblom underlined that Sundberg had been first in Sweden to emphasize the duty of the Church towards the modern Labour movement![8]

Söderblom was anxious to warn the Church against being tied to any class or social programme, and on the other hand, with W. Herrmann, pleaded with socialism to liberate itself from a materialistic ideology. For this very reason the Church did well in following, not with suspicion, but with interest, such Christians who in their political and social activity threw in their lot with the Social Democrats.[9] For the Church to preach contentedness would mean death to social and human progress. Therefore the right to strike must be upheld, although Christian socialists must aim at solutions through arbitration.[1]

His main concern was to demonstrate the necessary, albeit illogical, connexion between worship and service. The incompatibility between Jesus' eschatological message about the Kingdom and his positive practical service in the world was the 'great despair of logicans and theologians'.[2] He even went so far as to criticize Luther's neglect of the Church's task to challenge the social structure of his time in order to make his point: 'The heavenly does not steal time from the earthly, but gives all the more strength to eager, patient and faithful service.'[3] Much of what the young pastor of 30 was saying sounds as an anticipation of the Archbishop's message in connexion with another Stockholm Conference some thirty years later, in the same way as the programme of this Stockholm Congress of 1897 anticipated the professor's and the Archbishop's attitude to the relationship of Christianity to the religions.

When three years later, once again in connexion with a World Exhibition, a congress was held at Paris, in 1900, on the Study of the History of Religions, both Fries and Söderblom felt that this event was a continuation of their own Stockholm conference. Fries, the official Swedish delegate, said so. In his address to the congress

---

[8] Ibid. p. 102.
[9] Ibid. p. 123.
[1] Ibid. p. 127–30.
[2] Ibid. p. 100.
[3] Ibid. p. 105.

at Paris he expressed the hope that the work begun at Stockholm would find its 'more complete and perfect manifestation' at Paris.[4] There were features at Paris which must have reminded Söderblom and Fries of the Chicago Parliament of Religions. Among the delegates were Swami Vivekananda, Mlle Rev. Mary Baker, Eddy and H. S. Olcott. Above all, however, Paris was a congress of scholarly debate and thus a forum where the two Swedish friends felt at home.

Söderblom as a Parisian had shared with Albert Réville and Jean Réville, Léon Marillier and others in the preparations for this important meeting. It gave Pastor Söderblom an opportunity for fellowship with the leaders within his own special field. He established contacts with the European academic republic of scholarship and research and he was to regard himself as one of the founding fathers of this particular scholarly fellowship.

'The capital of the world', Söderblom called Paris in a report to Archbishop Sundberg.[1] From this vantage point he widened his geographical and cultural horizons and established contacts in a number of directions.

He had of course a special opportunity to study French Church life. During his Paris years he wrote some thirty articles on Church life and social conditions for Swedish newspapers, under the title 'From Paris' religious horizon'. These show that he had established interesting contacts with Catholic social concerns and leaders, as e.g. abbé Lemire. He could follow the beginnings of French modernism, a theme to which he was going to devote a thorough study in his *Religionsproblemet,* of 1910. Alfred Loisy's fate exercised him, and he followed his development with keen personal interest; he was to visit Loisy in 1908 and in 1926. His friends he found among the contemporary generation of French Protestant scholars and pastors: Paul Sabatier (a distant relative of Auguste Sabatier), R. Allier, Armand Lods, F. Ménégoz, Wilfred Monod, Jean Réville.

The future ecumenical leader could follow at close quarters an interesting process of Church integration in French Protestantism at this time. There had been serious tensions between the Orthodox and the Liberal fractions in the French Reformed Church, but in 1896 at Lyons, a reconciliation conference was held where a 'brotherly commission' was formed with a view to strengthening the unity

---

[4] *Actes de Premier Congrès Internationale d'Histoire des Religions* (Paris 1901), I. p. 6.
[1] Söderblom, *Om den Svenska kyrkogärningen i Paris* (1897) p. 32.

of the federated Church: the Reformed family of France was reunited in a living sense of belonging together.

Analysing this development, Söderblom could note with satisfaction that the two parties were agreed to leave aside the differing
dogmatic views; but he delved deeper, to the underlying cause of
this new readiness for understanding.[2] He felt that this was mainly
the result of the role of the theology of Sabatier and Ménégoz.
Thinking in Sabatier's categories of the body and the soul of the
Church, he found that the orthodox section had misunderstood the
nature of the body of religion, while the Rationalist group had
been mistaken about the nature of its soul. With the modern sym-
bolo-fideistic theology, a new formulation for an integrated Church
had been formed. There cannot be much doubt that this controversy
and its solution was to influence Söderblom, when forming his views
on the nature of Church unity.

His visit to Germany brought him in contact with the burning
issues of Social Ethics, as seen in the German churches and in German theology. 1896 was a tense and agitated period in the German
situation. It was at this time that the well-known leaders in German
Christian social thought, A. Stöcker and Fr. Naumann dramatically
parted company. Söderblom was also impressed by the social reformer Paul Göhre: Göhre's studies of the rural proletariat in Prussia
interested him; thirty years later, as Archbishop, he was to call for
a similar study into the conditions of rural workers in his own
diocese. It was in the Evangelical–Social Congress at Erfurt that
Söderblom had his most important contacts with these German leaders. He met personally some of the foremost thinkers in German
social reform on a Christian basis: the already mentioned Friedrich
Naumann (in 1903 Söderblom wrote an introduction to a Swedish
edition of Naumann's *Hilfe*), together with Max Weber and R.
Sohm. Here at Erfurt, it was brought home to him in unmistakable
terms that a pastor must be the intrepid herold of justice and charity
in the face of any social injustice. There were tensions in that group
of some one hundred or more delegates at Erfurt. But Söderblom
was at the same time impressed, as he wrote after Erfurt, seeing how
theologies of different schools of thought, were united in common
and convinced action in the experience of the renewing power of
the Gospel.[3] It was as if one could sense an anticipation of the

---

[2] Söderblom, in [S. A. Fries], *I religiösa och kyrkliga frågor*, 33, 1897, p. 135–39.
[3] Ibid., p. 112; cf. Karlström, *op. cit.* p. 179 f.

programme of Practical Christianity through which, a generation later, Söderblom would attempt to unite the churches of the world. He was no less interested in the social debate in *England*. In August 1896, Anna and Nathan Söderblom spent a busy weekend in London, one of Söderblom's many visits to England as a scholar and a Church leader. Leaving Calais by steamer, Friday at noon and returning the following Monday, the young couple managed to get through the following programme: Friday evening studying social work in London done by the remarkable Swedish lady, Agnes Welin. The whole of Saturday was spent at a Socialist Congress held in Crystal Palace (with Anna particularly admiring the remarkable fireworks in the evening!). Sunday morning they attended the worship in Westminster Abbey; this was followed by a burial service taken in Swedish by Nathan Söderblom. They then attended a Baptist service in the London Tabernacle, with Archibald Brozen preaching; and the late evening, Söderblom preached in the Swedish seamen's Church.

The Monday gave Nathan Söderblom an opportunity of visiting the British Museum Library and seeing the Assyrian collections in the British Museum, which were of particular interest to him. They had also managed to get tickets for the Houses of Parliament. They thus combined church interests with scholarly, political and social activities; their rapid tour reflected the wide range of interests pursued by the young couple.

He was debating with himself, even at this time, and with his father at Norrala to which special field of theological research he should devote his life: It depended to a certain extent on the changing academic opportunities in Sweden with only two theological faculties. Always closely concerned with Biblical research, he felt, in April 1900 that he might apply for a chair in the New Testament exegesis, 'the most important and highest branch of theological knowledge, and I try to follow what is done there'.[4] He did indeed; he had in 1898 published a highly competent book on *The Sermon on the Mount and Our Time*. But he had in fact already decided to try his chances in the History of Religion. From Uppsala it had been reported to him that his teacher and friend Professor J. A. Ekman who held the chair devoted to *Religionsgeschichte* had become Bishop of Västerås in 1898, two years later to be translated to the Archiepiscopal see at Uppsala.

---

[4] Söderblom, April 16, 1900 to his father.

He was going to apply, and as he applied he thought—of his father: 'I count it as a sacred duty', he wrote to his father, 'to make a bid for Uppsala. Therein lies something inherited. Father ought to have been there. Now I want at least to try. Father would have done it with greater right and assured success.'[5] As a professor he was going to take up again the father's role.

An academic competition for a professorial chair in Sweden is, notoriously, a harsh and brazing affair. Many feel called, but of course only one is elected, or appointed, on the merits or otherwise of his printed works. The applicants are judged by a panel of three or four experts who might need some six months or more for their task. In this particular case there was a serious factor of uncertainty: The chair was called Theological Prenotions and Theological Encyclopedia. This was a comfortably vague term allowing for different interpretations of what the Chair was really about.

There were five applicants for the post. Two of these were among Söderblom's best friends from his student days, L. Bergström and N. J. Göransson. The others were a philosopher, Docent J. A. Bensow, and Docent J. A. Eklund. The experts were four: Bishop von Schéele of Visby, who himself had been an incumbent of the chair in the 1880's prior to J. A. Ekman, professor (Dean) Berggren (Dogmatics), and Stave from Uppsala (Old Testament) and a professor from Finland, C. O. Rosenqvist.

The experts soon found the choice to lie between Eklund and Söderblom. The former had to his credit studies in the Philosophy of Religion, together with a book on Nirvana. Rosenqvist who definitely preferred Eklund, was not concerned with the fact that Eklund's study was based on second-hand sources; Eklund had no knowledge of Sanscrit or other Eastern languages. Rosenqvist insisted that Eklund's printed works fitted the particular name of the chair. Söderblom on the other hand, he said, was a 'shining intelligence who also liked to shine', but tended to be superficial. In his statements on the dogmas of the Church, Söderblom, he thought, sometimes would strike a note which was unworthy of a serious teacher of the Church! Dean Berggren vacillated; he wanted Eklund, but was persuaded by Stave to join the majority report. In this report, signed by Berggren, Stave and von Schéele, Eklund was represented as having produced 'the thoughts of a real genius', but Söderblom's undisputed superiority because of his knowledge of the

---

[5] Nathan Söderblom June 30, 1898 to his father.

languages of Avesta, was emphasized by a special expert, the professor in Sanskrit, K. F. Johansson. This determined the issue: Söderblom was preferred.

In the Faculty, professor Danell (Dogmatics) and Quensel (Practical Theology) voted for Eklund, while four, Berggren, von Schéele, Stave, and Lundström (Church History) voted for Söderblom. Söderblom in Paris could not be sure of the final outcome and considered taking a vacant living in Gävle which had been offered him. He wrote to Archbishop Ekman about this, but before he could get an answer from his bishop, he had been appointed professor.

Professor and Pastor

Gentlemen, there are today many that pity you. I must congratulate you. ... I speak in order to congratulate you with all my heart on your present occupation, on forwarding the study of theology in this time, and on your future vocation. ... I congratulate you on those with whom you will hold converse, an Amos, an Hosea, an Isaiah, a Jeremiah, a Paul, an Augustine, a Francis, a Luther, a Pascal, a Kierkegaard, and high above them all the Master, Jesus the Lord, who grows before our eyes, the nearer we come to Him, and whom you, freed by being tied to His yoke, will show to your brethren. The heart of man will reveal to you its innermost secret, its longing after God; even in gloomy periods, in the darkness of ignorance and sin, this longing will shine to you as a holy fire, in the light of which you will divine or apprehend much that was contradictory or hidden from you. In the superstitious rites and the confused animism of the savage, for which the ignorant have only contempt, you will discover the sense of the infinite. In those dogmatic formulae of the Christian Church which are most remote from the ideas of the contemporary world, formulae for which the ignorant have only rejection, you will discover the consoling truths of salvation. ... You have a secret confidant in every human heart, in so far as you serve the cause of Christ. By revealing the truth you will commend yourself to every man's conscience in the sight of God. The Lord kindle and preserve in your hearts the holy fire.

With these words' bold clarion call, Church and theology in Sweden entered upon the new century, and with a sudden, new expectation. Perhaps, after all, the Church had a future? It was Professor Nathan Söderblom, who after his inaugural lecture at the Uppsala University, on September 24, 1901, here turned to the young students of theology. The rapid and easy flow of those glorious words, the golden voice, the unmistakable power, conviction and joy in that young man—the impression of that moment was to live and linger for long.

He was unknown to most of his Uppsala listeners. Coming from far-away Paris, the cadence of his phrase partly revealed this con-

nexion with France. In fact, it can be shown in some detail that
Söderblom's words were inspired by, almost based on, Auguste Sabatier's speech to his French students in Paris, November 2, 1896.
Here Sabatier had spoken of 'the divine fire ... which will warm
you and enlighten you and justify you. Let it not be extinguished',
and here it was that Sabatier had quoted that word which was to be
Söderblom's motto (also to be engraved in his own tomb stone in
the Cathedral of Uppsala), Luke 17:10. When ye shall have done...

As Söderblom spoke, he could remember the inflexion of that
other, French voice, to which he had listened five years earlier, and
often after that. Or was it an echo of that word of his father's in the
Confirmation class, twenty years earlier: 'the tinder of devotion'?
The year of 1901 was to Söderblom not only a new beginning. It
was also the occasion for two poignant farewells. Sabatier had died
in April 1901 and the dying *maître* had held his hand in his and
told him, 'You do not know how much you have become a good
and dear friend to me'.[1] And in June, his father, Jonas Söderblom
had passed away. Nathan just managed to reach Norrala two days
before his death. His father turned to him: 'Are you home, Nathan?
And you, poor boy, were to be entrusted with such a high post!' He
gave him an apostolic injunction: 'Not as lords over your faith, but
as helpers of your joy.'[2]

At thirty-five, Söderblom had lost his father in Norrala and his
teacher in Paris. As a new professor at his old university, he entered
a new phase of his own development. He returned from Paris to
Uppsala. In Paris he had been a pastor who was also a scholar. In
Uppsala he was to be a professor who was also a pastor.

These two, Church and Academy, faith and science, were they
not worlds apart, could they be held together? This was Uppsala's
problem at this time, and that of the West as a whole. It was also
Söderblom's personal problem and he found an answer.

'Nathan Söderblom, Professor' is a theme in itself to which one
could devote a lengthy study, dealing with Söderblom's academic
contribution to Religionsgeschichte and the history of ideas. For our
purposes this chapter must be understood in terms of Söderblom's
preparation for his task as the ecumenical archbishop. We cannot
however dispense ourselves from a rapid survey of the development
and interconnexion of his theological categories. As a scholar he was

---

[1] Söderblom, Diary, April, 12, 1901.
[2] Ibid., July 27 and 28, 1901.

to establish wide international contacts to which we shall refer. But neither can it be overlooked that Söderblom, the professor, was always a pastor of souls.

Söderblom was soon to discover that his position in the Faculty was far from assured. In fact, from the outset he was to meet with determined opposition. Returning to Sweden and Uppsala he hoped that his friend Samuel Fries was to be his colleague at the Faculty, and in 1902 Fries applied with three others for the chair in the New Testament. There was no doubt that Fries was the most original and creative of the applicants; nor that he had enthusiasm and passion for scholarly research. Söderblom saw Fries becoming 'a shining light in the kingdoms of Sweden and of the sciences and not a smoking flax in the vestry of church politics'.[3] But at this time of the Faculty's development there were all kind of connexions between that vestry and certain members of the Faculty, and in the event Fries was placed at the bottom of the list, and the chair went to A. Kolmodin. The following year, 1903, Söderblom's brilliant research student, Torgny Segerstedt, defended his doctoral thesis, *On the Origin of Polytheism*. Söderblom was full of praise and hoped to see Segerstedt as his assistant professor. The majority of the Faculty decided, however, that the thesis lacked 'Christian substance', and against Söderblom's embittered protestations it was rejected. The 'Segerstedt case', or scandal, took on great proportions in the university: it estranged Söderblom from the Theological Faculty (as he returned home that evening, his wife remarked: 'I have never seen him so full of sorrow and indignation') while it definitely established his place in the Council of the University.[1] The great scholars of the Arts faculty, Hjärne, Noreen, Schück and H. Almkvist, were all for Segerstedt and felt Söderblom to be their ally against obscurantism. Söderblom had his first serious attack of bleeding ulcer that summer: it is conceivable that the struggle in the Faculty and the illness were closely related.

All the more established was his position as a professor to the theological students. He was an inspiring lecturer and generous leader of seminar meetings. His series of lectures were devoted to the World Religions; the contact between Christianity and the religions; but also to the great personalities and movements of the Spirit, in

---

[3] Söderblom, May 6, 1902, to S. A. Fries.
[1] Anna Söderblom, *På livets trottoir*, II (1956), p. 69. Estrid Ancker, *Torgny Segerstedt* (1962), p. 273. Ingrid Segerstedt Wiberg, *Torgny Segerstedt* (1955), p. 18.

general and in Swedish Church history. This teaching gave impulses and visions which were decisive for generations of young students.

His lecture-load was three to four lectures a week and one seminar a fortnight. The time for his lectures was 8 o'clock in the morning. In order to teach, the professor thus had to start early from his Staby manse, outside the town boundaries, walking through snow or slush and rain, or again in glorious sun-shine, to the University. As the table shows he devoted his lectures, in the first years to the History of Religion, and in the latter years, to the Phenomenology of Religion. In the seminars he discussed students' essays in the field of Philosophy of Religion and of Psychology of Religion. He had his special interests. His Luther lectures of 1904 contain the embryo of what became, in 1919, his book on *Humour and Melancholy in Luther*. He lectured on Swedish Theology in the nineteenth century mainly concentrating on his beloved E. G. Geijer, and he lectured on Socrates: these studies from 1905 were published much later, in his Gifford Lectures volume, *The Living God*.

Term	Lecture, and attendance	Seminar
1901 A.T.[a]	Hist. of Rel.: General Survey 60	Philosophy of Rel.: H. Höffding
1902 S.T.[a]	Hist. of Rel.: Babel and Bible 40	
1902 A.T.	Hist. of Rel.: India 60	Philosophy of Rel.: A. M. Fairburn 30
1903 S.T.	Hist. of Rel.: Greek and Roman 56	Philosophy of Rel.: A. M. Fairburn; H. Eucken 28
1903 A.T.	Hist. of Rel.: Swed. Theology 19th cent. 50	Philosophy of Rel: Troeltsch 28
1904 S.T.	Hist. of Rel.: Swed. Theology, 19th cent. 44	Philosophy of Rel.: E. Troeltsch 18
1904 A.T.	a. Luther and Mysticism b. Personality Mysticism 56	Psychology of Rel.: Sufism
1905 S.T.	Socrates, Plato, Stoics 40	Psychology of Rel.: Sufism; Guyon; St. Augustin 35
1905 A.T.	Rel. Texts: India 67	Socrates 50
1906 S.T.	Rel. Texts: India; The Cosmic Periods 68	Avesta Texts; Antigone; Philoktetos 30

Term	Lecture, and attendance	Seminar
1906 A.T.	Study of Rel.: Introduction 64	Rel. Legends: St. Francis legends
1907 S.T.	Hist. of Rel.: Persia 42	Psychology of Mysticism: Teresa, Guyon
1907 A.T.	Indian and Biblical Rel. 65 Greek Rel.	Psychology of Rel.: Prayer, Prayer in the Psalms
1908 S.T.	[No attendence figures; N. S. Sickleave]	Socrates
1908 A.T.	Socrates the Mystic 64	Philosophy of Real.: E. Boutroux 20
1909 S.T.	"Religionsproblemet i katolicism och protestantism" 112	Philosophy of Rel.: Buddhism 25
1909 A.T.	Primitive Rel. 40	H. Bergson: The Subject of knowledge and the Nature of Reality 14
1910 S.T.	Tyrrell and Newman 41	Luther's Catechism in the light of Hist. of Rel. 28
1910 A.T.	Phenomenology of Rel.; Prayer 45	Luther's Catechism in the light of Hist. of Rel. 14
1911 S.T.	Phenomenology of Rel.: Gods, myths, legends 49	Egyptian Mystery Cults 5
1911 A.T.	Phenomenology: Eschatology 53	Popular piety in Sweden 25
1912 S.T.	Phenomenology: Holiness; Eschatology 62	Philosophy of Rel.: Pehr Eklund
1912 A.T.	History of Rel. and Natural Theology 37 [to Leipzig]	None
1913 S.T. (28.3–14.4)	Phenomenology: Holiness; From Primitive Rel. via O.T. to Milton 64	Popular piety in Sweden 13
1913 A.T.	Leave of absence	
1914 S.T. (9.3–28.3) 12 lectures	Ritual and personal fellowship with God: Rites, sacrifices, prayer 74	

^a A.T. = Autumn Term.   S.T. = Spring Term.

In Emerik Stenberg's monumental painting, The Theological Faculty at Uppsala of 1911, Söderblom as the Dean that year is the central figure, chairing a meeting.[a] Reality was more harsh perhaps, than this illusion of art, for Söderblom's position in this group, after ten years in the Faculty, was not as central as the painter would have us believe. From his chairman's vantage point he could survey the Faculty and register the reactions of the members. He had his occasional supporters of course. The figure standing on Söderblom's right, H. Lundström, tended to side with Söderblom, from time to time. As a church historian Lundström was said to have established the Swedish claims of unbroken episcopal succession. He was known to hold a central, middle-of-the-road position in the Church, highly esteemed by those in the Episcopate who regarded themselves as more Lutheran than others, e.g. Bishop von Schéele of Visby. The mustachioed figure on the far right in the picture was Söderblom's old friend N. J. Göransson; now the professor of Dogmatics. A cautious logician, he was bemused sometimes by Söderblom's rapid jerks of thought and association; but too loyal to his old friend ever to allow himself to be drawn into any party intrigue against him. Next to Göransson in the picture is Einar Billing, professor of Christian Ethics, the youngest in the Faculty, a noble visionary and an inspiring force in the 'Young Church' Movement. The men on either side of Söderblom were his determined opponents: Kolmodin, professor of the New Testament, spare, lean, thin-lipped, he represented a Pietistic biblicism to which Söderblom's standpoint, or lack of such, seemed worldly and opportunist; and Erik Stave, a Swedish, somewhat abridged edition of B. Duhm's Old Testament, a broad heavy peasant of Dalecarlia, with a sharp glint behind his deceptively rimless glasses.

Quite frankly, Söderblom did not always feel at ease in that group of colleagues. He found himself in opposition to the majority of them in certain important matters of preferment, and felt this to be a personal defeat. He found an outlet in the more or less pious daydream on which he wrote to Fries: 'We seem to get rid of Danell to Luleå [as bishop; Danell was then one of the associate professors; later bishop in Skara]: Just think if Stave and Kolmodin were to go the same way.'[2]

If he had occasional difficulties with Uppsala, he felt the more united with the predominantly Liberal members of the Theological

---

[a] Facing p. 81.

[2] Söderblom, September 9, 1903, to S. A. Fries.

Faculty at Lund: Dean Pehr Eklund and M. Pfannenstil, systematic theologians. Lund was, at this time, and not only in geography, closer to the Continent and the world than hyperborean Uppsala; these contacts were important to him both as a professor and later as archbishop.

His colleagues in the faculty may have had reason to think that they did not know where he stood theologically; Söderblom, on the other hand, realized that he knew *their* positions only too well. No, it was in the Higher University Council consisting of the leading professors from all the faculties of the academy, that he felt at home. There were some giants among them: Harald Hjärne, History, and H. Schück, Literature, were his close friends. Then there was the group of gifted language scholars: H. Almkvist and K. Zetterstéen, Semitic Languages; A. Noreen, Nordic Languages; Danielsson, Greek; P. Persson, Latin; K. F. Johansson, Sanskrit; these were his close associates; it was easy for them to find their way to Söderblom's house. These were the men with whom Nathan Söderblom experienced his richest intellectual fellowship throughout his Uppsala years, as professor *and* archbishop; they also became co-workers for Söderblom's ambitious undertaking, *Främmande religionsurkunder*, texts translated from the world religions. They were experts in difficult languages, an accomplishment for which Söderblom always showed unbounded admiration. And, above all, these were the men for whom scholarly work was more than a job or a métier; it was a passion and a 'form of life'.

Returning to Uppsala as a professor Söderblom had the opportunity of renewing his earlier contacts with that master of historical research, Harald Hjärne, He represented the scholar's 'form of life'. In the Council of the University the two worked together. Söderblom became the pastor of the Hjärne family. In 1908, Hjärne published a book 'Swedish and Foreign'; on the frontispiece, the book dedicated to Nathan Söderblom 'these remembrances of exchange of thought throughout the years'. Hjärne combined patriotism with a relatively radical attitude in social questions, a standpoint which Söderblom appreciated. We emphasize this contact with Hjärne, for wherever Söderblom as the ecumenical Archbishop, was to move later on, his historical and geographical perspectives were related to the visions and patterns of Hjärne and to that of his remarkable seminar of young History scholars.

Söderblom would interpret for his students what he felt in the presence of men like Hjärne.

Young friends, have you seen the scholar? I meet him sometimes. I sit and listen as the problem becomes ever more complicated to him. ... He wants to get at the thing itself. It is as if to be initiated into a mystery, and at least, as I analyse my own attention, I find a good portion of religious awe in it. ... Windows are opened to tremendous vistas. I see the scholar himself. ... He has completely forgotten himself ... and I in all humility feel proud to be man.[3]

To Söderblom the situation in Uppsala presented its problems. He confided to a friend that 'Church people banish me in *partes infidelium*'.[4] After he had at last decided to go to Leipzig, his colleague Lundström wrote to him expressing regret that Söderblom should leave: Just now as the [E.] Billing element begins to be predominant, you are indeed needed'.[5] The development in 1911 and 1912 of the Segerstedt struggle may have been an additional factor.[6]

To the Swedish Church as a whole, Söderblom's participation in a so-called 'Heretics Meeting', at Örebro 1910, had made his position problematic. Bishop von Schéele, in Visby, was dismayed to see that Söderblom's name had been included in the draft programme for an international Lutheran meeting in Uppsala, 1911. Söderblom's name had been mentioned at a preparatory meeting at Magdeburg, Germany, but rejected, 'because he was regarded as not Orthodox enough', and von Schéele succeeded in replacing this suspect name by a more reliable, that of Professor Lundström.[7]

All the more Söderblom's international position as professor of History of Religion was enhanced through his important writings in this period. It was his Dutch friend Chantepie de la Saussaye who had suggested to Tiele that he approach the young Swedish scholar for a new edition of Tiele's *Compendium* of Religionsgeschichte. Söderblom accepted this offer because of his loyalty to and admiration for Tiele. It was no easy task. He chafed under the burden and wrote to S. A. Fries: 'Bored to death I am trudging along with this Compendium. It would have been a thousand times better if I had written a new book of my own.'[8] The Tiele in Söderblom's guise appeared in 1903 (the third edition of 'Tiele'). In 1912 a fourth totally revised edition followed; this time with sections on Jesus

---

[3] Söderblom, 'Vetenskapen som livsform', in *Tre livsformer* (1922), p. 106.
[4] Söderblom, April 17, 1908 to Bildt; Ebildslätt.
[5] H. Lundström, July 31, 1912 to Söderblom.
[6] E. Ancker, op. cit., p. 314.
[7] von Schéele, October 28, 1910 to H. Lundström; Uppsala.
[8] Söderblom, August 25, 1902, to S. A. Fries.

Christ and on the Christian religion. He also prepared the above mentioned ambitious series of texts from the History of the Religions, published in three volumes in 1907, under the title *Främmande religionsurkunder*.

Through the congresses of Religionsgeschichte Söderblom found an honoured place in the European academic republic. Here he established personal fellowship and friendships with the great leaders, young and old, of his particular métier: Frazer and Lang, Réville and Vallée-Poussin, Chantepie de la Saussaye and van Vollenhoven, Goldziher and Pettazoni. At the Congress in Basel in 1904, he represented the Swedish Government. At Oxford 1908 he lectured on Holy Triads, a comparison of Buddhism and Christianity, 'the two important religions of the world',[9] and with his friend S. A. Fries, he participated in the 1912 Congress in Leiden, the name of which to Söderblom was always closely connected with that of C. P. Tiele.

One of the current stereotypes about Söderblom is of the Liberal historian of the religions who, finding himself appointed Archbishop, had suddenly, there and then, to think up a theology of sorts.

This is very far from being the truth, however. It can in fact be demonstrated that it was as Biblical theologian and Church historian that the young Söderblom, in order to establish the unique quality of the revelation through Jesus Christ, turned to *Religionsgeschichte* as his general frame of reference. His study *Uppenbarelsereligion,* (Religion of Revelation), 1903, is in fact the contribution of a Biblical scholar taking his firm stand in a debate with other Biblical scholars in the 'Babel-Bible' controversy at the beginning of the century.[1]

Söderblom's *Religion of Revelation,* 1903, was an original theological contribution. Here he presented his two well-known phenomenological distinctions. Firstly, between 'prophetic religions', derived from a personal founder, and with a dualistic and eschatological emphasis, and 'religions of nature' or of 'culture'. Secondly, between 'mysticism of the infinite' and 'mysticism of personal life'. It is noteworthy in this connexion that already in 1893 Söderblom had anticipated this distinction. In his little book on Luther's Religion of that year he drew a line of distinction between what he

---

[9] *Transactions, Congress History of Religions,* Oxford 1908, II, p. 391.
[1] His friend S. A. Fries on February 21, 1903, gave an important lecture where, against F. Delitzsch, he insisted on the independence of Israel. S. A. Fries, *Bibel och Babel,* 1903.

called nature mysticism *and* mysticism in the sense of inwardness (*innerlighet*) and depth.

In conscious opposition to the somewhat dry moralistic and rationalistic tendency of the school of Ritschl, particularly in W. Herrmann, Söderblom insisted on 'something irrational in existence'. With Duhm and Sabatier, and later von Hügel, he pointed to a secret, an enigma, the heart-beat of prayer, in religion. This concern always lay at the root of Söderblom's insistence on what he called *mysticism*, albeit that he traced important phenomenological dividing lines between different types of mysticism. He was aware of the fact that his usage of the term 'mysticism of personal life', as applied to Luther in particular, was not uncontested; yet he persevered in using the expression. He showed a special interest in some of the great Christian personalities, the Swede W. Rudin; the Indian Sadhu Sundar Singh; the Spaniard St. John of the Cross. There was in him an affinity with the element of ascesis and discipline, an attitude where he felt that he represented a concern of his father's.

On the other hand, Andrae has pointed out the difference between his statements *on* religion where his sympathy for mysticism is clearly seen, and his statements *in* religion: his own message which largely belonged to the world of trust and forgiveness.[2]

This is obviously not the place for a thorough analysis of the complicated theme of 'Söderblom on mysticism'. For our purpose it must suffice to say that the all-embracing term mysticism allowed him a more generous, a much more comprehensive approach to the ecumenical question than might have been the case without it. He applied the epithets 'comprehensiveness' and 'universality' to one of his own great authorities on mysticism, Friedrich von Hügel, and to that extent there was also in Söderblom himself a close connexion between his interest in mysticism and his comprehensive ecumenical approach.[3]

---

[2] T. Andræ, in [Karlström, ed.] *Nathan Söderblom in memoriam* (1931) p. 61.

[3] Söderblom, *Religionsproblemet*, p. 268. In connexion with the attitude to mysticism, Söderblom's attitude to Psychology of Religion should be mentioned. He took a keen interest in psychology; his studies in Luther are concerned with the Reformer's psychology. But Söderblom's point was that psychology of religion should in the main be applied to 'the great personalities', such as Luther, St. John of the Cross etc. He was therefore critical of certain tendencies in William James' approach as the latter, in his view, made too much of the sociological method in his psychological study. Söderblom's lecture notes on Psychology of Religion, 1907. More cautiously he voiced this opinion in his *Studiet av religionen* (1907), p. 73. In this particular book he says however: 'Psychology of Religion and History of Religion are the two legs of religious study which it must use in order to move at all.' Ibid., p. 16.

But this interest in mysticism did not result in Söderblom forgetting what he called the prophetic emphasis. Quite the contrary. Söderblom's Biblical study had led him to emphasize the qualitative role of prophetic religion. If Söderblom's own scholarly speciality, Avesta, made him include Zoroaster's teaching in the prophetic religions, it must on the other hand be stressed that his intention and conclusion was to bring out, not the agreement, but the difference between Zoroaster and Biblical revelation. The latter points to God's action in history; and the founder, Moses, was followed by a succession of prophets with an increasingly rich message and creative religious genius perfected in Jesus Christ, in the New Covenant.

His concern was to bring out what was unique and characteristic in the prophetic, Biblical, and Christian religion, understood against a background of 'general revelation'. In his Gifford Lectures, *The Living God,* where he was in a position to gather and sum up his life's thinking on religion, he did this particularly in the chapter on Religion as Revelation in History. It was once again to the Old Testament, more particularly to the forbidding figure of Elijah that he turned. 'There could not be a more striking contrast than that between the tolerance of India and this fanaticism in the name of the Lord.'[4]

The Elijah story appeared to him as 'unique in the history of religion' because it stressed 'the difference and contrast: the prophet against the prophets. The prophet of Jahve, the prophet of the jealous god who revealed himself to Moses and in history against the virtuosi of the nature-gods, the spirits and the culture divinities.'[5]

This theme is also treated in the remarkable paragraph in the fourth edition of Tiele–Söderblom's Compendium, on 'Jesus Christ'. It is characteristic that this interpretation is placed as a paragraph, albeit the culminating one, in a chapter on 'Religion among the Western Semites'. But the emphasis is on the uniqueness of Jesus the Christ: his self-consciousness as Messiah and the Son of Man, expressed in the power of his personality. The distinctive marks of that personality were the purity of heart, and the quiet power of serving and forgiving Love; and his care and concern for each individual who met him. With this standpoint he held a conviction derived from his personal religious experience. It was faith, 'true inwardness' which could discover the particular revelation in Jesus Christ.

---

[4] Söderblom, *The Living God* (1932), p. 287.
[5] Ibid, p. 298.

The age-old problem of general and particular revelation was one to which Söderblom devoted much thought. He did this against a very wide background. 'In our own epoch of world missions, world communications and of a world history, which is beginning to flow, at last, in *one* common stream, it is important that the Church be acquainted with the thought of God's general revelation.'[6] The emphasis on Christian world missions in this connexion is of interest, for Söderblom was to place a special emphasis, indeed a particular interpretation on its challenge to the world religions at the time.

It is here that he introduces the concept of *'tävlan'*, contest or struggle. The term has an almost surprising emphasis in his writings, and he applied it not only to the meeting of religions, but also, in his ecumenical thinking, to the meeting, or confrontation of churches.[7] It has never been brought out that this concept of his was related to Benjamin Kidd's book, or rather a translation of Kidd's book. Together with many in his generation, not least in the Student Christian Movement, Söderblom was influenced by Kidd's *Social Evolution*. Kidd both represents nineteenth-century evolutionary thinking and wants to overcome one particular aspect of it. With his propagandist energy he drove the point home that, in human evolution, the decisive factor was, not economic forces or the intellectual factor, but the religious element. It is here that the problem of translation comes in. The Swedish edition, published in 1895, has translated Kidd's two terms 'rivalry' and 'competition' with the one, loose and attenuated word *'tävlan'*, as if Kidd had been referring to a sporting contest. It is in this somewhat blurred Swedish version that Kidd influenced Söderblom: Söderblom throughout speaks of *'tävlan'*, which in his text conveys the meaning of a noble and healthy contest. Söderblom gave his individual variation to Kidd's concept in that he saw Christian missions as the victorious agent in the contest.[8]

[6] Söderblom, *Uppenbarelsereligion* (1903), p. 13.

[7] In 1915 he was to claim that Christian universalism had to be expressed through different churches regarding themselves as co-workers in harmony or *in contest*. If a new *corpus evangelicorum*, a functioning Catholicity, is to appear, we need deeper understanding of the genuine charisma of each church. Söderblom, *Sv. Kyrkans kropp och själ* (1915), p. 58.

[8] It was at, or immediately after, the Stockholm Congress of Religious Study 1897 that Söderblom met Kidd's ideas. He made a page-long foot-note on it in the proofs of his Stockholm 1897 lecture. Söderblom, *Die Religion und Die Sociale Entwicklung*, p. 95 f. Religionsvetenskapliga Kongressen i Stockholm. 1897, p. 142. The Swedish version 1895 of Kidd's book was a translation by O. H. Dumrath, from the twelfth edition of Kidd; it had an important Foreword by the Swedish author Viktor Rydberg.

It was to the great and broad themes of his science that he turned. Holiness, Life, the Triads in Christianity and in Buddhism, these were some of his objects of study in the world of religions. This emphasis on broad and comprehensive concepts was an inheritance from the nineteenth century, in the tradition of Herbert Spencer and his contemporaries. He was influenced by their ambition to establish 'laws' and 'principles' for the development. He had learned much also from Tiele on this score, and from Kidd.

With this background Söderblom made the Phenomenology of Religion into a meaningful and challenging approach to the understanding of the world of religions.

Over against a moralistic emphasis, Söderblom underlined throughout the genuinely religious aspect. He did so in his Religion of Revelation, 1903 and in his study of 1913 on the concept of 'The Holy', well before R. Otto's well-known book on the subject of 1917. 'Holiness is the great word in religion'; Söderblom said here, 'it is even more essential than the notion of God. Real religion may exist without a definite conception of divinity, but there is no real religion without a distinction between holy and profane'.

In his *Religionsproblemet,* 1910, Söderblom has developed his theology of Revelation on a new line, in that with the prophetic understanding of revelation, he now combined an interpretation of 'existence (*tillvaron*) as life'. Together with this generation, Söderblom had found in 'life mysticism' of this period, a philosophy which corresponded to his own attitude. Henri Bergson made this contribution possible in that he appeared as 'the prophet of life', to use Söderblom's expression in a later (unpublished) essay of his on Bergson. Söderblom suggested to Bergson personally that there was affinity between his philosophy of 'creative evolution' and what he called the prophetic view of history. This affinity testified, according to Söderblom, to the fundamental Jewish structure of Bergson's thought. 'For the comprehension of Reality, Being—under the symbol of purpose, realization, insistence, progress, power, energy, life —has its origin in prophetic teaching.'[9]

Intuition and faith instead of intellectualism; active participation in the 'mystery of existence' rather than uninterested observation of ontological phenomena: for these ideas Söderblom found his authority in Bergson (and in Emile Boutroux). They gave a new accent to his thinking as far as it had been expressed in terms of

---

[9] Söderblom, 'Henri Bergson, Nobelpristagare', December 10, 1928, typewritten draft.

that other Frenchman, Sabatier, and his antinomy 'body-soul, institution-spirit'. They were in the last resort to influence Söderblom's whole ecclesiology and ecumenical vision for the terms *'Life and Work'*, or in French *'Vie et Action'*, were not fortuitous but carefully chosen terms, which, as Söderblom always claimed, were as closely related to the Bible as to Bergson and Boutroux.

'Truth is not static (*färdig*), but it emerges ... truth and life must accompany each other. The one does not emerge or grow without the other.'[1] He had anticipated this view already in 1899 when speaking in Uppsala: 'Being cannot be grasped in repose; being is grasped in becoming.'[2] A remarkable variation of this existentialist theme is to be found in the lecture of 1910, 'Jesus or Christ': 'Take reality seriously. Grasp it so firmly that it opens its eyes.'[3]

He expressed this insight to an international student conference at Constantinople in 1911. 'In God's Kingdom you can see nothing so long as you are standing as a mere spectator; only those who serve God fully and self-sacrificingly can perceive God's will.'[4]

A daring, further development of his theology of revelation meets in Söderblom's emphasis on 'continued revelation'. This concept was worked out about 1910 under the influence of Henri Bergson's *'evolution créatrice'*. He was convinced that the divine revelation according to the Biblical tradition and more particularly in the personality of Christ was 'for all times valid and inexhaustible'; but for this very reason, it was to him necessary to count with the idea of a continuation. Söderblom found this continued revelation of God, firstly, in genius; secondly, in history; and thirdly, in the rebirth of the individual.[5]

Daring as the concept was, his boldness was particularly marked in the emphasis on genius as a channel of continued revelation. He felt that he was influenced by Old Testament scholars, such as B. Duhm, Rudolf Kittel, but also by Geijer and by Carlyle in the formulation of this concept. It was to condition his view of the Church and of Evangelic Catholicity. 'Geniuses' he said 'are placed as interpreters of God's creation'.[6] The leaders of the nations—he thought above all of Gustavus Adolphus—belonged to this exclusive

---

[1] Söderblom, *Religionsproblemet* (1910), p. 160.
[2] Söderblom, *Tal och Skrifter*, 3, p. 52.
[3] Söderblom, *När stunderna*, (1935), 1. p. 299.
[4] Report, *W. S. C. F. Conference, Constantinople* (1911) p. 69.
[5] Söderblom, *Ett bidrag till den kristna uppenbarelsetrons tolkning*, 1911.
[6] Ibid p. 8.

group, but primarily 'the heroes of religion, who on their knees had been given a new assurance of the direction of God's ways'.[7] It was here that he gave a place of honour to Martin Luther: 'With Christ, Socrates, St Paul and the very greatest, he shared the conviction of his own importance'.[8]

We recall Söderblom's Luther research in this connexion. We have noticed the importance of his two books on Luther in 1893. In his *Religion of Revelation,* of 1903, Luther was presented as the prototype for what Söderblom called 'mysticism of personal life'. He was convinced that Luther's personal experience of the fear of God and of the assurance of salvation in Christ Jesus went deeper than with any other personality. It is because of this that Luther fascinated him, and it was to this psychological study of the personality of Luther that he was to return in the war years. It was about the time of the Reformation Jubilee 1917 that he devoted particular time and interest to his Luther research, the result of which was his book *Humour and Melancholy in Luther,* 1919.

From this concept of the religious hero he derived his idea of the saint: 'When the great geniuses wholeheartedly and consciously serve God they become saints,' and he went on to give his definition of saints: 'those who in life, personality and action clearly and unmistakably demonstrate that God lives.'[9] These ideas are expressions of Söderblom's never-ceasing interpretation of the concepts of personality and of history; one cannot claim that they have been generally accepted. For our particular purpose they are important for the understanding of certain aspects of Söderblom's ecclesiology and his Evangelical Catholicity.

Söderblom himself could see to it that his theological vision did take a permanent, plastic form. This happened in this wise. In 1908, K. A. Wallenberg, financier, decided to build at Saltsjöbaden near Stockholm, a church to the glory of God. The architect, F. Boberg, in 1909 contacted Söderblom for ideas for the interior decorations. He could not have chosen a more interested theological adviser. 'Few tasks have given such an unadulterated joy,' Söderblom wrote.[1] For it was at this very time that Söderblom was making notes and preparing his draft for what was to become his lecture on 'Continued Revelation' (published 1911). He got ideas as he made a thorough

---

[7] Ibid p. 10.
[8] Ibid p. 14.
[9] Söderblom, Uppenbarelsereligion (ed. 1930), p. 138.
[1] [G. Lindberg, ed.], *Uppenbarelsekyrkan in Saltsjöbaden* 1913–1938 (1938) p. 98.

inspection of Westminister Abbey. On August 30, 1908 he went round the Abbey, a notebook in his hand. The rose window in the south transept captivated him. He discovered that the artist had surrounded Our Lord with prophets and apostles together with Plato, Aristotle, Aeschylus, Zoroaster. 'Why not Socrates?', he wrote to his wife that day.[2] The place which his beloved Athenian philosopher had thus been denied in the Abbey was found for him, through Söderblom, in the 'Church of the Revelation', for this was the name which on Söderblom's suggestion was given to the Church at Saltsjöbaden. Here the saints of Sweden and Finland were represented, and Martin Luther and King Gustavus Adolphus, but also Socrates and Plato.[3]

The connexions between the Swedish Church and the University faculties of Theology were still active at this time. The professors of the Uppsala faculty were, as such, the members of the Archbishop's Chapter and Söderblom regularly attended the weekly Chapter meetings. This gave him, long before he became Archbishop, an invaluable insight into the affairs and problems of the arch-diocese and he felt that the faculty professors had a special contribution to give. Söderblom worked harmoniously with the shy and reticent Archbishop Ekman, who tended to consult him as adviser in matters of international Church relationships.

As professor, Söderblom had in fact a parish of his own. Swedish professors of theology were still prebendaries of country churches near the Cathedral town. Söderblom's own prebend, Holy Trinity of Uppsala, had its special character and charm. The parish was primarily rural and the great majority of the parishioners were farmers. The parish church was in Uppsala itself, close to the Cathedral and the Archbishop's House. It was a wonderful thirteenth-century structure, although badly in need of repair when Söderblom took it over.

---

[2] In his Diary 1908, p. 50–51, he drew a picture of the Abbey rose window to remind him of the scene.
[3] Professor J. Roosval, the Swedish Arts historian, said of the creation of the Saltsjöbaden Church: 'I had an opportunity of noticing the powerful personalities who were at work. How their will stated its goals . . . Nathan Söderblom's ideological contribution cannot as far as power and quantity are concerned be compared with the works of the great medieval artistic bishops or abbots, such as that of Berward in Hildesheim or Suger in St. Denis, but there was something of the same kind in this; one could better understand the ideas of the old prelates ... when he had seen the concern of the great Archbishop for prophets or philosophers. [Lindberg ed.] op. cit., p. 58 f.

He gave much time and thought to the restoration of the church and to the relief on the High altar. After the restoration in 1905, Holy Trinity appeared as one of the jewels among churches in the whole of the diocese. Söderblom's friend Sörensen-Ringi had made the altar scene, Jesus and the Apostles at the Last Supper. This was framed by two sculptures, Eldh's Mother and Sörensen-Ringi's Geijer: a peasant woman and the University professor representing the two categories of those in Holy Trinity's pews.

Above all, Söderblom became a pastor to students. Long decades were to pass before the Uppsala students got a chaplain of their own, but professor Söderblom at Holy Trinity was in fact a chaplain to students and a pastor of souls. Whole generations of students of University faculties were drawn to Söderblom's church. Why? 'It purled and whirled of life about him', one of them told us. And another 'How edifying he was, in the Trinity Church and elsewhere, when one was beset by doubt, vacillation, hesitation, self-criticism. Perhaps it was a sermon at New Year's Eve, or an address on the Spirit ... and the Spirit is close to each one, and its fruits are love, joy, peace'.[1] At a time when secularization had set in, there still remained in the hearts of many a fund of religious quest and thirst. Söderblom through his ministry at Holy Trinity made it easier for many intellectuals to be believing Christians.

Sometimes, in the academic milieu, with that particular climate to which Uppsala was becoming accustomed, this was no easy task: A radical Liberalism with a certain critical attitude to the Church was represented by the student association Verdandi where Professors K. Wicksell and Hj. Öhrvall dominated; their ideas found expression in Upsala Nya Tidning, where Axel Johansson was now chief editor. He watched the scene with a sharp eye. When in the autumn, 1904, professor H. Almkvist died, Söderblom who had been Almkvist's student was called upon to bury him. He did so with much tact and finesse; the ritual was preceded by a short address, with the text from John 1: 47, 'an Israelite indeed, in whom is no guile'. A thoughtful choice for an address on a professor in Semitic languages, one would have thought, but no! The morning after the burial Söderblom received a very sharp note from Johansson: he and a number of Almkvist's younger and older friends had been 'deeply disturbed' by Söderblom's religious meditations on the occasion. Especially the comparison with Nathaniel: 'in that ambigu-

---

[1] K. B. Westman, in *Hågkomster*, XII, p. 277.

ous manner which is the Mark of Cain of Liberal theology'. The letter is interesting. It points out a new tendency in Swedish culture beginning about this time: to many of the Liberals in political and cultural matters, the Liberals in the Church and religion were abhorrent; to them, the Conservatives were preferable for they belonged, once and for all, to the past; the others had an uncomfortable habit of kicking. Söderblom replied, for once, in kind: 'Your letter gladdens me so far as it seems to indicate that you have acted, not by conscious calculation, but with the usual fanatical party zeal.'[2]

The Pastor in that Uppsala, which was very much part of Poverty-Sweden had a message for the Church's social responsibility. He thought of international precedents. The example of an Anglican League of High Church priests who preached 'pure socialism supported by Marx and the Church Fathers', inspired him.[3] At Canterbury in October 1908, he witnessed a group of unemployed making their way into the Cathedral demanding to be heard, and how the Canon-in-residence managed to win their confidence.[4] Less than a year after this in Uppsala, he was himself faced with a similar situation. In August 1909, Sweden had a general strike and Söderblom had promised to speak to the workers in the Socialist 'People's House' at Uppsala. The hall proved too small however, and the crush terrible. But the professor was undaunted. Boldly he invited the crowd to his own place, the Holy Trinity Church. They agreed; the procession of nine hundred moved its way from the People's House to the Church. There Söderblom spoke for two hours, standing in the choir. He explained the religious symbols and inscriptions in that church. A survey of the history of the Swedish Church followed, from the days of St. Ansgar. He felt the Church had stood for the respect of law and social solidarity. Concluding he suggested that the message of the Bible could be summed up in three words (the first two of which were names of noisy contemporary Socialist newspapers) 'Fire', 'Forward', and 'Consolation'. The last word, Consolation, stood for the gift of the forgiveness of sins.[5]

To Nathan and Anna Söderblom Holy Trinity in Uppsala seemed

---

[2] Axel Johansson, October 4, 1904, to Söderblom. Söderblom, October 6, 1904, to Johansson.
[3] Nathan Söderblom, *Sveriges Kyrka* (1908), p. 56.
[4] Söderblom, October 2, 1908, to Anna Söderblom.
[5] Söderblom, Notes to this lecture, August 31, 1909, in the Söderblom papers. Cf. G. Kyhlberg, in *Hågkomster XII*, p. 291.

to be a continuation of their ministry in Paris. And as in Paris they had held their Monday evening receptions for Scandinavian artists, so now in their manse at Staby, just outside the town boundaries, they received the students on Monday evenings; for talks and laughter, music and prayer. Yngve Brilioth himself, as a very young student, was taken by his elder brother to one of these receptions and has interpreted what this meant: 'Many a shy and faint-hearted youth gathered new courage through the inspiring personality of the professor, and was led to dream of great things. He seemed in possession of a magic wand that could transform the study of theology and the service of the Church, to many perhaps a heavy and depressing task, into a thrilling spiritual adventure.'[6]

The 'Staby Cabin' became a spiritual power-house for the 'Young Church' revival movement in Uppsala, under the leadership of Manfred Björkquist from 1908. The first decade of the century was a period when youth associations of various kinds, political, educational, religious, played a special role in Sweden, not least important as a sounding-board for the inspiration of writers, old and young. Björkquist's Young Church movement can from one point of view be interpreted as a function of a general trend in Swedish youth at this time. Through this movement whole generations of Swedish students were touched and inspired to a new vision of the Swedish Church as God's gift to the Swedish people: a new understanding of its tradition and a new hope for its future. Bishop J. A. Eklund and Professor (later Bishop) Einar Billing were, together with Söderblom, the Church fathers of this movement, although Söderblom always felt the responsibility to transform this national enthusiasm into wider, universal perspectives.

The bosom-friends of the house were laymen. Justice G. Ribbing and his wife, the latter of a distinguished Jewish family, belonged to these. Mrs. Fehr, Dr. Fehr's widow, had brought the Ribbings to Staby in 1901 and simply told the circle, 'Now you are to be friends.' This prophecy proved to be correct. Justice Olivecrona was another prominent citizen of Uppsala with wide interests, and his family was inseparable from that of the Söderbloms. Professor U. Quensel (of Pathology) and his wife Thyra were devoted friends. Quensel as chairman of the Town Council, and later as Pro-Rector of the University, had wide interests; he also had the responsible and difficult task of caring for Söderblom's very precarious health. Professor

---

[6] Y. Brilioth, in Söderblom, *The Living God*, p. 17.

Hjärne and his family belonged to the group. The only exception in this prominent collection of laymen was Söderblom's old friend Professor N. J. Göransson.

In the small world of Uppsala before 1914, this group met regularly in the members' homes, 'almost daily', preferably according to a strict rule where to meet on Christmas morning, New Year's Eve, etc. Staby as a matter of course tended to be the centre. There was Bach and singing, discussions of day-to-day events, and Söderblom would read from the latest book of poetry, perhaps from E. A. Karlfeldt, the poet of the province of Dalecarlia.

Söderblom was the pastor of these friends; he gave infinite care to special confirmation classes for the young and their friends. The group was united by a religious quest and highest cultural ambitions. Sickness and death also brought them together. After a particularly trying time of nearly fatal illness, Söderblom wrote to Mrs Quensel: 'After an experience of this kind, life may be as long as it may; it will, all the same, be lived on the thin, precarious edge close to the darkness of death. This rather concentrates everything in life and illuminates its value.'[7]

While he was encouraged by his innumerable contacts with younger generations, in Sweden and Scandinavia as a whole, he was also inflicted with personal trials. As we have pointed out, in 1903 there was the first attack of bleeding ulcer. In May 1908, this became very serious; there were times when he was hardly expected to survive.

At this time two lay members of the Church, inspired by Söderblom's personality and message, took steps that were to be very helpful to Söderblom personally. Harald Bildt, a young diplomat, together with three other friends put money aside for Söderblom, to be used for sanatorium care abroad. The following three summers Söderblom spent at Karlsbad; his health improved considerably.[8]

Still another financial offer greatly encouraged him. Mrs Anna Lindblad whom Söderblom did not know personally before this time, had been led to offer a considerable sum of money for what became the Olaus Petri Foundation. With these funds Söderblom could send young Swedish students on scholarships for church stud-

---

[7] Söderblom, November 29, 1906, to Thyra Quensel. Interviews with Mrs. Malin Adell, née Ribbing.
[8] Söderblom dedicated his *Religionsproblemet* to Harald Bildt and Hjalmar Wijk: his benefactors in this connexion.

ies to Britain and the Continent ('Söderblom's Peace Doves'); above all he could now bring outstanding lecturers to Uppsala.

From 1909, Söderblom was in a position to invite famous scholars of *Religionsgeschichte* and others to lecture in the Olaus Petri Foundation at Uppsala. From the outset he regarded this Foundation as a Swedish parallel to the Gifford Lectures in Scotland, with which to him Tiele's name was particularly connected.[9] In March 1909 Söderblom could welcome the first Foundation lecturer: Professor Rudolf Eucken. The University Hall, holding some two thousand, was packed. With his flowing white hair and beard, Eucken looked like a Zachariah of Michelangelo as he propounded the Ethics of Jena. Söderblom was elated. He acquired the generous habit of naming each one of his famous Olaus Petri lecturers a genius, or next to it. A number of the lecturers were scholars of History of Religion; a time was to come, just after the war, when Söderblom was to use this University foundation in the interest of his particular ecumenical programme, more than ever emphasizing the international aspect of the Foundation.

The pastor in Holy Trinity Church became wellknown as a preacher. This was a period of good preaching at Uppsala. In the Cathedral, J. A. Eklund was the great preacher. Söderblom's Holy Trinity nearby was far more intimate as a church, and his preaching at this time must be understood in this setting, while related particularly to the seeking, Nicodemus-natures in the University.

Once again Sabatier's name comes to mind. As a young pastor to Huguenot farmers and craftsmen in the Cevennes, Sabatier had learned how to preach simply in the form, as he used to say, of a personal letter. He confided his homiletic experience to Söderblom, and the Swedish pastor was anxious to learn from it. Obviously this was not a case of dependence on Söderblom's part; but just as unmistakably the contact with Sabatier gave him a new assurance for the type of preaching which became natural to him. There are sermons from his time as Uppsala professor which have a particular affinity to Sabatier's message (e.g. 'The Inner Guest').

Returning from Paris, it was in a rapid impressionistic style that he preached. Söderblom's sermons, like those of Sabatier, had the simple direct note of the personal letter. Often there was an unexpected turn in his introduction which attracted attention. This is how he began a sermon on All Saints Day: 'At home somebody is

---

[9] Söderblom, December 21, 1907, to Anna Lindblad, copy.

sewing. She follows a design, and when the work is ready, it is neat and nice. But it is made according to a design. This is not the way in which saints are made.'[1]

To convey an impression of Söderblom as a preacher is not easy. Unavoidably some of his sermons appear as dated now, even in the Swedish original. In this book, room cannot be found for more than a few brief extracts; they cannot reproduce the magic of the personality of the preacher or the atmosphere created in Holy Trinity Church at Uppsala. A few samples must suffice.

'*The Poor Mortals*', 1905, has a modern note:

We are down here. Is there anybody up there? We are out here in life. Is there anybody in the centre of existence? The human spirit is hungry for reality, and wants a plain answer. Is there any reality beyond, or within?

We are here below, with our labours, our culture, our history, our suffering. Is there anyone up there? Let me rather say, is there anyone within? There is nothing in space to look up to. We think of the universe as a whole, held together by a centre of gravitation. We understand Geijer's remark: In the depths, as in the heavens, lives God.

Our question is rather: Is there anyone who listens to us, in our innermost being, in the depths of our hearts, not merely an echo of our own voice, of our own being, reverberating from the hidden depths of our personality, but a reality greater than our own, someone to pray to, to trust in?

The innermost room, does it widen out, not as the men of antiquity thought that the graves widened out into a kingdom of the dead? Do the vital chambers in the hidden depths of our hearts, where we kneel and receive help, combine to form a kingdom of life? Is there anyone within? No science can answer this question. No arguments or demonstrations can convince anyone that there is someone therein. And the prayers —were they not meaningless, lonely cries in the universe? But I did not dare to stop praying lest [logic's] chilly conclusion would enter and make an end to it all. Then there appeared something like a revelation; to me as to so many, this happened through the image of the Crucified. Do not call out, for he is quite near to you. For what are you aiming with your efforts? Be still! What are you groping for? Here is the great gift.'

'*The Inner Guest*', of 1907, is a homiletic interpretation of Sabatier's *Dieu intérieur*.

The guest within cannot be met in the outer rooms of the soul. Do not neglect the guest in your innermost room! You make ready your house for

---

[1] T. Andræ, *Nathan Söderblom* (1931), p. 228.

all kinds of other guests. You are so eager to show them attention and courtesy. But meanwhile the Supreme Guest who awaits you within is forgotten.

Socrates felt completely secure so long as he followed the directions of his inner voice, how different it was with the prophets! They too felt within themselves the presence of an inner guest. But He was the Powerful One, who leads the peoples and shakes the earth, burning what he touches with the fire of righteous zeal. The Friend and the Lord are names for the inner guest. But for Christians his truest name is 'the Spirit'. This spirit is not an indefinite spiritual force but the divine Spirit of Christ. It involves participation in a higher reality, in divine life. Therefore we may speak of the Friend or the Guest.

The image of the Crucified can help and captivate, if any can. *O caput cruentatum*. This image can free me, if any can, from the self, the wretched self, round which powerlessness, moral or physical, compels the mind to revolve. We have the image of the Crucified. His suffering brings us consolation. The figure of the Crucified gathers and calms the mind.

Christ gathers us also in the sense that as we become familiar with prayer and learn to go into the stillness in order to recover and renew ourselves, we become convinced that the Father of our Lord Jesus Christ is the inner guest of the soul. The Spirit and the Son lead to the Father. The intimate friend, the inner guest, is, as Abraham discovered with his guests, God Himself.'

But this 'inwardness', or *innerlighet,* was always integrated with the ethical claim, the practical Christian task or calling. The sermon *The Calling* (1909) brings this out.

Nobody else can tell me what my calling is. But we find it, we are in the midst of it. Here is something that must be done. Well, let me try. For long stretches we must walk along blindly. Then dutiful faithfulness to a given task is a blessed help. Impatiently we beat against the material of life. It responds in a dull and dead way. The only thing to do is: carry on with the task. Surely the right sound of metal will then ring to us once again.[2]

'To carry on with the task.' What was that task to Professor Söderblom? We shall turn our interest to the *horizons* which in the light of subsequent history, seemed to prepare him for his ecumenical leadership.

In our study of Archbishop Söderblom's ecumenical thought and work we are likely to find that his concept of Evangelical Catholicity, while universal in intention, was related to a particular church,

---

[2] The sermons quoted printed in the collection, *När stunderna växla och skrida.*

President of the Student Corps, Uppsala, 1892.

Professor in Uppsala, 1904.

Professor Söderblom, 1912.

Mrs. Anna Söderblom, 1921.

Emerik Stenberg's picture of the Theological Faculty, Uppsala 1911.
See page 63.

the Swedish Church, in its geographical concreteness, with its history and its great personalities; kings and bishops and—incomparable rural church-wardens. But one can see the threads of this unmistakable pattern also in the young professor's extramural activity, in the Swedish province and in the international community, the latter more particularly referring to Leipzig, Lambeth, and Constantinople.

1. In 1901, the cosmopolitan scholar and professor returned from seven years in Paris to Sweden. He loved Paris and France, and continued to do so. In his last few years, he and Anna Söderblom would day-dream of an existence as pensioners living in a little flat in Paris within easy reach of the Bibliothèque Nationale. Yet, at 35, returning to Uppsala, he was a Swede of the Swedes, in a period in Swedish history characterized by a new awareness of Swedish tradition and of the values of provincial culture. The authors and the artists and the musicians—Selma Lagerlöf and Zorn and Stenhammar—received their inspiration from the Swedish province. Selma Lagerlöf had her Värmland, Zorn his Dalecarlia. And Söderblom had his province, Hälsingland. As a student he had been First Curator of the Nation of Hälsingland; as a professor he became the Inspector of this organization. But much more than this: his old uncle, churchwarden Sven Jonsson in Söderala, used to write to him, in Paris or Uppsala, in these words: 'Are you not coming *home* soon?' 'To feel at home in existence', was Geijer's ideal, and Söderblom in his generation expressed this ideal more faithfully than anybody else. He was at home in Hälsingland: its forests and valleys, its mighty Ljusnan river and the Dellen lakes. And among the free yeomen in the red wooden houses.

In Paris, Sven Kjellström, the violinist, had been a constant visitor to Söderblom's home. Pastor Söderblom used to accompany the violin on his organ. Both of them having now returned to Sweden, Kjellström and Söderblom organized the Hälsinge moots, usually in June or July. The first officially organized meeting was held at Midsummer 1908. Söderblom had prepared every detail, but was himself prevented from attending by his nearly fatal illness that year. Kjellström's participation was essential, for the meetings depended on the amateur bands of village violinists.

The nineteenth century Pietistic revival had declared the violin to be a tool of the Devil himself; now it was taken from its hiding place and was given free flow. Not without resistance of course.

6 – 684363 *B. Sundkler*

Some of the Pietist pastors in Hälsingland deplored this organized renewal of musical folk culture. David Granquist, who was to be one of Söderblom's firm opponents at the episcopal election in 1914 and during his time as archbishop of the diocese, complained. He wrote to Söderblom's colleague, professor Lundström, about what he described as lack of leadership in the Church. 'Has e.g. Professor Söderblom a preponderant influence in the Chapter, as rumour has it; if so, the outlook is not bright, for he has personally been one of those who have grafted dance and fiddler's tunes to the folk-life of Hälsingland.'[1]

Worship in the old parish church, music, and local crafts, with sports in the open air, all with a strong emphasis on temperance: this constituted the programme of these meetings. Söderblom as the untiring, inspiring leader enjoyed himself at least as much as anybody else. He knew every special tune of these old and young peasant violinists; if by chance he happened to meet such an artist in the streets of Uppsala, he would immediately ask him for this or that tune. No such Provincial Meeting was complete without Söderblom himself giving a lecture or speech interpreting the nature and the personalities of Hälsingland. But he widened the horizon: to the nation as a whole, with the common Swedish language: 'our common land, our common language: Can't you hear how beautiful it sounds?'[2] And as the sun was setting over the forests and lakes and the river, he would widen the perspective, to Europe and the world; mankind and the Church universal.

We shall insist here on a point raised earlier. Even as a scholar Söderblom was just as much concerned with, and engaged in, Church History as with *Religionsgeschichte*. And it was the inward (*'innerlig'*) dimension of the history of piety in the Swedish Church to which he turned his attention; quite naturally as it was always the inner pulse of mysticism which he wanted to feel. A perusal of his bibliography 1904–11 (prior to his going to Leipzig) bears this out. 'Ah, it is of course spiritual Church History that we need', he told his friend Emil Liedgren, the hymnologist.[3]

In 1903–04 he gave a series of university lectures on 'Swedish Theology in the Nineteenth Century'. This was a period when J. A. Eklund and others began to insist on 'Swedish' theology and when it

---

[1] D. Granquist, September 29, 1911, to H. Lundström, Uppsala. Granquist followed this up by an official memorandum to the Chapter.

[2] *Söderhamns Tidning*, June 26, 1911.

[3] Söderblom, November 28, 1908, to E. Liedgren.

was felt that Sweden must produce something of its own. Speaking to his Uppsala students Söderblom tackled the problem in his refreshing manner. He agreed that Swedish theology could well afford to aim higher than being nothing but 'a barge in German backwaters'. Yet, 'a Swedish theology unfortunately could not be fabricated as easily as Swedish galoshes or Swedish shoe-polish'. For theology was, after all, an international undertaking. Science and scholarship did not allow for chauvinism. Yet, after these warnings, he interpreted the faith and piety of leading Swedish thinkers in the preceding century; above all, he dwelt on E. G. Geijer, who, he felt, was to Sweden, what Carlyle was to Britain and Grundtvig to Denmark.[4] He knew what line he wanted Swedish Church-historical research to take: away from curates' salaries and Church politics over to the sphere of piety and inwardness.[5]

In his first year after the return to Sweden from Paris, Söderblom, the cosmopolitan who had become a Swede again could allow himself once or twice almost exuberant expressions of patriotism. A Hälsinge Day at the national Swedish shrine of Skansen, Stockholm, might tempt him to oratorical flights: 'Come home to thyself, thou Swedish people; come home from insipid admiration for anything foreign.'[6] But he soon found that his task was different.

Sweden had its political crisis. The Union with Norway was severed in 1905. In Paris, Söderblom had been as much a pastor to Norwegians as to Swedes, and at Uppsala in 1905 he took his share in calming noisy nationalists, not least in the Uppsala Student Christian association. In those years he gave a series of lectures on the Church of Sweden, published under that title in 1908. Here he meditated on the antinomy of national unity and the freedom of the individual conscience, and claimed with Pascal that it was the responsibility and art of the true patriot to hold together these two opposites.

In his inimitable manner he concluded his little book of 1908, on *The Church of Sweden;* 'Is it my faith which causes an acoustic delusion? No, my ear does not make a mistake. From different sides

[4] Söderblom, File with lecture notes 1903–04 Swedish Theology in the 19th century. Söderblom had the intention of publishing a volume, to be called *Piety of Swedes* (Svenskars fromhet). A posthumous collection of articles under this title was published by Anna Söderblom in 1933. It included studies of Schartau, Tegnér, Geijer, Strindberg and Fröding. A second collection under this title, 1941.
[5] Söderblom, March 24, 1908, to E. Liedgren.
[6] Söderblom, Skansen address, May 16, 1902, Söderblom papers.

I hear sounds indicating that, once again, the bells will toll for *Högmässa* in the Church of Sweden.' His readers and listeners felt that they knew who was that intrepid bellringer.

2. At the end of 1912, Söderblom's career suddenly took a new turn, in that he accepted the call to the University of *Leipzig*. There was a complex set of factors which made him decide to accept the invitation. In 1909 he had been urged by Harnack to come to Berlin, but as he wrote to a friend 'It is quite clear for me that I shall never voluntarily go into definite exile'.[7]

Söderblom was hesitant and undecided about the offer from Leipzig, but a personal appeal from Professor Hauck of Leipzig made him accept, after all, on condition that it was to be a two year appointment and that he should at the same time retain his chair in Uppsala.

The Leipzig séjour became in fact relatively brief, from November 1912 until the beginning of August 1914, and it was combined with lectures at Uppsala given in the Leipzig holidays. Immediately on arrival he was faced with an international problem: the family was offered a flat in the 'Sedanstrasse' in Leipzig: What would my French friends say to that? was Söderblom's exclamation, and another flat was found in the Stallbaumstrasse, a name innocuous enough. He found the Leipzig milieu stimulating.

Firstly, Leipzig was a German city, characterized by the bourgeois culture of Lutheran Saxony. The appointment to Leipzig gave Söderblom invaluable personal contacts with German theology, in those years of uncontested German domination in the field of theological research. Albert Hauck, Alfred Jeremias and Rudolf Kittel belonged to the ornaments of Leipzig. While he retained his Swedish citizenship the Leipzig appointment simultaneously made him a citizen of Saxony. Secondly, at least as interesting and significant for our theme, was the fact of the international horizon of pre-war Leipzig. The city, well on its way to become a 'Grosstadt', with some 600,000 inhabitants, was the centre of the famous international fair; production of musical instruments and books were attributes for which the city was particularly renown. The University represented this international aspect. The Chemist W. Ostwald had established his '*Die Brücke*'-movement with important contacts throughout the

---

[7] Söderblom, January 17, 1909 to H. Bildt; Ebildslätt.

world, not least to Uppsala. W. Wundt laid the foundations of a sociology with close affinity to nineteenth century Anglo-Saxon sociology. The historian Karl Lamprecht, at a time when in Harnack's words there was an opportunity not only for 'Gross-Industrie', but also for 'Gross-Wissenschaft', had produced enormous volumes on German history, but with a difference; his whole message was the universal aspect of history.[8]

Lamprecht promoted university co-operation with America and he had personal contacts with Scandinavia (Norway); his method was that of 'Universal' history, including East Asia, particularly Japan.[9] This was only one of the many traits in Lamprecht which must have reminded Söderblom of his Uppsala authority Hjärne: to Söderblom Lamprecht became, as it were, his Leipzig substitute for Harald Hjärne.

Lamprecht who was Vice-chancellor of the Leipzig University in 1910–11, showed special interest in Söderblom. They had met in Scotland in 1911, when they both became honorary doctors at St. Andrews University. On the same occasion, Harald Hjärne and Ad. Deissmann, of Berlin, shared that honour. Lamprecht welcomed Söderblom in most generous terms; he expected the Swedish scholar to provide the great concerns and wide horizons, and he wanted himself to be regarded as one of Söderblom's 'disciples'. He had established a Seminar for 'the universal history of culture'; he wanted the history of art, of law and of religion etc. to be included in this enormous effort. Lamprecht regarded Söderblom's fourth edition of Tiele's Handbook as a prototype for similar 'precise and reliable' handbooks in other fields of human knowledge.[1] To Lamprecht, the Swedish professor and pastor was the one theologian whom he could understand and appreciate; after his death, his daughter wrote to Söderblom: 'My father had hardly any contacts with theologians; I know only one who in the field of church and religion thought in the same wide and global terms as my father; yourself.'[2]

Söderblom was to find that the theological colleagues too had this international horizon: A. Hauck, famous church historian, was an expert on English Church history, and was to lecture, during the

---

[8] K. Lamprecht, *Americana, Reiseeindrücke*, Freiburg i. B., 1906 and idem, *Rektoratserinnerungen*, Gotha 1917, p. 12 f.

[9] K. Lamprecht, *Zur universalgeschichtlichen Methodenbildung*, Leipzig 1909.

[1] K. Lamprecht, July 15, 1912, to Söderblom, in file 'Leipzig', UUB.

[2] Marianne Lamprecht, October 23, 1915, and January 15, 1919, to Söderblom.

war, at Uppsala in the Olaus Petris series, on the relationships of German and English Church Life: C. Rendtorff was the chairman of the Gustavus Adolphus association movement, and had wide contacts with Protestant minority groups throughout Europe. There was established at this time The Associated Councils of Churches in the British and German Empires for Fostering Friendly Relations between the Two Peoples, and Söderblom naturally showed interest in this effort. As a professor at Leipzig, he made it his special concern to interpret Luther in England.

The outlook for *Religionsgeschichte* at this time in German universities was decidedly precarious. The great von Harnack was against the subject being taught in a Theological faculty, while on the other hand he was all for it being taught in the Arts faculty. There, research and teaching in the languages and history of overseas peoples could be assured, and dangerous dilettantism thus avoided. The Dane, E. Lehmann had been called to the Berlin University's Arts Faculty in 1909. In Leipzig it was the confessional Lutheran professors of the theological faculty who had worked for Söderblom's appointment, and they were grateful to find energetic support from Karl Lamprecht and others in the University as a whole.

At Leipzig Söderblom had a strenuous programme of lectures dealing with general themes of religious 'phenomenology', such as Holiness, Belief in God, Eschatology. A select group of graduate students took part in his seminar and found his teaching stimulating not least because of the helpful way in which he devoted himself to personal supervision.

The time in Leipzig was to Söderblom a period of concentrated scholarly work, more so than he had ever had before, or was likely to get after 1914. His two principal works were *Natürliche Religion und Religionsgeschichte* and *The Origin of Religious Belief* (Gudstrons uppkomst). In the former he took the position that 'natural religion' is 'never natural, but positive'. All religion is as such 'positive' in the sense of 'a concrete whole of rites, custom and tradition'. In the place of 'natural religion', modern Religionsgeschichte provided the frame of reference in order the better to understand and appreciate the message of Christianity and the uniqueness of Christ.

Above all, he succeeded in gathering the results of his many years of research in the book which can be regarded as his most important scholarly contribution in the field of History of Religion, *Gudstrons uppkomst,* 1914.[3] Söderblom's method in this book can be interpreted as typical of his comprehensive approach to religion and Church; it was a grand synthesis of his work in *Religionsgeschichte.* Tylor, Frazer, Lang; they had all been concerned with finding some one root, some one single 'origin' of religion. To Söderblom, this was 'a new form of the old illusion believing that with *one* key one could open all the locks of Religionsgeschichte and mythology.'[4] To him reality was always much too complex for any ready made explanation from one neat formula. 'Strangely enough reality was not constructed for scholarship's sake', he warned with a characteristic turn of phrase.[5]

Just as characteristic was his own three-fold explanation: This was a category with Söderblom. Faced with any complex situation he would almost always find that it was composed of 'three' factors or three types. In this case, the three were animism, mana, and the 'Urheber'. In the latter, related to Andrew Lang's and Pater W. Schmidt's *'Urmonotheismus',* the question of origin was dominant. The mana theory implied a concept of power and holiness. And finally in his inspired pages on animism Söderblom drew a bold line to Jahve and Sinai, as 'a genuine animistic appearance'. It was 'the deity as *will'* and as a personal moral Being with which he was concerned here, in his own particular interpretation of animism. The size of his concepts shows in his remark that animism had twice been of epochal importance for Western religion; first through the revelation to Moses; second in Plato. Both 'reveal the two fundamental tendencies inherent in animism, namely the interpretation of existence either as will or as spirit.'[6] In his theology and ecclesiology, Söderblom was to return to these concepts, and behind, or underneath his seemingly simple Biblical references there were thus daring perspectives of Religionsgeschichte whereby the Christian theologian and Archbishop identified himself with the common seeking and striving of all of mankind.[7]

---

[3] This book first appeared in Swedish (1914); in 1916 in a German translation, in 1921 in Danish. There was a second German edition in 1926. At this time, Söderblom tried to have the book published in English.

[4] Söderblom, *Sommarminnen,* (ed. Anna Söderblom) 1941, p. 170.

[5] Söderblom, *Gudstrons uppkomst* (1941), p. 6.

[6] Ibid p. 366–367.

[7] Söderblom, *Natürliche Theologie,* (1913), p. 50. It was in harmony with this attitude that in the book 'Natürliche Religion', he turned against Dean Inge. In this book, in German, published in 1913, Söderblom criticized Dean Inge for having aligned himself with the Aryan ideology of H. S. Chamberlain; this Söderblom said, was not worthy of Inge's position.

Analysing the different strands which make up religious beliefs, Söderblom finally, on the last page of the book, placed the results of his study in the perspective of emerging world culture. Christian Mission was playing a central role here. Once again he saw its contribution in terms of Benjamin Kidd's idea of 'contest'. Christian Mission brought about this contest, 'it called forth that global spiritual process whereby the victorious belief in God was to emerge as a possession common to all of mankind.' He felt that with mankind he was standing on the threshold of a new epoch where 'universal co-operation and contest is coming to the fore.'[8] Co-operation and contest were also the categories in which he saw the ecumenical problem, not least as he turned now to the relationship with the Anglican Communion.

3. In the perspective of history there was one of Söderblom's international contacts and activities which was to be of particular importance to Söderblom's own life and work and for the Church whose leader he was to become. This was the Swedish conversations with the *Anglicans* in 1909, following upon the Lambeth Conference of 1908. For an understanding of Söderblom's standpoint and role in these talks, it is of importance to underline that to him two churches were involved, the Church of England and the Augustana Synod in the United States. He had to consider certain ecumenical conditions within the Church of England at this time, as well as certain attempts by individuals in the Episcopal Church in the United States to enlist Swedish emigrants into Episcopal congregations. In fact, the talks with the Anglican delegation to Uppsala in 1909, were overshadowed by a consideration that had comparatively little to do with England. In 1909, the Swedish 'horizon' in these matters was America: America, or rather 'Swedish America' and the American Lutheran Augustana Synod, was then Sweden's nearest neighbour. Until about 1909 a quarter of the Swedish population had emigrated to the U.S.A. It was the peculiar American tensions that complicated the negotiations of 1909.

From the very first Söderblom identified himself with the matter. On October 25, 1907, the Uppsala professor made this note in his diary: 'Thanks be to God who joins things together, so that my old dream of a connexion with the Church of England seems to become

---

[8] Söderblom, *Gudstrons uppkomst*, p. 368.

a reality.'[9] How old was his dream? It is difficult to know. He may have discussed it with Archbishop Sundberg when in 1893 he was offered a post as a seamen's pastor at West Hartlepool. Both Sundberg and Söderblom were aware of the efforts made, particularly by the American Episcopalians, to establish contacts with the Swedish Church. The reference to an 'old dream' is characteristic of Söderblom;he always felt the need to emphasize the continuity of his own personal experience and active interest over long stretches of time; this he did as soon as he was confronted with an issue which was of particular importance to him, and the Anglican contact was such an issue.

In a visit to Archbishop Ekman, Söderblom chanced to see a letter to Ekman from the Swedish Ambassador in London, Herman Wrangel. Was this a coincidence? From Söderblom's own references to the matter, one gets that impression. Yet this may be misleading. Archbishop Ekman appreciated Söderblom's international contacts, and could rely on his advice in such matters. Söderblom was a member of his Chapter, and there were regular opportunities for the two to discuss common interests, more particularly international Church problems. At this time both of them were interested in the relationships of the Swedish Mission and the Anglican Church in South India, a problem to which we shall return later. It was also something of a tradition with Swedish ambassadors to the Court of St. James to take an active interest in matters ecclesiastical. Wrangel told Archbishop Ekman of a talk he had had with Archbishop Davidson, and forwarded the minutes of the Lambeth Conference, 1897, which mentioned the need for negotiations between the two churches. From that moment, Söderblom took over.

He moved rapidly as he corresponded with Wrangel in London. In his own mind he was sure that among the Swedish bishops, it was H. W. Tottie in Kalmar only who had any real contacts with the English Church and he should be sent to Lambeth. Tottie was the obvious choice, with his excellent English, his wide international contacts acquired in his time as general secretary of the Church of Sweden Mission. On his own initiative Söderblom approached Tottie. Tottie characteristically replied to Söderblom, on July 21, 1908, that he should make use of the forthcoming State visit of King Edward VII to Stockholm. On this solemn occasion, the British Ambassador Sir Rennell Rodd, ought to be approached with a view to put

---

[9] *Förbindelse* is here rendered as 'connexion'.

pressure on the Swedish Government to send a representative to Lambeth.

Söderblom was ready to make the Royal visit an occasion for an interesting statement on the relationship between the Swedish and English Churches, although he did not share the State-church view to which Tottie seemed to subscribe in this connexion. Not the Swedish Government, but the Swedish Church should send a representative to England, he insisted. In honour of King Edward, *Stockholms Dagblad* published a special English issue and Professor Söderblom made his first official statement on the subject which now occupied his mind; he called his article 'The Swedish Church and the English [Church]'.[1] It was an important statement, not least with regard to Söderblom's own development. His orientation until this time had been mainly French and German but the year 1908 showed a conscious effort on his part to orientate himself towards England.

The article in *Stockholms Dagblad* discussed the relationship of the two Churches. Lambeth had taken the initiative hitherto, in 1888, 1897 and 1908; now it was the Swedish Church's turn to act. It was time that the hand extended in brotherly fellowship should at last be grasped by the Swedish Church. This was more than an act of elementary inter-church tact; 'the Swedish episcopate has every reason to demonstrate at long last that the Swedish Church did not neglect the unity of Christendom, and particularly [the unity] with the sister church with which we are here concerned.' Reference was made to the Lambeth 'Quadrilateral' and the historic succession of Bishops. Historic research by Söderblom's colleague, Professor H. Lundström, had proved, he felt, this unbroken succession with full certainty. Almost defiantly he declared 'If a comparison were to be made, the *succession* of the Swedish Church would be historically more certain than that of the English Church, not the other way round'.

The concept of continuity fascinated him: 'in our Church perhaps purer and more unbroken than in the Church of England'. This to him did not only refer to the succession of Bishops, but also 'in

---

[1] *Stockholm Dagblad*, May 24, 1908. This was an England issue. The leader by Dr. V. Söderberg, the editor, made a deliberate attempt for Sweden to orientate itself more to Britain than heretofore. Writing from England to his wife in August the same year Söderblom wrote: 'I was right that it should be a church mission. I am very glad that I insisted. The Government's Commission was however to *our* Church princes (!) *conditio sine qua non*'. Söderblom August 30, 1908, to Anna Söderblom.

more real things; continuity appears with us for example in the Liturgy, which with us never had a fundamentalist emphasis as in England.'[2]

Söderblom was aware of one hitch. His eagerness for contacts with Canterbury might be misunderstood or misconstrued by the Augustana Synod in the U.S.A., but so far from allowing this complication to become a hindrance to Anglo–Swedish church relations, it might even solve a problem for Augustana itself: 'It is not inconceivable that this fellowship may stimulate the Augustana Synod one day into allowing its Bishops to be consecrated in the Cathedral at Uppsala'. The young professor very wisely omitted any suggestion to whom conceivably might be the consecrating Archbishop on such a hypothetical occasion; this was better left to history!

It is not without significance for subsequent development to note here that Söderblom's article was translated into English by an American Episcopalian of Swedish descent, Gustaf Hammarskjöld, priest in New York, with special commission to gather such Swedish immigrants who wished to join the Episcopal Church. The article was published in *The Churchman*, the Episcopalian quarterly, in 1908.

As a result of these efforts made particularly by Söderblom, the Bishop of Kalmar left for England. Furnished with the Swedish Government's ecclesiastical commission, Bishop Tottie attended Lambeth, 1908, and there succeeded so well that a commission was appointed by the Archbishop of Canterbury with a view to establish official contacts with the Church of Sweden.

In the autumn of 1908 Söderblom visited England. He was on sick leave from his University and had spent two months in the summer at the Karlsbad sanatorium. His doctor and friend, professor Quensel was very reluctant to allow him, after the enforced stay at Karlsbad, to take part in a Congress of History of Religion in Oxford; but Söderblom could not be contained.

Not only did he participate in the congress but he also established important preliminary contacts with some of those Anglican churchmen with whom he was to co-operate in the years to come. We shall, however briefly, refer to these contacts here. Söderblom, very much on his own initiative, took upon himself to present the Swedish case to some of the leading Anglican churchmen, especially those who were particularly concerned with the Intercommunion issue. He

[2] Söderblom, in 'Canterbury och Uppsala' in *Svenska Kyrkans kropp och själ*, p. 133 (This passage from 1911).

soon discovered that however much a professor he may have been, Anglicans preferred to regard him as a priest rather than a scholar. He wrote to Mrs Söderblom, 'In Germany I am of a certain renown and am [known as] 'Herr Professor'; in France I can wear the red ribbon [of the Legion d'Honneur], but here I am 'Rev'. It is remarkable how extraordinarily highly the Church is esteemed here. *Nothing* is superior to a bishop.' The Dean of Westminster glanced at Söderblom's visiting card, and thereupon introduced him as 'Prebendary of Holy Trinity'.[3]

In Canterbury he visited Archbishop Davidson who received him for lunch. This was the first meeting between the two men. Davidson was sixty, had been a bishop for seventeen years and Primate of All England for five. Söderblom was forty-two; a Swedish professor of History of Religion. In a letter to his wife he recalls the meeting.

We had begun eating, as he came in. Seated himself next to me. Below medium height, with burly eyebrows and under these: great glistening and penetrating eyes. He had been in Lund and Uppsala and knew that [Archbishop] Sundberg had been a mighty politician. He supported my plans for contact between [our] Churches. Promised to instruct the Bishop of London to give the Swedish chaplain permission to take burials in Anglican mortuary chapels. Has seldom time to stay in Canterbury. I [said] "London is more suitable for a second Rome than Canterbury". He smiled and said that our Archbishop too lives in little Uppsala. "But he does not have your worldwide task!" "Then he wondered whether we did not have too many Swedes in America. No, I said, but there are too few of them in Sweden." He appears to be a very impressive personality, and runs his job magnificently.

From Canterbury, Söderblom went to Bishop Wordsworth in Salisbury and Bishop Ryle in Winchester. The former, chairman of the Lambeth Commission on Intercommunion, was far from unfamiliar with Söderblom's concern for closer connexion between the two Churches. Wordsworth proved to be one of those strange Englishmen who had attempted to learn Swedish and was particularly interested in Swedish church history. They discussed together the Swedish practice with regard to Confirmation and Söderblom had to restrain the Bishop as he insisted on episcopal confirmation as prerequisite for Intercommunion. This, Söderblom told Salisbury, the Swedish Church would not accept; but they agreed on regarding con-

---

[3] Söderblom, September 3 and 30, 1908, to Anna Söderblom.

firmation as a sacrament in the sense that it was more of a blessing than a required confession. It was Wordsworth who arranged for Söderblom to meet Bishop Ryle in Winchester.

Apart from the three Bishops, Söderblom, in these weeks of convalescence visited and had important talks with W. R. Inge of St. Paul's; Dean A. Robinson of Westminster; Bishop Westcott of Chota Nagpur; heard Bishop Weston of Zanzibar preach ('Next to nothing' was the Swedish professor's testimonial, in his letter to Mrs Söderblom); he also had contacts with scholars such as J. G. Frazer.

Söderblom had taken a firm stand; he for one had no intention to give away the Swedish position when the meeting between the two Church delegations actually took place in Uppsala, September 1909. He may or may not have discussed with Archbishop Ekman the formula, which the Swedish Primate used in his letter of invitation: 'an alliance of some sort' between the two Churches. In the discussion Söderblom was to show both that he wanted Intercommunion with the Church of England and that he was keenly aware of the complicated realities of ecclesiastical politics which threatened his plan of closer contact. Accordingly he acted.

The Swedish delegation consisted of two bishops, Ekman and Tottie, together with the Theological Faculty of Uppsala. In the Anglican delegation there were three Bishops of whom two were Söderblom's friends from his visit in 1908, namely Ryle of Winchester and Wordsworth of Salisbury. There was also Bishop G. Mott Williams of Marquette, Illinois, and three priests. Two of the priests were English scholars: A. J. Mason, then Vice Chancellor of Cambridge University, and E. R. Bernard of Salisbury. The third had a well-known Swedish name, Gustaf Hammarskjöld; he was an American of Swedish descent and acted as Bishop Mott William's chaplain. To some extent he was also to be his Bishop's interpreter, although Mott Williams having made gallant efforts to learn Swedish could to a certain extent manage on his own. He in fact represented a definite pro-Swedish section within his Church. In the Episcopal Church there had appeared in 1895 a Report on the orders of the Church of Sweden, decidedly critical of Swedish claims and known as 'Dr. Percival's Report'. Bishop Mott Williams had taken it upon himself to disprove the Percival Report, and had therefore become known in the United States as a champion of Swedish episcopal claims, as can be seen from his book: *The Church of Sweden and the Anglican Communion*, 1910.

Because of this American Episcopal representation, Söderblom was faced with a real problem. *The Augustana,* the official organ of the Swedish synod in the United States, voiced nervousness and dismay at the Swedish-Anglican contacts. This was strengthened by Bishop von Schéele's attitude. When Archbishop Ekman approached the Swedish bishops about inviting the Anglican Delegation to Uppsala, von Schéele alone was opposed. 'Disgust' was the descriptive term he used:[4] he felt that because of his three visits to Augustana, he represented Augustana's particular interests; he was fearful lest a Swedish-Anglican rapprochement should strengthen the hand of Episcopal efforts in the States to enlist Swedish immigrants.

Söderblom grasped the nettle. He had various reasons for so doing. The steady flow of emigrants to America was an important problem in Swedish public opinion at the time. Deep down in Söderblom's heart were the childhood memories of those who had exchanged Hälsingland for Kansas and Minnesota. A Royal one-man Commission on Emigration had been appointed in 1907; by 1909 this question was one of the great controversial themes discussed in the Swedish press.

Söderblom had friends among Augustana's leaders who kept him informed about the situation, although others again were disturbed by his supposed 'Liberalism'. He keenly felt his responsibility at the Uppsala conversations. All this made Söderblom more cautious than he had been in that first snappy newspaper article of his. On the arrival in Uppsala of the Anglican delegation, in May 1908, he told Bishop Ryle as chairman of the delegation that in no capacity could Hammarskjöld be allowed to take part in the negotiations. Again, in the debate, when Bishop Mott Williams made a plea for Episcopal care of Swedish immigrants, Söderblom was the spokesman for Augustana interests. He describes the scene in his laconic diary notes. He was prepared: 'Then I had my say' (*nu drog jag mitt*). This was a well-prepared statement in English, scribbled at top speed in his terrible handwriting and with jottings in the margin, 'v. Schéele', 'Henson', etc to help him steer his particular course.

Augustana is our natural and nearest ecclesiastical relation in the United States. Founded by Swedish ministers [who in their turn had been] ordained by Swedish bishops ... Augustana was the Swedish Church of America ... which derives directly from our Church. ... She is flesh of our flesh.

---

[4] Von Schéle, 23 September, 1909, to A. H. Lundström. UUB.

This was the reason why Hammarskjöld could not be accepted as spokesman for the Swedes in America: if he was to be present, there should also be invited one or several representatives of the Augustana Synod.

In Augustana lies the future of the Swedish Church in the U.S.A., our daughter, although she has not finished her ecclesiastical education ...' [this was to indicate Söderblom's expectation of Augustana's accepting episcopacy. 'Marquette wanted our Archbishop eventually to approach the Bishop of New York. I [replied]: "nothing must be done." Salisbury grunted, became more contented when I mentioned that Augustana is mad with me. Winchester understood.

The Augustana–Episcopalian issue concerned the situation in the New World. It made the 1909 negotiations in Uppsala into something more complicated than a straight-forward bilateral Anglo-Swedish exchange of ecclesiastical ideas. It took a Söderblom to realize that there were three sides to the problem, and it was like him generously to claim that all the aspects had to be emphasized. Bishop Mott Williams recognized him as 'the genius of the Conference'.

Yet the bilateral exchange too was important, supported as it was by an impressive array of historical argument by the Church history experts, both English and Swedish. They dealt with the Historic Episcopate, the Diaconate, Confirmation. In a statement specially prepared by Söderblom and his Uppsala colleague, Einar Billing, reference was made to the doctrinal authority of the Augsburg Confession in the Swedish Church. They claimed as the Lutheran standpoint that 'no particular organization of the Church or of its ministry is instituted *iure divino,* only *iure humano.* The organization of the ministry of the Church as a whole was to be judged on its functional merits: 'It is valuable to the extent that it is proved to be a pure vessel of the Gospel.' He could bring into the discussion another point which was always important to him, the *'independence'* of the Swedish Church in relation to the State; on this point he felt that the Swedish Church was superior to the English Church, for was not the King of England 'Supreme Governor', and he asked, did they in reality have any election of Bishops? There was of course a theological reply to this, put forward by Wordsworth, but Söderblom was never shaken in his view of a certain tendency to Erastianism in England, which, he felt, did not appear to the same extent in the Swedish Church.

To Söderblom an act of worship during those days in Uppsala was even more significant and unforgettable than the theological argument. The first day of the Conference was St. Matthew's Day, September 21. In preparation for the meeting, Bishop Ryle had asked Söderblom to find for the Anglican group a church where they could celebrate Holy Communion. Söderblom was glad to place at their disposal Holy Trinity Church, next to the Cathedral. Ryle celebrated, and Söderblom, as Pastor of the Church, assisted, in his Swedish vestments, and also received Communion. It can be claimed that this was the first occasion when *officially* a Swedish priest communicated according to the Anglican rite.[5]

There was a sequel to this. *The Guardian,* London carried a report on the visit of the Anglican Delegation, and referred to the fact that a Swedish priest, Söderblom himself, had communicated 'in a black and silver chasuble'. That brought the wrath of Dr. Leighton Pullen, the Anglo-Catholic scholar of St. John's College, Oxford, on Bishop Ryle's head; had not the Bishop by this admission 'openly defied the Book of Common Prayer, and sacrificed the principles of the Church of England?' 'For the Swedish clergy,' claimed Dr. Pullen, 'were unconfirmed: Possibly they desire to be confirmed.'[6] The long-suffering Ryle, who knew his critics, was unmoved; he later wrote to Söderblom: 'In this particular case, I rejoice to look back upon that happy morning in your church. After you had allowed us to make use of your beautiful church for such a service, I should have been singularly lacking in the charity of our Faith if I had not included you in our Communion.'[7] To both men it appeared important that their theological debate should end not in words, but in Communion.

To Söderblom, these Uppsala conversations with the Anglicans were to be of special importance. He had had to carry most of the burden on the Swedish side, and he had experienced an ecumenical interchange on matters of faith and of the ministry in a setting sanctified by the sharing of Holy Communion in his own Holy Trinity Church. Later he made a point annually of sending special greetings to leading Anglicans for St. Matthew's Day. That day to him held the promise of greater things to come.

4. The Student Christian Movement gave Söderblom his opportunity of widening his horizon to the gate of Asia. He was called to

---

[5] In August, 1912, visiting [the then] Canon H. Henson at Westminster, Söderblom went again to Holy Communion in the Anglican Church.

[6] *The Guardian,* October 27, 1909.

[7] H. E. Ryle to Söderblom December 20, 1909.

lecture at the Constantinople conference of the World's Student Christian Federation, April 1911. Mrs Söderblom accompanied him on this journey, taking them through eventful Easter celebrations in Rome and Athens, until they were faced with the 'exotic spectacle' of Constantinople. Söderblom was deeply conscious of this unique opportunity in meeting the venerable world of the Orthodox Church and of Islam: He could not refrain from an impulsive gesture; he bowed down and 'kissed devoutly the earth of Asia'.[8]

The Conference itself and its delegates presented something of a watershed in Söderblom's international relations. On the one side were the Student movement stalwarts, reminding him of New Haven 1890: John Mott, Karl Fries, Robert Wilder. On the other side, there were new contacts to be made. He was meeting for the first time, the men who at a later date were going to be some of his most devoted co-workers in the ecumenical movement: a young Archimandrite, Germanos, from the island of Halki in the Bosphorus, director of the well-known Orthodox Theological Seminary; there were representatives of the world wide Anglican Communion: Silas McBee and E. S. Woods; a Quaker doctor from London and China, Henry Hodgkin; and, with him, a highly vocal Chinese church leader Chengting Wang, representing new and surprising pressures from the Young Church of Asia; there was the French expert on the Church in Africa, Raoul Allier (whom Söderblom, of course had met earlier); and there was the Scottish theologian from Aberdeen, D. S. Cairns. Of the latter, Söderblom was to write that same year: 'Hardly ever have I met a foreigner whose religious thought is so similar to my own.'[9] To ordinary people, these were nothing but a string of names; but Söderblom was extraordinary in that he realized the unique importance and potentialities of these people, and he was to cultivate and strengthen, as far as possible, the contacts with each of these men in the following years.

Constantinople 1911 was to Söderblom not only meeting people and seeing ecumenical visions for the future. He also had to give

---

[8] Söderblom, *Sommarminnen* (ed. Anna Söderblom, 1941), p. 226. 'One day [1911] we went by steamer across the blue Bospore ... to Kadikjöj, which was once Chalcedon. During the trip Nathan Söderblom suddenly became very meditative; then he said: "In a few minutes we will land on the shore of that Continent where Christ, Buddha and Mohammed have worked." As we landed, he knelt on the piece of Asia's soil where we were and devoutly touched the soil with his forehead.' Edv. Söderberg in *Upplands Nations Årsskrift* (21–22) 1958–59, p. 58.

[9] Söderblom, November 17, 1911, to Anna Söderblom.

his lecture. One wonders what delegates made of Söderblom's address, 'Does God Continue to Reveal Himself to Mankind?', a variation of his learned 'Promotion' lecture at Uppsala University, May 1911. Some of his ideas on the men of genius and the heroes of religion becoming 'saints' must have appeared unfamiliar, perhaps slightly academic. But Söderblom was not the kind of cold-blooded lecturer who manages to 'read a paper' and leave it at that. He sensed the need in those attentive students for the personal application of the message. Thus he said: 'The great Revelation of God is turned into God's transaction with me. History will be my history. It was done for me, 'given for you', 'shed for you'. The most important event of my life will be Jesus Christ.'[1] And to that, of course, Mott and Wilder, Germanos and Chengting Wang could say 'Amen'.

At Constantinople the group of young Church leaders was placed in a unique setting. The oriental Churches in their precarious situation in the Moslem world, were the hosts. To Söderblom, this meeting with the Orthodox at Constantinople was an earnest of things to come: to him the meeting was 'an important stage, definitely one of the most important in our generation, in an enormous task: increased awareness and realization of the unity of Christendom'.[2] The professor from the North caught a new glimpse of a great responsibility: 'In view of the renaissance in the East, Christendom ought to be driven to a new consciousness of its unity, and particularly we Swedes ought to discover the unique position allotted to us, as a focus for Anglicanism, the most important Church formation of the Evangelical world, for Lutheranism, its centre for a religious interpretation of Revelation, and for the active Reformed type of Christendom.' He saw a new ecclesiastical creation taking form, where together with the churches already mentioned 'the old piety-loaded cult Churches' would have their appointed task, together with the Younger Churches of the Far East. No wonder that from this conference with the young, in old Constantinople, he concluded: 'The history of Christianity is not at an end on earth; it has just begun.'[3]

Söderblom's service and interests thus took him away from Uppsala to those wider horizons receding still further as he went along. Occasionally he heard from his other university and the Cathedral at Uppsala. In December 1913, there was the news of Archbishop Ek-

---

[1] *Report, W.S.C.F., Constantinople*, 1911, p. 77.
[2] [Söderblom], *Sommarminnen*, p. 235.
[3] Ibid., p. 242.

man's death. Söderblom's friend, Dean Lundström, the Church historian, took charge in the sedisvacance. Söderblom wrote to Lundström:

'I hear little of the speculations of who will be next Archbishop in Uppsala. Certain it is that whoever will be appointed, his position will not be enviable, for in our time the post is more than usually delicate and loaded with worries.'[4]

---

[4] Söderblom, December 18, 1913, to H. Lundström, Uppsala.

Swedish Archbishop

It was as Archbishop that Nathan Söderblom became an ecumenical leader—not as professor, nor as secretary of meetings, nor as political or social reformer at large. And it was from Uppsala, the centre of his diocese and province, that he as Primate of the Church of Sweden planned his international ventures, *and* gave to the emerging ecumenical movement that particular stamp which was his, and his alone. He created a body aware of itself and its calling to be modern, social, and international, and endowed it with a spirit of prayer and worship. If the Archbishop did this, it is possible that he owed it to his calling and to his Church. We must consider Söderblom's position in his diocese and in the Swedish Church as a whole.

At the time it was by no means a foregone conclusion that Söderblom was to become the Archbishop. As we shall presently show, it was a great and, as we must believe, providential paradox that he was appointed at all. If in the election of one Swedish Chapter one vote, one tiny piece of paper, had been cast for another man, Nathan Söderblom would never have become Archbishop, and the Church of Sweden and ecumenical history would have been the losers. We cannot of course consider here Söderblom's archiepiscopate in its entirety; that would be the theme for another complete book, and one difficulty to be encountered in the attempt to write such a book is that there exists as yet no study of Swedish Church History for the first third of the century. We shall limit ourselves in this chapter to one aspect only, albeit to that aspect which, from the point of view of Söderblom's theology is the fundamental, the tension between 'body' and 'soul', institution and spirit. We shall first consider the facts of the election and of his consecration and then, sketched against the background of his time, shall attempt to give a description of him in taking the chair at meetings, in his daily work at home and in the diocese, and in his relations with political and other figures of the day. We also feel that it is as a conclusion of this chapter that a study of Söderblom's personality has its place;

not at the end of the book, but on the threshold from Sweden to the international task for the world; for in the last resort, it was the man, almost as much as the message, who made that movement possible.

The Election

In January, 1925, Bishop Gottfrid Billing of Lund died, and Söderblom attended the burial service. After the funeral, two priests asked Archbishop Söderblom for an interview. On behalf of their colleagues they wanted to inquire whether he would consider allowing his name being put up for election to the Bishopric of Lund. Söderblom confided in his diary what he answered them: 'Are you mad! Don't you realize that it was by accident that I ... managed to become Archbishop—but could not [succeed in becoming] bishop.'[1]

Accident, he said, and he was not far wrong, for it was surprising indeed that his name appeared at all in 1914, on that short list of three, from which the King, or the Government, had to select one, and even more surprising that he was appointed. These statements make it necessary to look at the intricate Swedish Archiepiscopal election procedure in some detail.

The Swedes, as is well-known, are nothing if not thorough, and in their elections of Bishops they are thoroughness itself. The general principle was that the clergy of the diocese voted for their Bishop; then the three names with the most votes were placed on a short list and presented to the King. As a rule the King would select the first name on the list, but he was by no means bound to do so. He could appoint any one of the three, but, and this was the democratic power of the electors, he could not appoint anyone who was not on the list.

In the case of the Archbishop, this same principle was followed, but there was an important and rather special provision, designed to emphasize that the Archbishop was to be the leader not only of a diocese, but of the Swedish Church as a whole.

In his case there were no less than sixteen electoral colleges, comprising the clergy of the archdiocese, the chapters of the thirteen dioceses, and the consistory of Stockholm. The Archbishop being, *ex officio,* Pro-Chancellor of the University of Uppsala, the Higher Council of that University also had a vote.

---

[1] Söderblom, Diary, January 20, 1925.

As the votes from each of these electoral colleges had the same strength, this meant that the clergy of the archdiocese had comparatively limited influence on the final outcome. In fact, more than in the case of the other bishops, there was in the election of the Archbishop, considerable scope for the lay vote. As an expression of the historical connexion between Church and School, the diocesan chapters consisted to a large extent of High School *lectors*—the learned provincial mathematicians, botanists, and philologists—voting together with Bishop and Dean. It happened of course that a Bishop, by his personal authority and example, could influence the vote of the members of his chapter, but many times any such episcopal effort might have the opposite effect to what was intended.

The lay element was of course particularly pronounced in the case of the Higher Council of the University, where out of a number of thirty professors, only six represented the theological faculty.

The strong lay vote constituted an element of uncertainty and almost hazard, which greatly added to the interest which Swedish opinion, then as now, showed towards the archiepiscopal elections. The clergy of Uppsala diocese particularly felt this problem, and in 1913, made representations to the Minister for Ecclesiastical Affairs, F. Berg; he generously declared that he was willing to consider their claim to a bigger say in the matter.

Energetic canvassing soon began. The obvious name was Bishop Gottfrid Billing of Lund; he had also been the leading bishop in Archbishop Ekman's time, but already in 1900, when Ekman became Archbishop, he had refused to move from Lund to Uppsala, and there were well-founded beliefs that at 72 he would be even less tempted this time to move. He soon declared that he would not stand as a candidate, and the interest could shift to other names.

There were two such names, both of Bishops—H. Danell and J. A. Eklund. The weekly clergy review, *Svensk Kyrkotidning*, in the weeks immediately before the election, published no less than twenty-one letters on the burning issue; they were all extolling the great merits of these two Bishops, together with those of the Dean of Uppsala, Professor H. Lundström. With one exception they all avoided mentioning Söderblom's name. When it was mentioned at all, this was in order to warn against it. Did anybody know where he stood in fundamental matters of faith and Church politics? Could anyone suggest that this professor had the necessary maturity and experience required for the highest office in the National Church? These were merely rhetorical questions. Only one daily newspaper, *Stock-*

holms-Tidningen, edited by Söderblom's good friend Rinman, supported the name of the professor in Leipzig.

Trial elections were held in different parts of the diocese, showing that the three candidates were Danell, Eklund, and Lundström. Söderblom's name did not appear. The clergy became the more determined to support the combination Danell–Eklund when they read the results of a trial election of the professors of Uppsala University. For the most part a Pro-Chancellor's task was a sinecure, and the professors could hardly expect their vote to be of any special, let alone historical, importance. They loyally voted for G. Billing and Danell, but as the third name in their trial election, they produced one which many of the clergy preferred to avoid, that of a certain Uppsala professor in Leipzig, Nathan Söderblom.

Bishop Eklund on the other hand, received no votes from the academics. Temperamental as he was, Eklund had on more than one occasion infuriated the professors with his pronounced, sometimes outrageous, views on cultural and national questions, and the University did not forgive him.

This anti-Eklund attitude of the professors, stimulated the clergy to new efforts and expectations on behalf of this very Bishop. Altogether, the situation was full of tension and drama; Söderblom, in far away Leipzig, was informed about developments by his faithful friends and supporters, and felt that for him, life would continue as that of a scholar among his books.

The election took place on March 18, 1914. As everybody expected, the Bishops Danell and Eklund received the highest number of votes, fifteen and thirteen respectively; but few had expected that in the third place, with six votes, would appear that professor from Leipzig, Söderblom. Whose were the six votes? The Uppsala professors placed Söderblom first, before Danell and Lundström, so did the liberal theological professors in Lund, who were identical with the Chapter of Lund Diocese. In four other chapters, Söderblom was put in the third place—in Härnösand, Karlstad, Västerås, and the Stockholm 'Consistory'. But even here it was only by sheer accident that he appeared at all: in Västerås three men, including Söderblom, got three votes each, and it was only the lot pulled by a young lector, Landtmansson, that enabled Söderblom's name to scramble on to the list. If in Karlstad, Eklund's own chapter, one of the lectors had given his vote for Lundström instead of Söderblom, the former would have been placed on the short list, and Söderblom would have remained in Leipzig.

The Uppsala chapter did not include Söderblom's name at all, neither did the clergy of the Uppsala diocese—on their list he was number five. The tendency of the electors seemed obvious enough. In the first place, both Danell and Eklund received seven votes, while Söderblom had only two. Somebody did some rapid calculations and added up the total of votes polled by the leading names in the sixteen colleges. These came to: Danell and Eklund, 273 votes each, Dean Lundström 143, and Söderblom, a poor fourth, 106 votes. Yet it could not be denied that Söderblom was one of the three, and that the decision now lay with the Crown. King Gustaf V was, indeed, interested and personally involved. Bishop Billing of Lund in an audience, had readily given his humble but very definite advice: 'Reasons to bypass Danell could not be produced; personally I want [to see] Eklund appointed; Söderblom, I consider, should not appear; it is not possible to appoint him. I believe I can say that the wishes of the King were identical with mine.'[2]

In February, 1914, there was a change of government. A bitter struggle over defence questions brought Karl Staaff's Liberal Government to its fall, and an upsurge of Swedish nationalism with religious and conservative overtones lifted Hammarskjöld's Conservative government into power. One would have expected this to have adversely affected Söderblom's chances; with the outgoing Liberal government he had influential friends, not least in Berg, the Minister for Ecclesiastical Affairs, who admired Söderblom. For the official 'Prayer Day Message' for 1914, always signed by the King and the Minister, Berg in 1913 had turned to Söderblom in Leipzig, and Söderblom was thus given an anticipation of collaboration with government on that particular point, a task with which, as Archbishop he was to be quite familiar. But three months later Berg was no longer Minister; whether his successor in the Conservative government, or any other minister, would support Söderblom, was indeed an open question.

There was however, a close affinity between the Government and the Söderblom-supporting Uppsala professors, more in fact than was generally anticipated. K. G. Westman,[3] the new minister for Ecclesiastical Affairs, at 38, young as Swedish ministers go, came from the same academic background as Söderblom. He was a member of

---

[2] G. Billing, May 24, 1914, to J. A. Eklund.
[3] Even Swedes find it difficult to differentiate between Professor K. B. Westman, of Uppsala, Church Historian, missionary, and Söderblom's co-worker, and Professor K. G. Westman, of Uppsala, historian of law, and politician.

the Hjärne school of history in Uppsala, and personally connected with Hjärne, H. Schück, the Vice-Chancellor of the University, and other strong supporters of Söderblom's name. There were at least two other ministers who shared his view; there was the Minister for Foreign Affairs, K. A. Wallenberg, the mightiest financier in the country. He knew Söderblom as that Uppsala professor who had inspired the architect and the other artists for his own Saltsjöbaden Church. He had as a matter of course an international outlook, and felt that this was also needed for the Church. The pro-Söderblom triumvirate in the Government also included Hasselrot, the Minister for Legal Affairs.

We do not of course know the details of the arguments in the Cabinet meeting when the new Archbishop was appointed, on May 20, 1914, or those prior to this occasion. Many felt that it was a foregone conclusion, and that either Bishop Danell or Bishop Eklund had to be appointed. The Prime Minister himself was anxious to follow the majority of the electors. Bishop Billing in Lund felt assured when, a few days before the appointment, King Gustav sent K. G. Westman to him. He could not but notice that Westman himself would have preferred to appoint Söderblom, but Billing, with his long experience of political affairs, understood Westman's visit, ordered by the King, to mean that the King was trying to gather support for his view.[4]

Professor Hjärne himself went to Stockholm on the day of the Cabinet meeting. He was a well-known guest in the Riksdag where he himself had been a member. But the meeting went on for a very long time: 'In the Chamber the majority thought that Danell would be appointed.'[5] Hjärne could not wait much longer, and eventually took the train back to Uppsala. On his arrival he heard that a telegram had already been received: 'Söderblom appointed Archbishop', and Hjärne, in the evening of 'this day, so important for yourself and also for the Swedish Church and our country' wrote his letter of congratulation to Leipzig.

The news soon spread over Europe, and Söderblom received a telegram from Rome which said, in Latin: 'Gratiam vestram etiam—si heterodoxam gratia nostra salutat. Pius.' He felt though that there was perhaps something fishy about the message, and soon could establish that this was Professor Henrik Schück, of Uppsala Uni-

---

[4] G. Billing, May 24, 1914, to Eklund.
[5] Ibid. Hjärne, May 20, 1914, to Söderblom.

versity, having a bit of fun while on an archives expedition in the Eternal City.

Church opinion in Sweden was stunned. Bishop Billing of Lund, who was always well informed about affairs, wrote: 'To nobody did this appointment come so unexpectedly as to me.'[6] The unofficial organ of the Swedish clergy, *Svensk Kyrkotidning*, found itself in a dilemma, and solved it in a way to satisfy everybody and nobody.

It published two editorials in the same number, one on 'Archbishop Söderblom' saying that he was not without his good points; he had international contacts, as no other Swedish churchman had; he was a man of fine Christian culture with a lively artistic temperament. While lacking any experience of the job to which he had been appointed, he had nevertheless a 'warm Evangelical Lutheran spirit', and the writer therefore ended by wishing wisdom and tenacious strength to him 'who is now the Archbishop of the land of the Swedes'. Whether this was a nice way of saying that the new Archbishop was lacking in these good qualities, or whether it was a genuine expression of Christian sentiments, is not altogether clear, for it was immediately followed by a second Editorial proclaiming that the appointment showed recklessness, bitter recklessness, towards the Church, and this had roused the feelings of the clergy and Church people of the country, 'this and nothing else'.

The paper wanted to know who was in a better position to know who was needed, the electors or the Ministers of State who had taken office only two months earlier. The Church had once again recognized the truth of Holy Scripture: 'Put not your trust in princes.'[7]

A fortnight later, the same church paper published the first circular from the Archbishop-elect to his diocese, with a programme of the consecration to take place on 'November 8, my Father's birthday', and of the many events to precede and follow this great act of worship, on November 6, 7, and 10. He also made known the inductions of incumbents which he was going to make on Sundays August 23 and September 6, and 13, and that in the meantime his address was to be Skolgatan 1, Uppsala.

He added: 'Nobody will take it amiss that during the summer I shall try to find time for retreat and quiet in preparation for the Consecration, and the task.'[8] Perhaps he was not so inexperienced after all, that man in Leipzig. Time alone would show.

---

[6] G. Billing, May 24, 1914 to J. A. Eklund.

[7] *Svensk Kyrkotidning*, 1914, No. 21.

[8] Ibid., 1914, No. 24, Circular from the Uppsala Chapter.

Consecration

Söderblom was not likely to waste any time. In August 1914, he and the family left Leipzig and Germany for Sweden and Uppsala. Europe was engaged in a war to the finish; the future was hidden, even to the most acute observer. In the more limited world of the family the situation was critical. Mrs Söderblom's health was seriously affected after the birth of her twelfth child, and she had to be cared for in an Uppsala hospital. As the Archbishop's House was under repair until the beginning of November, the eldest daughter took charge of her brothers and sisters in their old home at Staby Vicarage.

Söderblom himself found refuge in the two little rooms in Justice Ribbing's yard in Skolgatan which had previously, on occasional visits from Leipzig, been placed at his disposal. No Archbishop, at least in the Northern hemisphere, can have ever had more modest headquarters. It was here that Söderblom wrote his Episcopal Charge, prepared his Peace Appeal to the Churches, ran the affairs of his diocese and prepared for the consecration.

There had been no archiepiscopal consecration in the Swedish Church since 1670. In all other cases, the primates had already been in bishop's orders on their appointment. There was therefore little precedent to build upon for the occasion, and Söderblom devoted a great deal of thought to the preparations. The Bishop of Lund, Gottfrid Billing, was to be the consecrator, and on his way from Leipzig to Uppsala in August Söderblom discussed the arrangements with him. There was no constitutional provision in Swedish ecclesiastical law as to the minimum number of bishops required to take part in a consecration, and it is an indication of the atmosphere in which Söderblom started out as an archbishop, that it was by no means taken for granted that all the bishops would attend, but Söderblom informed Billing that he expected at least a few bishops.

Billing had promoted the idea of regular episcopal conferences ever since the first Swedish Bishops' Meeting in 1898, and he suggested to Söderblom that such a meeting be held in connexion with the consecration. Bishop Eklund complained to Billing on this occasion. He took for granted that the suggestion was Söderblom's and therefore a wrong one; such a meeting, he thought, was simply designed to demonstrate the 'Church triumphant', with the new Archbishop as a balloon, unlikely to be tied or kept down. (This was in the days of Count Zeppelin's contraption.) Billing told Eklund that the said proposal was his own idea, and as for the balloon, was there not something called 'ballon captif', and in this instance was there not the anchoring and moderating influence that the Bishops' Meeting might be expected to have? This would indeed 'teach Söderblom'.[1] In the event all but Eklund and old Bishop Ullman of Strängnäs took part in the consecration, and Eklund himself came for the Bishops' Meeting on the following day.

In the meantime, Söderblom prepared for the consecration, but only after discussing the preparations in detail with Bishop Billing. The correspondence with Billing on this subject is a study in deference and subtle suggestion on Söderblom's part. He knew that Billing as a good old Lutheran wanted to keep vestments and such things as far away as possible from the act. Söderblom felt however that he 'could not altogether avoid mentioning this, albeit very minor matter', and tried to place Billing in a position from which he would accept that he and his two assistants for the occasion, Bishops Rodhe and von Schéele, would appear before the High Altar in 'cope and with crozier, as our manual expressly mentions this, and it has had domiciliary right not only in the Ancient Church but also with us after the Reformation'.[2]

The international situation seemed to impose economy and caution on any ecclesiastical function at this time. In the Church, the voices which had been critical about the uncomfortable fact of Söderblom's appointment seemed to emphasize that the consecration should be kept as simple and as inconspicuous as possible. It is only as one recalls these harsh circumstances that one can fully appreciate the courage and imagination with which Söderblom visualized his consecration, seeing it, even in the midst of world war, as a great ecumenical manifestation. It goes without saying that this was an innovation in the Swedish Church.

Söderblom sent out an invitation in Latin, and addressed it to the Primates of the Nordic Churches, as well as to the Church of England, and churchmen in France and Germany. He invited the Archbishop of Canterbury and the English members of the Anglo-Swedish Church Commission—Bishop Winnington-Ingram of London, Dr. Ryle, formerly Bishop of Winchester, Bishop Chase of Ely, together

---

[1] G. Billing, September 16, 1914 to J. A. Eklund.
[2] Söderblom, Oct. 7, 1914, to G. Billing. Billing of course saw through Söderblom's attempt at persuasion. On a later occasion he began his letter informing Söderblom that he would not take his cope: 'You must not be mad with me more than for a very short while, as I must tell you I feel obliged to refuse your two suggestions'. G. Billing, Sept. 2, 1920, to Söderblom.

with Canons Mason and Bernard. In the copies of the invitation for Dr. Davidson and Dr. Winnington-Ingram and Dr. Ryle, Söderblom added in his own handwriting, *'manibus ponendis'*; he thus insisted that they should not only attend the act of worship but take part in the laying on of hands. From an Anglican point of view this was premature, and no steps were taken in this direction until after Lambeth 1920. The Archbishop of Canterbury appointed Bernard and Mason to represent him, but at the last minute the North Sea in war-time was regarded as unsafe, and there was no British representation. In the same way, the French Lutherans, *Inspecteur ecclésiastique* Jean Meyer and Pastor H. Bach were prevented by war from attending.

With regard to Germany the situation was somewhat different. Söderblom had sent his invitation to seven German churchmen, including his Leipzig colleagues, Professors Ihmels and Rendtorff. Three of those invited were prepared to go to Uppsala since they had been officially appointed by the Prussian Cultus Minister to represent the Prussian Evangelical Churches for the occasion. Two of them, Rendtorff and J. Jacobi, were from the church in Saxony with which Söderblom, as a Leipzig professor, had been connected; there was also the General Superintendent of Schleswig-Holstein, Theodor Kaftan. Kaftan, a great church leader with whom Söderblom had always felt particular affinity, at first regarded the consecration as 'an exclusively Swedish occasion',[3] but he soon discovered that the consecration as conceived by Söderblom had wide ecumenical dimensions.

Already during the negotiations with the Anglicans in 1909, Söderblom had worked for positive contacts with the Augustana Lutheran Synod in the United States, and he now sent a special invitation to Augustana: 'We are of the same language and blood and have a common history behind us', he reminded his American friends. The invitation particularly underlined that the Augustana representative was to participate 'by prayers and the laying on of hands'. The leading Church periodical, *Augustana,* pointed out that the Archbishop's invitation was addressed to pastors who had 'received the ministry without the mediation of bishops'.[4]

---

[3] Theodor Kaftan, *Lebenserinnerungen* (1924), p. 392.

[4] The emphasis which Söderblom placed on Augustana's presence at his consecration can be measured negatively by the fact that in answer to a suggestion from the Episcopal Church of America that they send a representative, Söderblom gratefully declined. Cf. Söderblom, July 24, 1914, to Bishop N. Lövgren, UUB.

The consecration was expanded into a programme of five memorable days:

November 6. Gustavus Adolphus Day; the Gustavus Adolphus Association of Uppsala was formed. Söderblom himself, and his former Leipzig colleague, Professor F. Rendtorff, officiated at the meeting. On that same day there followed no less than three lectures and addresses devoted to the subject of Gustavus Adolphus. First in the University Hall by the History Professor, L. Stavenow; second in Odinslund, outside the Archbishop's House, by Dr. E. Wessén, President of the Uppsala students: third in the Cathedral at 10 p.m. by Bishop von Schéele, with some two thousand people present.[5]

November 7. Laying of wreaths at the late Archbishop Ekman's grave in the Uppsala cemetery, followed by the unveiling of a portrait of Ekman in the Chapter House; on both these occasions Söderblom was the speaker. In the afternoon the triennial meeting of the Diocesan Bible Society, where Söderblom's former colleague in the Theological Faculty, an Old Testament Professor, spoke on 'The Political and Social Message of the Prophets'. There followed Evensong in the Cathedral with a solid, lengthy sermon, or lecture, by the American guest who represented the Augustana Synod, Dr. L. G. Abrahamson. Nor was this all. The day was concluded with a programme of motets in Holy Trinity Church led by H. Alfvén, the *Director Musices* of the Uppsala University; he and Söderblom had been friends from their youth.

November 8, 22nd Sunday after Trinity. The Consecration Day. At 10 a.m. His Majesty King Gustaf V was received on the steps of the University, and the King, the Archbishop and the University professors then proceeded to the Cathedral.

At 11 a.m. there was 'Swedish High Mass' with Dean Lundström preaching; this service was concluded by the actual consecration.

The procession approached the High Altar. The assistants were six Rural Deans from the archdiocese and Stockholm, all of them in vestments; Dr. Abrahamson of the Augustana Lutheran Synod and the Dean of Västerås; the Swedish bishops, of whom von Schéele and Rodhe, together with the Consecrator, all of them in copes, took their places before the Altar.[6] The

---

[5] In his vivid account of the days in Uppsala, Kaftan recalled that the Friday programme had in fact yet another item. The student choir invited the guests to one of their student 'Nations' where, at 11.30 p.m., there was more singing, and Kaftan gave a speech. He expressed the pious hope that the young gentlemen would, in the future, lead and influence the Swedish people, so that foreigners looking at the people of Sweden 'might rightly say: "This is Gustavus Adolphus's people." This produced uproarious jubilation'. Kaftan, ibid, p. 396.
[6] It should be pointed out that the Scandinavian bishops and the German church leaders present did not participate in the consecration but remained in their seats. The only non-Swedish assistant was Dr. Abrahamson of the Augustana.

Consecrator gave an address on the text John 1. vv 47–51, after which the assistants read Bible passages. Then followed the actual consecration.

3 p.m. dinner in the Archbishop's House, with speeches by Söderblom, Bishops G. Billing, Ostenfeld, and Tandberg, and Professors Kaftan and Rendtorff.

At 6 p.m. the Student Corps of the University led by B. Jonzon, offered their respects to the Archbishop on the steps of the Archbishop's House. In response, Söderblom spoke about the two sculptures in the Uppland Student Nation, by C. Eldh, and by C. Milles.

At 8 p.m. Söderblom performed his first church act as a consecrated bishop in 'setting apart' Pastor Paul Sandegren for his task as a missionary to India. This was at a service in the Cathedral where Söderblom spoke on John 15.16.

November 9. The Bishops' Meeting under Söderblom's chairmanship, where the following varied agenda was discussed: the new Swedish Bible translation; the place of Luther's Catechism in the schools; revision of the Church Handbook; preparing the Reformation jubilee in 1917; religious care for Swedish soldiers; clergy stipends; ordination of missionaries; a memorial day for the dead—a proposal from the Swedish Florists' Association.

In the evening there was a meeting of the Uppsala Union for the Humanities. Dr. K. B. Westman gave a lecture on the Origin and Early Development of the Uppsala Archdiocese.

November 10. 'Martin Luther's Day' in the Swedish calender. There was a meeting of the Chapter of the Diocese of Uppsala. On this occasion Söderblom handed over his Episcopal Charge (*Herdabrev*).

'*All* of Söderblom' was in this episcopal consecration, in this sacred act of setting him apart for the task of leader and servant of his own Church and of the Church Universal. Immediately on his appointment he wrote to Bishop Billing who as *facile princeps* among the Swedish bishops was to be the consecrator. He expressed his wish that the consecration take place on November 8th. Billing wanted to find out if there was any special reason for this particular choice of date, and in his answer Söderblom provided a key to the secret of his heart: 'On November 8th my beloved departed father, pastor in the Archdiocese, would have celebrated his ninety-first birthday. This is the main reason.'[7]

So while the venerable ritual of the consecration emphasized the age-long tradition of the Church, Söderblom also kept a date with his own destiny. Through Jonas Söderblom he was related to the liv-

---

[7] Söderblom, May 25, 1914, to G. Billing.

ing past of Lutheran Pietism in his diocese, and even to the very soil of Hälsingland, which contained his forbears' graves. He referred to this sacred memory in his Episcopal Charge. According to Swedish ecclesiastical tradition, it was taken for granted that the newly appointed bishop would write a pamphlet or a little book as a message to the diocese, this should ideally be printed and ready so that it could be officially handed over to the Chapter of the Diocese on its first meeting immediately following upon the consecration. With some notable exceptions, chiefly that of Bishop Eklund, these charges had tended to be dull and formal.

Söderblom's Charge too escaped dullness, partly by its being set in so personal a key, partly by the dénouement by which it closed. The whole charge was based on the words in II Corinthians 1. 24 'Not for that we have dominion over your faith, but are helpers of your joy'. Only on the last page of the book did Söderblom disclose his reason for selecting that passage from Holy Scripture. His father had entrusted it to him on his death-bed. It had been Jonas Söderblom's motto for his life and service; it was to be the new Archbishop's watchword for his life and work. Söderblom went on to say: 'If, as I believe, those of blessed memory can commune with us who are left, his ardent soul must now feel considerable disquiet. How will this end? But apart from this he is sure also to experience joy that my calling has now united me closer with the congregations which he loved and served according to the best of his ability.'

To Söderblom there were other overtones to this consecration. The consecrator, Gottfrid Billing, twenty-one years earlier had ordained him. Also, as he used the ancient form of the Swedish consecration ritual, Söderblom was more aware than anybody else of the fact that seven hundred and fifty years earlier, in 1164, another Bishop of Lund, Eskil, had consecrated the first Archbishop of the new province of Uppsala in the cathedral at Sens in France. Söderblom had made a special historical study of that consecration and of the consecration prayer used at that time, beginning with the words, *Deus honorum omnium*. All this brought to his mind the whole sacred history of the Church.

In our analysis of Söderblom's programme of Evangelical Catholicity, we shall point out the role played in Söderblom's ecclesiology by Swedish Church history and by the personality of Gustavus Adolphus. As he prepared the consecration, he wrote to Bishop Billing by May 1914: 'If there are any visitors from afar, Härnösand, Leipzig or perhaps England, they would enjoy the [Gustavus Adol-

Trönö Church.

The altar, Holy Trinity Church, Uppsala, planned by Söderblom as the vicar.
The Lord's Supper by H. Sörensen-Ringi, surrounded by the Professor (E. G.
Geijer) by idem, and Mother, by C. Eldh.

In journeys often.

Skolgatan 1, Uppsala: The two rooms on the first floor were Archbishop Söderblom's abode, August–October, 1914. Here he wrote both his Pastoral Charge, and his Peace Appeal to the Churches. Cf. p. 107.

The Archbishop's House, Uppsala.

phus] homage in Odinslund, an event ever beautiful to my student heart.'[8]

As he listened to Dr. E. Wessén, president of the Uppsala Students, he must have recalled the same occasion twenty-one years earlier when he himself had spoken on behalf of the students of Uppsala. It was then that he had called out 'Will the North once again give its watchword, and will the world in the next century behold a new and higher Gustavus-Adolphus epoch'? It had been youthful oratory then; what if he had such an opportunity now, greater than that of anybody else? Would he grasp it?

Naturally the active participation of his brother bishops as well as, on that occasion, the presence of the Uppsala congregations and of representatives from the Diocese as a whole, meant much to him. To this must be added the presence of the University professors. As Archbishop, Söderblom also became Pro-Chancellor of the University and was keenly aware of this fact. The programme of the four days surrounding this consecration emphasized the connexion. The celebration in honour of Gustavus Adolphus included as part of the programme had a double function; his church programme of Evangelical Catholicity had an important element in it of Swedishness, particularly related to the great King and his role in world history. There was also a certain personal note. In 1893, Söderblom had himself, as president of the Student Corps, given perhaps the most memorable of Gustavus Adolphus addresses at the University.

To those with an ear for the accidental ironies of a situation, and who could also conceive of more than one kind of Swedishness, Bishop Billing's consecration address provided food for thought. It was widely acclaimed as ingenious because the Bible passage referred to Nathaniel. Unfortunately for Billing, Nathan Söderblom's Christian name was not Nathaniel but Jonathan. This particular address was in fact written for the induction of a pastor at the Ivö parish in the diocese of Lund, and had nothing whatever to do with Söderblom, but phrased in very general terms it could presumably fit any situation. The old bishop suggested that the Master knew all about Nathaniel and could look through his disciples. So, he went on to say in a remark that possibly reflected more of Sweden's position at the time than anything of the new Archbishop's international commitments: 'What is the Lord looking for in us? He sees if we are

---

[8] Söderblom, May 25, 1915, to G. Billing, Cf. Söderblom, *Svenskars fromhet*, 1941, p. 113.

sincere in our hearts and if we are right Swedes and right members of our Swedish Church.'[9]

Though this Uppsala consecration had its ecumenical dimension, this did not reach as far as Söderblom himself would have liked. There were the inevitable limitations imposed by war, but the intention on Söderblom's part to make the consecration a great ecumenical event was an innovation in Swedish and Scandinavian Church history. It was expressed by the presence of the Scandinavian, German and American Church leaders. It was symbolized in that gift of a golden cross which the Archbishop of Canterbury, together with the delegates of the Anglo-Swedish Church Commission, sent as a token of the particular interest which the Anglican Communion showed in Söderblom and the Church which he was now to represent and lead. The universal dimension of Söderblom's episcopal office was vividly expressed by the act whereby he sent out, on behalf of the Church of Sweden, a young missionary to South East Asia.

In its entirety, this consecration period, beginning on November 6, reaching its climax on Sunday, November 8, and leading to the meeting of the chapter on November 11, was an expression of the new and creative will to *communicate* which this Archbishop of Uppsala was to demonstrate wherever he moved.

The Swedish Episcopate

What was a Swedish bishop like? In order to assess Söderblom's performance as bishop and as Primate of the Swedish Church, we must consider the Swedish college of bishops, the Swedish 'type', which, compared with the Roman Catholic or Anglican brand of the species, showed certain differences.

There were not many of them: only twelve (in Denmark, eight, Norway, seven, Finland, four). Scandinavian bishops were nominated after a process of election, and thus, at least in principle, not superimposed from above on a diocese. There was a tendency for the machinery of election to exclude the exceptional and the radical, and to prefer the stable, middle-of-the-road men, although it must be added that in the 1914 Uppsala election 'short list', both Söderblom and Eklund were far from being cautious middle-roaders. It is of interest to recall that well over half the bishops whom Söderblom

[9] *Sv. Kyrkotidning*, 1914, November 11.

joined in 1914 had been appointed as young men, forty-five or younger. This tendency was maintained throughout Söderblom's archiepiscopate. However, by 1914, some of them were rather old. As yet there was no pension system for bishops. The senior of them, Ullman of Strängnäs, 77 in 1914, waited till 1927 before retiring on a pension; Billing of Lund, 73 in 1914, died in harness at 84; von Schéele of Visby was 76, Lindström of Växjö, 72, and E. H. Rodhe of Gothenburg, 69. The new archbishop at forty-eight could hardly help feeling juvenile in this venerable gathering, and he did at this time, like a good Swede, begin his letters to his aged colleagues Ullman and von Schéele in proper form: 'Dear Uncle'.

With regard to social background, five (incl. Söderblom himself) of the twelve bishops were sons of pastors of whom two came from peasant stock. Two were sons of ordinary yeomen, one of a village organist and another of a village tailor; two of lower rank State officials, and one of a higher civil servant, Member of the Riksdag. Only one, von Schéele, was a member of the nobility. As a very young man, long before he became a bishop, he had taken his place in the House of Nobility. In this connexion it should be pointed out that prior to the Reform of Swedish Representation in 1866 the bishops formed part of the Second Estate, that of the Clergy, and were not members of the House of Nobility.

There was an interesting constellation in the nineteen-twenties when the clans of Billing and Rodhe (Edvard Rodhe of Lund was married to a daughter of Bishop Gottfrid Billing, sister of Bishop Einar Billing) showed a tendency to appropriate a considerable number of the dioceses: Rodhe Sr., bishop in Göteborg, Rodhe Jr. in Lund and Billing Jr. (Einar) at Västerås, 1920, while Billing Sr. (Gottfrid) was bishop of Lund until his death in 1925. Sweden had of course no 'public schools' in the English sense, and like Söderblom the other bishops had all studied in little provincial grammar schools prior to going on to University, either Uppsala or Lund.

The Swedish episcopal bench had a distinctly academic character, much more so than the bishops in Denmark or Norway. There was a solid core of former professors of theology. Together with Archbishop Söderblom himself, no less than six out of the twelve belonged to this category (G. Billing, Danell, Eklund, von Schéele, Ullman), while two others were distinguished biblical scholars, actively engaged in textual revision (Lindström and Personne). These two also had long experience as schoolmasters. Four of the bishops had a more practical background (Bergqvist, Lövgren, Lönegren and Rodhe). Some of them were recognized as distinguished preachers of a conservative type, such as G. Billing, others as performers of nineteenth century oratory with long and flowing periods, such as von Schéele; others again as preachers with original and creative power, such as Eklund and V. Rundgren (bishop in 1920).

Because of various historical circumstances there were great discrepancies in income between the bishops. The Bishops of Lund and of Karlstad were exceptionally well off, Lund, because of land in Skåne, and Karlstad because of the forests of Värmland. Billing's income in 1920 of some 75,000 Sw. Kr. (about £5200) was in a class all to itself. The majority of bishops with the Archbishop himself had an income of some Sw. Kr. 25,000, or £2000; but Skara, Härnösand and Luleå, at the bottom of the list had to manage on some 13,000 Sw. Kr. (£1000).

But even the poor ones were regarded as rich compared with their curates. Söderblom, with his big family and ensuing money problems, was challenged on this point. In the 'Prayer Day Message' (böndagsplakat) for 1920 Söderblom had courageously touched upon the glaring social inequalities in Swedish society and made the point, 'justly distributed, the bread will be sufficient for all'. He was taken up on that by an anonymous 'Clergyman' in Svenska Morgonbladet, who on January 8, 1920 put the question: 'Does the Archbishop regard it as "just distribution" that the twelve Bishops of the Church (himself included) receive in yearly income as much as 120 rural curates. Let the word of the Archbishop in this Prayer Day Message not remain simply dazzling verbal fireworks! Let the theory be translated into practice!'

The group of bishops was Swedish also in the sense that, generally speaking, they lacked an international horizon. With Bishop Tottie's death in 1913, the one international personality of an earlier generation had passed away. Bishop von Schéele had special contacts with Lutheran Germany, had twice visited the Augustana Synod in America, and had even been to Jerusalem. He was therefore *hors concours* as far as international contacts were concerned. As a rule Söderblom was to find his colleagues would beg to be excused when invited to represent the Church in the Anglo-Saxon world. The language difficulties would prove forbidding. It was not until 1925 when Edv. Rodhe became Bishop of Lund that this situation changed.

In Norway and Denmark there seemed to be a tendency for candidates to represent certain parties within the Church: Pietistic,

'Liberal', or Grundtvigian, or again combinations of these. The Swedish college of Bishops had at least one representative of the West coast Schartau movement in Rodhe of Gothenburg; and, from 1920, in Rundgren of Visby, a genuine representative of nineteenth century 'Church Pietism'. Somewhat later, for a period of two decades, the 'Young Church'movement was a platform for preferment to the episcopate. In Söderblom's time, Lövgren and Einar Billing of Västerås, and Eklund of Karlstad, had special contacts with this movement, though Eklund was too much of an individualist to be forced into any preconceived category.

The connexion between Church and State in Sweden was expressed also by the fact that two of the bishops were members of the Riksdag, or three if one is to mention that earlier on von Schéele had been a Member of the Riksdag. In a grave political crisis in 1917, one of them, Bishop Billing, was even called to the King who asked him to form a new Government. Billing in somewhat drastic terms refused and could return to the relatively peaceful Lund. As a matter of course both Billing and Bergqvist represented the Conservative Party; it was only at the end of the nineteen twenties that a Swedish bishop, Sam Stadener, belonging to the Liberal Party, was to play an active political role. Billing, Bergqvist and Stadener all exemplified the popular image of the true Swedish bishop, big and burly, and practical men of affairs, admired from afar. In the social climate of Sweden of that day, public opinion tended to force most bishops (there were exceptions!) into adopting an aura of unapproachability, out of which they were expected to emerge on rare occasions in human form. It was natural, therefore, to find in an obituary on Bishop Tottie, 'Everyone who came into contact with him felt a gulf between himself and the bishop',[1] though in this instance the gulf was the gulf of a real greatness.

Into this stereotype, Söderblom was quite unable to fit. Of only middle height, rapid in movement, quick to seek contact and impelled to show sympathy and interest, he broke through the preconceived ideas of what a bishop should be. It took many a little while to understand.

More Body than Spirit?

It was October 14, 1915, a year after Söderblom's consecration, and he now called his first *Kyrkomöte* or General Assembly. The sixty

---

[1] *Sv. Kyrkotidning*, June 18, 1913.

members, laymen, bishops, clergy, went to the Royal Palace in the capital, where on behalf of the Assembly, the new Swedish Archbishop addressed the Swedish King, Gustaf V. The speech was brief, two or three minutes only, but in his few words Söderblom managed to give the key-note to his whole work, his theme throughout life and throughout his episcopate. He quoted the well-known saying of Gustavus II Adolphus on 'the majesty of the Fatherland and the Church of God which dwells therein'.

Accordingly, he said, 'the Church constitutes the soul of the Nation'. This church had 'through that which is essential, i.e. faith and confession, but also through that which is less essential, namely certain institutions such as Episcopacy, connexions beyond the national boundaries'. But as the Swedish Church, he insisted, 'she is above all called to be the soul of the nation. Perhaps she is this more than [is generally recognized], but she ought to be this to a much greater extent'.

Body and soul, institution and Spirit, were Söderblom's theme. On the very first day, when he arrived in Uppsala after his appointment as Archbishop, he addressed a YMCA group, speaking on 'The Wind of the Spirit and the Church'.[1] He always returned to, and varied, that theme: there were the age-old institutions, venerable survivals or towering administrative structures; how was one to animate them with soul and spirit?

In neighbouring Norway at the very same time, a brilliant Norwegian church leader, Johannes Johnson, previously of Madagascar, addressed his Church in similar terms: 'Fill the institutions!' There were real differences in the two situations in the National Churches of Norway and Sweden, at this time, but the concern which prompted Söderblom and Johnson was very similar.

The General Assembly of the Swedish Church was a church institution of an official character, designed to represent the interests of the Church. It was a substitute organization accorded to the Church in 1866 (the year of Söderblom's birth) when, through a reform of political representation, the *Riksdag* of the four Estates (Nobility, Clergy, Burghers, Peasants) was succeeded by the *Riksdag* with two Chambers. In Söderblom's time the *Kyrkomöte* had sixty members and was composed equally of clergy and laity.

The Archbishop was *ex officio* the President of the Assembly, and Söderblom led the deliberations very expeditiously. He may even

---

[1] K. B. Westman, Diary, June 3, 1914.

have conveyed the impression that he enjoyed the proceedings. He certainly enjoyed the opportunity of meeting with a number of interesting people, and must have felt sometimes that he helped to promote decisions of historical importance for the Church. But in general he felt very much out of step with this kind of meeting. As the President he was not supposed to make any speeches himself, in fact only once in the six Assemblies held during his time (1915, 1918, 1920, 1925, 1926 and 1929) did he make a special intervention. This was in 1920; only once before, in 1898 had an Archbishop inter-vened in the discussions. After referring to this precedent, Söder-blom made one of the longest speeches in the history of the Assem-bly lasting over two and a half hours.

The speech concerned a matter which was very dear to his heart, the revision of the Swedish hymnbook, and as such, an expression of the soul of the Church. By his intervention he contributed very definitely to what became the solution of that problem. Instead of a revised hymnbook worked out by a Royal Commission, Söderblom proposed a temporary Supplement which would allow the Church eventually to produce a worthier hymnbook.

Söderblom, unlike some of his episcopal colleagues, felt that church politics was not really his special *métier*. 'Incapable as I am of anything called politics', he wrote to his friend Manfred Björk-quist in 1920. This statement should perhaps not be taken at its face value, it was more an indication of the picture he had of himself than a reflexion of the real situation. Whenever any of the bishops in the *Riksdag* gave a hint of a certain *ennui* with the chores of the *Riksdag*, Söderblom concurred. 'Thank you for [your] disgust with the Parliament', he once wrote to Bishop Gottfrid Billing,[2] but he must have known that as far as Billing was concerned, any such complaint was only temporary.

In the Kyrkomöte of 1925 a special committee was formed to deal with the liturgical books of the Church. Here Söderblom was free to develop his ideas and to shape some of the sacred forms of the Church's life. This was an aspect of the work in the Kyrkomöte which he found congenial.

While thus obliged as President to remain silent, he was of course not inactive during the long speeches of the meetings. One of the secretaries of the Church Assembly has recorded his impressions: 'I recall how, as I worked on the minutes, he suddenly instructed

---

[2] Söderblom, October 7, 1914, to G. Billing.

me:"Find out what Churchwarden G in Y is called by his Christian name! ... Is that not Ellen Key sitting in the gallery? You must immediately see to it that she gets an Agenda and a Members' List, and that she is shown to a seat here, near the Speaker, as she is hard of hearing. ... There is a German professor waiting for me in the Speaker's Room. Go to him and entertain him for a while ... Please send this telegram to NN in America".[3]

As with the Kyrkomöte on the national level, so on the diocesan plane the Diocesan Chapter was part of the 'body', to use Söderblom's term, or of the official State Church organization. The Swedish chapters in the University towns of Uppsala and Lund had a special character in that they consisted at this time of the Professors of the Faculties of Theology. During the War, a Commission under Bishop Bergqvist's chairmanship revised the organization of the Chapters, but Söderblom insisted that Uppsala and Lund should be allowed to retain their representation from the theological faculties. 'The theological and ecclesiastical expertise is invaluable and altogether irreplaceable when we have to deal with rescripts of an important nature.'[4]

In the Chapter of course, Söderblom felt very much at home and the work agreed with him. It dealt with his own diocese, with the life of which he had been concerned for so many years. Already in his first years as Archbishop he had shown a surprisingly detailed knowledge of the local parishes, their problems and needs. The Uppsala Chapter was particularly important as it acted as centre for administrative matters remitted from the Government in Stockholm. Söderblom was thus in a position to express his views on a great number of questions of Church and school administration at that time.

In the Bishops Meeting, too, it was the spiritual concern which he wished to emphasize. One of the critics of the Bishops, professor Stave, of the Uppsala Faculty, once claimed that this Meeting was a secret conclave whereby a small minority tried to impose their will on the Church. This was very far from the truth. There were too many personal differences between those men for them ever to appear as a compact power group or conclave. It would be an exaggeration to claim that Söderblom as Archbishop dominated this group.

---

[3] Manfred Björkquist in *Nathan Söderblom in memoriam*, p. 216. Ellen Key (1849–1926) well-known Swedish authoress and reformer.
[4] Söderblom to O. Bergqvist in Letter Drafts, 1915.

In fact, he often felt ill-at-ease in this company, and he hardly ever, it seems, looked forward to those meetings. It was G. Billing who dominated during the first years of Söderblom's episcopate and Söderblom rightly referred to him as the Patriarch of the Church of the North.[5] This changed, as we shall see, after 1925, the year of Billing's death and of the Stockholm Conference. But Billing as the accomplished politician with his unique combination of experience, wisdom and personal authority, as a matter of course had the real influence in that select group. Söderblom had to experience defeats. In March 1919 he suggested that the Bishops' Meeting send a message of good will to the Swedish Free Church Conference which just met in the capital. 'Aware of the vital interests which on the deepest level unite all living followers of Christ in different camps', they drafted their greeting. With its reference to 'vital' and 'living', the draft was unmistakably Söderblom's! But a minority within the group opposed this measure, and the message was never sent.

Three years later, they discussed another spiritual matter, the care of souls. Söderblom had managed to win some of his colleagues for a statement on this subject to be addressed to the whole Church of Sweden.

First of all, the preaching must be made more central than as a rule it was at that time. Because, for what do men long? Certainly not for all kinds of analyses, but the simple Gospel of forgiveness and peace. 'While aware of the priest's duty of silence and the need for teaching about confession before a priest, [it must nevertheless also be said] that one does not need to be ordained in order to exercise the sacred right of Christian men to confess, and to receive, the secret anxiety of the soul.'

While the other Bishops shared the concern expressed in these words, they had misgivings against an official statement on the subject. It was perhaps not without significance that these doubts were expressed by G. Billing and J. A. Eklund, joined by O. Bergqvist.

Söderblom was dismayed and took the unexampled measure of writing in the minutes: 'I regret still another lost opportunity for the Bishops of the Church of Sweden through care of souls to come into closer contact with parishes and clergy. Because nothing is more needful than that we consider and emphasize that our calling is above all a spiritual personal task.'[6] He also quoted this complaint

---

[5] Söderblom, July 29, 1922, to G. Billing. E. Stave, in *Kyrkomötet 1915, Minutes*, No 13, p. 8.

[6] Bishops' Meeting; minutes April 20–21, 1922.

of his in his personal diary 1922 and added, 'One [attempts to] summon, but there are some who do not lift the wing.'

Söderblom was as aware as anybody else that the Bishops Meeting was a useful institution and he emphasized its role; he extended it when in 1922 he took the initiative to convene the first meeting of Northern Bishops, and there cannot be much doubt that he felt more at ease in this wider group than in the more limited Swedish one.

Both in the General Assembly of the National Church and in his Uppsala Chapter, Söderblom was confronted with the problem of the relations of Church and State. Entering upon his task he had in the first two years approached the subject in an optimistic, almost light-hearted mood. He studied with great interest the views of his friend Samuel Fries. After Fries' death in 1914, at the early age of forty-seven, Söderblom assisted in the publication of a posthumous volume called *Principles of Church Politics,* and wrote the Foreword. The Swedish nineteenth-century philosopher Boström had conditioned Fries's views on this matter—the State Church was the State itself, positively organizing its religious concerns.

In his own programmatic book, *The Body and the Soul of the Swedish Church,* Söderblom did not go as far as that, but he was sure that the State Church, more than any other form of organization, symbolized 'God's unmerited grace'. With the Uppsala Council in 1593 the Church had acquired a considerable independence for herself, he felt, and this self-government of the Church was reinforced by some of the great seventeenth century bishops in Sweden. In his Episcopal Charge of 1914 he showed that he visualized the possibility of a Socialist regime in Sweden and claimed in terms which for a churchman at the time were comparatively generous to the active Swedish Labour movement: 'It goes without saying that the sympathies of the Church lie with those in society who bear heavy burdens, and with such movements as seriously espouse their cause.'

While disclaiming any party affiliation, Söderblom nevertheless expressed himself in such a way as to make his leftish sympathies obvious. Not that this earned him much praise in the Socialist Youth organization. In 1914 they warned against him. 'The new Archbishop, Söderblom, through his glib and deceitful tongue must be one of the most dangerous enemies which Socialism has had in Sweden for a long time.'

With the end of the War, the Social Democrats launched a heavy attack against the State Church. Their most prominent spokesman was a young editor and member of the Riksdag, Arthur Engberg. Söderblom knew him well for he was born in Hassela, Hälsingland, and he had followed the gifted young student's career with generous interest; he had even once tried to win him for the ministry. There were formulae in Engberg's anti-Church propaganda that reminded Söderblom of Samuel Fries, for Engberg had learned from Fries' authority, Boström, that the State Church was 'the State as religiously organized'. With Engberg, however, this view was placed in a Marxist perspective. The Church was a class institution, he declared in the hunger year 1918, and, as the rising, underprivileged masses took power, the State Church system would be obsolete.

In fact Engberg very soon modified this view. In December 1919 he concentrated his attack on the Church Assembly which he hoped to abolish. Its right of veto against State measures was to be repealed, and such limited independence as the Church did have was to be even further reduced so as to make the Church into 'an organ for the religious activity of the State'.[7]

The Church had now to take its stand, and the Archbishop did so with great determination. This surprised some of the onlookers; they knew that Söderblom had good contacts with the powers that were, and that he cultivated such contacts. He had of course proved ever since the 1890's that his understanding and sympathy lay with social reform; as he had said, in 1919, in the official Prayer Day Proclamation signed by the Minister for Ecclesiastical Affairs, 'If justly distributed the bread will suffice for all'. But the Conservative *Göteborgs Dagblad* challenged this formula, 'exactly like the election propaganda phrases from the [Socialist] People's House', and suggested that it should be interpreted in the same manner as 'unreliable Socialist agitation, to which there exist no problems with regard to distribution, but everything is easy and simple as with the Bolsheviks'.[8]

If this was the reaction in Gothenburg, a conservative paper in Malmö was no more lenient. 'We see [Söderblom] literally woo the Liberal and Social Democratic parties in order to strengthen the sinking shares of the Church; the Primate of the Swedish Church on the Archbishop's throne, a free-thinker ... is not fit in these times to head the Swedish Church. His efforts to convert Radicals and Socialists have failed; his wordly church politics have suffered ship-

---

[7] Cf. C. A. Hessler, *Statskyrkodebatten* (1964), p. 188 f.
[8] *Göteborgs Dagblad*, January 5, 1920.

wreck. His performance belongs to the saddest pages of the history of our Church.'[9] Newspapers of this tendency were confirmed in their views as they learned that Söderblom had invited Fabian Månsson, a radical Labour leader, to address the General Church Meeting, March 1920.

If there was therefore a tendency in the Conservative camp to regard Söderblom as a dangerous Socialist there must have been some second thoughts as Söderblom took up the cudgels. He did so in the press, and collected his articles in a thought-provoking book, *Religionen och Staten*. It was however characteristic that he launched his attack particularly in the General Church Meeting of March, 1920. The General Church Meetings had first been organized in 1908, though unofficially, and not legally enacted as was the General Assembly. The 'Meetings' represented a platform for concerted Church opinion and it is obvious that Söderblom found these meetings congenial. Here he had full freedom to act; he was not tied as he felt he was in the General Assembly. Here was a place where the 'Spirit' could express itself and animate the institution of the Church. Nowhere did Söderblom meet and influence the whole Swedish Church with the same inspiration and conviction and vision as in these Meetings.

In the General Church Meeting of 1920 he spoke on 'The Church's Claim of Freedom', and it was against Arthur Engberg's propaganda that he directed his argument.[10] He knew that he had helpful partisans in the Labour party; H. Hallén, a pastor and Labour Member of the Riksdag, had withstood his party colleague Engberg in Parliament, and Söderblom recognized that Hallén was fighting the Church's cause of 'freedom' there. He felt that as a politician, Hallén was freer than he to express some of the things that needed to be said on behalf of the Church. 'I am tempted to be envious,' he wrote to Hallén, 'of anybody who is allowed to fight for his life's ideals without the heavy, entangled machinery and armour which my position entails'.[11]

Yet in the General Church Meeting he had freedom to act, and it was on and for freedom that he did speak. (We are aware of the fact that this blessed word was of course also Engberg's and Hallén's, but that is not the point here.) Söderblom attacked Engberg squarely.

[9] *Skånska Aftonbladet*, December 30, 1919.
[10] *Samtal om Kyrkan* (1920).
[11] Söderblom, June 14, 1918 and February 17, 1920 to H. Hallén.

'The motion is signed', he said, 'by a Member of the Riksdag whose speciality is animosity against Christianity and against the Church and its men. With boastful threats he has publicly declared that the Church must be smashed and crushed.' Engberg wanted to remove the right of veto accorded to the Kyrkomöte: To do this can have no other meaning than that the religious community quite simply is going to be turned into a slave. ... If somebody ... puts out the light and destroys it, what is he? Definitely not a friend of the light but an enemy of the light.

A deadly blow has been aimed at the freedom of religion. This is intended to be the beginning of a systematic struggle against the Church. They want to remove the independence of the Church . . . in order to kill or at least to weaken the Church and congregation of Christ. This is not attractive. It is un-Swedish ... it goes against the free traditions of our country. It is not modern. Further ... it is a tyrannical measure warring against the principles of freedom. Those [in the Labour Party] who try to revive the secular clause in the Party's Manifesto are motivated by enmity against religion.'

As a positive measure he suggested the modernisation of the Kyrkomöte so that it would be built on a definitely democratic foundation; there must be freedom from the tyranny of the enmity against religion; freedom for anybody to leave the Church; freedom for the Church to work and to create such conditions, particularly for the clergy, that they should be free for their essential task. He suggested that the question of Church and State be determined by referendum and claimed that the State could not, with impunity, do without the preaching of the Gospel.

There are stars so distant that they go on shining long after they have become extinct. Many who believe that they have put out the light of the faith, or to whom it seems that this light has gone out, still live in its light. If they manage to put it out, then in the end a deep darkness will come.

But the Church must realize that the greatest danger is her own worldliness, lukewarmness and fear. There must be glowing hearths of Christian love and Christian zeal in our parishes.

It was one of Söderblom's great days. He added dramatic significance to his performance in the Blasieholmen Church in that he took the opportunity of welcoming the great Socialist leader Hjalmar Branting. It was one of those occasions where Söderblom excelled. From the chairman's seat he had discovered Branting's face among the spectators in the gallery. Branting was invited to appear before the meeting and Söderblom gave one of his incomparable improvised speeches.

At the General Church Meeting, 1920, Hjalmar Branting, the Labour Prime Minister made a surprise call and was welcomed by the Archbishop. Fabian Månsson (Socialist), Söderblom's friend, addressed the Meeting.

Söderblom's friend Fabian Månsson spoke on the same occasion on the Gospel and the Renewal of Society. Månsson had already seen the first indications of a certain lack of inspiration in the Labour movement, and he felt that the masses would receive new strength from the Old Book, particularly from the Sermon on the Mount and the Lord's Prayer. It is a simple fact that Månsson's appearance on that occasion would have been unthinkable without Söderblom.

His interest in social problems—which we should summarize here —had been established much earlier. Here again is an instance of tenacious consistency in this agile church leader. The beginnings of this interest were from the 1890's, if one does not draw the line even further to the boy's observations in Hälsingland, then very much part of Poverty-Sweden of the 1870's. We recall the stages of his development in this field. Wilhelm Herrmann of Marburg provided him with theological arguments for a positive attitude to the Social Democratic movement. The Evangelical-Social congress at Erfurt in 1896 and the message of men such as Friedrich Naumann and Paul Göhre inspired him. Söderblom's lecture at the Stockholm Conference in 1897 and his book on the Sermon on the Mount (1898) are important documents showing a considerable degree of theological reflection. The Church had achieved an un-Christian dichotomy between cult and service, between worship and social service, between liturgy and diaconia:[1] His concern was to reintegrate the two. He was not prepared to indentify the interests of the Christian cause with those of Socialism but did already at this time stress the role of trade unions for establishing social peace.[2]

In the final analysis, he insisted, the springs of social revolution are not in new institutions but in new men who place love instead of hatred, solidarity instead of the war of everybody against everybody.[3]

In his Episcopal Charge of 1914 he returned to the problem. In the nature of things, he said, the sympathies of the Church are with the oppressed in society and with such movements as made their cause their own. He put his finger on the economic inequalities in society.[4]

One cannot very well claim that Söderblom had a neat and well defined system of social and economic thought. Perhaps this was too much to ask from a Swedish archbishop at the time. But at least he was keenly aware of some of the needs in the fields of employment, housing and economic justice. He would express his economic conviction in the somewhat broad terms to which we have already referred: 'Justly distributed, the daily bread will suffice for all. Justly distributed, work will not be oppressive to anybody. Both must be justly distributed. Anyone caught in the mud of selfishness will die the spiritual death.'

At the same time, he stressed that salvation was something more than social justice; the final goal of the Church's pilgrimage was not the fleshpots of Egypt, but Canaan.[5] The task of the National Church was therefore, 'to express the participation of the State in an eternal movement.'

From these presuppositions he ventured forth challenging the actual cases of social inequality in both rural and urbanized Sweden.

---

[1] Söderblom in [S. A. Fries, ed.] *Religionsvetenskapliga kongressen 1897*. p. 87 and 100.
[2] Söderblom in *Skåne-Tidningen* April 12, 1898.
[3] [Fries ed.]. Ibid p. 16.
[4] Söderblom, *Herdabref* (1914) p. 19 and 16.
[5] Söderblom, *Religionen och Staten* (1918) p. 189.

Paul Göhre's studies of the rural proletariat in Eastern Prussia were among the factors inspiring him to encourage one of his young priests in the preparation of a similar study of Swedish rural workers on the estates of Southern Uppland, in his own diocese.[6]

His visitations to the congregations in some of the poorer suburbs of Stockholm were at times dramatic occasions because of the Archbishop's outspoken comments. In 1921, he visited the Stockholm parish of Solna, which included the township of Huvudsta, a place where, at this time, unemployment was rampant.

It was common knowledge that the social conditions in Huvudsta were outrageous. It had been reported to Söderblom that the land-owner had managed effectively to hinder the laying of water pipes and electric lines to the workers' houses. As he visited the parish he went into the matter. He was not content with proclaiming pious generalities. He took up the question in the midst of the congregation, standing in the pulpit addressing the packed church. 'Is estate-owner Wibom here?', he called out. 'Let him now, as estate-owner in Huvudsta, inform us how he intends to organize such important amenities of life as hygiene, water and light.' The question echoed through the hushed church, and in most of the Swedish newspapers afterwards. Mr. Wibom had not availed himself of the opportunity of coming to church that day and the Archbishop went on: 'It cannot be allowed that a few among us usurp advantages and rights, placing burdens on the shoulders of others. The right of the capitalist is not always moral right.'[7]

The following day, the intermezzo was reported in the papers, most endorsing the Archbishop's action. Some of the papers, to be sure, took Söderblom to task for his temerity: he had displayed clericalism in his belief that the Church should be concerned with social problems.[8] The landowner himself could take courage from such expressions of dismay. Interviewed by the Stockholms-Tidningen, Mr. Wibom gave his view of the case: 'I cannot believe that the Archbishop has said anything of the kind. He has of course not referred to water and light in the mundane meaning of the word, but of the water of life and of light in a spiritual sense. The health of the body is looked after by other powers who perchance might manage without the interference of the Archbishop. Obviously

---

[6] *Uppsala Ärkestifts Prästmöte* 1927. *Protokoll och handlingar,* p. 230. R. Littmark, *Mälardalens nomader,* 1930.

[7] *Visitationsberättelse,* Solna, 1921, Diocesan Archives, Uppsala.

[8] *Upsala Nya Tidning* and *Sv. Morgonbladet,* both November 25, 1921.

Dagens Nyheter had the caption: 'A minute with the Archbishop'.

the Archbishop's words have been reported by somebody who cannot distinguish metaphor from ordinary prose.'[9]

With all his emphasis on the Spirit, Söderblom had a very keen sense of the all too ordinary prose of poverty and misery in the Sweden of those days, and in Swedish society he made his mark as Archbishop by his widely observed attitude. He shocked the bourgeois by establishing and maintaining close personal contacts with Fabian Månsson, rumbustious politician and author, then regarded as standing on the far left wing of the Labour party. He missed no opportunity of encouraging Hjalmar Branting, the Swedish Labour leader, or daring Social Democratic priest-politicians, such as Harald Hallén. It goes without saying, however, that he was not a member of the Labour Party. The social reforms he advocated were far from revolutionary. Both in the diocese (through the *Stiftsmöte*) and in the country as a whole he worked for harmonious co-operation between employers and employees. Together with Erik B. Rinman, editor of the Liberal *Stockholms-Tidningen*, he encouraged efforts for better conditions for workers. It was this spirit which informed

---

[9] *Stockholms-Tidningen*, November 22, 1921.

the Swedish Committee preparing the statement on social problems for Stockholm, 1925.

It is probably fair to state, in deliberately general terms that while Söderblom had no precise programme of the Church's social and economic action, he managed to dramatise the needs of the labouring masses as he understood them and thereby contributed towards changing the climate of Swedish society.

The Archbishop's House

Back in Uppsala, his day would begin at 8 a.m. when, occasionally, he would attend prayers in the Cathedral (there was, and is, no chapel in the Archbishop's house). Breakfast at 8.30 with those of the family who were not at school. The secretary was seated next to the Archbishop; they would open the first mail and Söderblom would make suggestions or dictations as to answers by letter or telegram.

From 9 a.m. dictating letters, articles, reports, and memoranda until lunch, supposedly at 1 p.m. ('We *always* had to wait for him at meals.') 3–4 p.m., another spell of dictation; 4 p.m. tea, often with guests. 4.30–7 p.m., correspondence, etc., as above. 7 or 7.30. Dinner, often with guests. 9 p.m. Evening prayer with the family. The 'Gunilla' bell from the Castle would ring at 9, and windows were opened to let the sound in. A hymn; Bible reading by the Archbishop alone, or by the family and guests reading one verse each. Prayers by the Archbishop with responses in Latin. *Sursum Corda*: *Habemus ad Dominum*. Blessing, and a hymn. The musical family of old and young comprised an excellent choir and it was the Archbishop's special joy to practise this family choir after prayers. Many a guest retained indelible memories from these occasions in the Archbishop's House.

There was also what we would call his 'extended family' which in fact was ever increasing. The central core of it was the family's circle of old friends, and in Uppsala of those days it proved easy for the members of this group to meet very regularly. There had developed a certain regime, whereby on the great Church festivals, such as Christmas and Easter, they met in the various houses in a happy fellowship; Söderblom as a matter of course being the centre of the party.

There was a regular, sometimes almost daily series of official or informal dinners, with guests from abroad, some of whom would stay for shorter or longer periods in the Archbishop's House. The

Olaus Petri lecturers or the delegates to ecumenical conferences and committees stayed in the Archbishop's House. Town and gown in Uppsala, together with ambassadors and high officials from Stockholm would be invited to meet them; the host displaying his prodigious linguistic ability and range.

The constellation of these two, the Archbishop and his Ärkebiskopinna (as the Swedes have it) formed a remarkable team. Next to the image of his father, Anna Söderblom was his censor; the diary bears this out, in the references to her courageous and high-minded role in the home, Church and society. We can only make a guess at the extent to which his sermons, addresses and speeches were formed with her exacting censorship in mind. As a young fiancée she had told him: 'I will follow you wherever you go, even to Constantinople!' She followed him far and willingly on his spiritual journey, to a certain limit. While Söderblom was prepared gladly and generously to adjust himself to a wide variation of expressions of Christian belief, Anna followed her own line. Certain pious meetings she found definitely suffocating and would have as little as possible to do with them. The noble, high-minded, ethical conviction which had characterised Dr. Fehr's Confirmation class followed her as her ideal. Early on in life she had contacts with Jewish piety in Stockholm, and was in fact a resolute Sionist in later years. She was far from being content with any easy acceptance of the faith; in fact with all her religious conviction, she was a doubter into her old-age. She looked like a beautiful seeress, and she had no small talk. At a dinner given in honour of the graduation of one of her sons, she had a young friend in the house as her partner at the table, the son of their neighbours, the Governor of the Province. She turned to him, saying 'Dag', for it was young Dag Hammarskjöld, 'I assume Dag is reading Pascal.' She probably inspired him to do so.

The week also had its regular rhythm. At weekends the Archbishop would as a rule be away for visitations in the Diocese; Wednesday mornings were set aside for the Chapter; Thursdays for business in Stockholm, with Church Boards, and in the evening, for University matters, with the Secretary to the Chancellor of the University.

He would make notes in his own hand in his little blue notebooks; or dictate certain passages here and there for a book; these preparatory notes would be gathered in envelopes, with the title of the chapter on it. Thus prepared he would begin to dictate a book. Any other work, except the most urgent, would then be relegated to later.

He could go on hour after hour, day after day, dictating. He was unwilling to come for meals. He would walk to and fro over the floor, rattling his bunch of keys as he went along. Occasionally he would climb a ladder to get a book from the upper shelves in order to make a quotation, or he would instruct his secretary to get down 'a thin little pamphlet, green, on the third shelf, from the top, near the window', or he would make a reference to 'Fru (FRU = Främmande Religionsurkunder; i.e., Texts from Other Religions) III, page So and so'.

He would dictate as rapidly and surely in French, German and English, not making any changes in the text as he went along. He only said 'This is not good, but write it down. We can change this later'. Or he might add: 'That piece was not too bad, don't you think?' As he dictated he always spoke as if there was an audience in front of him, and his flow of speech was accompanied by his characteristic gestures. For a change he would lie down on a sofa, with his Tartan blanket over him, continually dictating.

In the middle of dictation, somebody from the Chapter or University might come along with papers for him to sign, or an urgent telephone call from Stockholm or elsewhere would be allowed through; he simply went on dictating, while at the same time he answered the phone or rapidly put his signature to a number of documents.

In the parishes

His habit of devoting the week-ends to the episcopal visitation of the local congregations was his recognition of a venerable institution in the Swedish church, some would have said an outdated one that fulfilled no function. To be sure, a visitation could easily become a dreary, starchy affair. An ecclesiastical dignitary came along and made his enquiries; he put his set questions and respectful answers were, or were not, given. There would follow an endless series of pious speeches. To some, no doubt, this very dreariness and starchiness conveyed an impression of that dignity and social respectability which in the Swedish milieu was sometimes mistaken for, or identified with, religious reality. This may be something of caricature; and it must be admitted that, in spite of all, many of the Bishops made their visitations into splendid and memorable events.

Whatever may have been the case in other dioceses, Söderblom obviously had a special *charisma* for this task. To him the bishop's visitation was pre-eminently his very precious and longed-for opportunity of establishing personal and spiritual *communication* with the parishes and, as far as possible, with their individual members of all ages, sorts and conditions. He felt that it was here that he could in the most real sense exercise his episcopate. He wrote on this aspect of the visitation to Archbishop Johansson in Finland:

I was asked the other day by a journalist what aspect of my work I treasured most. I replied that without any doubt the visitations are dearest to me, and I added my experience that the bishop on these occasions, like all servants of the Church, must use the word as a sword. The concept of the bishop as a kind of Inspector or General Manager is not unusual in the world, but here in the far North it is our special task to emphasize and demonstrate that the bishop too it the servant of the Word, a *Seelsorger*.[1]

To another brother bishop, Headlam of Gloucester, he reported on one of his visitations made immediately prior to the Stockholm Conference. It concerned his own Trönö where he had been born. He wrote in his own English to Headlam:

I have just come back from a visitation trip to Norrala and Trönö, where the Rector and le Vicaire had read to the parishes the announcement of my coming, of which I give you a copy in Swedish, with the date Gloucester. It is always refreshing, even if it takes much spiritual and bodily effort, to have a concentrated visitation.

On Friday afternoon 6.30, I had to consecrate a chapel with a parish-house in Stugsund near to Söderhamn, and immediately after that to lecture in the Church of Söderhamn to the annual assembly of the Church youth on the 'heroic soul of Martin Luther'.

The following morning I started in the big Church of Norrala, six miles from there, with the young people and the parish Council and many visitors at 10 o'clock. We made a procession in the rain to the tomb and commemoration house of the Apostle of Hälsingland, S:t Staffan, who was killed by the heathen about 1060. Then, after the children had been sent home, I looked through the essential treasures of the Church and then, following the report given by the Rector, I discussed with the members of the parish Council different temporal and spiritual affairs and needs of the parish until 2.30, p.m. At 5 o'clock the same thing was [done] about five miles from there in the annexed parish of Trönö, in the new, very much too great Church, with place for 1200 people in a very wide parish with about 1800 members. Norrala has about 4000. I came back to the rectory in Norrala about 11 o'clock in the evening.

On Sunday at 11 o'clock procession with priests from the neighbouring parishes [in alb and chasubles] and the four church-wardens. Installa-

---

[1] Söderblom, March 1, 1924, to G. Johansson.

tion of the Rector before the Altar. That is one of the occasions when the Bishop has always in our Church been invited to be dressed in cope, mitre and staff. After that, High Mass, and then I began a conversation with the young people in the choir and continued with the crowd that filled the big sanctuary. Then 'Visitationsstämma', that is, a meeting with the assemblies of both parishes for telling them what I have found during the visitation and discussing some parish problems. I had a rather serious thing to say to my friends. After I had asked if there were any complaints of the clergy, I went to the Altar. Then followed a short exhortation, then Benedicamus and the Blessing. All that lasted nearly until 3 o'clock. At 6 o'clock the same thing in the other parish. But I preferred to go into the old Church from the 12th century. Amongst other relics there is a very fine little reliquaire, made in Limoges in the 13th century, representing the murder of Thomas à Becket and his burial. I had visited the martyrdom in Canterbury exactly a week before. Then with motorcar a little more than 70 miles to Gävle, where we arrived at midnight.

The following day back to Uppsala.

That gives you a description of a very much too concentrated and short visitation.[2]

Even the most seasoned research worker cannot withhold an expression of amazement at the very large part of the Archbishop's time, year after year, which was spent in visitations. Increasingly, his ecumenical work took its fair share and more of his strength. His international travels took him away from the diocese from time to time, and sometimes this could be as much as a full month in the Baltic in July 1922, or even the best part of four months in the United States at the end of 1923. Apart from international conferences and visits, there was also the time given to relief work in the years after the War.

In spite of all this Söderblom insisted that the diocese was his first and foremost responsibility. He said so to his clergy in their Synod in 1927:

The diocese is large. The pastorates are many. The essential calling of the Bishop of Uppsala is first and last his diocese. Everything else must take second place. Let this be said officially and emphatically against misrepresentations of various kinds.

However assertive this statement may have appeared there was an unmistakable apologetic tone to it. He knew that his international commitments took a very large part of his time. He still could not

---

[2] Söderblom, July 10, 1925, to A. C. Headlam (Lambeth Arch.).

alter the tiresome fact that there were only so many days in the year and only a very limited number of Sundays in the Church's year. As he began his episcopate he planned a series of visitations to all the two hundred and fifty-five parishes in his diocese and found that he might do the round in fourteen years. This as he knew was much too long an interval, and he attempted to do much more than that. He established a plan whereby every parish should have a visitation every seven years from the Bishop and the Rural Deans in turn. He knew that this was an aspect of diocesan work which needed special attention. He felt that both Sundberg and Ekman, his predecessors, had been too stationary, partly because of their age. Ekman in his twelve years had visited eighty-eight of the parishes.

Söderblom must also have felt that the war restrictions on international travel should be turned to the advantage of the diocese. In the four or five war years he concentrated with unmoved resolution on his diocesan work. If asked to preach or lecture outside his diocese he would refuse in those early years with a formula of this nature: 'I do not dare to take on any task outside my diocese because my diocese requires all my strength.' When he consulted his diary he would find that he had no free day whatsoever for months on end. Under this strict planning he visited no less than forty parishes in 1916; this meant many long week-ends away from Uppsala, or even seven days (as in the visitation to the important town of Gävle). It also meant busy hours dictating the minutes from the visitation, upon his return to Uppsala. Also later he managed to squeeze in an amazing number of visitations in a year. In 1924, the year between his extended American tour of 1923 and his Stockholm Conference, there were thirty-nine such visitations; in 1925, the year of the Conference, there were twenty-two.

The congregations and their conditions varied greatly. Broadly speaking, each of the three provinces within the diocese had its own character; Söderblom would refer to Uppland, Gästrikland and Häl-singland as Judea, Samaria and Galilee. There was of course little doubt that he loved his own Galilee with its Sea Gennesaret–Dellen for he seemed to know every house and person in that part of his domain. There was a very marked difference between the congregations of Hälsingland and those of Uppland with regard to church attendance. The tradition of Church pietism loyal to the National Church was still a power in Hälsingland, while Uppland from this point of view belonged to the tragic wasteland of empty churches in central Sweden, but in spite of this, maintaining an amazing loyalty to the good old order of church and priest, and proud of its incomparable Jerusalem, the city of Uppsala with its Cathedral. Gästrikland was more industrialized than the other provinces and presented most of the problems and opportunities typical of industrial regions everywhere. To these must be added the capital, Stockholm, which was part of the archdiocese, and Söderblom frequently paid visits to city parishes in what became in 1941, the Diocese of Stockholm.

These visitations he planned with great care on some free day in the autumn, for the whole of the following year. William Temple, when asked during the First World War, 'when are you going to begin your campaign on Life and Liberty?' replied: 'I have begun already. I have bought a Bradshaw.[3] Söderblom was a great believer in the Swedish equivalent of the Bradshaw, *Statens kommunikationer*. He enjoyed planning combinations of rail, bus and boat. He sent a draft programme to the parish in question asking for comments and counter-proposals, then he sent a very solemnly styled proclamation to the parish: 'By virtue of the episcopate which has been accorded to me in the Uppsala archdiocese I greet X and Y Christian parishes. Grace be with you and peace from God our Father and our Lord Jesus Christ ...' There would follow a detailed programme.

As Söderblom had written to Headlam, he found the contact with local parishes refreshing. He had that sure touch and acted with that combination of authority and personal charm which endeared him to, and amazed, both the clergy and the parishes. He came well prepared, but even to the best prepared unforeseen things may occur. So it happened as he visited the Bergsjö parish in Hälsingland. He was to re-dedicate the church but found that the golden crozier had been left behind in Uppsala. He was undaunted, however. On the Sunday morning he went out in the forest nearby and cut a young birch, trimmed it, keeping the leaves only on top. With cope and mitre, and with this living crozier he entered the church, exclaiming with his melodious voice: 'It is spring that I let in to your church and parish', and made an occasion which might have been embarrassing into something memorable and beautiful. On another occasion there was an induction of a new vicar. The church was packed at Alfta, Hälsingland, on that Midsummer Day, 1920. Because of the great number of people, some were seated in the choir and near the altar rails. The procession with the Arch-

---

F. A. Iremonger, *William Temple* (1948), p. 249.

bishop, his assistants and the new vicar, slowly wove its way through the crowd and arranged itself in a semi-circle with the Archbishop at the altar. After the first hymn, the Archbishop's clear, well-articulated voice intonated: 'In the name of the Father ...' There and then the new vicar fainted and dropped to the floor ... The young assistants carried him out into the vestry, cared for him, and returned. Söderblom was unperturbed. He read out his text, 1 Cor. 3: 10–15 and began his address 'For other foundation can no man lay. ...' Even as he spoke he slowly moved down the steps and forward to the altar rail, and as the young priests returned from the vestry, through the crowd, he asked them in a hushed voice how the vicar was (without interrupting his address to the congregation). He instructed them 'Find out whether he is ready to return'. (Then, to the congregation: 'People are seeking many foundations, but there is only one, Jesus Christ).

A young priest returned from his explorations and whispered that the vicar was prepared to come in two minutes if allowed to sit on a chair. The Archbishop concluded his address and was now prepared to read an abbreviated form of the ritual of induction. The whole act was carried through quite smoothly; a proof of this was that the new vicar's wife, seated in the front row, had no idea of the drama. Reporting on the Alfta induction, a priest added: 'We were humbly proud of him. He was after all our 'Nathan'.[3a]

In the inductions of vicars and dedications of churches the Archbishop slowly but surely let black gowns give way to colourful liturgical vestments. That is, when allowed to do so. On Trinity Day 1919, Söderblom was taking an induction at Hassela in Hälsingland. He was planning the procession together with clergy and church wardens. Some of the clergy insisted that there be vestments. The churchwardens, good old Lutheran Pietists, dampened this enthusiasm. They would not allow vestments: 'All here think that is old and catholic and that it should now be abolished.' The Archbishop followed their advice on this occasion.

In his Söderala visitation, July 1923, he came to the village of Östanbo. Paragraph II of the Visitation Minutes reads:

The Archbishop mentioned the historical places which mightily bear witness to the liberating power of the truth of the Gospel. One was Wartburg, where Luther by translating the Bible to the language of the people, created the most important condition for the life of spiritual freedom. The other

---

[3a] E. Birke, in *Julhälsningar till församlingarna i ärkestiftet*, 1965, p. 84.

place was Lincoln College in Oxford, an old house with recollections of both the English Reformer John Wicliff and of John Wesley and thereby the point of departure for that spiritual revival which through Methodism was conveyed to Christendom.

Even more graphic this ecumenical education at the grassroots became, as the Archbishop managed to take along some of the ecclesiastical dignitaries from exotic countries. Thus Dr. Glubokovski of Petrograd (as the city was then named) or Bishop Irenaeus of Novi Sad or Albert Schweitzer from Lambarene or a number of other personalities would follow the Archbishop, who on such occasions would act as interpreter. Or he might quote to a village group in Uppland or Hälsingland what the ecumenical leaders had just said. In 1916, in the middle of the war, Professor Hauck of Leipzig, the German church historian, had given Olaus Petri lectures on 'Germany and England and their mutual Church relations', at Uppsala University. He had quoted Goethe's word which was really from Sophocles:

> Nicht mitzuhassen,
> Mitzulieben bin ich da.[4]

Söderblom developed this theme to his village congregation and emphasized the significance of this word being quoted at that time and in connexion with that particular series of lectures.

This was a time of increasing secularization in the Swedish school system. Hardly anybody was more aware of this inevitable change in Swedish society and its significance than Söderblom. The elementary schools were, in principle, taken out of Church control in 1919, and the few secondary schools were no longer under the authority of bishops or Chapter. Yet a tradition of close contact of church and school was still very much alive in many parts of the country. Söderblom developed this and emphasized the importance of the schools, and to a surprising degree his visitations included the schools, for he would spend two days of every visitation of three or four days on them. His task as Pro-Chancellor of the Uppsala University on the one hand, and on the other these visits to hundreds of elementary schools in the countryside, made him emphasize on different levels the Church's role for the culture of the people.

The visitation to Hälsingtuna in September, 1916, included a few hours in Fiskeby village. At 9.30 a.m. he visited the infant school; at

---

[4] Not to hate, but to love do I exist.

11.30 the Fläsbro lower elementary school where he listened to and took an active part in the teaching of Reading and Swedish history. The following day he spent the best part of the morning and forenoon in another elementary school, listening, teaching, encouraging, singing, praying and blessing. He would enjoy teaching on such occasions and did not confine himself at all to Scripture lessons. Arithmetic, history, geography, these learned subjects came to life as he touched them. Together with the children he went in procession to the church where he spoke to them about the life of the Church.

There was also something else which he may have had in mind as he devoted his time to the children in the church. In his ecumenical contacts with the Church of England he had been reminded of the negative fact that the Swedish Church, although episcopally constituted, did not have episcopal confirmation, this being, in principle, delegated to the local priests. Söderblom was aware of the value in the Catholic position which established a personal bond between the Bishop and every mature member of the diocese. He was of course realistic enough to see that this aspect could not be reintroduced into the Swedish situation with its very large dioceses, but on the quiet he did the next best thing. As the children assembled in church, and after he had addressed them on the history of their parish or the history of the Swedish Church, or possibly a passage from the Gospel, he would bless them, laying his hands on each one of them.

Not long ago, I asked a fellow member of the Uppsala Chapter, a lay member from Hälsingland, if he had any recollection of Söderblom. Yes, he said, as a boy of eight he had been in church with the others of his school. The Archbishop had spoken to them and then, laying his hands on each one of them, had blessed them. This was something that he would never forget.

If, as we would suggest, Söderblom made his episcopate into a 'ministry of encouragement', this was applied not least to the teachers, both young and old.

In the nature of things he had to work through the clergy in order to reach the diocese. There existed a special institutional platform in the Swedish Church for contact between bishop and clergy, in the Priests' Synods, which however met only once in six years. There were three conferences of this nature in Söderblom's time, in 1915, 1921 and 1927. The diocese had not voted for him. They had placed their confidence in others at that time. Yet, he very soon established contacts with the clergy. The younger generations especially were immensely proud—as well they might be—of their Bishop. There were always a few die-hards who could never be sure that their bishop had the right theology, that is, their theology, and who therefore kept at a distance. He had his own sympathies and anti-pathies. He was impatient of those who he thought were lazy, and a combination of supposed laziness and all too obvious obesity was not popular with him. A priest should have what he called a certain 'distinction', something whereby he in some measure excelled. He had a foible for the scholars among them. Once he wrote: 'As I look at the map of the diocese, the priests engaged in research are con-spicuous. There one writes on Bonaventura. Another is Sweden's foremost expert on the Rosa. Still another is a specialist on Ma-nichaeism, yet another on Islam, or on Arabic folklore. . . . Normally these activities increase, rather than diminish any qualifications for the ministry.'

Unmistakably it was the younger generations of priests whom he regarded as his best co-workers in the diocese. This showed partic-ularly in the work of the Diocesan Conference, or the *stiftsmöte*. This was an important innovation in the life of the diocese, a volun-tary body, first organized in the diocese of Västerås by Bishop Löv-gren. The Uppsala equivalent first met in 1920. It met once a year and was led by a Diocesan Council where the Archbishop was chair-man. Söderblom tried to devote time to this group. He felt particu-larly at home when the younger clergy formed something of a pres-sure group within this organization, and he spent three memorable days with them at Storvik, April 1926. In the nineteen-twenties the lack of new priests was felt as particularly devastating for the diocese. Söderblom wrote to Professor Eidem in Lund in November 1925: 'The lack of new priests, hitherto unendurable, is soon superhuman . . ., at present it looks hopeless.' He had his tussles from time to time with his brother bishops in the adjoining dioceses over young candidates for the ministry, and he thought of various devices in order to find new men.[5] Some of those who did come were of remark-able quality, possessing that 'distinction' which Söderblom wished to

---

[5] Söderblom appreciated the role of the Young Church movement for the re-cruitment and supply of new priests in his time. He was not uncritical of the movement, but wrote to J. A. Eklund, January 24, 1916. 'For me it would be much, much more difficult to be a Bishop than for you if it were not for this blessed movement. But one becomes desperate in the face of all pretentious talk of Church loyalty and youth-work, while reality shows nothing but a few nice young girls as the pastor's real domain of activity.' UUB.

see. Some even had the particular distinction of being both young scholars and hailing from manses in the diocese, such as Bengt Jonzon and Torsten Bohlin (both later bishops). At Storvik a young priest by name of T. Ysander (later bishop) took the initiative. His personal background was solid west-coast Schartauism, although modified by contacts with modern theology and the Young Church movement. He also specialized in the History of Religions, an additional merit in Söderblom's eyes.[6] At the Storvik meeting Ysander struck a note which Söderblom recognized as familiar; the tension between old forms and the dynamic life of the Spirit. The Diocesan Conference as a place where the new dynamic forces could operate should be accorded greater influence also with regard to the age-old organizations such as the Diocesan Chapter. Söderblom was sufficiently inspired by this apparent awakening to make a speech at the Stiftsmöte where he went far with his characteristic emphasis: 'Nature around us is like a wedding hall. What banns have been published to-day? Ah, the wedding is to take place between God and the soul. They have found one another and celebrate their union.'[7]

Söderblom's concern in his visitations was to animate an old institution and infuse it with a spirit of personal contact and communication. He knew that, even in religion, the organization and the machine tended to take over. He had the courage to oppose this tendency to institutionalize. He also had the vision to establish, with his diocese, as far as possible immediate, personal relationships instead of safe but cold, depersonalized attitudes.

In Söderblom's case this concern did not exclude, but rather implied an awareness of the values of tradition and history. Of course it was renewal for the Church that he wanted. But this could not, and should not, be had at the price of neglect of tradition. So it came about that in his contacts with the local parishes he always insisted on continuity with the past and with the long and sacred tradition of the Church. He had felt that need, in his own case, with regard to his consecration; he had made a learned study of the consecration, held seven hundred and fifty years earlier, of his first predecessor as Archbishop of Uppsala in Sens Cathedral: in a similar manner, the local parishes needed to be made aware of their living

---

[6] Ysander was asked by Söderblom to write the chapter on Judaism, in the sixth edition of Tiele–Söderblom's Handbook on History of Religion.

[7] Stiftsmötet minutes, July 21, 1926.

past, in their historical monuments, particularly the Church buildings, with their sacred treasures and old documents. In his visitations he would bring out those treasures, lift them up amongst the people, make them feel the grain of old pieces of art; and realize anew, or for the first time, the value of those possessions. He took endless pains over this matter. He took it to the Bishops' Meeting in 1917, and on behalf of the Meeting wrote to the Government about it. He wanted the churches to have resort to technical advice by art specialists so that those possessions should be well preserved for new generations. Here again his emphasis was on renewal and spiritual awareness. The objects of art were meant to be, 'not curiosities useful for scholars and sought after by tourists; but in their way, they must be servants of life to be respected by generation after generation'.[8]

It can be argued that the roots of this concern of his were to be found in his childhood experiences. As one reads his temperamental sallies against misguided church architecture in his own diocese or elsewhere in Sweden, one is reminded of the two churches at Trönö, where Söderblom was born and spent his first years. There was the simple, yet beautiful mediaeval church, the picture of which Söderblom had entered into his *ex libris,* and half a mile away a horrid nineteenth-century 'wedding-cake' of a church. The comparison made him for ever sceptical towards some experts in the field of art. So it was with church restorations too. He never tired of referring to the Söderala church in Hälsingland, where the learned experts in the 1890's had made the congregation rebuild the Church out of keeping with its ancient style. The old local church-warden at the time had launched a solemn protest against this outrage and had his protest placed in the vestry, in the frame of a picture of the undefiled Church. To Söderblom, it was of special importance that this church-warden, Sven Jonsson, was none other than his paternal uncle.

The same concern which Söderblom showed over what he regarded as mistaken restorations of church buildings, he also demonstrated with regard to the debate on the Swedish hymnbook, and for the same reasons. Throughout the centuries the hymnbook had been the most popular and beloved book in Sweden. The church was said to have its Hymnbook Christians! If ever there was such a species, Söderblom belonged to it. He knew his Swedish hymnbook, and carried it in his pocket. He told his wife one day, that he would always carry the hymnbook in the back-pocket of his trousers, but she,

---

[8] Söderblom, March 6, 1917, to the Swedish Government.

always his exacting super-ego, an expert on the Hymns in her own right, drily retorted: 'Better to carry it in one's memory'.[9]

Söderblom's intervention in the Church Assembly debate in 1921 on the Hymnbook—an address of some 16,000 words—was as we have mentioned earlier an exception to the rule that the President should not participate in the debates. A commission consisting of Bishops Gottfrid Billing and J. A. Eklund (himself one of the great Swedish hymnwriters of this century) and Dr. E. N. Söderberg, i.a., had prepared a hymnbook which was in essence a revision of J. O. Wallin's hymnbook of 1819. Söderblom was prepared to accept this but had second thoughts when he discovered three fundamental weaknesses in the proposal. Firstly, it had dared to make changes in Wallin's hymns; and here Söderblom stated: 'a literary fall from grace is not a religious merit.' There were attempts to smooth and modernize Wallin's verse. This was abhorrent to Söderblom. Secondly, there was no real place for the songs of the nineteenth century revival, an omission which would sever a link between the Swedish Church and other Christian denominations throughout the land, and thereby threaten the expression of ecumenical relationships. Thirdly, there was not sufficient place for the new treasury of hymns that were being written by that very generation, a religious poetry expressing the new world-view in the post-War situation: 'that God was great and the world little.'

As Archbishop, he gave particular attention to the episcopal consecrations, the more so since episcopacy was a cornerstone of his programme of Evangelic Catholicity. It was on this account that he changed the robes of the Church from their melancholy black to their ancient resplendence of joyful white, red and purple. Of course there was more behind this than mere concern for colour or form, and indeed he often repeated what he once expressed in his English: 'The Church has no time to debate questions of toilet, we have something more weighty to fight for.'[10]

Nevertheless, in November 1914 he would have liked to fashion his own consecration as beautifully as possible, and as the Handbook allowed him to do. But then, of course, he was bound by the wishes of Bishop Billing, his consecrator. Later on, when he was in command, he was able to go further. There was a dramatic occasion at the consecration of the Bishops of Västerås (Einar Billing) and Visby

---

[9] Söderblom, Diary, Oct. 1924.
[10] Söderblom, in The Constructive Quarterly, 1915, p. 307.

(V. Rundgren), on September 18, 1920. This shook the country and the papers were full of it for weeks.

The drama was provided by the fact that the consecration suddenly made the Church and people in Sweden realize what was going on in the ecumenical contacts between their own Church and other episcopal Churches. It was on this occasion that Lambeth sent two bishops, Hensley Henson of Durham, and Woods of Peterborough. But that was not enough. Also present was the Orthodox Archbishop Germanos, coming all the way from Constantinople, and not only did he give lectures at the University but he actually took part in the procession in the Cathedral.

The irony of the situation was of course the fact that Hensley Henson's participation had suggested to the Swedish critics dark papal machinations. This was the stereotyped reaction which any brand of Anglicanism evoked at this time in those Northern parts of the world, while in reality Hensley Henson was as good a Rome-baiter as any decent Swede.

Dagens Nyheter, the Liberal paper, wrote: 'The consecration must have beaten all records as far as pomp and circumstance go. ... [Through the presence of the foreign bishops,] the consecrations became a demonstration of the Catholicity of the Church, ... Even Solomon in all his glory was not arrayed as one of these! One forgot that one was in a Protestant Church and only waited to see acolytes appear with their thuribles. All this dazzling, futuristically reckless joy of colour evoked, we are sure, in many the thought that we witnessed a spectacle and not worship in Spirit and in Truth. ... One could not withhold the reflexion, of course, that Nathan Söderblom is a glorious archbishop, but what a shining success he would have been as a stage manager.'[11]

The local Liberal paper, *Upsala Nya Tidning*, and its editor Johansson, always ready to deride Söderblom's efforts, delivered a particularly morose criticism. Johansson had started out in life as a theological student but exchanged the church for the press; he had recollections from his theological labours and used these to good account. Now he was alarmed.

This sudden efflorescence of church parades goes straight against our Evangelical Lutheran drabness. ... Here in Sweden we do not have (as in Catholic countries) a higher clergy who can manage these old ceremonies and ecclesiastical forms so as to put into them a substance of contents which could be grasped by the faithful. Here the Prince of the Church is

---

[11] *Dagens Nyheter*, Sept. 19, 1920.

one day as ostentatious as a peacock and the next as simple as the commonest sparrow. Here lies something which to many appears as a ridiculous contradiction. A Cardinal Archbishop of Paris or a Prince of the Church of any category lives and moves and has his being on an altogether other plane and in altogether different circumstances from those of our own dignitaries.'

There was an outcry in the press. Editors and clergy and ordinary laymen were mobilized in this battle. Söderblom himself did not hesitate to state his case. His article in *Stockholms-Tidningen* 'Was Jesus in the Cathedral?', September 27, 1920, is especially noteworthy. It gives much of his personal reaction to this problem of Institution and Spirit.

[My] confession regarding ceremonies and organizations, institutions and all these formalities: what a comfort it would be to toss away all this lumber and to breathe freely and easily! Who has not many times had that feeling, especially if he without being asked, has had loaded on his shoulders an official burden, heavy and cumbersome. Vestments in themselves are a simple matter. My concern is with the total heavy and complex machinery. ... Forms must exist. If we put them away, new ones are introduced in their place. Then into the bargain one has to obey the changes of the mode.

What did Jesus look for in the Cathedral? He looked for worship in Spirit and in Truth. I know He was there. Because many to our humiliation felt His presence and went out inspired and strengthened to serve God's Kingdom. As I have given this answer, I hope I have therewith contributed to the decent burial of an emerging ritualism which makes an unnecessary case as to whether external forms should either be removed or retained.

The Consecration that day, September 18, 1920 had a double effect. Whatever Söderblom said or felt, he was from that day widely regarded as having Roman Catholic sympathies, a serious allegation at the time. From that date he was also good copy in the Swedish press. Whatever he did, wherever he moved, the press followed him because it was anticipated that something unexpected was bound to happen. There was perhaps inevitably a subsidiary effect. People like Johansson in *Upsala Nya Tidning*, did not believe his protestation that he wished to toss away the whole lot. Did not the very splendour of those ceremonies call the bluff of that episcopal statement? It was of course not easy for the outsider to realize that hidden under the splendid golden cope was an ascetic and a mystic who knew that, after all, 'this one thing' in life and in religion, was prayer and the breath of the Spirit. It was not easy to understand this as, quite frankly, Söderblom seemed to take delight in the old ceremonies.

Communication

Communication was the urge of this expansive, outgoing, generous personality. He had a message to convey, and therefore was anxious to persuade, sometimes to cajole, his fellow-men to see his vision and to join the movement. Typical were the tactile expressions of this communication. The difficult Polish Church Conference in Uppsala, March 1921, was concluded by Holy Communion. The two Lutheran leaders and contestants from Poland, Bursche, the Polish nationalist, and Blau, the representative of the German minority, were seated in different rows of the Trinity Church. Söderblom stretched out his hands to both of them and walking between them led them to the altar where the three knelt together for the Communion. This kind of thing could be applied to more down-to-earth situations. There was not much love lost between the two churchwardens in a certain Uppland parish. On his visitation to the particular parish Söderblom heard of this and at Holy Communion he went to these two men, placed his hands in theirs and led them to the Lord's Table. Not everybody, nor every archbishop, in ceremonious Swedish society could get away with this kind of thing; but Söderblom did.

We have not finished with this point about Söderblom's tactile communication. His fine hands and fingers played their role. In December 1926, he had a glorious week in his beloved Paris, the first visit there after many years (and, as we shall see, after certain tensions and crises). He asked the Swedish Embassy pastor, Bjurström, to take him to the bouquinistes on the river near Notre Dame. Bjurström was a musician like the archbishop, and they discussed a tune. Neither could remember it off-hand. Were they not on their way to visit Henri Bergson, and was life not perfect, at that moment? That tune, he must find it. The Archbishop of Uppsala, in his clerical coat and pectoral cross seated himself on the parapet, stretched out his feet as if feeling the pedals of a church organ and stretched out his hands and fingers, playing in the air, until he found his tune!

It was the same sense of tactile communication which, when on a visitation to a parish, he would show the congregation some medieval treasure belonging to their local church and pass this around in the pews, for both old and young to feel the venerability of an old specimen.

The Swiss ecumenical secretary, Ad. Keller, himself more sensitive than people generally realized, noticed this hunger for communication in Söderblom.

He needed people in order, himself, to function fully. No sooner were they before him, willing and attentive, than his spirit began to well forth in an inexhaustible but effortless richness of ideas, suggestions, far-sighted visions, short-time practical proposals and witty remarks. The flowing streams of his personality did not make debating with him easy, in commissions for instance; he spoke, and the others listened. If he met with opposition, he did not use the chairman's power, but humour, in order to overcome this. In this he was as irresistible as life itself.[1]

Letter-writing was an important means of communication. Official correspondence was rapidly dictated, in 1915–17 to Yngve Brilioth and from September 1919–1931 to the incomparable Gerda Rodling. But the Archbishop also found time for notes or longer letters written in his own hand. There were the occasional moments waiting for a train at Ljusdal or Gävle. These were golden occasions for notes in all directions: To close friends, 'Dear So-and-so, We think of you. If only you were here. Yours ever', or the letters to great artists and authors. To Selma Lagerlöf: 'Optima Selma', or 'Selmissima'. She had consented to give an address at the Stockholm Conference. After anxious weeks of waiting, the manuscript did arrive, and Söderblom could prepare translations of it into three languages for the printing. Then, a telegram from Selma asking him immediately to return the manuscript for correction. Söderblom informs the great authoress by telegram: 'Sending manuscript of the address so worthy of Selma and the ecumenical cause.' Then again, in December that year, when writing to Selma to thank her for her latest novel: 'What can I give in return? The only enduring book in the writing of which I have shared was the Ecumenical Conference, which possibly will be read and meditated upon for centuries. But for that, you yourself wrote the most beautiful chapter.'[2]

Altogether surprising is to notice how this impulsive man, this archbishop with an immense burden of work managed to keep up a correspondence for years and decades. With persistence and faithful-

---

[1] Ad. Keller, *Von Geist und Liebe* (1933), p. 201.
[2] Söderblom, December 2, 1925, to Selma Lagerlöf.

ness he remembered his old and new friends, ever anxious to keep in contact and to strengthen his net of relationships.

His books and articles in reviews and newspapers were another means of communication. The Söderblom bibliography shows that there were some four hundred of these in the years 1914–1931; some very ambitious volumes such as his collections of sermons (two volumes, 1915), his Luther studies (1919), *Christian Fellowship* (1923), his book on the American tour (1924) and on the Stockholm Conference (1926); his great Lent book, 470 pages (1928), and finally his Gifford Lectures, published posthumously. He had always a little blue notebook with him, when on trains, or waiting for a bus to arrive, or for a preacher to finish, he would jot down his ideas for his lectures and books.

One could see him as he had welcomed a lecturer, or preacher, hailing him or her as the greatest authority of all time on this or that; Söderblom would follow the general theme of the lecture with apparent interest; at the same time he would suddenly remember important things to be noted down for a lecture or book: he would rapidly unbutton his Swedish clergyman's gown and find the notebook in his breast pocket, make his notes, which most probably had no connexion whatsoever with the current lecture or sermon; then slide the notebook into the breastpocket, button the gown, and be still for a moment. Very soon the same complicated process, in which possibly the audience would show increasing interest, would start all over again. Not all lecturers or preachers liked this.

Very seldom could he afford the time to write down his text in his own hand; he became wholly dependent on dictating to Gerda Rodling who was ready to take down in her rapid shorthand, chapters or articles, letters, telegrams; and this at all times. And indeed in all places. She might find the archbishop at an Uppsala or Stockholm street-corner, showing the sights to a Rumanian bishop or a Yale professor. He would beckon to her, and there and then dictate a few messages: the shorthand of this had to be crowded onto the back of a laundry bill or some such piece of paper. But it was all part of the game, and done in good humour, and everybody was happy.

For letters and articles, this method was of course inevitable; in the production of a book it was not always the best. Some of his writings show the marks of haste, although one should not forget the more important thing, that they *were* written, and published. To his book on Luther (1919) he had given great care. On the other hand, there were passages and indeed chapters in his mighty volume (960 pages!) on 'Stockholm 1925', which obviously are out of place and should have been tucked away in some other corner of the book. Mrs Anna Söderblom was a severe literary censor and she had at least as high ambitions for the quality of his books as he had himself. Reading the proofs of his Lent book she suggested that if *only* he had given more time to it, the book might have become a classic. This went deep, perhaps, but the book became a classic.

His spoken word had a new directness which made people listen as if hearing great news. We have seen how he had learned from Sabatier that a sermon should be as direct and simple as a letter. Even when Archbishop he stuck to this rule. But there was always the chance that something unforeseen might happen in the course of his sermon. Preaching at Gävle in 1916 he shocked the good burghers of the town by suddenly referring to a newly published book by the Left Socialist Fabian Månsson. This name at the time symbolised revolution and barricades; but Söderblom for good measure had brought along a copy of the book and showed it to the congregation, insisting that they must read it. As it happened, this was an autobiographical novel, called *Justification by Faith,* and in fact a valuable contribution to the understanding of Swedish piety. Only as one tries to visualize the stolid unmovability of the ordinary Swedish middle class congregation can one imagine the surprise conveyed on that day to unsuspecting church-goers. In fact, Söderblom, often, both in sermons and lectures, used a turn of phrase, devised to *épater les bourgeois,* only to modify it in the next sentence: This was the kind of thing:

'What we need is a new confession of faith. I do not mean any alteration in the old creed, but . . .'

This sometimes made him an easy target for those who did not stop to listen to the qualification or who felt that an Archbishop should not produce qualifications but utter pronouncements on eternal verities.

He might have to go to Stockholm for meetings, two, three or more times a week by train. The late train back to Uppsala taking some sixty or seventy minutes was not generally regarded as a very pleasant ride; the day had been busy, the hour was late, and the passengers, businessmen, scholars and others, were tired, and the stiff backs of those Third Class carriages were not inspiring. Söderblom had just passed through the open carriage with its thirty-forty passengers. He left his briefcase in the Second Class compartment and returned in order to chat with those he knew. At the journey's end, the surprised commuters compared notes and found that the Archbishop, moving from seat to seat had managed to call upon everybody in the carriage, with a word of encouragement or sympathy.

The Man

He had received and developed this incomparable charisma of communication. As a bishop he made his service into a ministry of encouragement, finding fruition in an instrument—himself—which it had helped to create. But behind the instrument, what was the driving force? Söderblom himself gives some clues when he speaks on 'The Christian Character', as he did in 1927 at Malmö to a General Church Meeting, an occasion which naturally drew out from him his best. A Christian, he said, must not be content with the outer shell, for an ornamental book-binding may hide any manner of contents. St Paul teaches that the Christian should have a stamp of his own or, in Greek, a character. 'We should in our essence and our life express the thoughts of the Creator. Kierkegaard says that each man's life is to be a poem, as if we are each to write or compose ourselves. But 'a Christian allows God to write his life's poem'. E. G. Geijer, he went on, interpreted the thought of the Creator when he declared that every single person, in his sphere, could do something better than all others; this individuality eminently characterises the Great Artist's creation, his handiwork, man.[1] The means or the method will be a combination of two things: the free and spontaneous impulse of faith; *and* discipline. The burden of his message was an emphasis on the latter: discipline, order, a rule of life, perhaps because in his own personality faith was indeed free and spontaneous.

This concept of personality, as a kind of bipolar development and balance, was central in Söderblom's understanding of himself and others. Thus to Söderblom his best friend, S. A. Fries was a solid square piece of a man who had 'early in life become complete'. As he made that observation he may have felt that, by comparison, he himself had needed a much longer time for his development and achievement of balance. Searching for integration of his own personality, he was keenly aware of the promise in his rich endowment of varied gifts, and the danger of their being dissipated in their own anarchy. In the Paris years he had written in his diary a challenge to himself: 'To be simple and true.' But how to be simple when

[1] Söderblom, *Tal och Skrifter*, 4, p. 14.

he was so complex, with that broad and colourful register of human abilities?

Occasional expressions of his thoughts, like a door ajar, would reveal, at all times in his life, the underlying torrent of emotional and intellectual force that discipline must channel and set to work. There were those rapid jerks and sharp transitions in the presentation of an argument, which revealed only how much lay hidden. There were the sudden flashes, meant to be illustrative but which dazzled the pedestrian steps of his hearers on the path of his thought. To the ordinary listener, the strong personality behind it all seemed to gather and unite the different ideas. The golden voice, the goodness of the man, the fact that he imparted the obvious impression that he had something infinitely important to say: all this conveyed to most people a sense of wholeness, in spite of the occasional gulfs, or the whims and fancies. Others were less willing to approve: some of the professor's colleagues in the Uppsala Faculty, some of the Archbishop's colleagues in the episcopate, certain journalists.

In his Malmö lecture he had quoted both Kierkegaard and Geijer. These two Scandinavians were contemporaries and yet centuries apart. Söderblom made a point of quoting Kierkegaard, but in his understanding of personality he was closer to Geijer than to the Danish father of Existentialism. Not even his years in Paris in the decade of the symbolists and impressionists had shaken his nineteenth century, Geijerian belief in personality as ideally a finished piece of art, a well-chiseled sculpture, the end result of life's strivings and of the struggle of the spirit.

He knew the dangers of this essentially classical understanding of personality. He saw it in Goethe, and said of him: 'He plays himself, he registers himself, and he is seated at the same time in the stalls, finding everything rather good ... this chilly, perfect, and self-observing spirit.'[2] Söderblom saw this danger of introspection in some of the great men of mysticism such as von Hügel. But he also knew the way out: in acts of self-forgetting service, in a charity which had neither time nor interest for self-observation. 'The soul does not find time, as the photographer, in order to notice how it looks. It has no time to gaze into the mirror, but becomes a mirror itself, reflecting ... God's power.'[3]

His appreciation of art was coloured by this view of things. He sometimes felt his own aesthetic and literary ambition as a tempta-

---

[2] *Religionsproblemet*, 1910, p. 385.
[3] Ibid., pp. 281-2.

tion. This was the Pietist in him warning him; the father-image of Jonas Söderblom of pietistic Norrala entreating Nathan to keep to the Saviour's Cross. Once when Lydia Wahlström, his and Anna's good friend, complimented him on 'some of the most ebullient articles' in a book of his on the Swedish Church, he answered sharply and with a hushed voice, 'Yes, but those are dangerous things'.[4] People saw this Church leader with his obvious delight in processions and in the drama of the liturgy and of the Church's year: Was this not revealing? Was not the Archbishop perhaps an actor? So they asked, some of these North Europeans, overlooking the fact that they themselves were acting out a role; a role less obvious because more stereotyped than his: tin soldiers in uniform, immobile snowmen in high places. Of course, he acted; he could not help turning any little occasion, any chance meeting, into a memorable and dramatic event. Of course, he was aware of, and wished to use, any good means of stage-management. But the role-performance of this archbishop was lifted into the service of his cause and of his Master.

In his Malmö lecture he had referred to self-discipline, and asceticism and discipline played a central part in his life. He often, almost alarmingly often, used one metaphor for this: the race-horse and his rider. The good horse can achieve its highest capacity and its greatest speed only under the sure hand of the rider. So it is with the soul. Kirkegaard using the same image had said of the apostles: 'they were well broken in.' This applies to Christ's disciples at all times. 'Only with God's good hand and strict bridle can the soul be helped to give its best.' In using this metaphor he was speaking out of his own soul and heart. He needed that bridle, that discipline, that asceticism. His disciple, Tor Andrae, who knew him well, spoke of his 'superhuman, I would be tempted to say inhuman, self-discipline'.[5]

This was his severe and very demanding super-ego, his censor. On a deep level it was the image of his father, Jonas Söderblom. He had struggled with him as he grew up, but he had been reconciled with him, and this return and reconciliation with the earthly father was at the same time reconciliation with the Heavenly Father. He would try to arrange the decisive events of his life, such as his consecration, to fall on dates related to his father's. The father's image followed him. He told K. G. Westman, the Law professor and Government minister who had signed his appointment as Archbishop, that he was

---

[4] Lydia Wahlström, in Hågkomster, XII, p. 229.
[5] Tor Andrae, Nathan Söderblom, 1931, p. 208.

ever aware of the departed father's presence. He felt this communion with the exacting and loving figure right up to the gate of death. Two days before his fatal illness he prepared a Diocesan Letter on Evangelism, dated July 2, 1931; significantly it contained a word about his father. Bishop Landgren, he said, had pointed out to the peasants of Hälsingland a man, Jonas Söderblom, saying: 'He can show you the way to heaven.' On the last stage of the same road, the son returned to the bishop's word.

Hard work was part of the discipline and ascesis. The Archbishop's superhuman load of work was felt by him to be a help; he seemed to carry it lightly, as if the burden carried him. One of the great technocrats of our time, Lord Reith, himself a pastor's son, refers to the profound satisfaction in being fully 'stretched' by the opportunity to encompass a seemingly impossible amount of work. Söderblom did not speak of being 'stretched' but would certainly have recognized the reaction as parallel with his own. It is indeed hard to imagine what would have happened to him if he had not, in 1914, been saddled with that burden of responsibility. He became Archbishop at a terrible moment in the history of mankind; yet another might have seen no opportunity for a churchman in a small and neutral country distant from the main conflict. To Söderblom it was a καιρός, an opportunity loaded, filled to the brim, with tragedy and hope. He grasped his destiny, conscious of having been prepared for the task. He coined a new word, in Swedish 'ansvarsglädje', the joy of responsibility. But he knew that all depended upon his gifts and powers being held together by that discipline of the will.

He undertook his work with the determination of a man who knows that he is about the King's errands. There were no neurotic inhibitions in him. Only once do we come across apprehensiveness and in that instance it was probably more assumed than real. Taking his seat in the Swedish Academy, in 1921, he was due to give an address on his predecessor. Three weeks before the great event he wrote to his poet friend, E. A. Karlfeldt, the Secretary to the Academy, 'I am fretting like a schoolboy and postponing my preparation as if I was a boy at high-school shirking his homework'.[6] This was probably only a roundabout way of telling Karlfeldt how honoured he felt in being elected to the Academy, 'the greatest honour that could befall me'. The overwhelming impression is one of decisiveness. A doctor who was close to him told us, 'He was the very image

---

[6] Söderblom, December 2, 1921, to E. A. Karlfeldt.

of a General, incapable of giving anything but exact instructions and commands, "Do this, Go there".[7] His healthy readiness to reply to a charge against him in the Press, whether from right or left, corroborates this impression. There have been times before and since when Church leaders have told themselves that by keeping quiet and appearing subdued they would at last be forgotten and left in peace. Söderblom had another ideal for his Church than this.

To this cult of work was related a heightened sense of the value of time, of using the unforgiving minute to the full. 'Time is elastic, almost anything can be fitted into it', he used to tell his clergy, and if they looked sceptical, this was followed by another of his oft-quoted words: 'You must work yourselves to death—but slowly, please.'

Resolute as he was, he liked to take rapid decisions and move without hesitation. But he could wait. He had the patience to bide his time. He was to endure seeing the conferences that he planned postponed more than once, but he never sulked. He simply kept on towards the goal. He might have been tempted to push through the matter of a new Swedish hymnbook during his own tenure of office. That it did not appear till almost two decades later was due to his own intervention. It was preferable to a hasty solution.

At a deep level of self-discipline there was to be found a further trait in his character, illuminating to anyone who seeks to understand his particular approach to opportunities and decisions. Facing any important choice, he would relate it to some much earlier experience of his by which the present seemed to have been foreshadowed or anticipated. 'Thirty years ago, I had hoped to do this' he would declare. Or, 'Realizing my old dream' of this or that. The backward glance would also, as like as not, be combined with a prophecy of the distant consequences of the act now contemplated. He seemed to wish to bind together, not only his own gifts, but past and future in his own life. This urge for continuity and cohesion in his life was seen by him as equally significant and necessary in Church and Society. His fascination with history and tradition is possibly a projection of the deep urge within him towards integration of every sort. His amazing faithfulness in keeping up a correspondence over many years and indeed decades is another indication of this side in him.

The emphasis we have given to his determination, indeed to his cult of the will through asceticism, must not hide the fact that he was

---

[7] Dr. S. Richter, who operated on Söderblom in 1931, had first met Söderblom in connexion with the dedication of the Engelbrekt Church in Stockholm.

at the same time like some generous, self-renewing, scintillating fountain of joy and humour, even of a puckish humour. The Swedes
were not used to this in their clergy, let alone in their bishops. A
Swedish bishop should be solemn and, above all, dignified: this very
dignity was, at some unconscious level, a kind of guarantee that the
figure and the acts of worship he performed in their name were
truly acceptable to the Deity. It was difficult therefore to know how
to accomodate the contradiction, a humorous archbishop. Perhaps it
was best to accept that he had Danish blood; for a Swedish stereotype about the Danes holds that in the Scandinavian family they
represent humour and witticism. This helped to explain and excuse.

As it happened, Söderblom himself at the time was giving thought
to the hereditary springs of humour. In his book, *Humour and
Melancholy, and other Luther Studies*, he examined 'the fountain of
humour in Luther's soul'. 'If we are not too mistaken, we can recognize in this humour an inheritance from his father, increased to
the proportions of genius.'[8] What in Luther's case he took to have
been a gift from the father's side, may in Söderblom's have come
from his mother's.

But again, in Söderblom, as in Luther, humour and melancholy
went together—the bow of humour drawing music from a life made
taut by sorrow, and compassion. There is an element of the biogra-
phical in Söderblom's book on Luther: interpreting Luther, he is
really writing the story of his own soul. Luther is presented by him as
unique in the history of great Christian personalities. While St. Paul
and St. Augustine, Calvin and Pascal, lacked humour, Luther alone
by this gift could break through the ascetic, well-formed, type of
piety. Söderblom himself needed this outlet.

Söderblom writes on Luther—and on Nathan Söderblom—'The
safety-valve of humour saved him from a ridiculous and inflated
pomposity. This humour was a gracious gift at birth to one whose
poor human soul was to comprise heaven and hell. The experience
of life and education has increased the gift and its use'.[9]

Yet, just as surely, this open and friendly Archbishop knew how to
preserve a distance; with all his exuberant kindliness there was—
even in the most personal contacts—an unmistakable aristocratic
reserve.

This radiant personality of Söderblom's knew frustrations and

---

[8] Söderblom, *Humor och melankoli*, p. 4.
[9] Ibid., p. 48.

disappointments, even if he hardly ever showed this to the outer world. The personal diary was the outlet for this kind of thing. There were the special days of self-scrutiny: his own individual Judgment Days. New Year's Eve, and Good Friday, and his birthday were such occasions. While his fiftieth birthday was the signal for much praise and adulation, Söderblom wrote in his diary on the day after: 'How to find a form for this kind of existence; spiritual toil instead of this easy recognition for having said a few words. Today miserable, dull. I ought to flee to the desert and live on wild honey and locusts'.

He could shake off criticism with good humour and a witty retort in the Press. But some of the barbs stuck. The wounds show in the diary. No doubt these exclamations were conditioned by his uncertain health, sometimes preceding grave attacks. One occasion was in 1921. The popularity of two recently published autobiographies, one by Sven Lidman and the other by Ivan Oljelund, brought a suppressed misery to the surface:

Perhaps my toil in Paris might have been appreciated ... [but now] if I say anything, if I do anything, which is right, *I* have not the right to say or do it. They watch me! They hound me down. Anyone has the right to do what he wants against me. That has merit. That way shows piety. It's Liberal. They learn from me, but build themselves a pedestal, however mean, from which to brow-beat me ...

Oh, if I were to move from this fine house ... where for seven years I have been ill at ease, and moved instead to a draughty cold little cabin, like the one in Staby, oh, the regret; but that might earn me much praise for Christian behaviour, and personally unspeakable happiness. But perhaps God wants someone to carry this load. To be for a whole lifetime invariably for service, at hand, and being rebuked for it, never one's own, free, out of the throng; well, it is no enviable office. I could maintain myself without the Church; I have been a professor and called hither and thither. I am almost comparable with all these gentlemen who sit in judgment over me.

To pray! God, canst Thou yet use me?[1]

Besides, these somewhat morose reflexions of his he was soon prepared to transform into an engaging study of Lidman's and Oljelund's books after a lecture of his in the Uppsala University. The relationship between the note in the diary and the article is a study in resilience.[2]

[1] Söderblom, Diary, December 23, 1921.
[2] Söderblom, Den sista tidens omvändelseböcker. Tidn. *Upsala*, December 14, 1922. Några omvändelseböcker, *Vår Lösen*, 1922, p. 66.

But there was not only criticism, of course. On the contrary, he was acclaimed, more particularly in the latter part of his archiepiscopate as we shall see presently.

What did this archbishop feel about it himself; about this adulation, the 'Söderblom myth'? He took it in his stride, it seemed: at one level, he needed response and thrived on it. But there was another, and deeper level where his personal struggle was fought. He allows us some glimpses of it in his diary and in his letters to his wife. In April 1924, when he arrived in Birmingham for the great Copec conference, he was acclaimed as the great ecumenical leader of his day. He writes 'How they discuss education and I feel so helpless, a failure, incapable. The one thing I have is my love for him.'

The diary provided an outlet. He wrote [1922]:

How mad was that theology which invented a Purgatory in the beyond. Such people [did] not know what worry is. As if Purgatory *here* was not enough. The pain is many-sided in its inventiveness, nothing is left untried. I could write a book [about this], it would appear in many editions; thus accrue some income for my heirs.

[Or again, 1927:] My Lord, I know that it is never so desperate or wretched and painful that it could not become worse. I thank Thee that Thou hast allowed me to take one day at a time, and that the future is hidden behind a veil. But in this darkness, in this painful uncertainty, no! in this certainty of despair, I keep to Thee. Thou will not cast me out. I do not understand. Thou dost understand. One thing only I do know: in Thee alone is my life, my salvation. Thy mercy exceeds everything else, even the cry of my anguish and my despair. To Thee be praise. To commune with Thee is my sole consolation. [1928:] Today during the installation service [of a vicar], I saw light. What I need is total submission. That does not allow for brooding and worry. That is what I have to learn.

[And, finally, two lines:] Anna says: Those who walk in sunshine see no stars.

But a diary is only an outlet for the throbbing heart, and of the cry of a soul. That pain and worry had to be turned to a nobler use, in the service of others. A Lent book perhaps? A series of meditations on Gethsemane and Golgotha? In 1922, the year when he had his first experience of *angina,* he made his first diary notes in preparation of a book ['Passionsboken' he called it then] which was not to appear until 1928, as *The Passion of Our Lord Jesus Christ.* Those notes deal with the question of the Sons of Zebedee, now pages 14 and 15 in the printed book. The Sons of Zebedee wanted seats of honour in glory with their Lord. Söderblom went on to say:

Do not say that this prayer was dictated only by pride and vanity and a naïve lust for glory and power. No, the two wanted to be seated next to the Master on his great day, when they together with him and their fellow-disciples were to sit in judgment over the tribes of Israel. However the question does not concern the place in the Kingdom of Glory, but the imitation of the Master on his way. [His question is:] Can you drink the cup which I drink?

This side of the personality also belongs to the picture. This also was Söderblom, although nobody knew, and nobody could guess from that radiant, expansive, happy and communicative personality. This was where humour, for Söderblom, was saving grace.

It was matched with the deepest of religious experience, that of the mystic. The 'Gelassenheit' (he uses the German original in his Swedish text) 'of mysticism, its unconcerned peace in God, can in humour find a corresponding view of the world and of men'[3]. Yngve Brilioth wrote of Söderblom at his Stockholm conference, 1925: 'He had mastered then as always the art of *vacare Deo,* to keep the inner chambers of the soul serenely ready for high visitations in spite of the din in the outer rooms'[4]. Söderblom wrote to his daughter Yvonne Anderberg: 'Did I not say to you about prayer that I could not live one day without unceasing prayer?'

Prayer and this supernatural peace—the foundations had been laid long before he became Archbishop. Yet it might have been noticed that about 1919 they received a deepening, thanks to a profound alteration in his theological emphasis after the war. The World War had shown him that 'the evil in the world was worse than the world believed'. The only religion which now was of any account was 'a new irresistible sermon of the Cross', he said in 1919, and in his last year he was to sum up his faith in the words: 'The centre of my theology is the atoning passion of Christ.'

No wonder then that John Landquist, the Swedish critic, would sum up his repeated impression of the man in these words: 'On the surface an exuberant surge of liveliness, and in the deep peace and determination.'[5]

Landquist remarks on his liveliness of mind as well as gesture. It was the way the comparatively heavy lines of his face were splendidly lit to a beauty all their own by a sudden movement of life, and the rapidity of his thought as it followed or leapt ahead and devel-

---

[3] Söderblom, *Humor och melankoli,* p. 65.

[4] Y. Brilioth, in *Söderblom in Memoriam,* p. 328.

[5] J. Landquist, *Möten,* 1966, p. 73.

oped or shared the thought of those he was with. Emanuel Vigeland, the Norwegian painter, who made a remarkable portrait of
Söderblom in cope and mitre gives an example of the amazing fa-
cility Söderblom showed in switching his thought and expression
with great rapidity from point to point. As the Archbishop sat for
his painting, or rather stood, Vigeland mentioned his love for Russian authors, particularly Dostoyevski and his Raskolnikov. 'Oh, the
poor little student!', the Archbishop immediately broke in. 'How
hard it was for him standing there, ringing the bell to the pawn-
broker's shop'. Vigeland at once mentioned Paris and Zola's 'Mas-
terpieces'. Without a second's hesitation Söderblom carried on:
'Claudius, Claudius, thou art also in other countries than in France.
That is the tragedy of great art.'[6]

His mind was, not restless, but ever active, remarkably positive
and productive. Playing his piano or organ, or listening to music,—
Bach, Schütz, Beethoven, Händel,—inspired him particularly. 'How
many of his great thoughts came to him while he listened to music',
said Gerda Rodling. She noticed that it was as he listened for instance to Bach's Matthew Passion, Hohe Messe, or, noblest of all, the
A flat in Beethoven's C minor symphony, he would take out occasionally one of his blue note-books and jot down a few rapid sentences to be worked on later. Music integrated him. Through a
day's meetings with men and their problems, he seemed to carry with
him a deep undertone of melody, or to be carried by it, breaking
out into a bar, hummed to himself, from 'Verily, verily', or from 'I
know that my Redeemer liveth', out of Händel's *Messiah*.

He would sometimes express what he referred to as his 'musical lay
reflexions' on Bach, particularly his Mass in B Minor or the St.
Matthew Passion. Söderblom's interpretation of *'et incarnatus est'* in
the Nicene Creed, according to the Mass in B Minor, was penetrating:

'It is Christmas which is depicted here, the idyll, the child in the
manger. Yet, here the Mass does justice to its name B Minor. There are
the basses' heavy, solemn B Minor notes descending, in triple time, to
ever more profound depths and finally, almost reluctantly, agreeing with
the expressive dirge of the upper voices; above this, the violins play a sequence of notes which might be groans and falling tears, and the alto begins to sing a theme in a minor key which touches one to the quick,

---

[6] Em. Vigeland, in *Hågkomster*, XIV, p. 156. Cf. B. Sundkler, Ärkebiskop Nathan Söderbloms kyrkogärning, in *Kyrkohist. Årsskrift* (65), 1965, p. 13–31, and
idem, Upplåta och sammanbinda. Nathan Söderblom 1866–1966, in *Julhälsning
till församlingarna i ärkestiftet* (51), 1965, p. 39–51.

placing the beginning of Christ's passion to the first days of this life on earth and not only to Golgotha ... Bach's interpretation ... [is of] the atoning power of the Passion. For then, the wonderful choir allows us to hear in 'Crucifixus' the mystery of salvation.[7]

This was the man who on becoming Primate of Sweden at the beginning of the World War made Uppsala the cradle and first home of an integrating movement of the Churches of Christendom. The orchestration of gifts in that personality was directed and held together by a sense of ethical responsibility and by a life of prayer. It was his conviction that an orchestra of the Churches could be brought together and held by a common social task for a world in need. There was a clear parallel between the two, between the Archbishop and the emerging world movement. It was as if he had projected his life's deepest experience on to the struggle of the Churches for peace, brotherhood and unity.

---

[7] *Tal och skrifter,* 4, pp. 9–10. The quotation is from an address on Church Music, November 13, 1926.

The Archbishop and the War

> Not to dare anything but what,
> according to wordly calculation, must succeed.
>
> Söderblom's diary, December 23, 1914.

Christmas and New Year's Eve were red letter days in the Archbishop's calender and in his household. Söderblom sitting in his study could hear the cries and laughter of children at play in the adjacent rooms, but for him, Christmas, 1914 was filled with apprehension. Late at night there was occasion for self-examination, for what the Norse bard, Ibsen, called 'keeping Judgement Day with oneself'. Even while children's hands were eagerly placing candles in windows and on the soaring Christmas tree, the Archbishop was keenly aware that 'the lamps are going out all over Europe'.

In preparation for a Christmas address, Söderblom jotted down in his diary passages from the Old Testament prophet Isaiah referring to Assyria, Egypt, and Israel. He was going to apply Isaiah XIX to the warring nations of Europe. Then suddenly those ironic words, like piercing darts, are pencilled in the diary: 'Not to dare anything but what according to wordly calculation, must succeed' (and how he detested that word '*uträkning*,' calculation, in religion and church!).

He must dare. He had a vision and he had a position. One met many people of course, in Uppsala and elsewhere, with intense convictions about justice and peace and reconciliation, but they were not heard, they did not have a platform or a position from which to speak. And there were men in high places without, alas, ideas or vision or courage.

Söderblom had both position and vision. Or had he? Archbishop of Uppsala—this *was* something, in Uppsala at that time and in Sweden as a whole. But beyond the borders of neutral Scandinavia, in that cataclysm of war? Just another black coat with a pectoral cross. And the vision? What was this vision? And what was a vision in comparison with the march of armies?

He must dare . . .

Peace Appeal 1914

When war broke out on August 1, 1914, Söderblom happened, on his doctor's advice, to be in a Bohemian village on the frontier between Saxony and Austria. He thus experienced those first days of enthusiasm in Germany. In his Episcopal Charge published a few months later, he recalled how his friend Professor Deissmann had referred to a *ver sacrum*, a sacred springtime. In the same breath he quoted noble expressions of national sacrifice in France and Britain: 'England is now described as a people at prayer', he wrote in his Episcopal Charge. This was a cathartic experience, 'doubtless there is a purification. Much which is unessential and harmful is swept away'. In a sermon in September 1914 he expressed admiration for the 'blessed power which lies in modern nationalism', but hastened to add: 'Nationalism can and should be religiously deepened through the knowledge that every people, as well as every person, has its calling in the inscrutable ordinance of God.'

He used the same term for the confrontation of nations as that which, as a Christian apologist, he had used with regard to the meeting of religions; there must be *contest* between the nations, and the best would presumably win.

If [our duty] means struggle and contest, nevertheless, the prayers of the contestants can meet before the same God. The patriotism is taken up into worship of the God Who bids: Love your enemies. Then, and only then, [patriotism] is baptized and sanctified.

While there were according to Söderblom certain admirable expressions of nationalism, there were also hideous forms. His thoughts turned Eastwards: 'We recognize the god of nationalism, the same in all ages. It is not long since the Tsar Nicholas declared: 'The god of the Russian earth is a mighty god.'[1] Presumably arms would determine, then, which god was the mightier. He mentioned examples also of German, French, and English idolatry, and suggested that the same applied to neutral Sweden.

During September and October he prepared two widely publicized statements on the War: his Appeal, and the chapter in his Charge on the Church and the War, published in connexion with his

---

[1] Söderblom, *När stunderna växla*, II, p. 107. For this chapter as a whole we refer to Nils Karlström's thesis, *Kristna samförståndssträvanden under världskriget 1914 –1918*, published 1947, in Swedish. It is a highly competent and exhaustive piece of work of no less than 724 pp. It includes the relevant documents.

consecration. In the Charge he declared that the Swedish Church might have to take on the task of trying to achieve reconciliation between the belligerents. At the end of September, he formulated his Appeal for Peace. The words are an unforgettable *document humain* of great power:

> For Peace and Christian Fellowship.
> The War is causing untold distress. Christ's Body, the Church, suffers and mourns. Mankind in its need cries out: O Lord, how long?
> The tangle of underlying and active causes which have accumulated in the course of time, and the proximate events which have led to the breaking of peace, are left to history to unravel. God alone sees and judges the intents and thoughts of the heart.
> We, the servants of the Church, address to all those who have power or influence in the matter an earnest appeal seriously to keep peace before their eyes, in order that blood-shed soon may cease.
> We remind especially our Christian brethren of various nations that war cannot sunder the bond of internal union that Christ holds in us. Sure it is that every nation and every realm has its vocation in the divine plan of the world, and must, even in the face of heavy sacrifices, fulfil its duty, as far as the events indicate it and according to the dim conception of man. Our Faith perceives what the eye cannot always see: the strife of nations must finally serve the dispensation of the Almighty, and all the faithful in Christ are one. Let us therefore call upon God that he may destroy hate and enmity, and in mercy ordain peace for us. His will be done!

However he was not satisfied by merely publishing pious words. He attempted to enlist the co-operation of church leaders everywhere. With K. B. Westman's assistance he sent out the appeal in English, French, German and Swedish for their signatures. There were characteristic differences in the response to the appeal; the churchmen in neutral countries readily affixed their signatures. Professor Shailer Mathews and Dr. Charles Macfarland of the Federal Council of Churches, signed on behalf of the whole council; church-leaders in the Netherlands, Switzerland, and the Scandinavian countries, including Archbishop G. Johansson of Turku (Åbo), Finland, also signed.

Churchmen in the belligerent countries, on the other hand, decided that they could not allow themselves to sign Söderblom's document. It is difficult to determine how far this appeal in wartime did reach. When the text of the appeal was published at the end of November, 1914, in seven languages, English, German, French,

Dutch, Danish, Norwegian and Swedish, it was widely acclaimed as an expression of the Una Sancta. It was also sharply criticized, from two quarters, by radical pacifists for not being radical enough, and from Church circles engaged in bolstering the war effort, to whom Söderblom's Appeal was, at best, unpractical idealism. Söderblom was sustained by a letter from Robert H. Gardiner, the secretary of the young Faith and Order movement in the United States, who wrote on January 15, 1915: '[The Appeal contains] the substance of the idea which I think ought to be presented constantly to the world until Christian unity and International Peace are secured.' Gardiner had understood the idea behind Söderblom's effort, the concern for peace and reconciliation wedded to the concern for Christian unity.

In issuing the Appeal, his first international act, Söderblom had responded to a wave of expectancy which met him as he took Archiepiscopal office at the outbreak of war. From that terrible August of 1914 exists a file of letters to Söderblom, both signed and anonymous, by simple folk and the highly placed and cultured, voicing this expectancy.

Nobody expressed it as beautifully as did Söderblom's friend in Aberdeen, Professor David S. Cairns. Söderblom had sent his Appeal to him, the 'Apostle of Scotland', as he used to call him in his sometimes exuberant language. Cairns knew Söderblom well, and shared much of his background in continental scholarship, his orientation in the history of religion, and concern with the Student Christian Movement and the world missionary endeavour. In his reply Cairns said: 'You seem to me, if I may say so, predestined, above most other men in Europe, to take a leading part in the great work of reconciliation.'[2]

Cairn's letter was important also from another point of view. Churchmen on both sides of the ever widening abyss shared one argument against the Appeal. This was the question of its timeliness; the Appeal from Uppsala was made before its time, it was premature. With one exception, all the Churchmen approached, Dryander at Potsdam and Davidson at Lambeth, Dibelius in Berlin and Cosmo Gordon Lang at Bishopthorpe, York, and Meyer in Paris, agreed that Söderblom's words, while noble and probably well-meaning, were nevertheless spoken at the wrong moment.

Cairns saw, perhaps not further, but certainly deeper than this; he wrote:

---

[2] D. S. Cairns, January 18, 1915, to Söderblom.

I cannot help hoping that when the storm has cleared away, you will have a very great deal to do in bringing the Churches and the divided nations together again, and whether this endeavour on your part meets with present success or failure, it is of vital importance as publicly initiating your further mission. It is a great act of faith, and faith is always a going against appearances. I cannot believe such acts done in real faith can be lost, for in their very nature, they are a part of that future, which will supersede the past and present alike.

Not always, if ever, were the expectations which met Söderblom from outside Sweden and within, expressed in such terms, but he was encouraged by these hopes especially when expressed by men like Dr. Cairns.

The Appeal of the Swedish Archbishop was welcomed with approval in another quarter. This was within the World Alliance of Churches for Promoting International Friendship. Mainly inspired by Anglo-Saxon Christian idealism, Quakers in England and the United States, together with leaders in the American Federal Council of Churches, and with Anglicans engaged in social reform and movements for international reconciliation, this Alliance had been preceded before the War by conferences for fostering friendly relations between England and Germany.

The first meeting of the Alliance took place in Constance on the very day of the outbreak of war, August 1, 1914. Some of the men with whom Söderblom was to work very closely for reconciliation met at Constance. Significantly the Church of Sweden was, as yet, not represented on this occasion, yet the *internationale* of the Alliance soon discovered Söderblom and were anxious to work with him. A dominant theme in Söderblom's international activities during the War and immediately after, was to be his relationship to the Alliance. He gave loyal co-operation, but eventually decided to 'go it alone'.

In Söderblom's wartime involvment there is a pattern of action and reaction, appeals from the outside followed by Söderblom's prompt reaction to them, and certain moves on Söderblom's own part resulting in international action and co-operation: a pattern to be discerned first in 1915–1916, and then again in 1917–1918.

Both parties were concerned to establish co-operation in the interest of international reconciliation, but through the interplay of initiative, action, and reaction, Söderblom's concept of ecumenical movement and encounter was to take on its own special profile.

Thus increasingly Söderblom was to emphasize the importance for the movement of its being nurtured by worship and prayer. It was to be this kind of ecumenical movement rather than an alliance of secretaries. It was surprising, perhaps, and certainly providential, that an archbishop in a neutral country was to take up this great burden of responsibility. He could not do otherwise for he was constrained by a high calling.

Co-workers

'There was a time when the Archbishop's house in Uppsala *was* the ecumenical movement.' So said Dr. Visser't Hooft in Uppsala in 1965, commemorating 'Stockholm, 1925'. They were well chosen words, but they need modification, for, in reaching out to the world—even in the midst of world war—Söderblom was not alone. He had a number of co-workers whom he had found and inspired, and who served the cause with incomparable devotion. They were for the most part young Swedish pastors, who, through Söderblom, had this unique opportunity of serving the Church Universal. It was largely the conditions of war which made it necessary for him to rely mainly on Swedes, though here his co-operation with churchmen from other Scandinavian countries should not be forgotten.

There were different categories of such co-workers, in fact one could speak of three or four concentric circles, so long as it is understood that the image of 'circle' should not be over-emphasized. All was arranged on a voluntary and *ad hoc* basis, but such was the appeal of Söderblom's personality and of his cause, that a certain number of young men were prepared to be assigned by him to the various tasks which he had in hand.

Firstly, the inner circle, comprising three men—Yngve Brilioth, K. B. Westman, and, to a certain extent, Karl Fries.

Born in 1861, Karl Fries belonged to Söderblom's own generation. An old acquaintance of Söderblom's from their student years in the 1880's, and during the War, Fries became so closely associated with some of Söderblom's international activites, that it is not without cause that he should be counted with Brilioth and Westman as a member of the innermost of the concentric circles.

He had been a YMCA secretary from 1888 and had acquired his particular style from this work. His fresh and dynamic personality had something of the practical Anglo-Saxon mission leader of the

John Mott type. He had prepared himself for a missionary career in Ethiopia and his doctoral thesis of 1892 on Semitic languages, dealt with an ancient Ethiopian text. This Scandinavian with his hearty laughter and warm and friendly personality was a recognized leading figure in international youth organizations. He was also the first secretary of the Swedish committee of the World Alliance, from 1916 to 1918, and Söderblom relied on him for contacts with the Alliance, as well as with the international missionary movement. Fries—no relation to Samuel Fries, who was a friend of Söderblom's but died in 1914—was useful also from another point of view, seemingly trivial. He lived in Stockholm, unlike Brilioth and Westman, and he could there establish and maintain contacts of special importance to Söderblom.

The extent to which Brilioth and Westman assisted Söderblom in those years is largely unrecognized, and particularly so in Sweden. After Söderblom's death, both of them wrote fairly extensively on Söderblom's ecumenical work[1] but neither ever hinted at the fact that they had carried a considerable part of the burden.

They were young men, Westman thirty-three and Brilioth twenty-three, when, in 1914, Söderblom enlisted their co-operation. Both historians; disciples of the great Harald Hjärne; and specialists on the Swedish Middle Ages, a field which at its best gave to the student a universal perspective combined with a national outlook. Both were also excellent linguists and handled the correspondence in the European languages both classical and modern, with surprising ease. Both were inspired by Söderblom's ecumenical ideals.

Yngve Brilioth was, of course, hors concours. Before he was twenty, he was recognized as a Greek scholar (he took the exacting Swedish examination of 'Fil.Lic.' in Greek when only nineteen), and his Greek calligraphy stood the ecumenical cause in good stead when, after the War, he wrote Söderblom's personal letters and addresses in Greek to the Patriarch of Constantinople. At the early age of nineteen, he had however decided to exchange Greek for history and became a member of Hjärne's famous seminar. Here he chose for his Doctoral thesis, *The Papal Taxation of Sweden Until the Time of the Great Schism:* thereafter, the two years, 1913–1914, when he visited Rome searching the Vatican archives, introduced him to Catholic Christendom.

---

[1] Y. Brilioth, *Den Ekumeniska Gärningen*, in *N. Söderblom in Memorian*, 1931, pp. 272–347. K. B. Westman, *Minnestal över Nathan Söderblom*, 1934.

In 1914, when Private Brilioth, like other young Swedes, was enlisted in the army, a letter from the new Archbishop found him on the little island of Fårö in the Baltic, supposedly guarding his country against danger from the East. Söderblom, remembering him among those who came to his receptions in old days, had decided to invite the shy but brilliant young man to assist him.

From June, 1915, Brilioth worked for Archbishop Söderblom. There are four big books of letter drafts extant in which, at Söderblom's dictation, Brilioth, in pencil now very faint, has taken down messages in Swedish, German, English, French, and not a few in Latin or Greek. Between June, 1915 and December, 1916, Brilioth wrote—according to these drafts—1328 letters, of which 1061 were in Swedish and 267 in English, German, and French. Söderblom's activity and energy are legendary, but the young secretary's achievement was hardly less amazing, particularly in view of the fact that at the same time he prepared his doctoral thesis *and* his Cand. Theol. examination.

The fellowship between the young Archbishop and the young scholar became one of increasing depth and strength, and in 1919 was cemented still further by the marriage between Brilioth and Söderblom's eldest daughter, Brita. Söderblom and his son-in-law were different in many ways: the one an extrovert, optimist, enthusiast, and trusting; the other shy, cautious, withdrawn, with just occasionally a furtive smile, lighting up the big, shining eyes of that splendid, rather dark face. But while there were differences, there were also similarities. They were both sons of the manse, both historians with a love for theology, both were devotees of the cult of the will, and as they were yoked together in a great and exacting task, each admired in the other the immense rapidity of thought, determination of will and breadth of horizon.

The co-operation was mutually advantageous: Söderblom stimulated Brilioth's interest in English Church History, '*The Anglican Revival*', and in the post-war years 1919 to 1922, Brilioth did his remarkably fruitful research work in England. This also gave him an *entrée* into Anglican Church life, and provided personal contacts with Henson, Headlam, Bell, and others who were of particular importance to Söderblom and the ecumenical cause. Seen in a larger perspective, it appears significant that Brilioth, later to become the Chairman of the Faith and Order commission, received his basic ecumenical training under Söderblom.

K. B. Westman was almost ten years older than Brilioth, yet he was not much more than thirty when he began his work for Söderblom.

He was a learned scholar, equally at home in twelfth century Swedish society, medieval and twentieth century China, or among the Appalachian battlefields of the American Civil War. Tradition-and-renewal, Uppsala as related to the conflicts and prospects of the international scene—these big themes of Söderblom's were also very much a part of Westman's thought. In the first years, while the younger Brilioth was acting as the Archbishop's private secretary, Westman was becoming Söderblom's adviser and emissary abroad. He represented the Archbishop at Berne in 1915 and was also responsible during that year for the enquiry into war attitudes among European churchmen. He accompanied Söderblom to that most important meeting at Oud Wassenaar in 1919, and later went to Germany, Britain, and France, as Söderblom's roving ambassador.

One particular task which Söderblom entrusted to Westman was the correspondence with prospective Olaus Petri Foundation lecturers: During 1918 and 1919, these university lectures were made by Söderblom into an instrument of ecumenical contact, and Westman considerably furthered this aim; but then he could hardly do otherwise since it was owing to the bounty of the Olaus Petri Foundation, that Söderblom could put aside occasionally a few kroner for services rendered.

It was Westman who organized the Neutrals Church Conference in December, 1917. At this time, he took over from Karl Fries the secretaryship of the Swedish Committee of the World Alliance, and this committee showed its appreciation by voting the staggering amount of 150 Swedish kroner (£10) for his work.

Söderblom admired this faithful friend. It is quite conceivable that Westman's work cost him the Uppsala chair of Church History in 1920. In the tough and bracing atmosphere of Swedish academic life, there was a premium placed on the quantity of scholarly output, and Westman's long months and years devoted to Söderblom's cause may have allowed his competitor to win the race.

Ever resourceful, Söderblom was planning an endless series of other possibilities for Westman. Looking at the chess-board of Europe, he tried to place his knight, now as Swedish pastor in Berlin, now as Bishop in Visby. His notes and letters to Westman toyed with these ideas week after week. Above all, he hoped that Westman would become the Executive Secretary of the 'Life and Work' movement. Keenly interested in the Swedish mission project in China as Söderblom was, he could not bring himself to agree that Westman should become the leader of the work there, that his knight should of his own accord jump off the chessboard, as it were. As chairman of the Church of Sweden Mission Board, he voted against the decision, but was outvoted by the majority, and later nostalgically wrote from time to time to Westman, trying to persuade him to return to Sweden in order to take over the secretaryship, close to Söderblom himself. Eventually, in 1930, Westman was to return from China to Uppsala as a University Professor of Missions.

In the archiepiscopal election in 1931 after Söderblom's death, the Church put Westman in the first place, a proof of its great confidence in him. He devoted much of his time to the International Missionary Council. Söderblom, the pioneer of 'Life and Work', had thus as his closest co-workers two men, of whom one was to be the leader of the Faith and Order Commission, the other a prominent spokesman in the International Missionary Council.

The second concentric circle of Söderblom's international co-workers consisted of those who were or had been Swedish legation pastors. Söderblom himself had been one such, in Paris, and he felt that his contacts from that time were particularly valuable. But this was not all. As Archbishop, he allowed himself to act as if he thought that men with similar experience from London, Paris, Berlin, or Copenhagen, formed a special category. They were Swedish priests who could be expected to have a wider horizon than others, with an unusual international background that could be made to serve the common ecumenical cause.

London was represented by J. Lindskog and A. Hellerström. Söderblom was impressed by Lindskog as a systematic theologian and as a priest with a keen social concern. In spite of the unwieldy machinery of Swedish ecclesiastical preferments, particularly during the War, Söderblom managed to find what he wanted—a parish for Lindskog in Stockholm. He simply sent him a telegram which—unexpectedly enough in war-time London—reached its address: 'Apply for Braennkyrka. Söderblom.' Lindskog, now near at hand, was to become his confidential adviser in Faith and Order matters, particularly at the Lausanne conference in 1927.

Lindskog's successor in London, A. Hellerström, rapidly established himself as a key figure in the relationship between Uppsala and Canterbury. Having a keen interest in liturgics, this knowledgeable Lutheran priest felt at home in an Anglican *milieu*. His contacts with the Archbishop of Canterbury and with G. K. A. Bell seem to have been remarkably close, and whenever Söderblom visited Britain—April, 1921, June, 1925, July, 1926, and later—it was Hellerström who arranged his contacts with leading churchmen.

Paris brought Söderblom into contact with Sam Stadener who had succeeded him as Embassy pastor in 1901. Born in 1872, Stadener, received as a theological student strong impressions from the liberal Lundensian school. He was a complex personality, dynamic and ambitious, and Söderblom, who knew a brilliant person when he met one, made repeated attempts to engage Stadener in his ecumenical endeavours. Stadener was early recognized as one of the foremost Swedish preachers of his generation—with those long and flowing sentences which were still possible and even admired at the time— and was asked by Söderblom to preach in Uppsala Cathedral on the last day of the so-called Neutrals Church Conference in December, 1917.

He sought Stadener's services for difficult tasks where diplomatic skill and a knowledge of France and the French were particularly needed. Thus Stadener became a member of the Church delegation of 1923 sent to report on the condition of German prisoners in the Ruhr, then occupied by French soldiers. Again, in the early part of 1925, Stadener acted as Söderblom's emissary to the Orient. His proficiency in French helped him to establish contact with Greek, Coptic and Armenian patriarchs in Alexandria and Jerusalem, and he tried to persuade these worthies to attend the Stockholm meeting.

This pilgrimage to the East, however, was to end his ecumenical endeavours in Söderblom's service. He had developed too keen a sense of what was going to be, in the long run, profitable in Swedish church politics to stake his whole future on Söderblom. He now decided to devote himself to the Association of Swedish Priests, 'A.S.P.', reputedly more 'Lutheran' than 'Ecumenical'. Soon he was to proclaim, with an address which no one could fail to read, that in Sweden the leadership of the Church consisted of 'illusionists who commit the age-old Swedish mistake of playing politics on the Continent while the home front is weakened'.[2] Stadener was not going to make that kind of mistake; after all, too much was involved.

Nils Widner was another typical member of this group. He had been legation pastor in Copenhagen, and was appointed to a parish near Stockholm, eventually to become *Pastor Primarius* there. To Söderblom it was obvious that with this background, Widner should be responsible for the organization of Sweden's ecclesiastical contacts

---

[2] Clarence Nilsson, *Sam Stadener*, 1964, p. 228.

with the Nordic countries. This was to be an important matter during the War years.

In this connexion we should mention Söderblom's close contact with some of the Swedish ministers plenipotentiary and other diplomats. Only in a rather indirect way could they be described as Söderblom's co-workers, but such was the impact of Söderblom's personality—it was definitely a matter of personality rather than of any survival of a state church system—that Swedish envoys would give particular attention to Söderblom's ecumenical cause, and this was true in the case of Harald Bildt. Söderblom and Bildt first met in Paris in 1900; Bildt was a man of independent means, and he gave Söderblom generous financial support in times of sickness or any other adversity. Particularly during his time as envoy in Cairo, Bildt furthered Söderblom's interests, and on his behalf, established ecclesiastical contacts with patriarchs and archbishops in the Orient. As a result of 'Stockholm, 1925', a 'Fellowship of Unity' was formed in Cairo, representing about ten different churches, and Bildt became the first President of this organization. Through Söderblom, he was included in the Swedish delegation to the Lausanne Conference on Faith and Order in 1927.

Söderblom's most effective representative in the East was, however, J. Kolmodin, a brilliant historian and one of the most gifted of Sweden's diplomats of the time. We shall have much to say of him in the chapter 'Uppsala and Catholicity'.

Another concentric circle of co-workers consisted of the special ecumenical envoys or delegates *ad hoc,* whom Söderblom sent out from time to time as circumstances demanded and allowed. Herman Neander was the first of these: it was through Söderblom and the Olaus Petri Foundation that Neander, from 1910, had been given the opportunity of studying modern Greek and Russian. As we shall see presently, he became Söderblom's special emissary to the prisoner of war camps in Germany, and above all in Russia and Siberia. In the 1920's he was sent to make contact with the Orthodox Churches. After the War, besides Neander, a number of young Swedish priests were sent out on errands of special urgency and importance; in 1920, F. Sjöberg to the churches in Poland; in 1921, O. Nystedt to Czechoslovakia and Hungary; in 1923, as already mentioned, Stadener, together with the Swede A. Wihlborg and J. Oman from Britain, to the Ruhr; in 1924, and in 1926 and 1927, Paul Sandegren to Lithuania.

This was something altogether new in the life of the Swedish Church, and produced an exhilarating feeling of international responsibility.

Communication, fellowship, friendship—these contributed to the charisma of Söderblom's role as an ecumenical leader. Through his expanding circles of co-workers, he reached out to new groups and other lands. This was particularly so in connexion with his co-workers in the other Nordic countries.

Söderblom's intimate co-operation with the leading bishops in Denmark and Norway created another of these concentric circles. When Söderblom made his appeals to the world for peace and for unity, he did so in letters signed conjointly by Copenhagen, Oslo, and Uppsala. This was a significant and creative initiative on the part of Söderblom, and far from being the accepted thing at that time. In fact, never previously had the three Scandinavian churches thus appeared before the world as a united whole.

E. Berggrav has recalled the difficulties and suspicions which had to be overcome, and which were, to a large extent, swept aside by Söderblom's refusal to accept that such hindrances should exist at all: ' . . . [Söderblom] always counted on the Scandinavians, and he never did the least thing that might have suggested a wish to domi-nate our churches. He had no intention of doing this. But we on our side were a little afraid of him—that is true. Especially at the begin-ning, we thought ourselves subtle and clever when, behind the ex-pansion of Uppsala we believed we could sense a certain tendency to overlordship.'[3] That such fears were unwarranted soon became obvious.

Harald Ostenfeld in Copenhagen and Jens Tandberg in Oslo had that much in common, that they represented a comparatively Liberal churchmanship with a genuine interest in social problems. As perso-nalities, the two bishops were rather different. 'Ostenfeld was always more pastor than Bishop',[4] with a horror for the representative side of his office. Tandberg was a man of fine culture, who loved to cultivate the episcopal manner. Together with his colleague, J. Gle-ditsch in Trondhjem, he found it difficult to manage the vocal Pietistic movement in the Church with its intransigent anti-Liberal tendencies. From the point of view of Söderblom's particular ecu-menical approach, this made the Norwegian situation different from that of either Denmark or Sweden. Tandberg, who signed the 1917 appeal of the Scandinavian Primates, did not himself attend the Neutrals Church Conference in Uppsala—much to the consternation and dismay of the younger Norwegian generation, particularly Berg-grav.

---

[3] E. Berggrav, 'Nathan Söderblom', in *Kirke og Kultur*, 1931.
[4] P. G. Lindhardt, *Den Danske Kirkes Historie* VIII (1967), p. 112.

Söderblom also worked very closely with the younger men: V. Ammundsen later Bishop, Haderslev, Denmark, was a brilliant Church historian and linguist, and he used his gifts to the full in the ecumenical movement. On the social side, and with regard to the Church's relief work, Dr. A. Th. Jörgensen had wide experience, on which Söderblom could rely; and then there was Berggrav himself, the young Norwegian pastor and journalist, destined to become bishop of Tromsö and later, Oslo.

The relationship between Söderblom and Berggrav merits a study of its own. This should be a psychological study in depth which would show how both these men knew that, for themselves, and what is more, for each other, the most fundamental influence on their lives was that of their fathers—Lutheran pietistic pastors—and how they deeply respected and loved one another because of this, quite apart from the obvious congeniality between the two. Berggrav worked very effectively with Söderblom in the Neutrals Church Conference in 1917; it was he who took the initiative for the Polish Church Conference in Uppsala in 1921, although he was himself unable to attend on account of ill-health; and after Stockholm, 1925, Berggrav wrote a little volume—a 'contour'—on the Conference, critical and generous at the same time. He said there about Söderblom what nobody else managed to express, stating, with unerring aim: 'Here was a Churchman who was not first and foremost organizer but *soul*.'[5]

After the war, bishop J. Gummerus of Borgå and Tampere became his special co-worker in Finland. Finland's archbishop, old Dr. G. Johansson of Turku (Åbo), became increasingly estranged from Söderblom. His Beckian theology made him intensely suspicious of his Swedish colleague's new-fangled ecumenical endeavour. All the more Söderblom relied on Gummerus, solid historian and congenial with Söderblom's international outlook. It was particularly with regard to the Baltic churches that Söderblom engaged Gummerus upon his ecumenical tasks.

But the concentric circles of Söderblom's co-workers expanded beyond the borders of the North.

A step taken in 1915 by the Swedish S.C.M.[5a] can in fact be regar-

---

[5] A. Johnson, *Eyvind Berggrav*, p. 147. After Bishop Bell's death, Berggrav said in an obituary: 'Bell baptized me as an ecumenist.' Berggrav's biographer, Bishop Alex. Johnson adds: 'That is hardly right. Bell "confirmed" him on that occasion in 1939, but it was Söderblom who "baptized" him, who gave him faith in the ecumenical movement.'

[5a] S. C. M. = Student Christian Movement.

ded as an extension of Söderblom's attempt to maintain, in spite of war, contact with Church leaders on both side of the great divide. The S.C.M. addressed an enquiry with two questions to a number of churchmen and theologians in Germany, Britain, and France—asking them to comment on the effect of war on religious life, and the possible role of the Churches for reconciliation during and after the War. There were twenty-three answers, fifteen from Germany, five from Britain, and three from France. They were published in 1915 in a volume called *The Struggle Behind the Frontiers.*

The little book is interesting from many points of view. There were at this time comparable ventures by other Swedish academics to gather information from the belligerent nations, such as that by a young radical politician Ernst Wigforss (later Minister of Finance) called *World War and World Peace, Documents and Reflexions,* I–II, 1915. The S.C.M. volume by comparison was limited in that it concentrated on the views of Christian leaders.

From our point of view we need to notice how those who contributed to the S.C.M. enquiry were not there by chance, picked out haphazardly from some university or Church calender. They represented, in fact, a characteristic sample of Söderblom's friends on both sides; and it was obvious that the names had been selected only after consultation with Söderblom—who himself wrote the preface to the volume.[6]

The list of names itself gives an indication of the friends abroad with whom Söderblom corresponded throughout the first years of the War. As a churchman in a neutral country, he had probably at this time a much wider international correspondence than others, yet, the number of people with whom he could in fact maintain contact in wartime, was comparatively limited. The copies of the correspondence allow us to determine the range of these international contacts. To the names already quoted must be added, for Britain, the Archbishop of Canterbury, as well as Canon A. J. Mason of Canterbury, a member of the Anglican Commission to Sweden of 1909, and also Professor Cairns of Aberdeen.

The American correspondents were limited practically to two men,

---

[6] The Swedish title of the S. C. M. volume was *Kampen bakom fronterna.* The correspondence for it had been carried on by K. B. Westman and P. Hasselrot. It is a volume of 184 pages; the first part of the book contains the letters, the second part certain representative statements, such as war sermons. K. B. Westman had a concluding interpretation of the material thus collected, under the characteristic title: 'The unity and dividedness of Christendom with reference to the present world situation.'

Dr. C. S. Macfarland for ecumenical matters, and Dr. L. G. Abrahamson for contacts with the Augustana Lutheran Synod. In France the correspondents included old Paris friends such as Wilfred Monod, Eugéne Ménégoz, André Bertrand, and Madame Barbe de Quirielle. There was also an intermittant exchange of letters and telegrams with Bergson. Hoping against hope, Söderblom tried to get him as an Olaus Petri lecturer and—almost succeeded. Among Parisian correspondents we should also include the name of his close friend, G. Nordling, a Swede in Paris.[7]

Söderblom thus had, beside the leaders of the World Alliance, other international connexions which he cultivated as far as conditions allowed and used for his particular ecumenical tasks in various parts of Europe. Yet it was the World Alliance programme to which he was first related.

Before treating this we must, however, sketch the background of world war as experienced in neutral Sweden, affecting, as it did, Söderblom's plans and actions.

Swedish Attitudes to the War

The Swedish Archbishop and the World War—the problem is more complex than the words would at first suggest. It is not enough to follow Nathan Söderblom from one peace appeal to another, from one conference to another; he must be seen also in relation to the politics of his own country, to the changing fate and fortune of Sweden in a time of world war and after. That this should be so may seem surprising. A Church leader, some would love to believe, should have made up his mind once and for all—from a Christian standpoint; so that with unwavering adherence to principle he may guide his flock.

In fact, of course, a Church leader, in this case an Archbishop of a national church, is, by definition, a representative figure. His choice of alternatives for action in time of war is particularly limited. He can and perhaps must, make certain critical statements—possibly 'prophetic'—on various aspects of the politics of his country, but generally speaking he does so within the framework of a given overall political situation.

Söderblom's position must be understood within the framework of Sweden's attitude and position, in themselves more complex than

---

[7] G. Nordling was the father of Raoul Nordling who 'saved Paris' in April, 1945 ('Is Paris burning?').

the general neutrality formula would suggest. We are aware of the difficulties of showing things in the right perspective as with a few strokes of the pen we attempt to sketch this framework.

If Sweden, like its neighbours Denmark and Norway, was neutral in the War, this was not to say that Swedish wartime politics were identical with those of these two countries: geography, history, and economics conditioned certain very real differences in outlook. Nor was opinion in Sweden homogeneous. From a Swedish point of view, the role and rule of Russia was a factor of particular importance. All through history Russia had been the traditional enemy. Every Swedish schoolboy in the little towns along the Baltic coast knew the circumstances under which his particular town had been burned, his province ravaged by Muscovite soldiers centuries earlier. The same schoolboy, when indulging in some prank at home, would be called to order by his mother exclaiming: *'Ä du alldeles rysk!'*—'Are you completely Russian?'

Much of Sweden's attitude was determined by the Russian threat, or bogey, as the case may have been. If the Conservatives, generally speaking, tended to be pro-German, they were so not merely because of the traditional strong German cultural and political influence, but also because they looked upon the War as 'primarily a trial of strength between Germany and Russia'.[1] A German victory on the Eastern front would—it was felt in the first years of the War— remove what was, rightly or wrongly, regarded as a threat from the East to Sweden's independence. Furthermore, such an outcome would bring liberation to the Finnish and the Baltic peoples, with whom Sweden had historically of course been closely linked. This general attitude was, in certain academic circles, not least in Uppsala, rationalized at the time by grandiose 'geo-political' speculations —the adjective was well-liked and expressed an attitude of some consequence.

On the other hand the two Left-wing parties tended to side with the Allies, and Branting, the leader of the Social Democrats, was uncompromisingly pro-French; but this of course, did not make them any the less opposed to Imperial Russia. Thus one could find several well-known Social Democrats among the small but vocal groups of activists, who were calling for Swedish military action against Russia. It is only fair to add that these were expelled by their party.

An anti-Russian theme was also apparent in the Swedish literary

---

[1] H. Tingsten, *The Debate on the Foreign Policy of Sweden, 1918–1939* (1949), p. 11.

tradition of the nineteenth century. Victor Rydberg influenced opinion to a large extent when contrasting the Hellenistic-Occidental spirit of civilization with the Oriental and its supposedly barbaric tendencies. During the War, Ellen Key in her book *A Deeper View of the War,* 1916, reiterated these ideas. Nobody could suggest that Ellen Key was pro-German, yet this was the suspicion to which she exposed herself when in August, 1916 she called the West European countries to join forces 'for peace, freedom, and culture against the barbarian which dominates Eastern Europe'. This was, according to her, 'great strategy', as contrasted with the 'little strategy' which was tearing apart the great powers of the West.[2]

In all this Söderblom the Archbishop was pulled in two directions by his warm and well-informed sympathies. He admired the traditions of religion and culture on both sides, and he had friends and colleagues in both camps. Wistfully he hoped with Lord Roberts that 'England and Germany will win, during the fighting, each other's respect'.[3]

As Archbishop of Uppsala, Söderblom was too much of a Swede to be unconcerned for the possible threat from Imperial Russia. Just as deeply as Ellen Key and others, he was in the first years of the War, convinced that the struggle between Russia and Germany was a decisive contest between Eastern barbarism and occidental civilization, the latter represented by that Germany which he knew from the University of Leipzig. We must be careful in pointing out that this attitude was not expressed officially in print but in some of his letters, particularly to Germany in 1915, he stressed this view.[4] His keen interest in the fate of the Baltic peoples was translated into a hope that the outcome of the struggle between Germany and Russia would be 'a chain of new frontier states liberated from Russia'.

Söderblom had one main overwhelming concern—peace, and peace as soon as possible. He was aware that this attitude could be misunderstood, and that at a certain point in the bitter conflict, a declaration for peace would be seen as a demonstration of solidarity with the Central Powers. Yet in April 1916, when Branting, the Labour leader, had stated in *Le Temps* that he did not want a speedy peace, Söderblom disagreed, however much he might be in

---

[2] Ellen Key, *En djupare syn på kriget* (1916), p. 19 f.

[3] Söderblom, March 19, 1915, to David Cairns, Aberdeen. In possession of Prof. Cairns jun., Aberdeen.

[4] Söderblom, June 22, 1915, to Pfarrer Teschner, and October 12, 1915, to L. Ihmels.

sympathy with the broad aims of Branting's political activity. He commented in a private letter: 'I hope that Branting made a false assertion when he stated that the Swedish Social Democrats did not want an early peace. Lamentable.' Söderblom on the contrary hoped for 'an immediate end to this slaughter'.[5]

These all too short political references must be supplemented by a brief indication of peace attempts in and from Sweden during the first part of the War. A general Swedish Peace Conference was held at Varberg in 1915 and sent a greeting to the Pope; K. P. Arnoldsson's Swedish organization for peace and arbitration was active, and also Professor K. Wicksell and his wife Anna. Following upon the famous step taken by Henry Ford, a 'Neutrals Conference' on peace was held at Stockholm in April, 1916, and a well-meaning peace appeal was sent out from there. Leaders in Church and State in Scandinavia, Holland and Switzerland were challenged to declare where they stood in these matters; among some ten leading Swedes who refused to sign, the most prominent was Archbishop Söderblom; and this is interesting, since it places Söderblom's peace work in perspective.[6] He wrote to Bishop Ostenfeld in Copenhagen: 'The good intention is obvious, but we cannot offhand sign or bless, with a good conscience, this aunty-like naïvety.'[7] These reactions on Söderblom's part to political efforts in his own country in time of War serve to show up his own position in stronger relief. For a variety of reasons he did not feel at home at this time with pacifist plans; he felt that he had his own contribution to make in the shape of a united effort by the churches, and in challenging them to see this as their particular task. To a certain extent he had to do this on his own, yet he was not without his group of supporters and co-workers, both inside and outside his connexion with the World Alliance, to which we must now return.

A World Alliance in a World War

It had been among men of the World Alliance that he found the keenest response to his Appeal of November 1914. While many regarded this Appeal as premature, some of the Alliance leaders in London, particularly members of the Society of Friends such as J.

---

[5] Söderblom, April 24, 1916, to O. Håkansson. Letter draft.

[6] *En rundfråga om villkoren för en varaktig fred* (Stockholm, 1916), p. 119.

[7] Söderblom, October 13, 1916, to H. Ostenfeld. Letter draft. The reference is too brief to allow one to state with assurance to which series of peace appeals this letter refers.

Allen Baker, M. P., and Dr. H. Hodgkin supported his move. Immediately on their return from Constance, August 1914, they had written to Söderblom in terms which showed that they were aware of the time factor but that they took a different standpoint from that of the cautious churchmen in other communions. 'It is not too soon', they wrote very gallantly, on August 7, 1914, 'to begin to think out the new situation which will arise at the close of the war.'

In 1915, they proposed another Alliance conference, this time in Berne. We have already seen that the Church of Sweden was not represented at the conference at Constance, in 1914. The more eager were the Alliance men now to secure a qualified representative from Sweden for Berne.

In January and February, 1915, Dr. B. Battin, Quaker and American from Swarthmore College, visited Söderblom, with a view to inviting him to the Alliance conference at Berne in August. Battin found Söderblom very responsive to the general aims of the Alliance and ready to discuss the specific problem which Battin raised with him—the case of the Prisoners of War. Battin had been asked by Dr. Siegmund-Schultze, the German social reformer, to ask Söderblom whether he would 'visit prisoner of war camps in different countries', thereby dramatically drawing attention to this crying need.[1] Battin hoped to bring together Söderblom, Dr. Mott and Siegmund-Schultze in Berne, in order to discuss this problem. He begged Söderblom to attend the World Alliance meeting at Berne: 'We wish to launch our movement in a broad and far-seeing way, and count much on your knowledge and wisdom', he wrote to the Archbishop.[2]

Söderblom felt however that he could not afford to leave his diocese in order to attend the Berne Conference. He in fact never once travelled outside Scandinavia during the War. Nonetheless he was anxious to secure a competent delegation from the Church of Sweden, and he managed to do so, for the group included K. B. Westman of Uppsala, his adviser in ecumenical matters, and Professor Edv. Rodhe of Uppsala. Söderblom also invited N. Widner, of Stockholm. Widner was a cautious man and expressed his caution in terms which Söderblom was to meet many times in those years:

The problem is whether in times of the wolf such as these, it is at all possible to achieve anything by a Conference. What now must be done for peace must be done in times of peace. I am a little afraid of fiasco.[3]

---

[1] B. Battin, June 7, 1915, to Söderblom.
[2] B. Battin, ibid., and June 21, 1915, to Söderblom.
[3] N. Widner, June 17, 1915, to Söderblom; the Swedish representation in Berne included also Principal K. A. Jansson and Wilhelm Gullberg.

However, this fear was overcome by Söderblom's insistence, and Widner became a valuable addition to Söderblom's little ecumenical team.

One can notice at this time a shift of interest on Söderblom's part with regard to the World Alliance. His contacts with the organization were handled on two levels, the international and the national. In the international relations he was aware of the expectations which his activity and his position aroused in some of these leaders. On his side he responded with an initiative of his own with regard to the Alliance.

He instructed his young secretary Brilioth to make a proposal on his behalf with regard to a possible follow-up of Berne. (In the next few months he also wrote at least twice to Karl Fries, urging him to try to bring the World Alliance conference to Uppsala.) Brilioth wrote to Battin: 'I have to add that the Archbishop would of course be very glad to receive the Congress at Uppsala at any time (if it suits the members of the future congress to come to his place), where everything is well prepared to receive them.'[4]

These few lines are important, for they constitute the very embryo of an idea which was to become 'Stockholm (and Uppsala) 1925'. We cannot refrain from making the more general point that this invitation to the American Quaker from Swarthmore College was extended by the Swedish Archbishop, the future leader of the Life and Work movement, and written for him by a young historian who was to become the future chairman of the Faith and Order movement.

Söderblom's attitude to the national, Swedish, branch of the Alliance also changed. He did not agree at first to become chairman of the Swedish committee of the Alliance formed in 1915, while in Copenhagen, on the other hand, Bishop Ostenfeld took the chairmanship of the Danish committee as a matter of course. Söderblom suggested his colleague, Bishop von Schéele, as Swedish chairman, and he intimated to Battin that 'it was proposed that Bishop von Schéele of Visby, the oldest bishop in the Church, should take the lead'.[5] He had of course good reasons for this suggestion. His own diocese took up all his time and by comparison the diocese of Visby was a sinecure. He also felt that he must pay deference to von Schéele because of his international contacts.

Old as he was, von Schéele, by comparison with other Swedish

4 Y. Brilioth to B. Battin; draft letter in Brilioth's letter-copy book, end of June, 1915.
5 B. Battin, *Report on Foreign Work*, March 5, 1915.

bishops, had close relations with pacifist leaders in his country.[6] Söderblom felt that for the time being he should leave those interests to von Schéele, while he himself attempted to gain the attention of the international leaders of the Alliance for his own plans. As we have seen, he was already beginning to envisage or conceive a plan for an international meeting to be held at Uppsala. He could not of course know as yet what form it would take, and it seemed inevitable then, and for some time to come, that it had to be part of the emerging World Alliance organization, carried as this was by strong American and Anglo-Saxon interests. Even when, two years later, in September, 1917, Söderblom wrote to Herman Wrangel, the Swedish envoy in London, about his new appeal of 1917, he underlined that it was 'a follow-up of the Berne Conference which has been insisted upon from different quarters'.[7]

At the same time this was to provide for him a platform from which he could promote his own programme. Under these new conditions he was prepared to take responsibility for the Swedish branch of the Alliance, and at the end of 1917 he agreed to become chairman of the national organization, succeeding von Schéele.

However, his eventual position with regard to the Alliance at home and abroad owed something to his Nordic connexions, for it was here that his own particular approach to ecumenical relationships, through united prayer, work, and worship rather than through a largely administrative alliance, began to emerge. We shall therefore have to give some attention to war-time Nordic co-operation as it developed under Söderblom's guidance partly as a result of the Berne conference and partly in independence of it.

At Berne, the Swedes had been joined by other Scandinavians who were going to play an important part in the Nordic co-operation on Alliance lines during and after the War: V. Ammundsen and H. Larsen from Denmark and C. Hansteen, F. Klaveness and N. B. Tvedt from Norway.

The Germans Siegmund-Schultze and A. W. Schreiber gave a survey of the Prisoners of War situation. It became clear that the problem had to be tackled on as large a scale as possible.

On their return to Sweden, the three Swedish delegates duly reported to Söderblom. About this time the Archbishop had an important visit from Dr. A. C. Harte, an American YMCA secretary

---

[6] Cf. *Nordic Peace Calender*, 1916, p. 47.
[7] Söderblom, Sept. 10, 1917, to H. Wrangel. Draft letters, 1916–19.

sent by Dr. Mott to enlist Söderblom's help, and Swedish assistance generally, for the care of Prisoners of War.[8]

Söderblom did not feel that he was himself in a position to follow Siegmund-Schultze's impulsive suggestion that he visit the camps, but he did the next best: he called his man Herman Neander, then a young pastor in his diocese. Neander, as one of Söderblom's first peace doves, was promptly sent to Prisoner of War camps at first for a year, among Russians in Germany, and then from March, 1916, among German and Austrian prisoners in Russia and Siberia. In his case, there was established significant co-operation between the Archbishop and the Swedish Red Cross: Neander, together with Pastor W. Sarwe, was among the first Swedish Red Cross delegates to Russia. There he could work with, among others, Elsa Brändström. He also established contact with the Danish YMCA emissaries to Russia, thus forging another link in war relief work between Söderblom and Bishop Ostenfeld in Copenhagen.

Other activities in which Söderblom was engaged during these years were exchange of Prisoners of War between Germany and France, correspondence on the identification of prisoners, and the establishment of a Swedish Committee for the distribution of books to the Prisoners of War. Somewhat later, in 1917, he arranged for the translation into German of a little soldiers' Prayer Book of his. This was distributed to German prisoners of war in Russia and Siberia. We are told by K. B. Westman that Söderblom was at this time once more about to increase his Prisoner of War work. In November, 1915, however, the Swedish Red Cross, under the presidency of Prince Carl, called an important conference at Stockholm, with representatives of the Central Powers, Russia, and Sweden. Here the spiritual care for the Prisoners of War was given special attention, and Söderblom, who had been among the first to respond to the challenge of the situation, now felt that this enormous task could best be handled by the Red Cross.[9] While as a matter of course he continued to give his assistance in this field, as the situation demanded, this was from now on an activity where he had initiated certain tasks which could be taken over by others with greater resources in personnel and finance.

---

[8] Cf. C. P. Shedd, *A History of the World's Alliance of YMCA* (1955), p. 547, and Karl Fries, *Mina minnen* (1939), pp. 152 ff.

[9] There are two long letters from K. B. Westman to W. Dickinson of the World Alliance, December 8, 1915, and January 4, 1916 (draft letters in lead pencil), on these matters. K. B. Westman papers.

Nordic Fellowship

Thus, while during the War he did not move beyond the Northern
countries, he did concentrate all the more on common Scandinavian
tasks. Bishop Ostenfeld said of him: 'He looked upon the Nordic
Churches as a unity.'[1] This vision was not as self-evident as it would
seem to the outsider looking at these small countries at the top of the
world map; in fact each of the Churches had its own distinct personality, and the exchange of traditions and ideas was limited. The
conditions of war changed this, and there were new contacts in the
political field. The meeting of the three Monarchs of Denmark, Norway, and Sweden, in Malmö in 1914, gave a promising lead. Conferences between Prime Ministers were held, a Baltic exhibition at
Malmö in the summer 1914 led to new contacts.

In the ecclesiastical field, there was now an overwhelming common
task where the contribution of neutral countries was necessary—the
prisoners of war—and we have noticed how Söderblom and Ostenfeld co-operated over this, and how Söderblom's Appeal in 1914 had
had, among other signatures, those of Bishop Ostenfeld of Sealand
and Bishop Tandberg of Oslo; and how he had even had the satisfaction of securing the assent of his Finnish colleague, Archbishop
G. Johansson of Turku (Åbo), who later on in life was to be one of
his most churlish critics. In this connexion we shall anticipate later
developments by pointing out that the invitation to the Neutrals
Church Conference in 1917, went out over the signatures of the three
primates (Ostenfeld, Tandberg, and himself) at the insistence of
Söderblom.

For his Nordic connexions, Söderblom counted on Nils Widner
as his special emissary. As we have pointed out, Nils Widner had
been a Swedish envoy pastor in Copenhagen, and he was as much
at home in Denmark as in Sweden. At Söderblom's prompting, Widner organized the first meeting of Nordic pastors at Nääs in Western
Sweden, September, 1916. Some thirty clergy met there, among them
E. Berggrav, Professors L. Brun, O. Michelet from Norway, V. Ammundsen from Denmark, Dean Pfannenstil, Professor Edv. Rodhe,
and Dr. M. Björkquist from Sweden.

Söderblom worked with Widner in planning the Conference but
could not attend the 1916 meeting himself. If he made a special
effort to attend the 1917 meeting at Copenhagen, this may have been
related to his discussion in the meantime with Widner as to the

---

[1] H. Ostenfeld in *Hågkomster*, XIV, p. 64.

possibilities of the Nordic organization. Widner may have been pusillanimous over what seemed to him the too lofty plans of the World Alliance, but when he could approach the ecumenical problem from the Nordic angle, he felt more at home, and he soon proved to be something of a strategist in this area.

In May, 1917, Söderblom and he discussed the matter, and Söderblom asked him to formulate his ideas on paper. Widner wrote: 'I imagine that the three Nordic Churches, both on account of their national similarities, and because of the Lutheran Confession which they, at least *formaliter*, have in common, should form a crystallization point for the other Evangelical Churches. . . .' The Bishops must be the leaders, 'for preference with the Archbishop of Uppsala at the head'. He suggested frequent Nordic Conferences, exchange of literature, etc. 'This organization should also devote itself to Scandinavians abroad as well as to common tasks in the mission field. By thus being assigned certain common responsibilities, they would inevitably foster Nordic solidarity. This Nordic Church group . . . [would] easily attract to itself the Churches of Germany and England, or could at least become a bridge between them.'

Widner had met Dr. Battin in Karl Fries' home in Stockholm prior to writing his letter. He was not altogether satisfied by what he had seen of the Alliance meeting on that occasion. He told Söderblom: 'In the [Swedish] Alliance Committee there were some very odd people!' He was bewildered by the ethos of the World Alliance, and he went on to state in his letter to Söderblom: 'In particular therefore, I regard it as desirable that the initiative in these things should remain in your hands, and that it should be churchmen, not all kinds of sectarians and "peace friends" who will form the majority. If not, it would all be only a farrago of an Alliance.'

Widner referred Söderblom to the experience of his meetings at Nääs. From the point of view of the Nordic national churches he wanted this group to be the nerve centre of Nordic [co-operation]. The Nordic Churches under the presidency of Archbishop Söderblom, and with representatives from Holland and Switzerland, should become the 'foundation stone for a "*corpus evangelicorum*".' Nordic Church co-operation, while cultivating that which was specifically Nordic, should thus aim to go outside itself. 'I have for a long time not dared to think of anything far-reaching, but it now looks as if events speeded the programme more than I at least expected two years ago.'[2]

---

[2] N. Widner, May 31 and June 9, 1917, to Söderblom.

This vision interested Söderblom considerably. Attending the second Nordic clergy meeting at Copenhagen in November, 1917, he employed some of Widner's terms, with Widner as the Chairman of the meeting, without, as far as we can see, mentioning his previous discussion with him. The minutes now have the following wording:

'Archbishop Söderblom defined the aim of the Committee's work: in the future in Scandinavia, there would appear a stronger ecclesiastical coalition (*sammanslutning*), a *"corpus evangelicorum"* which, without any encroachment whatever on the activities of the individual churches, could show the way to unity and concord for divided evangelical Christendom. As far as Scandinavia was concerned, co-operation was all the more important on account of the World War, and would be even more so after the War. Such great tasks would be placed on their shoulders, for instance as regards missions, scholarships, student work, etc., "that they could only be solved if they stood shoulder to shoulder".[3]

This little speech was a characteristic Söderblomian performance. Speaking on this occasion he went along with his chairman, using Widner's expressions, yet widening the perspective. Widner's idea was to attract the other churches, of Germany, Britain and elsewhere, to a 'Nordic bloc'. Söderblom was as determined as Widner to emphasize Scandinavian church co-operation, but only insofar as this would serve a wider, international family of Evangelical churches.

1917: New Plans

The year 1917 by no means saw the end of the war. Yet, it brought fundamental changes in the overall situation and with that some hope of peace. The turning point occurred in February and March with America's entry into the war and the revolution in Russia. From a Swedish point of view, and that of the Archbishop, the cataclysm in Russia also implied a chance, a lease of life, for Finland and the Baltic provinces.

It was under the impact of the March revolution that the Socialist 'Stockholm Conference' of 1917 was called together by the executive committee of the International Socialist Bureau. Not that the partners were all agreed as to the policy to be followed, in fact there were strong tensions within the group. On the Swedish scene Söderblom was confronted with this, when at the beginning of May, a group of Radical Social Democrats, including Söderblom's friend

---

[3] Minutes of the meeting, N. Söderbloms papers. Cf. Karlström, *Kristna samförståndssträvanden*, p. 631.

Fabian Månsson, rebelled against the Labour leader Hjalmar Branting and formed the 'Social Democratic Left'. But in spite of national and international tensions, the Socialist Conference was called by a Committee representing the Dutch and Scandinavian Social Democratic parties.

Meeting in Stockholm from the middle of May, the conference established contacts with the Russian revolutionary leaders—a few weeks earlier, a famous figure, Lenin, had passed through Stockholm on his way to Russia. There were plans, albeit abortive, to call new sessions of the Stockholm conference in August and October, 1917, and definite peace proposals were discussed.

The very name of 'Stockholm' awakened keen expectations. The German leader Scheidemann, writing nostalgically after the war, expressed himself in Biblical terms: 'Over all the trenches, the thought of Stockholm appeared like a new star of Bethlehem which was to lead to the crib of the Child of Peace.'

In the German Reichstag in July, 1917, Scheidemann, together with other leaders on the left, managed to carry through a peace resolution. In the same month, in the House of Commons in London, Ramsay MacDonald made an effort to secure a positive response to this German feeler for a negotiated peace, but failed. There was a note in MacDonald's speech which particularly appealed to Söderblom—'The God of Christianity is not a village idol or a national idol. He is universal'. After this, Söderblom was to take a special interest in MacDonald's political contribution. Later in the year in November, Lord Lansdowne—'an extreme Conservative, to his bewilderment taken up by the Radicals',[1]—also made a move in the same direction.

In this connexion it should be pointed out that 'Stockholm 1917', the Socialist peace conference in the Swedish capital, could not but challenge Swedish opinion. A number of Swedish peace appeals were formulated. Of special importance to the Church was the sudden activity of the Swedish branch of the World Alliance.

Bishop von Schéele of Visby, chairman of the Swedish committee, had a plan, or at least an idea, however hazy. He felt that he had to act within the framework of the World Alliance. He wrote to Karl Fries, secretary of the Swedish committee:

I am considering the possibility of setting in motion some kind of opinion in the interest of peace, or rather for the constitution of an international

---

[1] A. J. P. Taylor, *The Trouble Makers* (1958), p. 150.

court of peace and arbitration for preventing war in the future. Utopia? Yes, but for such we must fight in order to get going at all.[2]

Von Schéele's suggestion did in fact result in an appeal for peace published in the name of the Swedish committee of the World Alliance in May, 1917, but it is important, at least for our purposes, to emphasize that this was made possible only because of the contribution of Söderblom and his co-workers. It was after a meeting in the Archbishop's house in Uppsala, on May 17, 1917, between Söderblom, Edv. Rodhe, and Westman, that a draft broadly on the lines of von Schéele's idea was proposed. This proved to be important also from the point of view of Söderblom's relation to the Alliance, for it was now that the old Bishop von Schéele, decided to relinquish his duties and to hand over the chairmanship to the Archbishop. With his keen interest in the political 'Stockholm' conference of 1917, Söderblom saw a duty to call together, in some connexion with the World Alliance, a religious equivalent to 'Stockholm'. This appeal to 'the Christian People of Sweden" implied: 1. Desirability of a lasting peace. 2. Duty of Christians to work for the reconciliation of the peoples. 3. Extension of ecumenical contact. 4. Establishment of a rule of law, a legal order 'whereby as far as possible war will be prevented in the future'.[3]

There were similar appeals about this time from the theological faculties in Lund and Uppsala—of which of course, Westman and Rodhe were members—and from the Swedish Free Churches.

Two international appeals from religious leaders were particularly important to Söderblom. These were issued from opposite sides of the ecclesiastical spectrum, one from Rome and the other from London. Pope Benedict who in September 1914 had sent out his *Hortatio,* now in August 1917, on the eve of the fourth year of the War published a bold, far-sighted peace appeal. In it he maintained that right must replace might and violence. His message contained definite proposals for methods of negotiation and simultaneous and mutual disarmament. The papal plan even went so far as to propose that each side among the belligerents should return territories taken during the War—Belgium and Alsace–Lorraine on the one hand, the German colonies on the other.

On the opposite side of the religious firmament, the English Society of Friends, in May, 1917, took a step which was to make a

---

[2] K. H. G. von Schéele, March 16, 1917, to K. Fries. Söderblom collection.
[3] K. B. Westman, Diary, May 17, 1917.

particular impression on Söderblom. In May, 1917, the yearly meeting of the Friends in London, issued an appeal 'To Men and Women of Every Nation who seek to follow Christ'. As we recall, in November 1914 they had been almost alone in feeling that Söderblom's appeal was *not* premature. In May, 1917, they took up this theme of timing: 'The longer we stand by consenting to the death of our fellow-men, the more clearly we show our disbelief in Him as the Saviour of the World from its present distress.' At the meeting of the Message Committee in June, 1917, they emphasized: 'The time is fully ripe for the calling of such a gathering.'[4]

The Friends wanted a peace which would be 'both just and lasting', and to that end appealed to Christians in characteristic terms to give themselves to prayer, whether in international conference, in small groups, or in solitary communion'.

They were not content with pious phrases but were bent on action. In July 1917 there was formed the British Council for Promoting an International Christian Meeting. The organization which grew up had unmistakable traits of an energetic pressure group. The nucleus comprised J. Allen Baker and Dr Henry Hodgkin, with Marian Ellis as secretary who in the first few months drafted and distributed a million copies of an appeal.

Söderblom had corresponded with these leading English Quakers of the World Alliance since 1914 and now from this date in 1917 he strengthened his contacts. Though he was far from being a Quaker himself, the prophetic courage and definite stand of the Friends greatly appealed to him. Besides, the English Friends began from now on to take a leading part in supporting Söderblom's appeals. If 'Uppsala' at this time became a name to be conjured with, a Christian parallel to the Socialist 'Stockholm', it was largely the result of pressure for action on the part of the London Quakers. The British Council began to have effect.

It drew in men from the Church of England and the Free Churches, such as Hubert Burge, bishop of Southwark and, later, Oxford, William Temple, E. W. Barnes, Alfred Garvie, Hugh Martin, Dean Inge, Mrs Creighton, wife of the Bishop of London, and Lord Parmoor.

The last-mentioned, and Willoughby Dickinson of the World Alliance, were leading Church of England laymen, courageous and

---

[4] At the June meeting of the Friends it was decided: 'Some leading men and women in other denominations should be asked to act in co-operation with us in an advisory capacity.'

versed in public affairs. Together with William Temple, they shared a twofold interest dear to Söderblom's heart: the International Christian Conference, and the League of Nations Society.[5]

This is what Temple had written in an editorial following upon the failure of the Socialist 'Stockholm, 1917':

We are sorry. . . . But the failure of Labour makes an opportunity for the Church. . . . The world is longing for the manifestation of something greater than warring nationalities. The Church exists to be that greater thing. Will it not act? The time is ripe and opportune.[6]

A week later he spoke again. In measured words with a prophetic note Temple challenged the Church to take the initiative.

In Christ, he felt, 'and nowhere else is what the world is longing for'. 'Here is something which unites the most passionately hostile.' 'We believe that an immense service to humanity could be rendered by an earnest attempt on the part of all sections of the Christian Church to say this thing unitedly to the world.'

'We desire, then, to see summoned an international interdenominational Christian conference, the primary aim of which shall be the proclamation of Jesus Christ as King, [and how to] promote obedience to the law of Christ in international affairs. Further, we would see [the churches] test how far they could reach agreement on the principles that should determine the terms of peace and the settlement of Europe, Asia, and Africa. It is at least conceivable that they would thus materially shorten the war. But as an act of witness the conference would be of incalculable importance. It would immensely increase the opportunity of the Church to guide the world when the war is over. After the war men will respect the Church in proportion as during the war it has been something more than national.'

In July 1917 it was Dickinson who suggested a novel plan for overcoming the difficulties of war-time travel: a 'Double Conference', one for the Allies, in Britain presumably, and the other in Germany for the Central Powers, with the Neutrals represented at each. A vigorous debate ensued but, though the idea of it and Dickinson's efforts deserve mention, nothing came of it, and it was William Temple, writing in *The Challenge,* who was the occasion of the first effective link with Söderblom's hopes and plans. Let Söderblom tell of it in his own dramatic words as, thirteen years later, in Oslo, when receiving the Nobel Prize for Peace, he looked back to that moment:

In the summer of 1917, rather downhearted after new setbacks, I went by train from Stockholm to Uppsala. . . . Quite near to Uppsala I pulled out

---

[5] Cf. H. R. Winkler, *The League of Nations Movement in Great Britain, 1914–1919* (1952), passim.
[6] *The Challenge,* September 21, 1917, p. 324.

of my pocket an English paper. On the first page I met the heading: 'The British Council for Promoting and International Christian Conference.' I could hardly believe my eyes. This was exactly what we in the North had planned. I sent a telegram, and my invitation was soon ready.[7]

After referring to the plans as conceived by the British Council, he went on to analyse the impression that William Temple's editorials and other articles had made on him.

Söderblom's shift of interest towards his British contacts coincided with a movement of opinion in Sweden as a whole: a change of government in Stockholm in the autumn 1917 made the country politically and economically look west. But in Söderblom's case the reason was the response he found in Britain towards his ideas.

In order to act he had to follow up the Scandinavian co-operation which he had already promoted. In the same month of March he had turned to his colleagues, the Primates of Denmark and Norway and suggested that together they should convene a Church Conference of Neutrals, comprising Scandinavia, Holland and Switzerland, and proposed August 1917 as a possible date. This would fit the general strategy he had conceived and was putting into effect through Nils Widner. Söderblom might also point to the International Student Conference planned to be held that year in Sweden. At this stage, too, on account of the fourth centenary of the Reformation, he could draw attention to the Protestant character of his proposed Conference. He hoped to gain the support of his Nordic colleagues for a renewed Peace Appeal. In the end the Appeal was sent out independently of any Conference, at Whitsun 1917, duly signed by the three northern Primates and by Church leaders in Holland and Switzerland. It was this appeal whose echo came back to him redoubled from the British Council and from the columns of William Temple's paper, the Quakers in demanding a 'just and lasting peace' even repeating a phrase which he himself with his desire for solidarity with all genuine efforts for peace had taken over from the International Socialist Movement—a righteous and durable peace. In its final form his Appeal contained the words: 'We therefore keep the hope of peace alive, and we bless all efforts for a righteous and durable peace.'

To this the British Council decided to send on 1 August 1917 'a sympathetic and affectionate response to the signatories of the Manifesto'. In so doing, the British groups also suggested that the invita-

---

[7] *Les Prix Nobel en 1930–1931*. Stockholm, 1931.

tion be sent to 'an ever widening circle, including the Roman and Greek churches'. By this suggestion they initiated a series of enquiries and proposals which were to be of great importance to Söderblom: certain members of the Council immediately set to work to try to establish contacts with Roman Catholic leaders, such as Cardinal Bourne, who in his turn referred to Cardinal Mercier of Malines, Belgium.

The correspondence in the following months with the British Council and with William Temple—an exchange of views in which Hellerström, the Swedish legation pastor in London played a valuable part—helped to clarify the issues, and define the aims of the hoped-for Conference. Scandinavians, in the year of the Reformation jubilee, tended to emphasize the Protestant programme, but the challenge from the British Council found Söderblom more than willing to attempt the suggested widening of scope.

Temple brought up another issue which was to be of particular importance in subsequent planning on Söderblom's part. The Scandinavian plans had, as a matter of course, been related to the idea of the World Alliance; this was natural in the case of Denmark, where Bishop Ostenfeld had from the beginning been chairman of the National Committee. In November, 1917, Söderblom himself took over the same post in Sweden. He succeeded Bishop von Schéele, and in this new capacity was eager to further the interests of the Alliance, the more so as already in 1915 he had suggested that the Berne Conference of the Alliance should be followed by a similar Uppsala Conference. Writing in *The Challenge* on November 23, 1917,—the article was significantly signed 'St. Birgitta's Day [October 7], 1917' —Söderblom said:

'We deem it wise to connect the proposed conference with the World Alliance. ...' In this connexion, he took the opportunity of explaining to the British public the proposed purpose of the Conference. This was to manifest 'the unity of the Church as something beyond and above nationality'. As distinct from the Papal peace appeal, Söderblom underlined that discussions of the causes of the War and of the political conditions of peace were to be definitely excluded—here he took up a point which, among others, Dr. Davidson, the Archbishop of Canterbury, had raised. Instead the Conference would 'strengthen the conviction of unity in all believing Christians, and promote that temper which makes for justice, goodwill and peace in the intercourse of nations'.

There was much in this with which William Temple could concur, but on one point he took a very determined stand, by dismissing the idea of co-operation with the Alliance. He was disappointed, he said.

So important an event as an assembly of representatives of all branches of the Christian Church in the middle of a world war should stand entirely upon its own basis. [The World Alliance] is an alliance of individual Christians belonging to various denominations. ... To make the supremely important event which we desire, an appendix to a branch meeting of this Alliance, seems to us to involve such a misrepresentation of the true proportion of things as to damage the chance of any effectiveness.[8]

Temple concluded this argument by expressing his hope that Söderblom would

repeat that effort, with better auspices, for a date when it may be possible to secure representatives from all countries for a conference that shall not be appended to anything else, but shall be its own occasion as we are sure it will be its own justification.

Temple's argument and appeal did not have an immediate effect; the invitation emphasizing co-operation with the World Alliance, signed by the three Scandinavian prelates, had, in fact, already gone out. In a longer perspective though, Temple's view was to make its impact.

Temple, theologian and Anglican churchman, emphasized his particular point with some energy. He wanted the Church conference to be independent, and thus to be free from any entanglement with the World Alliance. Söderblom's idea appeared more comprehensive. He wanted the World Alliance to be part of the conference. It was for this very reason that about this time he had agreed to be the chairman of the Swedish branch of the Alliance. He knew of course his own mind. He wanted a church conference on his own terms, in his own Uppsala. It was primarily to be a Nordic church conference, as a nucleus of a wider Evangelical fellowship, to deal with international and social problems. But on these terms he was prepared for the Alliance to send representatives, as necessary partners in the common undertaking.

Söderblom's invitation to the Uppsala meeting included the following:

... The necessity for mutual understanding with regard to arbitration and disarmament is not only proclaimed in many quarters but is universally

---

[8] *The Challenge,* Nov. 23, 1917, 'Notes of the Week'.

13 → 684363 *B. Sundkler*

acknowledged. The Pope speaks in the name of the whole Church when in championing peace he asserts those principles. But they need support from a strengthened sense of our unity in Christ. The present condition of the world insistently demands a manifestation of that spirit which excels patriotism or nationality, namely Christian brotherhood.

We consider it our duty to make an effort to use this opportunity. On December 14th the Committees representing the Scandinavian countries in the World Alliance for promoting International Friendship through the Churches will assemble in Uppsala, Sweden, to discuss their future policy (especially with regard to a possible conference of the Alliance in Scandinavia after the end of the War), and we hereby beg to invite some representatives from both groups of belligerent countries to take part in this meeting of the Committees.

On this occasion there should, of course, be no discussion of the causes of the war, nor of the political conditions of peace. The task of the conference should be to take up, without prejudice to national loyalty, those complicated questions that have arisen concerning international Christian fellowship. Above all we would by prayer and mutual understanding strengthen the conviction of unity among all believers in Christ, weighing the duty of the Church to resist the passions of war and promote that temper which makes for justice and goodwill in the intercourse of the nations.

We would emphasize that we consider it essential to have representatives of the belligerents from both sides. If—contrary to our expectations—one side should send no representatives, it might be necessary to revoke the invitation to the other side.

When this letter reached churchmen on either side of the abyss, the response was significant. The matter of timing was raised, as it had been on the occasion of Söderblom's earlier appeal in 1914. Generally it was felt to be premature, and also that the time allowed for preparation was too short. Temple underlined this in *The Challenge,* and the Archbishop of Canterbury, Dr. Davidson, agreed with him.

Davidson's main criticism, however, was of what he called a 'possible ambiguity' in the purpose of the Conference. He pointed to the difficulty of drawing a clear dividing line between 'matters purely religious in their character', and considerations of a political or semipolitical nature. Reactions from France and the United States and from elsewhere in Britain were similar: the idea was well-meant, but at that particular juncture in the War it was impossible to send representatives, quite apart from the problem of securing passports for them. From now on, at least in Britain and the United States the name of Söderblom tended to evoke the image of a somewhat impetuous man who would rush in where Anglo-Saxons feared to tread. From another point of view, it could be argued that Söderblom did in fact hesitate and wait. His British advisers—Anglicans and Quakers alike—had urged him not to omit the Roman Catholics and the Orthodox from his conference. There is no doubt that this idea greatly appealed to Söderblom, but it was a matter of timing and of the right approach. In fact, as Nils Karlström has shown, there was no invitation to the Vatican for the initial Conference in December, 1917. To be sure, the Pope was invited, but not until 1918, as we shall see presently. On the other hand, individual Roman Catholic leaders received an invitation from Söderblom for the 1917 meeting. These were the Cardinal Archbishops of Paris, Gran [Hungary], Cologne, Brussels (Mercier), and Vienna, together with Archbishop Kakowski of Warsaw.

There were two replies from these dignitaries. Cardinal von Hartmann of Cologne referred to Pope Benedict XV's own peace endeavour, and said it was for Catholics to align themselves with this. It was with particular joy that Söderblom read the generous answer from Archbishop Kakowski—in spite of the fact that his letter did not arrive in time for the Conference itself. In historical terms—thereby striking exactly the same note as Söderblom himself would have done—the Polish Archbishop expressed his joy that a conference was to be held on Swedish soil, which,

through the royal blood of the Vasa was united with Poland's own past. It was [he continued] meet and right that all Christians, without doctrinal differences, should find a common platform for the work leading to the fulfilment of the command of Jesus Christ: 'mandatum novum do vobis, ut diligatis invicem.' May the Almighty bless your work and allow you to harvest the fruits of your seed.[9]

Söderblom's relation to the Vatican is a problem in itself, to which we shall return, but however difficult it was at the time, he was always to refer to the concrete fact of Archbishop Kakowski's letter. As late as 1930–1931, he quoted it in full in this debate with Max Pribilla. To him it was the proof he needed to show that however rigid the official attitude of the Roman Catholic Church might be, there existed all the same individual Catholic bishops whose attitude was much more generous.

---

[9] Karlström, 'Rom u. die Stockholmer Bewegung. Ein chronologischer Beitrag. *Kyrkohist. Årsskrift*, 1931, p. 100–112. A. Kakowski, December 12, 1917, to Söderblom. Neutrala Kyrkokonferensen.

In testing beforehand the German reaction to a Conference, Söderblom turned particularly to Siegmund-Schultze, and this proved useful. The chief difficulty as far as Germany was concerned lay in finding the correct addressee (because of the German system of lawyers as Church Presidents). But Söderblom had found the right approach, Siegmund-Schultze thought, in inviting the oldest theological member of the German Evangelical Kirchenausschuss, as a kind of primate of the Prussian *Landeskirche*.

Siegmund-Schultze felt that the Swedish Archbishop had acted with caution and circumspection, 'in that he had invited those Church leaders whose spirit and wisdom and irenical attitude seemed to him assured'. Siegmund-Schultze was thus all in favour of German representation at the Conference. However he could not convince the official committee—the Kirchenausschuss—of the German Evangelical churches; the risks were regarded as too great. But individual German churchmen were prepared to accept the invitation, and in the end a highly qualified group, including Professor Ad. Deissmann, Mission-Director Axenfeld, and Siegmund-Schultze, was formed. Even Dr. Dryander, the German leader with most prestige at the time, wanted to attend, but was prevented on medical grounds. Not that those decisions were arrived at without certain inner tensions. It was war after all, and some of the German Church leaders did not trust Söderblom's intentions, neither could they be expected to express themselves in very complimentary terms when referring to the Allies.

One of them, who knew Söderblom from Leipzig, warned Siegmund-Schultze, in terms which show some of the suspicions with which Söderblom had to contend at this time; incidentally, the letter-writer tended to mix his metaphors in an alarming way:

I see you intend to go to Uppsala. You have thus been caught by the Söderblomian glue. That will be some egg-dance. ... Well—I am telling you—If you accept, so that in the eyes of the hypocritical English and Americans who regard Germany as a moral wrong-doer, some kind of apology is given—and that may be what Söderblom is aiming at—then it is goodbye to our friendship.[1]

Söderblom engaged the German minister in Stockholm and the German pastor, E. Ohly, for the negotiations. Siegmund-Schultze prepared a valuable memorandum where he pointed out the intended combination of the Conference plan with that of the World

---

[1] C. Paul, November 27, 1917, to F. Siegmund-Schultze. Soest, Ecum. Archives.

Alliance; he felt free to accept an invitation for a meeting with the Alliance.

Siegmund-Schultze's analysis of Söderblom's ideas, from the vantage point of wartime Berlin, is interesting. He referred to the meeting as arranged by Archbishop Söderblom in conjunction with Ostenfeld and Tandberg:

> Although this undertaking will coincide in space and time with the action of the World Alliance—the three Scandinavian Primates are at the same time chairmen of their respective Alliance committees—there is all the same a question of an enterprise extending beyond the circle of the World Alliance, which the Primate of the North undertakes on the ground of his earlier appeals and messages as a certain parallel or antithesis to the Primate of the South. Of course, in order to avoid this comparison, Catholic representatives too are invited, although, as I guess, without much hope that they will attend. By writing to them, there would also be the wish to make the Anglican Church—placed between Catholicism and Protestantism—more co-operative, and possibly also the Russian Orthodox Church.[2]

The British had suggested that invitations should be extended to the Romans and the Greeks. It is characteristic of the situation in 1917 that Söderblom, in thinking of the Orthodox, had in mind the Russian Orthodox Church. (Through Neander, he had personal contacts with the Church in Russia.) In the case of Germany, he had contacted the pastor at the German legation in Stockholm, and he used similar channels for the Russians. Provost Roumjantzeff of the Russian Orthodox congregation in Stockholm, was instructed to forward two invitations to Petrograd. These were for the Minister for Religious Affairs, Kartascheff, and the Metropolitan, Venianin. However, conditions in Russia being what they were at that time, no reply was received to these individual invitations.

In view of the fact that representatives from both the belligerent parties could not be secured, the invitation to the Germans was revoked as had been anticipated and the International Christian Conference was, at the last moment, re-organized as a Neutrals Church Conference. The days in the beginning of December, 1917, when this decision was taken by Söderblom were particularly hectic. The correspondence by letter, difficult at best in war time, was now turned into a nervous exchange of telegrams with as many of those concerned as possible. What Söderblom and his co-workers, greatly

---

[2] F. Siegmund-Schultze, Memorandum, November, 1917.

daring, had conceived as an international meeting, now became a conference which was virtually a meeting of Scandinavian churchmen. This was a limitation, yet, within the limits which the harsh necessity of war had drawn, there was a strength also in this Nordic concentration, a nucleus of what Söderblom at this time thought of as a *corpus evangelicorum*.

'*Uppsala, 1917*'

There were two non-Scandinavians at the Conference, both of them Professors of Theology—J. W. Pont, then of Amsterdam, and P. Böhringer from Basel; in the midst of war they represented at Uppsala a welcome contact with Europe, and with the World Alliance, treated as the special international envoys of the Alliance.

Paul Böhringer (1852–1929), a liberal theologian of the Biedermann school, and a diligent historian like Pont, a Swiss and the only non-Lutheran in the whole conference, was engaged as much in the Society for prevention of cruelty to animals as in the Swiss section of the World Alliance; a forceful preacher with a gift for the graphic illustration. This was his interpretation of the Uppsala Conference:

It is the case of the first effort to bring the Protestant Churches out of their unreal isolation from the drama of the world in order to realize in common the common ideals which everywhere emerge mightily into daylight. The Conference culminated in the ordination of young Swedish pastors who received the blessing from all participants.[1]

J. W. Pont (1863–1939) had likewise been sent to Uppsala by his national section of World Alliance, the Dutch. While Böhringer's travels had brought him to Palestine, Pont had overseas contacts with South Africa and was one of the Dutch authorities on the relations with that country. A pastor and history professor of one of the Lutheran minority groups in Holland, he was involved in attempts to unite the two Dutch Lutheran communities; at the same time, he had personal contacts with British Quakers. In December 1914 he had been engaged in helping two daring Friends from London who attempted, in the midst of war, to reach Berlin with a view to establishing peace; in the service of World Alliance he had a brief spell in the prison of Berne 1915, suspect of espionage. A generous

---

[1] *Totenschau zum Jahrgang 1930 des Schweiz. Pfarrer-Kalenders*, p. 413; *Schweiz. Protestantenblatt* (Basel), 1917, p. 5.

and dynamic Dutch preacher and lecturer, Pont thus had a dramatic story to share with his Scandinavian friends.[2] Apart from these two delegates, Uppsala, 1917 was altogether a Scandinavian conference. There were sixteen Swedes, ten Danes, and six Norwegians present. The Swedes included two bishops (the other was E. Lönegren, who in 1928 was to be the first Swedish bishop to take part in an Anglican consecration). There were six theological professors from Uppsala and Lund, and three Free Churchmen with close contacts with the World Alliance (these were the only Free Churchmen present).

Two of these, W. Gullberg, of the Swedish Missions Covenant and K. A. Jansson, a Methodist, had represented their Swedish Free Churches in Berne 1915 (Gullberg was also present at Constance 1914). Gullberg as well as the Baptist delegate, J. Byström, were members of the Swedish Riksdag. This triumvirate thus represented international contacts and World Alliance connexions, and were keenly interested in social and international problems.

There were also, characteristically, four members of what we have termed Söderblom's 'concentric circles of co-workers'; Westman, acting as General Secretary of the Conference, and Fries, Stadener and Widner. General O. B. Malm, a high ranking army officer with Pietistic and YMCA connexions, was included. This was his first experience of ecumenical work—eight years later he was to become Söderblom's trusted helper as administrator of the Stockholm Conference.

Even though the Conference was now overwhelmingly Scandinavian, the members did not lack an international background. As one would expect, the delegation of sturdy Norwegians brought with them the tang of fresh sea breeze into the stuffy academic atmosphere of Uppsala. Both Bishop Stoylen of Kristiansand and Dean Hansteen of Bergen had been pastors to seamen, the one in Cardiff, the other in New York; this they had in common with the host of the Conference. N. B. Tvedt was another Norwegian with long international experience. Stoylen had other things in common with Söderblom: a keen interest in the Scandinavians in America and in hymn-writing. Stoylen and Hansteen were, at this time, recognized leaders of the Pietists in Norway, while F. Klaveness, as far as theo-

[2] J. Loosjes, Naamlyst van predikanten etc. der Lutherskerk, Den Haag, 1925, p. 253. Handelingen en Levensberichten van de Maatschappij der Nederlandse Letterkunde 1941-42, p. 113; Oecumen. Berichten, 1940, p. 1. Letters from and interviews with J. W. Pont (Junior); L. C. Pont; A. C. Nielson.

logy and churchmanship were concerned, was regarded as a liberal, open to all new ideas, and with pacifist leanings. There was also that young journalist, E. Berggrav.

The Danes, likewise, included determined internationalists. Bishop Ostenfeld, as he was wont, did not say much at the Conference, but what he said was very much to the point: 'The Church of Christ is universal and international.' Pastor Hans Koch was among his closest friends, and had in fact succeeded him in the Copenhagen parish which he relinquished when he became bishop. Koch, too, had international contacts, particularly with social and Socialist interests in the Church of England. While the modern progressive school was thus represented, there were also leaders of the Pietistic Inner Mission. Dean J. Götzsche, later Bishop of Viborg, was to be known as 'the Bishop of the Inner Mission'.

An old friend of Söderblom's in the world of scholarship was also included in the Danish group, Chief Librarian H. O. Lange, one of the leading Egyptologists of his time, co-worker of Chantepie de la Saussaye. Lange was one of the great lay leaders of his Church. Lange the librarian, had brought an interesting colleague, for H. Larsen was also librarian, but to the Conference he was better known as the editor of the Danish pacifist review, *Fredsvarten*. He was to make the debate on peace in the Conference eventful.

The conference was held at Uppsala, a fact of great importance to the host of the meeting. Because of this, Söderblom could shape the conference according to his own design, and 'Uppsala 1917' helped him to work out in broad outline the pattern of a Church conference on international affairs.

To the worship of the conference he gave special attention. The debate was placed in a setting of worship and active church life, in and around the Cathedral. The broken bread in Holy Communion, participation in ordination, members of the conference preaching in the churches in Uppsala and Stockholm; this was also one of the main reasons why Söderblom, whatever anyone else was saying, insisted that the Conference must be held in Uppsala.

Professors Pont and Böhringer were placed by Söderblom in an unprecedented situation. On the Sunday of the Conference, there was an ordination in the Cathedral of Uppsala, and Söderblom ordained four young priests with his Norwegian colleague Bishop Stoylen assisting him. Söderblom made this occasion into a significant act of ecumenical fellowship, for, at his invitation, Böhringer and Pont also took part in the laying on of hands.

While the other assistants at the ordination service, all of them Lutheran, appeared in vestments, Böhringer and Pont, on Söderblom's suggestion appeared in their ordinary black suit as they took part in the procession and the ordination service itself.

The agenda of the Conference, proposed by Söderblom and Westman, had the following five themes:

1. The Christian's supramundane and supranational unity in Christ.

2. The War and the Christians.

3. Christians and the system of law.

4. How to overcome hatred, strengthen brotherhood and thus prevent war.

5. The supranationality of Missions.

These themes were discussed in the two days available, and resolutions were drafted and accepted. In fact there were not only the days, there were also the nights which were left for the drafting of resolutions. This was the time when in the Archbishop's study, Söderblom, Westman and Berggrav worked together as an incomparable team.

Berggrav, recalling these hours, makes the point that Söderblom enjoyed opposition and being contradicted:

> We two secretaries (the other was K. B. Westman) sat in his study far into the night. We sat in our shirt-sleeves and struggled with our respective languages—German and English—and Söderblom walked the floor to and fro, gesticulating and dictating. He found wonderful formulae—he was a master in that! and we very loyally registered the nuggets. ... Yet, I do not know how many times—in the beginning with some trepidation— we said: 'No, Archbishop, that won't do!' He laughed as he heard our arguments, and then said: 'No, you are right', and thus merrily started anew.[3]

Söderblom gave the introductory keynote address, on 'the Christians' Supramundane and Supranational Unity in Christ'. There are extant, a few pencilled notes in his hand and a few pages of an address of his, allowing us to get some faint idea of what he said on the occasion. These few indications are interesting both in themselves, and in what they do *not* contain.

At this time, at the end of 1917, he had not altogether found what was soon to become his constant and ever-recurring themes in his

---

[3] Berggrav, 'Nathan Söderblom', *Kirke og Kultur*, 1931, pp. 344–345.

ecumenical addresses, yet there was sufficient here to show where he stood in these matters, what was to be his line of approach. The fundamental antinomy between body and soul is present, and there is the faintest anticipation of his vision of an ecumenical movement through 'Evangelical Catholicity'.

The War is tearing apart what we hoped would grow together. The faith in evolution has gone bankrupt—but not the Christian faith. The Church is looking for reconciliation; the secret of sacrifice; the power and fellowship of suffering; a unity at the Cross.

a. The unity we seek is not confessional. The Faith and Order approach is aiming at an organizational Church conference. *We* must believe ... in the impossible.

b. The Evangelical ideal must also be contrasted against the approach of Rome. Why do we seem to do what the Pope is doing? [referring here to Pope Benedict's recent Peace Appeal]. There is no competition. We must rejoice at everything good which is being done. Yet, the Catholic Church is a State. This system is not anything for which we could strive, but rather it is fatal for Christendom as a whole. In attempting to force the Churches into an outer unity, stifling the unique peculiarities of the individual communities, Rome does not lay sufficiently deep foundation for the unity of the Church.

c. What is needed is an inner (*mer innerlig*) and Evangelical concept, of what the Creed refers to as a *Una Sancta Catholica Ecclesia*. Humanly speaking the future of Evangelical Christendom depends upon its ability to form for its spiritual purposes, a *corpus evangelicorum*. But a body without a soul deserves only to be buried. The outer unity of the Church is in no way useful if it is not animated by love and faith. The divine light has been broken into different colours. We do not regard them as of similar value, and we must not shirk our convictions, but we see those common [factors] which unite: we meet at the Cross.[4]

There was a deep sense of fellowship and unity in the group, yet there were also strong tensions, and this became obvious over the peace issue. Some of the Danes tended to take a pacifist standpoint; in particular Larsen urged that the Conference be a 'prophetic voice which could issue a watchword for the Christian attitude against war'. War was sin, he said, and even went on to suggest that the State itself was of the Evil One, and must be shunned by Christians. But, as Berggrav recalls, there was a Norwegian answer that 'no Conference, not even a neutrals conference, could, or even should,

---

[4] From the scribbled pencil notes in Söderblom's hand, and from his article 'Kyrkans enhet' in *For Kirke og Kultur*, 1918, pp. 1–4, the text has been reconstructed by the addition of prepositions etc.

try to act as prophet'. The Swedes, including Söderblom, seem to have tacitly concurred with this view. Söderblom was thus at his very first conference faced with an issue which, of course, was going to follow him to Stockholm, 1925, and beyond.

In the end, resolutions were agreed upon and published:

Christian Unity

When our Christian confession speaks of one Holy Catholic Church, it reminds us of that deep inner unity that all Christians possess in Christ and in the work of His Spirit in spite of all national and denominational differences. Without ingratitude or unfaithfulness to those special gifts in Christian experience and conception, which each community had obtained from the God of history, this Unity, which in the deepest sense is to be found at the Cross of Christ, ought to be realized in life and proclamation better than hitherto.

Christians and social life

The great mission of the Christian community is to be the salt of the earth and the light of the world. This the evangelical Church can and must fulfil only spiritually by means of her teaching and *life*. The Church ought to be the living conscience of nations and of men. Together with Christians in all belligerent countries, we feel deeply the opposition between the war and the spirit of Christ. We therefore wish to emphasize some principal points concerning the conduct of Christians in social life.

1. The Church, which has unfortunately not seldom laid more stress upon that which divides than that which unites, ought to enforce the ideal of Christian brotherhood, arouse and strengthen the judgement upon selfishness and employ all its powers in the work for the removal of the causes of war, whether these be of a social, economic or political nature.

2. Christians ought to feel their share in the responsibility for public opinion; they ought to serve the cause of truth and love in public national and international life as well as in personal relations, and try to understand the assumptions that lie behind the utterances, thoughts and deeds of others.

3. The Church ought to educate the nations to a higher degree of self-government.

4. The Church ought to work for international understanding and the settlement of international controversies through mediation and arbitration.

Christians and the system of law

According to the Christian conception, the consciousness of right and wrong and the system of law and political order that arise from this consciousness, are good gifts from God to man. The Gospel requires for its work at least an elementary legal order . . .

For this reason the Church has in the name of Christ to vindicate the sanctity of justice and law, and to demand its further development. In the first place, the Church ought to do this with all its might within each separate country, but it is also its imperative duty to support, as far as lies in its power, the effort for the international establishment of justice embodied in law. It ought therefore to fight against any glorification of violence and force at the expense of justice and law, and to lay stress upon the axiom that even the acts of nations and states are subject to ethical principles just as much as those of the individual, and that the commonwealth of nations ought to be built upon the principles of truth, justice and love.

The Church ought humbly to confess that it has failed in this respect, and ought to strive with all its might to rectify its shortcomings . . .

In taking farewell of this first largely frustrated attempt at holding an international Christian conference, it will be well to consider its contribution to the future. 'Uppsala 1917' was not only a quite limited affair, restricted as it was almost entirely to three Scandinavian countries, but, more important, it was *felt* to be limited. It was not exclusive: it was rather as if empty chairs cried out to be filled. Nevertheless, the enforced limitation allowed the members to brood on the theme discussed earlier by Söderblom and Widner— the *corpus evangelicorum* of the Northern Churches. This in turn gave the members cohesion, inspiring them to new resourcefulness in expanding the scope of the Conference, so that Söderblom was already feeling his way towards new horizons, towards contact with Catholics and the Orthodox. So, too, the great themes of the Conference beckoned the members towards a future when these would be taken up internationally: even perhaps to a time when the problem of war could be considered by those now fighting each other. Already the relationship between the League of Nations and an international Church Conference was a live issue.

As Söderblom emerged as inspirer, convener, and leader of such conferences, 'Uppsala 1917' had its special importance. Having just become chairman of the Swedish branch of the World Alliance, he could measure the overall situation and recognize his freedom to establish his relative independence of the Alliance—Temple's words were bearing fruit: a Church conference of this sort was its own justification. Söderblom at this time also found what he was to regard as his very own concept of a true Conference: a Conference whose acts and deliberations were rooted in worship, centred on a great Church and its services, and thereby endowing the human participation of those few days with its own particular values, intuitions and memories.

Outside Sweden, also, 'Uppsala 1917' lighted the future. Christian leaders in other lands saw a beacon. As Canon Masterman, later Bishop of Plymouth, expressed it to a December meeting in Oxford: 'In these days, our brethren from neutral countries lay the foundation of a Christian International.'[5]

No 'Uppsala' in 1918

Before the 'Uppsala 1917' conference broke up, Söderblom had got agreement for the calling of an international Christian conference in 1918. April 14 was the date urged upon him in telegram by Mrs Creighton, now widowed but a still energetic member of the British Council. The three Nordic primates were entrusted with the sending out of the invitations—indeed some had already been despatched before the December conference.

'We must believe in the impossible', Söderblom told the Uppsala Conference. To call an international Christian conference *during* the War was widely held to be impossible. After the cessation of hostilities, yes, but not during the War. Söderblom was adamant. He also knew that he had the support of his Anglican and Quaker friends in Britain. Precisely while the War raged, the international Christian conference should be called and held. There are a certain number of undated drafts of the invitations for the 1918 Conference. allowing us to study the stages whereby the purpose and structure of this projected conference developed.

'The general plan' of the conference, as Söderblom called it at this time, could hardly have been more general or vague. The English text of the first draft stated: 'The general plan is inspired by the Lord's Prayer', then followed the five themes treated at Uppsala, December, 1917.

1. The spiritual unity in Christ of his disciples, without loss of loyalty either to the talents and duties entrusted to nations or to the creeds they profess; facts and their expressions.
2. Christianity and War.
3. Potentialities and duties of the Church in counteracting the evil passions of war and promoting that frame of mind which makes for righteousness and goodwill among nations.

---

[5] Söderblom, *Stockholm 1925*, p. 604.

4. The Christian Doctrine on the sanctity of law and on the work of international legislation.

5. Actual church problems viewed practically and universally, e.g. the Mission Field.

In a later Swedish draft, Söderblom, with lead pencil, has crossed out No. 2. and suggested in the margin of his copy: 'The attitude of the Christian Church towards a League.' This proposal again had to give way to the final formula: 'The shortcomings of the Church with regard to the realization of Christian brotherhood and the spirit of Christ in all human relations. Penitence of the Church.'

It was to be an international conference on as wide a scale as possible. The invitations were directed to the following:

The Churches that had been represented at Uppsala, together with Finland; the Federal Council and the General Council in the United States, together with certain leading churchmen from that country; the Church of England and the English Free Churches; the Church of Scotland and the United Free Church of Scotland; the Evangelical Churches in Austria, France, Germany, Hungary; the Roman Catholic Church (invitation to be sent on the one hand to the Pope, on the other to 'other [Catholic] churchmen in a leading position'); The Old Catholic Church; the Orthodox Churches in Bulgaria, Greece, Rumania, Russia, Serbia, Turkey. With that charming optimism of Söderblom's with regard to languages, the invitation had the following exuberant statement on this point: 'Languages to be used at a general meeting will be French, German, English, Latin, Italian, Russian, and Greek. Interpretation will be made, if needed.'

The term 'General Meeting' hid a problem. There had to be representation from the belligerents of both sides, and great care had to be taken in order to avoid delegates' meeting with delegates from 'enemy countries'. A method had been devised by the Red Cross. According to this plan the 'General Meeting' referred to a plenary session where, after a decision taken by all the parties concerned, the total group of delegates thus could or would, by common consent, but as an exception, be convened together.

However, the harsh and intractable facts of war made the convening of the Conference impossible after all; already about the middle of February, 1918, Söderblom had to announce that the April meeting was postponed. The date was now fixed for September 8.

In both cases one day only was mentioned—'April 14' and 'September 8'. It must be taken for granted that Söderblom and his co-inviters had intended to modify this. Having once brought all the delegates together to the Conference, they would have had to announce the intended length of the meeting. Yet, our raising this matter allows us an understanding of how Söderblom visualized his projected international conference. Particularly in view of later developments in the years 1919—1925, it is important that we should do so.

Söderblom constantly said that the main thing about an ecumenical conference was *the fact* that people were brought together for worship and common council. He did not conceive of these conferences primarily as occasions for technical debate over a protracted period of time.

We suggest that his almost lighthearted reference to a one day international conference in time of war—'April 14' or 'September 8' —must be understood in these terms and as the embryo of this kind of conference.

For weeks Söderblom was elated and full of hope; to his confidant, Kolmodin, in Constantinople he wrote:

It looks as if we will get a rather mighty ecumenical gathering but without sectarian Rome. The Polish episcopate has however, through the Archbishop in Warsaw, expressed unconditional agreement. From England, 25 delegates have been promised. The Moderator of the Church of Scotland will come. The Germans will send their best men. The Conference was postponed largely because the whole thing takes on much bigger propoitions than we thought at first. By September everything will be so well planned, that the Americans will only have themselves to blame ... if they fail to attend.[1]

In the same optimistic vein he could write to Siegmund-Schultze in Berlin and to Marian Ellis in London.[2]

Soon he sent a telegraph message to Kolmodin: 'Ecumenical Conference September eighth excellent prospects.'[3] Of course Kolmodin needed all the encouragement he could get in order to press the matter with the Orthodox.

In London, Hellerström, the Swedish legation pastor, kept Söderblom in touch with a number of British Church leaders, and reported on their reactions to Söderblom's overtures.[4] One difficulty

---

[1] Söderblom, March 3, 1918, to J. Kolmodin.
[2] Cf. F. Siegmund-Schultze (ed.), *Nathan Söderblom*, p. 26.
[3] Draft of telegram, April 25, 1918, UUB.
[4] A. Hellerström, Feb. 12, 1918, to Söderblom. The young pastor showed that he had an instinct for the tactics of diplomacy. According to the instructions of the Neutrals Conference, invitations to Britain went to the Church of England and

had not been foreseen, and this concerned a semantic problem. Hellerström reported that influential people 'objected to the use of the word *ecumenical* as it might be resented by the Vatican. In its place, the word 'international' was suggested.[5]

The reference to the Vatican was indicative of the emphasis which certain Britons—Anglicans and Quakers alike—at this time placed on inviting the Pope. Söderblom had informed Hellerström and Marian Ellis that the Pope of Rome and the Patriarch of Constantinople were to be approached and invited in accordance with the decision taken at Uppsala. One of those who had definite views on this matter was the Archbishop of Canterbury. Dr. Davidson had sounded a certain number of political and church leaders, and Dr. Bell expressed Davidson's attitude very neatly: 'The Archbishop saw both the importance, and even more clearly, the difficulties of the Uppsala proposal.'[6] The wording of Dr. Davidson's letter to Söderblom illustrates this:

If you are able to tell me that the invitation is accepted by the authorities of the Roman Catholic Church, that the Pope gives it his benediction, and that duly accredited Roman Catholic representatives from such countries as France, Italy, Austria, Spain, and the United States of America, will officially attend it, we shall feel it to be both a privilege and a duty that the Church of England should bear its part. Similarly we should desire to see duly accredited representatives from the Eastern Churches in Russia, in the Turkish Empire, and in Greece.

It was in this connexion that Archbishop Davidson, in his own way, pointed out the problem with that big new word for international fellowship: 'We shall not feel it to be possible to send representatives to a gathering, which, while claiming to represent the organized forces of the Church of Christ in Europe (you even use the word Oecumenical), was without accredited spokesmen belonging to the Roman Catholic Church and the Orthodox churches of the East.'[7]

At that time, Johannes Kolmodin in Constantinople and Harald Bildt in Rome, were working for the very thing for which Dr. David-

the English Free Churches, and the Church of Scotland and the Free Church of Scotland. Hellerström insisted that a special invitation also be sent to the Welsh Free Church: 'It is important that they should be included as Lloyd George is closely connected with them.'

[5] A. Hellerström, Jan. 3, 1918, to Söderblom.

[6] G. K. A. Bell, *Randall Davidson*, p. 885.

[7] R. Davidson, Feb. 12, 1918, to Söderblom.

son was pleading. It could possibly be added that if the efforts on Söderblom's behalf were not always as fruitful as he had expected, the fault was not altogether his. Hellerström felt that he could put the argument about the participation of the Russians to good use. 'If it were shown', he wrote to Söderblom about Dr. Davidson on February 12, 1918, 'that it would be absolutely impossible for the Russians to [get a permit to] go to Berne, he might change his view.'

Allied opinion was thus largely against holding a conference during the War. This was the view of Anglican bishops such as the Archbishop of Canterbury and Bishop Theodore Woods of Peterborough. In view of the active support given later to Söderblom by Bishop Woods, his attitude at this time is of interest. But Söderblom had at least one unwavering supporter in London, the secretary of the British Council, Marian Ellis. The interesting point about her amazing activity in the interest of an Uppsala conference was the international outreach of her appeal. She bombarded churchmen in the United States, in France, and in Switzerland, with her 'Uppsala' message.[8]

She was to find, like her co-worker Dr. Hodgkin, and like Archbishop Söderblom, that some of the most determined resistance to the plans came from American churchmen such as Bishop Brent and William P. Merrill. This was understandable in view of the fact that America was at this time beginning to bear the brunt of the War, and that all their energies had to be devoted to one task.

We cannot go into detail here and enumerate the reactions from other countries. In Germany, particular concern was shown over the fate of their Missions overseas. 'Uppsala, December, 1917,' had issued a statement on Missions, incorporating in its resolutions certain findings from a conference in Stockholm in 1916. German mission leaders would have preferred a stronger emphasis on the supranationality of missions and Director Axenfeld told Söderblom so.

Though Söderblom was sustained, and inspired to new efforts by the support from the Friends as well as from other individual churchmen, all these efforts by him and his co-workers in many lands proved in the end to be of no avail. As September, 1918 approached,

---

[8] One of her French Catholic correspondents, M. C. F. Honoré, writing from Lyndhurst, England, on November 2, 1918, said to Marian Ellis: 'Let us lift up our heads and face the truth: indeed why not "die" as "Upsala" and "ressucitate" (sic!) as "Jerusalem"? Would not that appeal to Selma Lagerlöf.'

it was once again impossible to secure visas for the participants in Oslo and Copenhagen, and on the actual date, September 8, they sent a telegram to those most concerned abroad. The wording was unmistakably Söderblom's: *'Our prayers hold ecumenical conference.'*

In working towards his projected 1918 conference, Söderblom used a great deal of energy and developed all his ingenuity and his considerable powers of persuasion to further the choice of the one place he had in mind, a certain cathedral town dear to his heart. It is worth considering why.

As early as December, 1917, Hellerström in London had told him that the British, almost without exception, wished the Conference to be held in Switzerland. The Anglicans, from the Archbishop of Canterbury downwards, were for this idea.

At the Neutrals Church Conference, invitations were extended from all the five countries represented: Switzerland, Holland, Denmark, Norway, and Sweden. In the correspondence during the following weeks, the possibility of Sweden and Uppsala was mentioned only to be rejected; it was difficult to get there in time of war. There was also another objection, that Sweden was, in certain church circles in Britain and the United States, looked upon as pro-German, and therefore out of the question. Allen Baker informed Hellerström that it would probably be impossible to get passport visas for Sweden.

Söderblom wrote long letters to Hellerström on this matter, on December 19, 1917, and January 3 and 30, 1918. On the latter date, Westman too wrote to Dickinson in the same vein, obviously representing Söderblom's views. The place Söderblom wanted was Uppsala.

Söderblom did not immediately say this in so many words. He referred to Scandinavia in general, and freely suggested Gothenburg or Oslo on a par with Uppsala. (In an early typewritten draft, one of his co-workers, Westman or Brilioth, had referred to 'Christiania' [Oslo] as the place, only to have the word crossed out by Söderblom who added 'or Uppsala'.) Soon however, Bishop Tandberg had to inform Söderblom that the Norwegian Government could not accept an international Church Conference in the capital during the War; this strengthened Söderblom's hand.

For the choice of place, there was more to it for Söderblom, than mere geography. He argued his case as he wrote to Hellerström in London:

Here in the North [he wrote] the Conference would be sustained by strong participation of the Churches and their men generally. Through the episcopal office we have both freedom of action and a concept of the Church common to Anglicans and Swedes, and thereby a connexion [with Britain] which is lacking in Switzerland.

In Uppsala (or Gothenburg) [he went on] the Conference would be given more sanctity and dignity, and also be arranged in a manner which to our belligerent brethren, particularly the English, would be reassuring.

[If Switzerland were chosen] we shall do our best there, but then, the ecumenical Church Conference would be just another Congress among others. In Uppsala or Gothenburg, it will be what *Challenge* wants it to be.

Another advantage [he continued] is that an individual particularly interested in the Neutrals [Church] Conference, has promised to put at my disposal money to cover all costs for the coming Conference, if it is held in Uppsala.

Söderblom had this last sentence in the typed draft for his letter to Hellerström, but then decided to wait till the right occasion presented itself, and crossed out the sentence with pencil. An Uppsala business man, Major A. Sjöstedt, who later was to appear as the financial benefactor of Söderblom's Conference plans, had already met Söderblom and given him certain assurances.

A fortnight later, Söderblom was prepared to play this card and make it known to Britain, through Hellerström, that 'a layman' had undertaken to carry all expenses if Uppsala was chosen. 'Now', he added, 'voices in favour of Uppsala as the right place were making themselves heard even more strongly.' In his need for arguments, he added one which was possibly lost on English Quakers, at least in war-time: 'In Uppsala we would be glad to show the Conference a unique exhibition of old Swedish ecclesiastical art.'

By the end of January he had built up five arguments in favour of Uppsala, which he presented to Hellerström:

1. 'The Russian Orthodox and such Polish churchmen as have been brought to Russia, could not get passports through Germany. ... Therefore to invite them to Switzerland would be almost a mockery, and we do not wish to meet without this part of the Church.'

2. 'The three inviting bishops could not travel to or through a belligerent country.' The task entrusted to the three Nordic primates is here used as an argument against the threat of a Swiss alternative. Westman pressed this argument one degree further in his letter of the same date to Dickinson: 'The three Scandinavian Primates', he wrote, cannot go outside Scandinavia during the War. No doubt other representatives could be sent from here, but I imagine it would be of special value for the conference if the inviters take part personally.'

3. 'The Scandinavian churches form a broader spiritual background. Nowhere is the Conference sustained by warmer interest and prayer.' Switzerland has no ecclesiastical authorities with the same freedom of action as the Scandinavian bishops.'

4. 'If the Conference were to be at Uppsala, an individual has placed all the necessary funds at our disposal.'

5. 'Further, the Olaus Petri Foundation at Uppsala University has decided to invite a number of lecturers to the University in April.'

He mentioned three of his friends whom he hoped to see as Olaus Petri lecturers: Dean Inge, Dr. Cairns, both from Britain, and Professor Glubokovski from Petrograd. He felt that the contacts through the Foundation were making Uppsala into an international centre, and Söderblom was anxious that Hellerström should press home this argument with the British: 'During the War, a number of Frenchmen have visited me. Next Autumn we expect Bergson. Tell this confidentially to Tatlow, Ellis, and others.'

These asides illuminate his manner of persuasion; the chances of getting Bergson and Inge were slender indeed but such was his conviction that people *must* see the strength of his argument, that happy anticipation was sometimes allowed to take the place of established fact.

It would be misleading to interpret this concern for 'Uppsala' as simply a manifestation of a certain ecclesiastical possessiveness on Söderblom's part. In addition to the general political, geographical and ecclesiastical factors just mentioned, there was the atmosphere of worship that had informed 'Uppsala 1917', centered as it was on the Cathedral there. Söderblom was already acting out, as it were, in the sacred drama of Swedish church life, what was soon to emerge as his ecumenical theology; he had already coined the formula 'Evangelical Catholicity', and he gave his first lecture on that subject in 1918, to a Swedish S.C.M. group.[9] The meeting with other churches, not least in the Neutrals Church Conference, quickened his appreciation of the values and potentialities of the Swedish tradition of episcopacy and Evangelical Catholic worship. He had stated in 1914, on at least two occasions, that the Church of Sweden had a uniting function. He did not use the term 'bridge-church', but the concept as such he held and applied it to his own Church.

---

[9] His lecture on 'Evangelical Catholicity' was given at Sigtuna, Aug. 13, 1918. As far as we can make out it was never printed. The manuscript is in the Nathan Söderblom collection.

All these considerations of his were involved in his plea for Uppsala. He felt that he wanted to form and fashion the very atmosphere of the Conference to be convened. All his care for the worship at 'Stockholm 1925' and his rather lukewarm attitude to 'Lausanne 1927' must be understood in this light.

The Olaus Petri Foundation—
Instrument of Ecumenical Outreach

When the ecumenical conference had thus been twice postponed, it had been a frustrating experience to have to inform those interested that there would after all be no conference. But Söderblom was not defeated. He set about finding other ways and means. 'I have been brooding,' he wrote in June, 1918, to Kolmodin in Constantinople. 'Now I see the solution.' It proved to be a solution of limited scope yet with a significance of its own, and characteristic of Söderblom's approach to ecumenical relationships at this time.

His solution was an invigorated use of the Olaus Petri Foundation, as we have already seen, an Uppsala university lectureship Foundation. It had not been inactive during the War. In 1916 Söderblom could welcome Professor Albert Hauck—a former colleague of his from Leipzig—for an important series on 'Germany and Britain, and their ecclesiastical relationship' (published the following year, in German and Swedish). Söderblom decided to invite a number of lecturers, practical churchmen and academic theologians, to Uppsala at the end of 1918 to lecture on their own churches, thus presenting a broad picture of the European church situation in the last months of the War. He explained to Kolmodin:

'We are anxious to see the Orientals here. It will be a meeting between Orthodox and Evangelical Christianity. We shall keep the Olaus Petri lectures as the fixed point. At all costs, see to it that the Patriarch sends a representative. He would be allowed to lecture in Greek. The emissary of the Greek Patriarch will be honoured here above all others. He will lecture first, after my introduction on September the 9th, then Old Catholics, Russians, Bulgarians, then Hungarians, Englishmen, French, Germans, etc. Do you accept my view that we should now concentrate on these lectures, which will be published together? Let the lectures be a *fait accompli,* a witness to *Una Sancta Catholica,* and a further preparation for the Conference to be held later.'

One can watch, while the Archbishop dictates his letter, the whole lecture plan emerging and taking shape before his eyes. He was now prepared to send his invitations in all directions. K. B. Westman and Yngve Brilioth acted as his secretaries, and possibly also advised him on whom to approach. But with Söderblom inviting the lecturers, one had to expect certain surprises. It is characteristic of Söderblom's loyalty to old friends and co-workers that he should turn to Chantepie de la Saussaye, the Dutch professor of History of Religions. Chantepie replied that, at seventy, he was too old for such an effort. He recommended Professor J. W. Pont in his stead. It goes without saying that Söderblom insisted that he should get some of his French friends for this purpose. As he was wont to do, he charged the Swedish Embassy pastor, in this case in Paris, with the task of enlisting 'either Adolphe Lods or Wilfred Monod or Paul Sabatier or K. Soulier'. He even considered the famous Catholic modernist Alfred Loisy but was a little hesitant as to his suitability in this connexion. He added: 'We shall see to it that there is no risk of contact with any Germans. Deissmann will not lecture until October.' That he had to act with care and circumspection became obvious when *Le Temps* carried an article attacking the dangerous idea of ecclesiastical contacts in neutral Uppsala. Söderblom the Prochancellor of the University of Uppsala, knew how to sidestep such criticism. In a telegram he assured *Le Temps* that the Olaus Petri Foundation was a Swedish university institution, altogether divorced from any church conference.

It is difficult to know whether Söderblom in every case expected his lecturers to have anything significant to say on the ecumenical problems of the time. In certain cases they were invited for representative reasons more than anything else: they represented sectors and traditions of the universal Church which had little contact with other parts of the world. In other cases Söderblom felt he had a right to ask for something creative. He therefore turned to such men as could be relied upon to deliver a prophetic message on social problems. He tried Wilfred Monod—but Monod who was already committed to a trip to the United States could not come to Uppsala. He was all the more eager therefore to get Siegmund-Schultze of Berlin. He was well aware of the brilliant and courageous way in which Siegmund-Schultze had edited his review *Die Eiche* since 1913. In his case, Söderblom wanted to inspire his lecturer to make a bold statement. He wrote in October, 1918: 'Would you treat the social-economic-democratic question? Here the Church is faced with a revolution. The Gospel must free itself from the chains of "good society" in order to become salt and light. I suggest to you that you treat this problem in an utterly radical and frank manner.'

We have already seen how Söderblom invited the Greek Orthodox to contribute to his Uppsala lectures. There were other Orthodox Churches to be approached. In the midst of the Bolshevik revolution, Professor Nikolai Glubokovski at Petrograd (now Leningrad) received the following telegram: '*Fondation Olaus Petri vous invite donner conférences dans Université septembre. Söderblom.*' Glubokovski was dumbfounded. Before the War, he had had some acquaintances but no close friends in the West, he said, but, he went on in a fine confusion of images, 'from 1914, after the outbreak of the War, the whole Occident disappeared from my horizon behind the smokescreen of human madness and the din of cannons'. About Söderblom and the Olaus Petri Foundation he knew hardly more than the names. Getting a passport and some money to buy a ticket in revolutionary Russia meant endless difficulties. These however were overcome by a new telegram from Söderblom: 'Come. Here we will arrange everything.'

Glubokovski lectured on Orthodoxy and attempts at union in the Orient. In him, Söderblom and his co-workers came into contact with a great and generous representative of Orthodox piety.

After the years of neutral Sweden's relatively forced isolation from the rest of the world, Söderblom himself found these new, or renewed contacts bracing and inspiring. It was with great satisfaction that he could make the following note in his diary for September 30, 1918: 'Bishop Henrik Geduly from Nyireghaza, Hungary, lectured lucidly and brilliantly. After the lecture the American, Donald A. Lowrie, lately active among prisoners of war in Russia, turned up in the Council Chamber of the University. Professor Glubokovski is staying at Kiplingeberg, Dr. Carlyle is in Stockholm, will return on Monday to conclude his series of lectures.' These brief notes may not appear to contain anything extraordinary or particularly interesting, but in actual fact, each of the names represented great efforts of persuasion on the part of Söderblom and his few co-workers, and meant important links with the churches and countries.

The important series of Olaus Petri lectures was introduced by Söderblom himself as inspector of the Foundation, with an exposition of his beloved theme 'Evangelical Catholicity'. Söderblom also spoke in this series on the peace efforts of the Church.

The lecturers were as follows:

Great Britain: A. J. Carlyle, James Cooper, H. T. Hodgkin, W. B. Selbie.

Germany: Ad. Deissmann, F. Rittelmeyer, R. Schairer, F. Siegmund-Schultze.

France: K. Soulier.

Holland: J. W. Pont.

Switzerland: Fr. Würz.

Hungary: H. Geduly, E. V. Révéz.

Russia: N. Glubokovski.

Northern countries: J. Helgason, A. Hjelt, A. S. Poulsen, Jens Tandberg.

Sweden: N. Söderblom, J. A. Eklund, Edv. Lehmann, K. B. Westman.

Swedish editions of the lectures were published in 1918–19, and in English in co-operation with Peter Ainslie, in *The Christian Union, Quarterly* in Baltimore.

The Olaus Petri lectures at Uppsala University from the autumn of 1918 were characteristic of Söderblom's approach. No one but Söderblom, Archbishop, Prochancellor of the University, and former professor, would have thought of using an academic foundation as a tool for furthering ecumenical contacts. Week after week, leading international churchmen and theologians found their way to Uppsala, in spite of visa difficulties and the other vicissitudes of the times. Söderblom showed that he possessed the magic wand to turn these academic occasions into something exciting and stimulating. The University, the Archbishop's house, and the Cathedral became a centre where people felt something of the reality of the Universal Church. A new generation of Swedes was exposed to new religious visions and widening hopes. For some of the lecturers coming from afar after the World War, the idea of distant Uppsala assumed a surprising significance. Söderblom himself acquired a deeper and more exact knowledge of personalities and movements in the Church after the War, for as a matter of course he used each one of these occasions to the full to establish personal contacts and, if possible, institutional relationships.

Finding the Way

The World War had come to an end, at long last. Wilson and Versailles had brought peace on earth—yet there was no peace. From his rooms at King's College, Cambridge, a young economist spoke for mankind:

> In this Autumn of 1919, we are at the dead season of our fortunes. The reaction from the exertions, the fears, and the sufferings is at its height. Our power of feeling or caring ... is temporarily eclipsed. Never in the lifetime of men now living has the universal element in the soul of man burnt so dimly.[1]

Keynes was prepared to give his own particular interpretation of that phrase 'the universal element'. One of the churchmen who had taken cognizance of Keynes' book was Söderblom himself; he had his version of the idea of universality.[2] At this time Söderblom tried to answer the question: Can we expect a renewal of Religion? 'The world formula has been changed', he said. 'We used to believe in culture and progress.' In 1919, people could no longer believe in such things, 'we can only believe in love and righteousness', proclaiming 'the invisible Kingdom of the Spirit as opposed to a merely earth-orientated existence. ... No anaemic old or new intellectualism is good enough'. He showed mankind to the 'source of life ... the secret of the Cross'. We do approach a renewal of religion, of this Söderblom was as sure as of God Himself. 'For God now visits the world. Do you sense how close He is to each one of us? To-day is the day of the disciples at Emmaus.'[3]

From this vantage point Söderblom looked at the world in 1919. The Götterdämmerung over Germany cast deep shadows. The hunger blockade led to starvation and suffering both in Germany and

---

[1] J. M. Keynes, *The Economic Consequences of the Peace* (1920), pp. 278–279.
[2] To F. Siegmund-Schultze, Söderblom wrote on Feb. 28, 1920, 'I receive an increasing evidence from Britain and America condemning in most serious terms the peace of violence. I take it for granted that you know Keyne's (!) book'. Siegmund-Schultze, *Nathan Söderblom* (1966), p. 50.
[3] Söderblom, *Gå vi mot religionens förnyelse?* (1919).

Austria. The war-guilt clause, Article 231 in the Versailles Treaty, caused bitter resentment; even a peacemaker like Siegmund-Schultze responded in *Die Eiche* (Dec. 1920) by drawing attention to a problem comparable to the matter of war-guilt, that of the guilt *after* the War.[4] It was also at this time that Oswald Spengler conceived and wrote his *The Decline of the West*.

As if they were one

As chairman of the Swedish branch of the World Alliance, Söderblom took certain initiatives directly related to the international scene. In November 1918, an intense campaign for a 'righteous peace' was carried on all over Sweden. Söderblom and the Alliance issued 'an earnest appeal to those in authority to try to bring about a peace that will, as far as possible, prevent the growth of new national hatred and desire for revenge, a peace that will lead to reconciliation and mutual confidence between the nations, a peace that will prepare the way for the dominion of love and righteousness in the world'. A series of some 1,200 meetings was held all over Sweden and the appeal gained well over 310,000 signatures.

In June 1919, Söderblom took the initiative again. A memorandum was sent to the Peace Conference at Versailles saying that the Peace Treaty 'should make provision for the spiritual forces of a religious and moral nature that are active in the World'. They specified two sets of problems which were regarded as particularly important: that of freedom of minorities, and that of the position of Christian missions. The other Scandinavian and the Dutch Alliance branches joined with the Swedish leaders in this appeal.

Söderblom followed the Swedish debate about the League with special interest. Conservative forces warned against having anything to do with the League of Nations: 'A power organization on the old imperialistic basis, to secure the fruits of victory and mask Anglo-Saxon world domination', was one comment (by R. Kjellén).[1] Even those Swedes who most fervently worked for the League, Liberals and Social Democrats, pointed out certain weaknesses in its organization.

Söderblom himself, anxious to promote the cause of the League, referred to the problem in terms of his antinomy, 'body-soul'. This

---

[4] *Die Eiche*, 1920, p. 162.
[1] Cf. H. Tingsten, *The Debate on the Foreign Policy of Sweden 1918–1939* (1949), p. 18.

was common in World Alliance circles in different countries at this time; Wilfred Monod in Paris, Siegmund-Schultze in Berlin, Talbot in Winchester, all of them leaders in their national branches of the Alliance, varied the theme of the League as 'a body which needed a soul', the soul being 'Christ the leader and the Captain', in Talbot's version.[2] To use Monod's expression, 'a League of Nations in need of a soul, a League of Churches',[3] slightly modified by his German fellow-Christian Siegmund-Schultze, who said: 'The task of the World Alliance is to give to the body of the League of Nations a soul, the League of Churches.'[4]

It was therefore not altogether original to Söderblom when he used this same concept and expression on different occasions. In January 1919, he persuaded the Swedish branch of the World Alliance to issue an appeal: 'As we are convinced that the great thought for the future has a Christian kernel, we recommend our fellow Christians to remember ... the League of Nations. In a Swedish lecture of that year he would state: 'The League of Nations must become religion. The peoples long for a supranational order of society, and its realization must become a religious concept."[5]

In his capacity as both chairman of the Swedish branch of the World Alliance and Archbishop, Söderblom, in November 1918, took another step which was of great importance for his contacts with Germany and Austria. He issued an appeal for help for German and Austrian children, thereby setting in motion relief work on a large scale in the summer of 1919. The first batch from Germany and Austria in the summer of 1919 comprised some 1,700 children. Being Söderblom, he was not content with mere words, however eloquent. With his infinite capacity for taking pains, he himself by letter, telephone and personal visit, attended to a large number of the cases. His initiative also inspired the Swedish Red Cross under the chairmanship of Prince Carl, and the Swedish 'Save the Children' organization to greater efforts, and Söderblom's initial vision and example had in this field an effect similar to that at the beginning of the war with regard to prisoners of war.[5a]

---

[2] Edward Talbot, *Spiritual Sanctions of the League of Nations*, 1919, pp. 10–11.
[3] *Christianisme Social*, 1920, p. 146.
[4] F. Siegmund-Schultze in *Die Eiche*, 1920, p. 217.
[5] *Handbook of the World Alliance*, 1919, p. 53, Stockholms Tidningen, April 12, 1919.
[5a] Siegmund-Schulze reports that the mean increase of each child in the three months in Sweden was about 20 lbs., the record being held by a twelve years old boy whose weight increased by 39 lbs. *Die Eiche*, 1920, p. 18.

The Swedish effort was largely independent of the measures carried out on the initiative of the other national branches of the World Alliance, but Söderblom kept in touch with international leaders of the movement in other countries, particularly Siegmund-Schultze in Berlin and Willoughby Dickinson in London. After the frustrating years of the war, the year 1919 was the time when the World Alliance had to act in order to live up to its challenging name, 'The World Alliance for Promoting International Friendship through the Churches'. In point of fact of course, the international organization of the Alliance consisted of little national groups in Europe: in Great Britain and France, the Low Countries, the North and the Baltic, together with Switzerland, Italy and Hungary. In most cases the national committees were made up of a few individuals, and any connexion with the Churches as such was tenuous. In the United States, it was the Federal Council of Churches which constituted the national representation, and this gave the organization its particular strength. From Söderblom's point of view at this time, it was the British Council that attracted the most interest.

During the war Söderblom felt that his ideas had met with especially effective response from Britain, and his contacts in this direction were to be strengthened in the nineteen–twenties. We notice in this connexion that this was the general tendency in Sweden at the time: 'During the 1920's Britain stepped into Germany's old place in the Swedish cultural world.'[6] There were other, special, reasons why Söderblom took an interest in the British debate, and we must digress for a moment to consider the British scene.

The World Alliance owed its existence to British pioneers, and the British Council was one of the strongest branches of the organization. The secretary, Sir Willoughby Dickinson, a lay leader in the Church of England, was at the head of a number of Liberal and progressive causes at this time. In 1915 he had become chairman of the League of Nations Society, and he indefatigably promoted the idea of the League. From 1918 the Executive of the British Council of the Alliance devoted its propaganda to the establishment of a League. When, after Allen Baker's death in 1918, the Bishop of Winchester, Edward Talbot, became President of the British Council, he supported this cause with determination.

Talbot was chairman of two important Church Commissions at

---

[6] H. Tingsten, *The Debate on the Foreign Policy of Sweden, 1918–1939*, p. 28.

the end of the war. The one, an Anglican Commission, had grown out of the national concern for repentance and hope, and dealt with 'Christianity and Industrial Problems', and Talbot shared the sense of urgency that characterized the members of his commission. These were years in the history of the Church of England when not only parsons, but even bishops were impatient, and Talbot was no exception.

The other commission was interdenominational, concerned with the Church and the Army. We suggest that something of the same *ethos,* a common approach, conditioned and coloured the reports of both these Church Commissions. They were of course expressed in differing theological terms, but theology and ecclesiology in the last months of the World war were modified by the existential and traumatic experience of war. Some of the men of the commissions had been through fire; they had suffered the terrible loss of their next of kin in the war. Talbot had had a heavy share of this: his son Gilbert was killed at Hooge in August 1915. Another son, Neville, as Assistant Chaplain-General, was to write the book *Religion Behind the Front.*

'Seen against the vast and terrible background of the trenches and the battlefield, ecclesiastical divisions looked spectral and unreal', said the report on the Army and Religion (p. 421). The Commission felt that this would lead to a 'new fellowship of the Spirit', out of which has sprung 'the Interdenominational idea'. The words were those of David Cairns, the Scottish Presbyterian who was the secretary of the Commission, but there can be no doubt that Talbot as the chairman who signed the report shared the view thus expressed. In a pamphlet on *The Spiritual Sanctions of a League of Nations* (1919) Bishop Talbot himself referred to what he called 'the influence of the War upon human morale; its creative moral power', (p. 7), in that it had brought out new capacities in character and new standards of value, 'in a way which we are all occupied in trying to understand'.

The Commission on industry mustered an impressive galaxy of Anglican leaders and theologians: Gore; Bell; Theodore Woods, then of Peterborough; Kempthorne of Lichfield; R. H. Tawney; the Principal of Cuddesdon, J. B. Seaton, its secretary later Bishop of Wakefield. This group signed the report with the following challenge in its introductory statements:

We use the word Church without any controversy and in the largest possible sense to mean 'all who profess and call themselves Christian'. We know and deplore the divisions of Christendom, and we do not in the least underrate the difficulties involved in healing ancient wounds and restoring violated fellowship. We do not underestimate the theological and constitutional questions involved. But we say deliberately that in the region of moral or social questions we desire all Christians to begin at once to act together as if they were one body, in one visible fellowship. This could be done by all alike without any injury to theological principles. And to bring all Christians together to act in this one department of life as one visible body would involve no loss and manifold gain. We should get to know and trust one another: we should learn to act together we should thus prepare the way for fuller unity: and, on the other hand, we should win for our action on social questions in town and country a weight and effectiveness which it is idle to expect from the action of a variety of sects and bodies. What we desire to see in towns, counties and villages is the organization of all who share the Christian profession to act together in the name of Christ for the making of a better England through the courageous application to the present-day situation of the fundamental ethical principles of our religion.

Söderblom of course knew Talbot by name. He had often quoted Talbot's words in his contribution to the Swedish S.C.M. enquiry on war attitudes in 1915. The Oud Wassenaar meeting was to give Söderblom his first opportunity of meeting Talbot personally.

In preparing the Oud Wassenaar meeting, Dickinson was well aware of Archbishop Davidson's cautious attitude with regard to Söderblom and his conference plans. The more eager he was to secure Söderblom's attendance at Oud Wassenaar. In the middle of August, Söderblom informed Dickinson that he could not go to Holland, and Dickinson expressed his disappointment, which, he said, would be shared by Bishop Talbot.

The most important business we have to transact is to arrange about holding a general Conference of all churches next year. In this matter we shall greatly need your advice. In fact it will be most difficult to settle anything of this nature without knowing fully what your wishes would be.[7]

He therefore urged Söderblom to reconsider his decision, and succeeded in persuading him to come. Dickinson, in his position, had no intention of raising with Söderblom another matter, that of the presidency of the Alliance, but this question had been broached with Söderblom by others, probably by Siegmund-Schultze. In March

[7] W. H. Dickinson, August 25, 1919, to Söderblom. Söderblom's letter to Dickinson was dated August 12, 1919.

1919, Söderblom informed his confidant in Constantinople, his friend Kolmodin, that he was being considered for the presidency of the Alliance.[8]

Oud Wassenaar, 1919

The issues at Oud Wassenaar appeared different to the individual parties involved. Anxious as Dickinson was to see Söderblom at the conference, he had perhaps tended to overstate, from his own point of view, the importance of the question of an international conference. In the year of Versailles, Dickinson personally was more eager than ever to promote the interest of the League, and to rally Christian forces behind the international organization. He could count on the support of his whole British Council for this concern.

The Germans and the French on the other hand, albeit from opposite sides of the trenches, were concerned with another problem, that of the war guilt, or '*la Schuldfrage*' as it was sometimes called in French! Siegmund-Schultze and Adolf Deissmann in Berlin, and Wilfred Monod, now chairman of the French branch, engaged their national groups in debates over this issue. The Germans among themselves even raised the question as to whether this bitter problem could be brought before a 'Bruderrat', a kind of court of arbitration consisting of Neutrals.

'Oud Wassenaar, 1919' was a World Alliance meeting, the first after the World War. It provided a platform for the Churches to 'speak to the world' and to address the League of Nations. There was no other platform for this kind of pronouncement, and Dickinson, Siegmund–Schultze and the others, believed in its potentialities for the reconstruction of the post-war world.

The dynamic American delegation had ten members, an earnest of the new, constructive interest that the American Churches were prepared to take in the building-up of war-torn Europe. This was their splendid idealistic response to the isolationist turn of the 'America First' and the 'Return to Normalcy' programme. Arthur J. Brown and F. Lynch, Charles Macfarland and young Henry Atkinson challenged the tendency to national egoism in their own country, and engaged their churches in a great campaign of generous giving in the interest of suffering Europe. Two hundred million dollars was America's contribution.[1]

[8] Söderblom, March 8, 1919, to J. Kolmodin.
[1] A. Keller, *Dynamis* (1922), p. 131.

It cannot be doubted, however, that it was the members of the Church of England who dominated this meeting. This appeared as a period of greatness in the history of Anglicanism: the National Mission called the Church to repentance and new resolve; preparations for the great Lambeth Conference of 1920 were being made; and the sister Church in the United States, in 1919, boldly took the initiative in going forward with its Faith and Order programme. One could detect, perhaps, two tendencies among the four Anglicans at Oud Wassenaar; at least so it seemed to Söderblom. There were W. Moore–Ede and Sir Willoughby Dickinson. One of their concerns was to represent the Archbishop of Canterbury. This meant in practice that they were not to be altogether enamoured of any hasty measures suggested by a Swedish Archbishop. There were on the other hand Bishop Talbot of Winchester and Mrs. Creighton. Both had supported William Temple's national campaign; both had close contacts with Söderblom's friend, Cairns of Aberdeen, and with the Society of Friends; both had been outspoken in their defence of the supranationality of missions at the important meeting at Norwood in 1916. By office and personality, Talbot was the most important member of the group. Archbishop Davidson's young chaplain, G. K. A. Bell, was also at Oud Wassenaar. He was not, however, included in the list of delegates.

The chairman of the French branch of the Alliance, Wilfred Monod, was unable to attend Oud Wassenaar, and France was represented by Jules Faivret and L. D. Parker.

Söderblom was to find that the Swiss delegation was particularly helpful with regard to his plan. In his book *Stockholm, 1925*, Söderblom was to say that it was one of the Swiss representatives at Oud Wassenaar, Otto Herold, who made 'the decisive positive proposal' with regard to the further planning of his own ecumenical conference.[2] Not that he fully shared Herold's somewhat restricted Protestant view of the composition of his ecumenical undertaking, but he knew that the Swiss delegation included men of particular competence in ecumenical matters. There was Herold, there was his friend Paul Böhringer who had attended the Uppsala Conference in December 1917, and the Swiss group also included Professor Eugène Choisy who was to prove an indefatigable co-worker in the nineteen–twenties.

The representatives from the Northern countries included a cer-

---

[2] Nathan Söderblom, *Stockholm, 1925*, p. 135.

tain number of those who had made the Uppsala 1917 conference a valuable experience. The Norwegian party included Tvedt and Klaveness. There was the Danish pacifist Holger Larsen, together with the Swedes, K. B. Westman ('invaluable', Söderblom wrote to his wife), and Wilhelm Gullberg. The young Danish Church historian Professor Valdemar Ammundsen now appeared on the international ecumenical scene for the first time; he was to be one of Söderblom's most effective co-workers. Finland and Latvia also had representatives; Arthur Hjelt of Helsinki was an old friend of Söderblom's from student days, and, coming from Riga, Pastor Irbe represented a part of the North for which Söderblom felt particular concern and interest.

The German delegation to Oud Wassenaar arrived late, but the main and great fact was that they came at all. They were few in number but constituted an eminent group, for their names were Adolf Deissmann, Julius Richter, F. Siegmund-Schultze, F. A. Spiecker, a director of Siemens with a wide international experience who devoted himself to social and ecumenical questions, and Reinhold Schairer of the German S.C.M.[3]

From their point of view, Söderblom and Uppsala were incontestably central on the international scene, and Söderblom had a few weeks earlier, in a letter to Siegmund-Schultze, expressed his sympathy with the Germans after Versailles: 'Terrible, an abyss is the World situation. One must ask oneself whether this is hell or the earth. God help us. Now much in the Old Testament becomes true for Germany—a new Israel.'[4] The Germans appreciated this, but a few statements of this nature caused Söderblom to be regarded, even at Oud Wassenaar, as pro-German. So he was, but one must not forget that he was at the same time, just as much pro-British, pro-French and pro-American.

However these pro-German sympathies of his did not commend him to everybody at Oud Wassenaar, and one or two of his best friends among the British raised the matter with him. This was 1919, after a World War, and very soon after Versailles.

Behold the scene at 'Oud Wassenaar', the aristocratic hotel near the Hague, October, 1–3, 1919. It was a measure of the isolation caused by the war that this was Söderblom's first journey beyond

---

[3] Söderblom had recommended Siegmund-Schultze to include Schairer in the delegation. Siegmund-Schultze, *Nathan Söderblom* (1966), p. 48.
[4] Ibid., p. 33.

the borders of Scandinavia since 1914. Söderblom wrote to his wife: 'This glorious place, a hotel magnificently arranged, in the middle of summer residences, parks, gardens. I enjoy the sun; a little verandah through which one can walk into the park.'

He met the British delegation: 'Cairns regards the Bishop of Winchester as the foremost man in the Church of England, tall, unkempt, bearded. I have just read his and his committee's admirable report on social and economic conditions. [He] is a 73 year old giant; bearded as an old Greek monk, little slits of eyes behind glasses. Humour and spirituality. One cannot help falling in love with the old man. With his stiff leg he has been on the Alp tops in Switzerland. He has lost in the War a highly gifted son, Gilbert. My journey has been worthwhile just in order to meet Winchester.'

It was the spiritual authority of the man that attracted Söderblom: 'Winchester's meditation and prayer on The Kingdom. Different from anything I have ever heard; devotional and natural. He would pause and keep silent; then he read a Bible passage or said something about the Kingdom. I have never heard anybody taking prayers in such a true and quiet and thoughtful spirit.'

He was walking in the park with Bishop Talbot, and he heard his English friend exclaim: 'But look, my old friend Spiecker!' The two old men embraced. 'It was the first meeting after the War between Germany and England which I witnessed.'[5]

Talbot was not less impressed by Söderblom than the Swedish Archbishop by him. Talbot told Bell: 'I could have fallen backwards. He was so mobile, so quick in his movements, so overflowing with information and suggestions, so indefatigable.'[6]

The conference provided opportunities in session and in private, for outspoken encounters between the Germans and the others. While Wilfred Monod of France was unable to attend the meeting, he sent a letter in which he raised the matter of violation by the Germans of Belgian territory. In answer to this, the German delegation issued a statement read at the Conference which acknowledged the violation of Belgian neutrality in 1914 as morally wrong.

Oud Wassenaar was an opportunity for making a declaration of the principles for which the Alliance stood. In a letter to his wife,

---

[5] Söderblom, *Stockholm, 1925*, p. 18.
[6] The Anglicans were impressed by the mobility of the Archbishop. Söderblom told his wife that Mrs. Creighton called him the Mercury-Archbishop. As Söderblom protested, H. Hodgkin suggested a kinder version would be the 'mercurian archbishop', which also could be interpreted as envoy.

Söderblom suggested there were different schools of thought represented in the commission, 'the Americans wanted the resolution to be more optimistic, [Talbot of] Winchester and I more apocalyptic, Hodgkin [of the Society of Friends] wanted 'more of God in us, not only God outside us'. Against the dark background of war, out of 'this day of the Lord,' they knew that the one hope for society and mankind was that the mind of Christ should be expressed in every human relationship. God's will was not only individual salvation but the transformation of 'the whole life of humanity and of all its corporate activities'. The final resolution was an effort towards reconciling these tendencies.

Special resolutions followed from this general principle. National Councils were recommended to enter into communication with Labour and Socialist movements, and there were expressions of deep concern for the fate of German missions and for Hungarian minorities.

But care for these concerns presupposed a united Church. Dr. Hodgkin made the point that Christian unity was a fact which needed to be demonstrated in practical service, while Otto Herold on behalf of the Swiss, spoke of the 'urgent necessity of uniting all Protestants', albeit assuring the different Churches full independence in matters of Faith and Order. He had approached the two Church leaders in the North and the West, Archbishop Söderblom and Dr. Macfarland, to 'take the first steps in this direction', and he felt that they would act accordingly.

Söderblom took a lively interest in these discussions. The accounts of the conference emphasize his power of communication, his gift of establishing and strengthening contacts. As the conference solemnly adopted the resolutions on the supra-nationality of Missions, Söderblom, in characteristic fashion, began to intone *Nun Danket Alle Gott*. The minutes of the conference record the following: 'After this the Archbishop of Uppsala led the hymn, Now thank we all our God.' It can be surmised however that Söderblom intoned the hymn in its German original!

In an account of the proceedings to his wife, he gave his own interpretation of the things that mattered at the Conference.

Tuesday evening I managed at last to arrange for us to take prayers together. I began with *Kyrie eleison*. Response: Glory be to God in the Highest. We said together *Veni Sancte Spiritus*. Cairns, apostle [of Scotland]; John 15 with comments. Silent prayer which was quietly interspersed by Deissmann, brief, deep and serious; Ainslie, sympathetic American from Baltimore; Ammundsen, personal faith; Hodgkin, something of a St. John, turned upwards bodily and spiritually; a French Methodist, Parker, perhaps too eloquent; and at the end, the glorious Mrs. Creighton. She said among other things, 'Thou redeemest the world without us.' Our Father, each in his own tongue. I gave the blessing in French. We sang 'Befiehl du deine Wege'. Then we joined hands together just as we do at home, as a sign that 'the living stream of Christ' ... must penetrate everyone of us and take away selfishness.

Yet we should not overemphasize Söderblom's role at Oud Wassenaar. Dr. Siegmund-Schultze has pointed out that Oud Wassenaar was characterized by 'sharp contrasts'.[7] In an interview in November, 1966, he emphasized that the tensions also concerned Söderblom's position at the conference. Precisely because of Söderblom's dominant role in later conferences, it is necessary to define as succinctly as possible his influence at Oud Wassenaar. His leadership was by no means assured at this time. In fact, in the actual discussions at Oud Wassenaar he preferred to keep somewhat in the background. Deissmann's report on the Conference reveals this since Söderblom's proposal concerning an ecumenical conference is only casually mentioned. Siegmund-Schultze, who in his *Die Eiche* had welcomed Söderblom's idea of a conference—'the plan of such a conference during the war was already an *act*'[8]—does hardly more than refer to the resolution as such. Not that these two great friends of Söderblom's in any way wished to depreciate his contribution—far from it, but it took a churchman from a neutral country, and one of Söderblom's stature, to look beyond the immediate issues and take a long-range perspective.

In November 1966, Siegmund-Schultze suggested to us that it was not only Söderblom's courteous deference to the Anglo–Saxon leaders of the World Alliance that demonstrated the relatively secondary role played by the Swedish Archbishop at Oud Wassenaar, there was also, he felt, a tendency to keep Söderblom somewhat in check.

This was revealed particularly in the debate for the nomination of the new president, J. Allen Baker having died in 1918. The Germans, and probably the Northerners, wished to elect Söderblom for his post. Siegmund-Schultze wrote Söderblom after returning from Holland: 'I am strongly convinced that a closer union of evangelical Churches at present will best be realized via (*über*) Uppsala,

[7] F. Siegmund-Schultze, *Nathan Söderblom, Briefe und Botschaften* (1966), p. 47.
[8] *Die Eiche*, 1919, p. 187, and ibid., p. 250.

partly for political reasons, partly for church-political reasons. The German churches see this as their great opportunity'.[9] We shall return to this problem later.

It was in this atmosphere that Söderblom presented his plan: a Proposed Ecumenical Conference. Anxious as he was to see his international conference convened at Uppsala, he had already, on September 8, 1919, the anniversary of the abortive attempt at a Conference in 1918, issued a message signed by the Nordic Primates, reminding those concerned of the standing invitation from Scandinavia.

... to meet in one of our countries, in Upsala, Kristiania [Oslo], or Copenhagen, or an[y] other place in Scandinavia during the following year. ... The Conference will not, in any part of the World, be [welcomed] with a warmer and wider and deeper sympathy and with more ardent intercession than in Scandinavia, while the need of such a manifestation of the unity of the Church, the preparation for the duties imperiously imposed by the time, have been alive and strong during these apocalyptic years. [The reference to Oslo and Copenhagen was possibly not as wholehearted as it may have appeared, for in the printed form, the message had a postscriptum] May I add for my personal part that, if Uppsala should be chosen, a modest hospitality will be offered to every member of the Ecumenical Conference, the cost of the Conference itself has been guaranteed without any initiative from my part.

As he read his paper, he well knew that there was hesitation with regard to the idea, but he took courage from the fact that it was his friend Bishop Talbot's turn to chair the particular session in which he was explaining his plan. As we have already pointed out, Talbot had shown him the Anglican report on Christianity and Industrial Problems, and Söderblom was gratified by being able to quote from this report both as a gesture of appreciation to Talbot, and as an expression of his agreement with the pragmatic approach of this competent Anglican group.

Proposed Ecumenical Conference. Memorandum, is the title Söderblom had chosen for his address, which was a mere fifteen hundred words long. After a rapid review of the efforts towards an international conference from 1914 onwards, the memorandum read:—

Now a few words (1) on the character of such a gathering, (2) on the comprehensiveness of it, and (3) on the place where it might be held.

---

[9] F. Siegmund-Schultze, Oct. 16, 1919, to Söderblom.

1. Our task is not to bring organizations together, but to unite hearts and minds and endeavours. True believers and followers of Christ have always been a minority even in the Christian communions, and they will ever remain a minority. But it is essential to use for Christian aims all communions of the Church, and all Christian organizations to which it is our privilege to belong.

Our ecumenical conference has to be clearly distinguished from the great task that is called the World Conference on Faith and Order. The Commission sent to Europe for that World Conference quite agreed with us in that respect. Our conference may be a most important preparation for the World Conference on Faith and Order, but it will not deal with Faith nor Order, but [with] some well-defined urgent practical aims.

Union for such purposes does not reqire unity in Faith and Order. I remind you of the doctrine in the Augsburg Confession and the Thirty-nine Articles in that respect. Dr. Carrolls renders the same doctrine in his Primer on Church Unity, answer 49. Uniformity is not necessary for common preaching and striving in actual needs of mankind. The Report of the Archbishop's Fifth Questionnaire says (page 2): We say deliberately that in the region of moral or social questions we desire all Christians to begin at once to act together as if they were one body in one visible fellowship. This could be done by all alike without any injury to theological principles.

I have tried to define the chief objects of the Ecumenical Conference in an article which appeared some weeks ago in *the Contemporary Review,* London. They seem to me to be: (A) Common doctrine and endeavour for international Christian Brotherhood and organized Unity of Nations; (B) Christian principles and action for social renewal of Society. Further (C) a common voice must be created for the Christian conscience. I advocate an Ecumenical Council representing Christendom in a Spiritual way.

2. As to the comprehensiveness of this proposed gathering, good reasons speak for beginning with Evangelical Christendom only, in order to create a common platform for our part of the Catholic Church before inviting the Orthodox and Roman divisions of the Church.

But there are also good reasons and warm sympathies for making the scope as comprehensive as possible at once.

3. As to the place of the Conference my brethren in Copenhagen and Christiania and myself have the honour of reiterating our invitation to one of the Scandinavian countries.

In order somewhat more fully to understand Söderblom's arguments on that decisive occasion, we have to supplement these notes with his view as expressed in an article appearing at the same time in English and in German. Here he expounded in broad outline how he visualized the organization of this ecumenical council.[1]

... Christendom calls for a common channel of utterance. From the throne of St. Peter, as well as from other parts of the Christian world, words have again and again gone forth which find echo in every truly Christian heart, and are spoken on its behalf. But a common platform is lacking. What I propose is an ecumenical council, representing the whole of Christendom, and so constructed that it can speak on behalf of Christendom, guiding, warning, strengthening, praying in the common religious, moral and social matters of mankind. It should be composed partly by the appointment of men specially qualified, partly be election on broad democratic lines. It is too much to hope that Rome, with its exclusive sectarian isolation, should as yet be willing to be represented in any common council. There remain then two ancient offices in the Christian Church which should qualify their holders without question for the ecumenical council; to wit, the Patriarchate of Constantinople and the Archbishopric of Canterbury. The remaining parts of the evangelical-catholic church in America and Europe should then be represented, according to their importance and characteristic influence, by three or more elected members. The first to be considered here would be the largest contingents of evangelical catholicism, which are found in Germany and the United States. After these, the Scandinavian countries, Finland and the Baltic provinces, and further, Hungary, Switzerland, Holland and France, where Protestantism possesses a spiritual and moral influence out of proportion to the number of individuals actually to be reckoned, etc. This ecumenical council should not be invested with any external authority, but should have and gain its influence according to the degree in which it was able to act as a spiritual power. It should speak, not *ex cathedra*, but from the depths of the Christian conscience.

Söderblom was at the cross-roads here. His relationship to the World Alliance was in the balance, and was to be determined by the debate of that very plan of his. With regard to Faith and Order he had already at the beginning of June met an American delegation in Uppsala, and now at Oud Wassenaar he referred to the results of that encounter. Here he felt that Talbot's Anglican report was an effective rejoinder to the proposal of the American Episcopalians, and it was from this report that he emphasized the 'as if' formula as a key to his practical approach to ecumenical co-operation. No

---

[1] The article appeared as 'The Church and International Goodwill' in *The Contemporary Review* (1919), Vol. 116, pp. 309–315, and 'Die Aufgabe der Kirche, Internationale Freundschaft durch Evangel. Katholizität', *Die Eiche*, 1919, pp. 124–136.

less an authority than Dr. Visser't Hooft has challenged Söderblom and his generation on this point. 'The "as if" answer is ... inadequate because it fails to take account of the importance of theological agreement for action itself.'[2] As a historian, the present writer has no brief to act as advocate for Söderblom and his generation. We simply try to understand why those men had to act as they did *in order to move at all,* and in so doing, we notice of course that the Anglican Report from which Söderblom quoted made a point of trying to counter precisely that kind of criticism.

As we have pointed out the report was signed by Anglo-Catholic theologians of some repute. It was true of these men as it was true of Talbot and Söderblom, that the existential experience of war had prompted them, with their theologies and all their doctrines, to look beyond these to the immediate and urgent tasks that had to be tackled here and now.

Söderblom in his generation felt that he was thereby showing the Churches a way, an ecumenical way, but he had to use the concepts and the frame of reference which he and his generation knew; therefore he advocated 'an ecumenical council representing Christendom in a spiritual way.'

This was a somewhat unusual phrase, in fact so strange, that nobody who has discussed the ecumenical implications of Oud Wassenaar seems to have noticed it! Yet anyone who recalls Söderblom's fundamental category of body and soul, institution and spirit, will discover that once again, in one of the most decisive statements of his life, Söderblom the Archbishop, blazing a new path for the Church Universal, revealed his dependence on that early influence in his outlook.

Söderblom, who had waited for so long, and had on three occasions met with the frustrating experience of seeing his Conference plans postponed, was sensitive to the currents in the debate. At first he was prepared to be optimistic. He wrote to his wife:

The Conference, the ecumenical, was dealt with yesterday. Now it will be taken over by us in the North. We have Bell with us, therefore, I presume, also Canterbury. Otherwise it will have to be with us, Germany, the British Free Churches, Holland, Switzerland, Hungary, America, without the Church of England. . . . Here is a wonderful, hearty atmosphere. On a couple of occasions we have positively had to stand up, crying, praying, singing.

---

[2] W. A. Visser't Hooft. *The Pressure of our Common Calling* (1959), p. 18.

But he could not be sure that he would succeed in carrying the hesitant with him. Above all, in that meeting of the World Alliance, he was not sure that the Alliance would provide the ideal platform from which to promote his Ecumenical Conference.

The Alliance men themselves also realized that an official Church conference of the nature advocated by Söderblom lay outside the competence of their organization. While thus expressing 'deep sympathy' with the proposal as such, the Conference decided to refer the matter to the national 'branches' of the Alliance for their consideration. On the suggestion of Pastor Otto Herold, it was agreed outside the actual programme of the meeting, that a committee with full powers to act was to be formed.

In his book on Stockholm, 1925, Söderblom, recalling the importance of Herold's proposal, said: 'The decisive proposal to plan the ecumenical undertaking was entrusted to the United States and the North.'[3] This was his somewhat sweeping manner of saying that 'Oud Wassenaar' unofficially asked Macfarland and Söderblom himself, together with Herold of Switzerland, to act. Before they left Holland they published an invitation to

the Churches and Organizations to whom this message is addressed to appoint not more than three members each, to meet at Paris on November 10. The appointed members should then be prepared to present as fully as possible the view of their respective churches and Church Organizations as to the Constitution, nature, scope and date of the proposed [Ecumenical] Conference.

Sensitive as he was, not only to the currents, but also to any counter-currents at Oud Wassenaar, a saddened Söderblom came to Siegmund–Schultze after the meeting and confided to him: 'It won't work, this approach through the World Alliance. We must choose another road.'

If Söderblom was dejected, this was a very temporary reaction. For he now knew that the Conference question was to be handled by 'us in the North', supported by the American Federal Council. He might be forced to take another road—the future would prove whether that road was to become the Ecumenical Way.

Paris 1919 and Geneva 1920

Canterbury was the crux. At Oud Wassenaar Söderblom could not shut his eyes to the sad prospect that Canterbury would advise his

---

[3] Söderblom, *Stockholm, 1925*, p. 135.

men, at least for the time being, to have nothing to do with this new enterprise. Söderblom tried every kind of device to win over the most sceptical. Oud Wassenaar had suggested that Scandinavia, America and Switzerland alone were to convene in Paris in order to arrange for the ecumenical conference. Accordingly Macfarland, ever constitutional and expeditious, made a list of names for Paris, as a matter of course excluding representatives of the Church of England. But Söderblom could not bear the thought of allowing such a list to go out. He told Hellerström in London:

I ought perhaps to mention to you in deepest confidence that the list for Paris of the secretary of the American Federal Council did not envisage the Church of England; only the Free Church Council. Through my intervention the Church of England was placed at the top of the list. ... I thus believe that the English Church has much to lose if it does not grasp the opportunity offered to take part in the Paris meeting. [He felt that this was important because of] the position of the Church of England in Ecumenical Christendom.

He probably thought of the prominent role on his Ecumenical Council that he hoped to accord to the Archbishop of Canterbury together with the Patriarch of Constantinople. The reply from Canterbury did not leave any doubt whatever where he stood in this matter. Davidson addressed himself to Macfarland but really dealt with Söderblom, of course. One can understand the wise and wary Archbishop at Lambeth. He had formed an image of his colleague at Uppsala, and this latest proposal from the North seemed to corroborate that picture: a churchman in a hurry, full of hazy plans which in the end did not amount to very much: this at least was the impression left by all those abortive plans to call an Uppsala conference in the midst of war.

Canterbury had problems of his own at the home base; particularly a certain pressure from vocal Anglo-Catholic groups to approach Rome. These considerations were among those which conditioned Dr. Davidson's reply. He was not prepared to send Anglican representatives to Paris as 'the matter was as yet in a purely preliminary stage'. But he called for clarification, for a more precise definition of the objects of the conference. A conference of that nature needed long preparation. It was natural to him to make comparisons with the organization of the World Missionary Conference at Edinburgh, 1910. That had required more than two years of preparation. Further, he went on, if the Conference is to be held it ought to be in the real sense of the word Ecumenical and include the Roman Catholics and the Orthodox Churches of the East. The Orthodox seemed likely to be represented, but Rome? The Church of England could not join in a Conference to which the Roman Catholics were not invited. The further question whether it would be wise to hold a Conference in which the Roman Catholics definitely decided to take no part of course must also be considered.

When Dr. Lynch, chairman of 'the committee on an Ecumenical Conference' in the American Federal Council visited him, he invited a group of bishops to meet Dr. Lynch. There Dr. Davidson said, according to Lynch: 'If this can be as big as the Nicaean Council and do as much for the Church as that Council did for faith and order, I can be interested in it. But I cannot be interested if it is just a haphazard meeting of leaders of the Church coming together for a week. If you are going to get the group together to be representative of the whole Christian Communion, as coming with the same force and authority as the Councils of the Church, I can be interested.'[1] The Archbishop was sufficiently interested, and worried, to follow this up with a letter to Dr. Macfarland emphasizing his qualms about the vagueness of the plan. 'It must be made plain from the start that the Conference has a definite objective in shape of certain definite tasks to be undertaken and certain definite questions to be tackled.'

Söderblom had had his presentiments of this, and he was informed by Hellerström in London about Davidson's actions and reactions. He did not understand Canterbury at that time; 'more political and cautious than whole-hearted', was the formula which Söderblom found for him in a letter in November, 1919, to Kolmodin. But he was determined that the Anglicans should be won for the cause: 'It would be fatal if the Church of England were not in from the beginning. The Americans, English Non-conformists and Scotland etc. would then go forward on their own.'[2]

Söderblom decided not to take Edinburgh, 1910 as prototype for his conference. 'In Edinburgh they had to illuminate and study a mass of problems in order to get a broad view of the whole world of missions. The Ecumenical conference, on the other hand, will have its greatest importance precisely in the fact of being convened.

---

[1] Minutes, American Section, Committee on Arrangements for the Universal Conference on Life and Work, Nov. 2, 1921.
[2] Söderblom, November 3, 1919, to A. Hellerström.

Only after it has been constituted, can it start to examine all the extraordinarily important problems which will be the concern of the Ecumenical Council of Churches. A comparison with the Lambeth Conference is more illuminating. It first meets, appoints its committees, takes a pause and meets again when the committees have done their work. In the same manner, I think, the Ecumenical conference should meet as soon as the Committee on an Ecumenical Conference, to be formed at Paris, has had time to approach the Churches and these have appointed (or refused to appoint) their delegates.'[3]

In preparation for the Paris meeting, Söderblom tried from Uppsala to secure a sufficiently strong Scandinavian representation. Söderblom himself could not attend. His idea was, as always, to send a Swedish embassy pastor, and he turned to S. Stadener who had been his own successor as embassy pastor in Paris. Söderblom's Norwegian friend and co-worker, E. Berggrav was to go with Stadener. But Berggrav was hindered by illness, and Stadener by visa difficulties. Söderblom then turned to another Embassy pastor, in London, A. Hellerström, who together with Y. Brilioth, studying at Oxford at this time, was to represent Söderblom and Scandinavia. Söderblom also considered sending K. B. Westman to the Paris meeting, but felt that the Swedish delegation ought not to appear too dominant. Instead he gave Hellerström and Brilioth his instructions.

Söderblom at that time considered that the Ecumenical Conference as such would meet in the summer of 1920, in connexion with the Conference of the Student World Federation, or, failing this, in 1921.[4] The Conference would have a full programme and primarily set up 'the Ecumenical Council of Churches, which may be considered as perhaps its most important task'. Details should be left to the Ecumenical Council, thus to be formed. In his letter to Stadener (November 1, 1919) Söderblom was quite definite about the place for the Ecumenical Conference—Uppsala: 'I have told you that if the Conference will be in Uppsala, I have guarantees for all expenses, for full hospitality, except travel which members of course have to pay themselves.'

Whether the choice of place for the November 1919 meeting was Söderblom's idea is difficult to say. He was concerned at this time

---

[3] Söderblom, November 4, 1919, to A. Hellerström.
[4] In a letter to Siegmund-Schultze at the end of April, 1920, Söderblom still hoped that 'the real Ecumenical Conference would meet in Scandinavia [in 1921]'. F. Siegmund-Schultze, *Nathan Söderblom*, 1966, p. 52.

about the lack of response from French Protestants, and he may have considered, at Oud Wassenaar, that holding the meeting in the French capital might have its positive effects on the French members.

The Paris meeting, November 17, 1919, was a small but important 'preliminary conference'. There were only eleven participants, of whom six were Americans, including Lynch and Atkinson, but also including two members of the transient Interchurch World Movement. Macfarland, on the other hand, could not attend. There were two Swedes, two Swiss, J. G. Choisy and O. Herold, and one representative of the French host country and Church, André Monod.

In his letters to Brilioth and Hellerström, Söderblom had as he was wont struck the note of urgency. One has, however, the impression that the Swedish archbishop's young envoys were impressed by the need for caution. Hellerström had arrived at this standpoint after discussions with Davidson whom he greatly admired. He suggested to Söderblom that in his correspondence Davidson appeared more negative to Söderblom's cause than he was in reality, and had to appear so because of consideration for 'the Romanist tendencies in the High Church party'. Söderblom's optimistic directive was toned down by Brilioth to 'plans for a greater committee meeting' in 1920. In the end, the Paris committee entrusted further planning to a one man committee, Dr. Lynch. Hellerström reported to Söderblom about Dr. Lynch's activity in the Paris meeting: 'He was quite clear about the idea of a Meeting, and insisted that it be an Ecumenical conference on the lines drawn up by the Scandinavian bishops'.[5]

There was only one 'pan-Protestant' protagonist at the Paris meeting. Herold of Switzerland repeated his plea from Oud Wassenaar, not without a certain bias against Rome. The Orthodox too had better be left out of the conference, he felt; they were after all very different from any Westerners. But Herold's plea did not meet with any response from the others in the group. In fact, later, as Dr. Lynch carried out his instructions, his hand was strengthend by the decision in the Federal Council in New York. In March 1920, this Council took the stand that 'the ultimate Conference should be inclusive of all Christian bodies of all countries, if this be possible'.

Far away from his beloved Paris, Söderblom at Uppsala waited anxiously for reports from the meeting. From his point of view,

---

[5] A. Hellerström, November 19, 1919, to Söderblom.

the result was disappointing, and he tended to feel that this was due to Canterbury's 'incorrigible caution'.[6] By contrast he saw himself as the daring visionary. In letters to his friend Kolmodin at this time he would refer to 'my ecumenical madness'.[7] It was all the more important for Söderblom to prepare the hoped-for great international meeting thoroughly. He did this as one who knew that the whole future of his plan depended on the result of this one stage. In order to make it easier to keep the meeting under his control, ever aware of the need for contacts with the Baltic States, with Russia, and the Orthodox, Söderblom insisted that the conference meet 'in Uppsala or somewhere in Sweden'. He hoped for 1920.

In the meantime, in World Alliance circles, the tension between the interests represented by Canterbury and Uppsala continued throughout the first half of 1920. In preparation for the important Alliance Conference at Geneva at the end of August there was held a small preparatory committee meeting at the beginning of May, where Söderblom was represented by professor Edv. Rodhe of Lund. Oud Wassenaar had had to table the question of nomination of President of the Alliance, and the committee meeting now attempted to prepare this question. To Rodhe, the debate appeared—he wrote to Söderblom—as a quiet tug-of-war between Canterbury and Uppsala.[8] W. Dickinson chaired the meeting and, as he had done at Oud Wassenaar, again promoted Canterbury's name. He did so, Rodhe admitted, 'in a masterly fashion'. Emphasizing Söderblom's merits in his support of the Alliance, he nevertheless felt he had to mention that, during the war, the Archbishop had been reported as not fully reliable because of pro-German sympathies. Having mentioned this, Dickinson added that he himself of course knew that that accusation was unwarranted. (By way of a parenthesis one might add that Dickinson himself may have been particularly sensitive to that kind of argument. After the publication of A. J. P. Taylor's *The Trouble Makers*, 1958, we know how much the Union for Democratic Control in England, to which Dickinson was related, was under the same suspicion.) Nevertheless Canterbury who occupied a more central position than Uppsala was preferable for the office of President particularly as regards the contacts with the Oriental Churches.

Siegmund-Schultze of Germany spoke for Söderblom; Rodhe on

---

[6] Söderblom, November 17, 1919, to A. Hellerström.
[7] Söderblom, February 11, 1920, to A. Kolmodin.
[8] Edv. Rodhe, May 9, 1920, to Söderblom.

the other hand became convinced that Sweden was of little importance and Uppsala far away, so he tended to support Canterbury's
name.

The election took place at *Geneva,* which was rapidly emerging
in the post-War world as the headquarters and centre for great international movements and their conferences. In August 1920 there
were, among others, three international conferences of importance to
our story. The first, from 9th–12th, was Söderblom's own, Life and
Work, followed at once by Faith and Order from 13th–23rd, which
in turn was followed by the World Alliance meeting, 24th–28th. At
the last, the political tensions as also the uneasiness due to the
suppressed question of war-guilt, were keenly felt and affected the
election of President. The German representative Spiecker spoke
against Canterbury's candidature, but the Anglicans were well represented by Bishop Talbot, and in the end Canterbury was elected.
It was claimed that with Canterbury as President, the Alliance would
be well placed to speak with authority on political matters to the
League of Nations. Söderblom was elected one of the eleven Vice
Presidents of the Alliance, along with some of his friends in the
ecumenical cause, such as D. S. Cairns, G. Janoska, and W. Monod.
But Söderblom's attention at the beginning of August was on his
own meeting and the fate of his movement at this critical moment.

On his way to Geneva the Archbishop sent a note to his wife:

This ecumenical business begins to frighten me. It must acquire 1:o spiritual contents, 2:o concrete form. [But a few days later he added:]
    I have attended many congresses, meetings, jubilees, conferences in thirty-
three years. Many that were more solemn, agreeable, distinguished and
great than this one, with more remarkable speeches, but none where a stub-
born will could achieve so much action pregnant with future. On this level,
no days of my short life can be compared with these.
    To Johannes Kolmodin in Constantinople he wrote: These were the
most remarkable and in a way the hardest days of work which I have experienced in my life.[9]

In fact, Geneva 1920 was the climax of Söderblom's ecumenical
efforts until that time. There were similarities between the two conferences at Oud Wassenaar and Geneva. It was at Oud Wassenaar
that Herold had suggested that the planning conference in 1920 be
arranged by Scandinavia and the United States; to which Switzer-

---

[9] Söderblom, August 31, 1920, to J. Kolmodin.

land was added. The representatives from these countries dominated Geneva. Out of the ninety delegates, more than a third were Americans; and from Sweden and Switzerland there were ten delegates each.

But there were also differences. The Anglican delegation had been vocal in 1919; from Söderblom's point of view its contribution had been of special significance. But they were absent at the Geneva 1920, Life and Work Conference, or almost absent. Officially they were not represented. But Bell, who in any case had come to the Geneva of conferences, was invited by Karl Fries to attend some of the meetings, and Söderblom reported to Mrs. Söderblom in his staccato manner about this contribution: 'Before [Bell] left yesterday morning, he managed to render invaluable service as Secretary. On Monday and in the French-German question: gallant, a man of honour, capable.'

The main difference between the two conferences was to be found on another level. Oud Wassenaar was held under World Alliance auspices; Geneva was something new and untried. At Oud Wassenaar there had been a tendency for Söderblom to keep, or perhaps to be kept, somewhat in the background; at Geneva the Swedish Archbishop was unmistakably and as a matter of course the central figure. For it was his idea and initiative, and it was convened to prepare his own ecumenical conference.

He did not come alone. The Swedish delegation was impressive, for it included Söderblom, Aulén, (41, professor of Systematic Theology, Lund), and Brilioth (29, Assistant Professor of Church History, Uppsala). There were Karl Fries, three pastors: J. Lindskog, Albert Lysander from Malmö, one of the early leaders of what was later to be known as the Swedish High Church movement, and H. Neander, Söderblom's emissary to the East. There were also three laymen, close personal friends of Söderblom: Gustaf Ribbing whom Söderblom somewhat romantically described as Sir Gustaf Ribbing; Major Anders Sjöstedt, business man from Uppsala where he had become one of Söderblom's most enthusiastic supporters, and finally K. E. Öhman. Söderblom had acted promptly concerning the selection of this delegation. He had seen to it that they were appointed by the General Swedish Church Meeting, March, 1920.

The American delegation included most of the Federal Council leaders who were to be Söderblom's co-workers in the following years: Peter Ainslie, Nehemiah Boynton, Arthur Brown, Frederick Lynch, Charles Macfarland, William Merrill, J. A. Morehead. Söderblom was particularly gratified to find as members the two American leaders of Faith and Order, Bishop Brent and Robert Gardiner, who had come to Geneva for their own Conference in the same month. The Swiss delegation comprised men with whom Söderblom had been working earlier and on whom he was to rely later very considerably: There was Paul Böhringer of Basel who had attended his Uppsala 1917 conference. There was Otto Herold, and there were Eugene Choisy and Adolph Keller. Both Choisy and Keller were to become two of the most devoted servants of the ecumenical cause in the nineteen twenties. In his estimation of the conference, Söderblom felt that together with the three already mentioned delegations there was at Geneva a further, fourth 'point of support' in the group of Scots representatives, James Cooper, J. A. McClymont and J. D. Mac-Gilp.

In the strong American representation the Reformed-Presbyterian–Methodist churchmanship was dominant. This also applied to the small delegations from Belgium, France, Britain, Holland, Hungary, Italy, and Spain. Even in the German delegation of five this same tendency was to be noticed. The Germans were anxious to emphasize that their delegation was not officially appointed by the German Evangelischer Kirchenausschuss.

It was a dramatic meeting. Some observers claimed that it was a badly organized meeting, so much so that Siegmund–Schultze wrote: 'The American way of preparing an ecumenical conference appears to us Germans often rather blasphemous.'[10] If thus there were faults in the organization, these were probably the result of a certain division of authority: Dr. Lynch was commissioned to attend to the preparations, while it was taken for granted by him and by others that Archbishop Söderblom would outline the programme for the Conference.

Geneva was related to Oud Wassenaar over another issue, that of war guilt. The French Protestants had to a certain extent held aloof from the planning of an ecumenical conference. The fact that the Preparatory Committee had met in Paris had hardly changed anything in this matter. Now at Geneva, Professor Raoul Allier, Church and Missions historian, read a declaration from the Council of the French Protestant Federation. It recognized the importance of what had been said at Oud Wassenaar by the German representatives with

---

[10] *Die Eiche,* 1921, p. 104.

16 – 684363 *B. Sundkler*

regard to Germany's invasion of Belgium in 1914. But this was limited to a few exceptional individuals. Do you not admit [he went on], that common action itself by Evangelical Christendom is made difficult as long as there is no authentic pronouncement on the part of Protestantism in Germany, Austria and Hungary to acknowledge this wrong? The Christian churches must show that they are ruled by justice. If that is not the case, there does in reality not exist any Christian fellowship'. *La Schuldfrage* was to follow the ecumenical encounter those years as a dark shadow until Stockholm 1925, and indeed beyond Stockholm. When it was first brought into the open it shook the meeting. Macfarland supported Allier's intervention. Söderblom was torn between sympathies in both directions. It must suffice in this connexion to state that Söderblom would always recall with gratitude the names of the men who by their statements and proposals on this question saved the conference, particularly A. J. Brown and F. Lynch of the U.S. Federal Council and the Italian Waldensian, E. Giampiccoli, 'a tall Christlike figure with eyes as Mater Dolorosa, pathetic, pleading for mutual forgiveness although he had lost a son [in the war].'[1]

For Söderblom, the main issue at Geneva was of course the fate of his Conference idea. That daring plan of his had been defeated earlier, on two or three occasions. It could have failed also this time. He felt keenly the risks involved. Meeting Dr. W. Simons, the German Secretary for Foregin Affairs, the archbishop referred to his plea as 'my wild idea'. But as he was aware of the dangers he was sustained by his young Swedish co-worker (and now son-in-law) Yngve Brilioth who told him: 'If only one attempts something really crazy, then one will succeed.'[2] Söderblom also knew something else. He interpreted this to the Swedish Church Assembly that year. 'The distress of war having been followed by the distress of peace ... Christendom begins to realize that its unity is not just a beautiful but unpractical, perhaps dangerous, dream of enthusiasts. It is quite simply a question of right or wrong, and of obedience to the clear commandments of Christ or an offence against the Spirit of the Gospel.'[3]

Söderblom arrived in Geneva with a draft Suggested Programme which he had prepared with Brilioth in June, 1920. The main con-

---

[1] Söderblom, *Stockholm, 1925*, p. 30. Letter August 13, 1920, to Anna Söderblom.
[2] Ibid.
[3] *Allm. Kyrkomötet Minutes*, 1920.

cerns of this programme were expounded in Söderblom's Introductory Address on 'Idea and Need of an Ecumenical Conference.'

In the Suggested Programme the aim of the Conference was defined as 'co-operation of Christendom over urgent practical problems', and by this definition a delimitation from Faith and Order and from the World Alliance was achieved. He drew particular attention to the Encyclical Letter from the Ecumenical Patriarchate, which had proposed 'a kind of league of the churches'. This and similar proposals have 'all the same, a chiefly practical, aim'. The scope of the conference was defined on the lines suggested by Söderblom later at Geneva under the title Most Urgent Needs. The draft programme adds: 'Other topics may be gathered from the Encyclical Letter of the Ecumenical Patriarchate in Constantinople and from other documents.' The Conference must not pass without creating definitive organizations: an Ecumenical Council was to be formed, 'consisting of a number of representatives of Christendom, of whom some were to be chosen *ad hoc* in the broadest democratic way by the Christian communions, some selected among leaders of important offices in the Christian Church. This Ecumenical Council which ought to have its official seat in Jerusalem or another historic place of our Christian Faith, should constitute a purely spiritual authority, without any mandate to interfere in internal church affairs.'

The Introductory Address, in Söderblom's rapid pencil notes, develops some of these ideas.[4]

Unity a commandment. I do not say that differences in traditions, experiences and conceptions should be a sin. But lack of love, unity and co-operation constitute a part of human wretchedness.

We are accustomed to divisions, take them as necessary, accustomed also to the powerlessness, the impotence of Christendom. [Cf] my friend P. Ainslie, Federal Council Bulletin. United Christendom is undefeatable.

The Epistle, Tenth Sunday after Trinity, 1 Cor. 12. One and the selfsame Spirit, Eph. 4. But Jesus, Jn 17, most severe in v. 23. Nous empêchons le monde de connaître que Dieu a envoyé le Christ et qu'Il nous [a] aimé. That is a horrid crime and Christendom takes it lightly.

Must be preached. If anybody considers unity and love amongst Christians as a beautiful [ornament] but as a thing of minor importance, then I don't see how he has read the New Testament.

---

[4] As far as I am aware, this address can now only be known from Söderblom's own pencil notes. Söderblom papers, UUB.

Christian unity which is recognized more and more as an obligation and a commandment [to be obeyed].

Most urgent needs

   a. Brotherhood in international affairs. Christian mind. *New heart*
   b. Lawful order and freedom
   c. Christian principles in the construction of Society, social, economical. *New Creed*
   d. Missions
   e. Religious minorities
   f. Christian ethics—from faith, against international as well as national evils
   g. *Council.* Tongue for the Christian conscience

Unity can be achieved in one of three ways:

   a. 'The Propaganda-way'—the method of Rome [to which we must say]: No.
   b. Faith and Order. Great and necessary undertaking. But besides this [there is]:
   c. [The] Ecumenical Way. Difference [from b]—urgent, practical aims. Not touch Faith and Order. Winchester Fifth report!!

American Council on Organic Union Quarterly, 1 Cor. 4, v. 9. [The Bishop of] Winchester, Fifth report!!
Holy Synod in Const[antinople] and Athens
   Creed, Council. *We cannot wait*
We have already federal councils for common tasks a) local; b) national; here were mentioned i.a., U.S. Federal Council, [Swedish] Bishop's conference. Not interfere in internal things
We must have an *ecumenical council*

   Possibilities
      Federal Council 60–70 millions
      Methodists 20–25 millions
      Anglicans 40–45 Winchester
      Scotland (Presbyterian Alliance) Holland, France etc.
      Evangelical Lutherans 60 million
      The Orthodox
      Three parts of the Catholic Church
      But our power is not in numbers, but in God, in
      His Spirit in our hearts. The Streams. . . .

Let Christ's voice be heard. We have lived part of this world's tragedy. Shall we use our short lives to do our utmost to let the Crucified reign in our hearts, in society, in the world? Do we feel the divisions and the impotence of Christendom as a burning shame?

Never was the world more in need of the co-operation of all Christians. No one among us could have imagined ten years ago that we should see a time when practically all people would agree that science and technical perfection and laws and institutions are not enough, but that the renewal, we say the conversion of human hearts is needed. The tragedy of the world war and revolution preach to the Church, that the only thing that can save humanity is Christianity but that it has been neglectful and feeble through divisions.

He was aware of the fact that he had cut his moorings with regard to other international Church movements, and was taking his ship into the open sea. Already at Uppsala in June 1919 he had faced the Faith and Order challenge and taken his stand. He had both Brent and Gardiner as his listeners when at Geneva he compared his own plan with Faith and Order. Faith and Order was a long-term affair he felt, and his was an urgent task which could not wait. Action and service (it was called 'work' in the formula 'Life and Work') was necessary here and now.[5]

He felt that he was showing a new approach, the 'Ecumenical Way', and in so doing he was anxious to enlist both Talbot's Anglican Commission—with that famous 'as if' formula—and the Patriarch's Encyclical for his own 'Ecumenical Way'.

In order to emphasize the radical nature of his proposal he added under 'urgent needs' something he called 'New Creed'. He was not to continue arguing this for long, but it was a recurring expression in his addresses at this time. It is characteristic of his attempt to find surprising statements in order to shake the complacent. Söderblom expressed this idea with a typical choice of words: 'What we need is a new creed. I mean no change in the old creed of the Church, not at all, but a clear expression of the teaching of Christ and of our Christian duty regarding the brotherhood of the peoples and regarding the moral foundations of society.' As far as can be ascertained, Söderblom's idea on this point did not evoke any comments—and this was perhaps just as well.

Söderblom's initial address gave the Geneva meeting its lead in preparing for the theme of the proposed Conference. Later he would

---

[5] Faith and Order convened in Geneva immediately after Söderblom's Life and Work meeting. He wrote to Mrs. Söderblom as he left Geneva, returning to Upsala: 'Now Faith and Order is giving long speeches for twelve days. Neander, although enchanted with the Greeks, [said] "No. Christianity is not speeches but action".'

always insist that he wanted his Conference to deal with only a very limited number of problems. The programme must not be crowded. He found already at Geneva that he had to recommend restraint on this point.

The three main areas suggested by Söderblom were as follows:

1. Christian brotherhood and righteousness in *international relations*. This was developed in the language of Söderblom, Edward Talbot and Wilfred Monod at the time: 'Creation of a Christian disposition of mind as a necessary soul for the commonwealth of nations.'

2. The Christian concept of the system of law as a gift of God. This was a theme which he had often debated with his friend Judge Ribbing, a recognized Swedish authority on international law, who, as we have seen, was one of the Swedish delegates at Geneva.

3. Christian principles in social life and in the social and economic reconstruction of society. Relation to the Labour movement.

With regard to these three areas there was unanimity, and Söderblom had the trying experience that having suggested a certain limited number of fundamental themes, the group was inspired to suggest a host of other very useful subjects and interests: home missions and diaconia; Christian education; liberty of conscience and the protection of religious minorities; intemperance; gambling; the protection of family life; recreation; recruiting for the Christian ministry and Bible school work. All these were accepted by the meeting after some discussion. Only the experienced Karl Fries could restrain the enthusiasts from embarking on the wide theme of foreign missions. The meeting finally decided to avoid duplication and overlapping by omitting foreign missions as being the concern of the International Missionary Council.

Geneva also attended to important matters of organization in which Söderblom was personally involved. On Dr. A. J. Brown's motion, the meeting decided to form three 'groups', for America, Europe and Great Britain, each with its own chairman, secretary and three other members with power to act in their own sphere. In 1921 at Peterborough, there was formed very significantly a fourth, Orthodox group. On the suggestion of the practical Dr. Brown, a Committee of Arrangements was organized with twenty-five members of whom no less than thirteen were Americans. No French or Germans were included. The America–Sweden combination which largely determined the character of the Geneva meeting as a whole, was indicated in the choice of officers to that committee: Söderblom became chairman, with Macfarland and Lynch as 'Interim General Secretaries'.

Söderblom himself was appointed chairman for the European group, and his far-reaching influence at the meeting was demonstrated by the printed List of Nominations, which contained names from some fifteen countries, almost exclusively suggested by Söderblom. This list was characteristic of his personal preferences, and the names read like extracts from his crowded Visitors' Book, and prove the extent to which Söderblom's movement at the beginning was part of his personal group of friends.

This is true not least of his hopeful references to the prospective representatives of the Church of England: The Bishops of Winchester, Peterborough, Oxford, Durham and Hereford, with Canons William Temple, E. A. Burroughs of Peterborough, and G. E. Newsom of Newcastle, together with his personal friends Lord and Lady Parmoor, Mrs. Creighton and Dr. Hodgkin of the Society of Friends. Making some corrections in his list, he crossed out with pencil the name of the Bishop of Durham. Our guess is possibly as good as that of anyone else when we surmise that it was Bell who, on being shown that list, convinced the Swedish Archbishop that Hensley Henson, however much he was Söderblom's personal friend, would not be taken seriously as a protagonist of 'Life and Work'.

Söderblom also put forward names for secretaries to this group. They were both North Europeans, Scandinavians, Swedes from Uppsala, yes, come to think of it, both really members of his own household, his inner circle of co-workers! K. B. Westman as general secretary and Yngve Brilioth as assistant secretary. Excellent choice! Characteristic, too!

Uppsala! Yes, that raised another important matter, the place for the meeting. Söderblom had only one place in mind. Obviously America would be best, he said, but it was too far for the Europeans. In Switzerland there were always so many conferences, but where else in the world could one see such a concentration of Evangelical Christendom as round the Baltic? If one town only had to be mentioned the most suitable place seemed to him to be Uppsala.[6] Here the layman from Uppsala, Major Sjöstedt, had strengthened his case for him. He eliminated other alternatives; London and Paris were

---

[6] *Die Eiche*, 1921, p. 115.

out of the question, he thought, if the Conference was to welcome Germans; Geneva already had the League of Nations and could not take another invasion, thus Sweden was the only alternative. Uppsala was the place.

Sjöstedt was something of a financier, director of the Uppsala Tramways and with financial interests in Swedish waterfalls. He supported Söderblom's invitation to Uppsala and added an argument that could not fail to impress: 'If the Conference were held at Uppsala, the expenses of the arrangements and for the Conference itself would be met by Sweden.' Ungrudging in his generosity, he was prepared to guarantee a very large sum himself. This decided the issue. The Conference was to be held at Uppsala. Nobody knew at the time that even happy Sweden would have its financial crisis shortly afterwards, and that Sjöstedt would lose all his money. This was to be for Söderblom another last-minute cause for anxiety.

If the Geneva meeting was thus willing to follow Söderblom's lead in the matter of the place for the Conference, the members were inclined to be much more cautious than Söderblom as far as the date was concerned. It was now considered realistic to think in terms of 1922 or 1923, 'or at such time as the Committee of Arrangements may decide'. Writing to his wife, Söderblom anticipated the great work of preparation for the Conference. 'Oh, now I catch just a glimpse of Berner Oberland round Die Jungfrau in Mürren. When are you and I coming here to see and to meditate. Perhaps after the ecumenical Meeting in Uppsala–Stockholm August–October 1922!'

Söderblom had to be accomodating with regard to the name of the Conference. He had helped to coin the phrase 'Ecumenical', but naturally had experienced the difficulties of a long and unfamiliar term. When he published his article on 'Evangelical Catholicity' in German in Die Eiche 1919, the salient phrase was rendered by the printer: 'What I advocate is an ecumenical council, an economical council of churces' (p. 136). Dr. Brown wanted the Conference to 'avoid embarrassments' by eschewing that big word. We can assume that Söderblom pleaded for the use of his beloved term 'ecumenical'. In the end, the minutes from the Committee of Arrangements as reproduced in the Conference record has this characteristic compromise: the name 'should provisionally be 'Universal Conference of the Church of Christ on Life and Work'. 'It is hoped that this Conference will be Ecumenical.'

The scope of the proposed ecumenical conference depended on the question of who would be invited to take part in it. It was the hesitation on this point which was the cause of the most conspicuous absence from the Geneva meeting. The Anglicans stayed away because the Archbishop of Canterbury did not feel that a sufficiently Catholic approach was assured. When this question was to be discussed, Söderblom achieved one of his most spectacular feats of drama. We have seen how he had kept in close touch with the Orthodox Church in Constantinople. He had invited the Metropolitan Germanos and colleagues to Geneva and Uppsala that summer. In a letter of June 6, 1920 to Neander, Söderblom had requested that the group of Orthodox dignitaries should arrive in Geneva the day before the beginning of the Faith and Order meeting. Söderblom wished to welcome them to his own conference on Life and Work!

According to Neander, Söderblom kept the proposed visit of the Orthodox bishops secret until the very minute of their appearance. Only the group of Scandinavian co-workers was informed. That morning in the Conference was a particularly Scandinavian one: Bishop Ostenfeld of Copenhagen was in the chair, Pastor Tvedt of Oslo took the devotions, and Söderblom of Uppsala, together with Neander, his Swedish envoy to the East, were the happy stage-managers. The time was August 11, 1920, at 10.00 hours.

'As soon as the chairman [Ostenfeld] had announced this news, the three Oriental prelates, to the amazement of the conference, appeared.' The Metropolitan of Seleucia, Germanos, the Archbishop of Nubia, and Professor C. Papadopoulos thus made their entrée into the incipient ecumenical movement in the Western world. Söderblom asked 'one of his Swedish priests', Herman Neander, to welcome the visitors in Greek, and this linguistic ability duly impressed the Conference. Archbishop Germanos replied:

The Greek Orthodox Church is glad that there will be conversations between the Evangelical Church and the Church of the East. We pray for the success of this conference. The [Encyclical] Letter of the Patriarch breathes the spirit which has always lived in the Greek Church. She has always in her worship prayed for the unity of all who belong to Christ. Therefore the Greek Church welcomes any effort to bring the Christian churches closer to one another. This delegation from the Greek Churches welcomes the announcement of the Ecumenical Conference and will inform the Patriarch accordingly. This news will gladden the hearts of all the Bishops and Metropolitans of the Greek Church.

Archbishop Germanos concluded his address by praying in Greek for the unity of Christendom.[7] After this brief but memorable appearance, the Orthodox group led by Pastor Neander left the meeting.

Söderblom reported to Kolmodin in a letter of August 8, 1920:

The question of whether we were going to accept the Greeks was rather critical. I presented the conference with a *fait accompli* in simply inviting the Greeks to proceed into the hall where they were solemnly welcomed— which all parties afterwards fully approved. Greater difficulties were experienced about Rome who however will now be invited. It is obvious that the Pope in his sectarianism will decline such negotiations.

To Söderblom, this visit opened the way to further and closer contacts with the Orthodox churches, culminating in the reading of the Nicene Creed in Greek by Photios, Patriarch of Alexandria, before the High Altar in his own Cathedral at Uppsala. But, at Geneva that day as he observed the amazement of this very Protestant group, he could not help but remember the efforts of a Swedish layman in Constantinople, Johannes Kolmodin.

No sooner had that brief but immensely significant *eisodos* of the East taken place, than the Conference turned to the other related problem, that of inviting Rome into the movement. The issue was not presented in those terms, but rather brought to the meeting under a general formula, moved by Bishop James Cannon of the American Methodist Episcopal Church: that instructions be given 'to invite all Christian Communions to participate in the proposed Conference'. The operative word here was *all,* thus including Rome.

There was opposition to this idea. Herold once again represented a fairly general Swiss Protestant attitude:

Our interpretation of Christianity is that of the Reformation, while the Roman Church represents such a different mentality that no co-operation with her is possible. The gathering of all Protestant Churches is already in itself a great achievement; any plan to comprehend too much had better be postponed.

Söderblom knew that Herold had Swiss, French and American supporters of his Protestant idea. After controverting him in the

---

[7] Archbishop Germanos's speech translated here from the brief paragraph (in German) in Siegmund-Schultze's *Die Eiche,* 1921, p. 113. Where Siegmund-Schultze has 'Die Kommission der griechischen Kirchen', we take for granted that the reference was to the delegation of which Germanos was at that moment spokesman.

debate, Söderblom confessed to his wife that he felt he had said some 'unnecessarily harsh things. ... Later I recognized how dependent they are on their own particular churches.'

He first tried a simple device in order to ease the tension in the meeting, and in his letter in Swedish to Mrs. Söderblom he quotes his English words: 'Let us first see if there shall be dinner or tea, and then see whom we shall invite.' Thus invigorated, the Archbishop held forth, saying that 'God demands of us to have wide visions'. He was sure that in fact and in practice the Ecumenical Conference would consist of non-Romans, but individual Roman Catholics might like to attend. He thought of that letter he had received in 1917 from the Polish Archbishop of Warsaw. 'Those who wish to come, we should not exclude.' The term 'ecumenical conference of Protestant churches' was a contradictio in adjecto (a contradiction in terms), he said.

He also reminded the Conference of the standpoint of 'the great Anglican family of churches' who would not participate unless the fellowship was fully inclusive. 'If we were to exclude any Christian Church, we would in our turn be sectarian. We must demonstrate that we are the real Catholics and thus challenge the Roman Catholics to see whether they place Rome above a Catholic ethos.'

After this eloquent plea only two diehards voted against the motion, in that conference of eighty-five from fifteen different countries.[8] To Söderblom this was a decisive victory. He had aimed at an ecumenical conference, and he would have nothing less than that.

Uppsala was to be the place after all. Yet, no sooner had Söderblom managed to persuade the Conference to accept Uppsala than he had second thoughts about this. What really caused him to modify the bid for Uppsala is not known, but one can at least guess at his reasoning. The experts told him that the Ecumenical Conference might last six weeks and comprise some five-hundred delegates. This presented the Swedish hosts with immense practical problems. The little hotels in Uppsala at that time had of course only a small capacity.

If there was one person in Uppsala who knew from practical experience some of the difficulties involved in caring for such a crowd in such a small place, that was the Archbishop himself. He must have

---

[8] Cf. Die Eiche, 1921, pp. 113 and 114, and Nathan Söderblom, August, 1920, to Anna Söderblom.

insisted of course that Uppsala and its Cathedral remain in the picture, but for practical reasons the Conference would have to be moved to nearby Stockholm. He reported to his wife: 'The invitation to Uppsala, diplomatically presented, was received with keen interest and applause as Sjöstedt promised to find the necessary funds. To-day as I changed to Stockholm, with the final session in Uppsala, even more gratitude was felt.'

Uppsala or no Uppsala, the ship was launched. His wild dream could now be translated into terms of reality. It had been a long journey of hard work in preparation for what he already anticipated as his Uppsala/Stockholm Conference, and as he attended the first day of the Faith and Order Conference, also in Geneva in 1920, and where he was the one to propose Robert Gardiner for re-election as secretary, he wrote to his wife: 'In a few days we have done a piece of hard, immensely exacting work. ... With God's help we have trodden a narrow and steep path and progressed farther than we had thought in the most daring dreams of our hearts. ... But this is just a start. Now we begin.'

Uppsala and Catholicity

I.

At the outset of a chapter concerned with Catholicity, it is well to ask what contacts the Church of Sweden did have at this time, and to hear what contacts clerical opinion expected it to have. Dr. Ekelund, a rural dean and incumbent of the Diocese of Karlstad, writing in the Yearly Programme for 1918 as put forth by the A.S.P., an association of Swedish priests, is a good witness. A learned theologian with a central position in the Church, and profusely decorated for his services, Theophil Ekelund must be regarded as an authority on the matter and as typical of many among clergy and laity in the Church at the end of the war, just at the moment when the Archbishop in Uppsala was beginning to take advantage of the new freedom to travel.

Ekelund was clear and assured. First he dismissed the alternatives: with the Romans, no contact was possible because they rejected *a priori* any approach; with the Orthodox, contact 'at present' seemed out of the question; with the Reformed Church, its 'exclusive character' seemed to stand in the way; outside the Lutheran fold there remained only the Anglicans, and who could say what would come of the feelers that had been put out?

Having circled the ecclesiastical horizon, Ekelund focussed attention on the only possible outlet: 'Our sister Churches in the North, the mother Church in Germany, and the daughter Church in America are those which for fundamental and external reasons ought to be the first concern of the Swedish Church, and which allow real co-operation to be expected.'[1]

---

[1] Paulus Holmgren, vicar in Gävle, early nourished his well-founded apprehensions as to what might happen. On October 1914 he wrote to his friend, Dean Lundström who had acted in the sedisvacance between Ekman and Söderblom: 'It has been exceedingly good to know that the chairman [in the Chapter] has devoted himself in the first place to the priests of the Diocese and left in peace the Patriarch in Moscow together with other even more exotic celebrities.' Lundström papers, Uppsala University Library.

It is ironic that Söderblom also saw the future in terms of family, a family of Churches. The practical difference in the working out of his vision, compared with Ekelund's, is a measure of the degree to which Söderblom's archiepiscopate meant an innovation in the life and history of the Swedish Church.

In this chapter we record not so much the progress of Life and Work, but the development of a Faith and Order programme of his own which Söderblom pursued, more in deed than word, from his central position as Archbishop in Uppsala. It is first necessary, however, to sketch the doctrine of the Church and the doctrine of Evangelical Catholicity on which the programme was built.

The Church: Body and Soul

Söderblom's pronouncements on the Church, and on what he called Evangelical Catholicity, must not be thought of as polished paragraphs in a theological system. They were made in concrete situations, polemic or persuasive, as the case may have been. In common with his teacher, Auguste Sabatier, Söderblom held the view that dogma was 'symbolic', and theological statements were therefore, in the nature of things, approximate and provisional: Söderblom's statements on the Church must therefore be placed in their particular historical framework and setting.

This applies particularly to his most original contribution in this field, with the startling title: 'The Body and the Soul of the Swedish Church', of 1915.

The introduction is made by way of a sketch of an ordination of priests in a Swedish cathedral, where the author enumerates in some detail the various vestments to be worn on such an occasion by the officiating bishop and by the ordinands. Without further warning there then follows this paragraph:

In the case of a living being we distinguish between soul and body. Doubt may be entertained as to how far downwards the soul may be traced in the realm of inanimate and animate creation. Where does the inspiring influence of the spirit end? Where does 'lifeless' matter step in? Is any matter really dead? Is it not sooner or later taken again into requisition for spiritual purposes? The model and material from which life has fled may once more become a channel for the soul, even as an old and rusted bugle which one may take down from the wall, for music; if a man knows the art he may win from it tones that a hundred years back carried a meaning from man to man, though it has since been mute. The downward limits of organic matter, the body, are not defined. According to its intensity, a spirit shapes for itself, out of created things and events, an organ and an impress far beyond the organism which it is wont to call its body. And it is not seldom impossible to fix the limits of the body upwards. Where is the dividing line between the soul and that which it inspires? Yet we make a distinction between the thing formed and spirit which dwells in it. So also in the living organism that is composed of the religious community, the Church, a manifest distinction is found between the body and the soul; the former consists of fixed shapes, which are at an early age set forth in ceremonies and organization, and, at a later phase, in formulated dogmas and creeds: and the soul consists of emotions, thoughts, faith, personal and collective experiences, that are more or less able to shape a body for themselves or to use for their organ a model already at hand,—or else they live, thronged and obstructed in a trying confinement which nevertheless has an element of test and discipline.'[1]

As it happens we know the exact occasion when this study of Söderblom's was conceived in its first outline. There is extant a little blue notebook kept by Söderblom in the days of April 16–18 1914, when, together with members of his family, he stayed in a hotel, Hohe Sonne am Rennsteig, near Eisenach, 'with a wonderful view over to Wartburg' as printed on the hotel bill (28.80 DM for three days—two adults and three children), which was left in the notebook.

Söderblom's situation at the time was one of great anticipation and tension. His name had been placed on the short list of three for the Archbishopric of Uppsala. The reports from Uppsala were conflicting, he might be preferred, he might not. Nobody knew. Yet, deep in his heart, Söderblom felt that he was to be appointed, and he projected himself now into the role of Archbishop in far away, and yet so close, Uppsala.

He was on his way to the cathedral of Sens in France, where the very first in the long succession of Swedish Archbishops had been consecrated in 1164. The thought, like a flash, woke to life a sense of the sacred tradition of the Church of Sweden, not just odd parts of it, but the whole nineteen centuries, and more, for the prophets of old were very much part of it. He rejoiced in that tradition. As he meditated on it, looking towards Wartburg, he remembered that he had brought his own copy of C. A. Cornelius, *The History of the Swedish Church,* and out of it he made notes in the blue notebook,

---

[1] Söderblom, in *The Constructive Quarterly,* June 1915, p. 284: 'On the Character of the Church of Sweden.'

from St. Ansgar, St. Eric, and St. Birgitta, the Reformers and the solid bishops in the time of Gustavus Adolphus, to Pietism and nineteenth century revival. They were all part of this same living tradition. There was the rub. Tradition—life. Tradition could stifle life, and yet, tradition was valuable, was necessary. This was Sabatier's problem and his own message: there was a necessary tension and reciprocity between tradition and renewal, between organization and spirit, between body and soul.

Anticipating his own unique call to service in the Church of Christ, he wrote down a few words which he was to modify as the manuscript was prepared for the printers. 'When the good tidings about Christ, that is, when the Spirit, became religion and church, this happened in connexion with *episcopal* organization. In its turn, Sweden too was thereby incorporated into Christendom. . . .'[2] This ecumenical pioneer, Nathan Söderblom, was—this is sometimes overlooked and forgotten by those who study his contribution to 'Life and Work'—not just any Alliance secretary, he was a Church leader in Bishop's orders, and very conscious and increasingly aware of that fact.

In order to understand this fundamental concept of Söderblom's, to which he always returned, that of the antinomy between body and soul, we must relate it first to his general theological theme of Revelation.

In the Swedish volume where Söderblom published his study 'The Body and the Soul of the Swedish Church', he also had an article called 'The Church of Revelation'. The occasion for this article was an interpretation of the art scheme in the 'Church of the Revelation' at Saltsjöbaden, Stockholm, where Söderblom had provided the architect with the ideas underlying its form; but the ideas themselves had a wider theological reference.

Revelation was Söderblom's fundamental theological concept, and the Church was related to the revelation of God in Christ and His Holy Spirit, and the *extension* of the revelation was, in short, the Church, or at least the prophetic 'spirit' of the Church. In an im-

---

[2] Notebook: 'Professor Söderblom' (in German letters), UUB. In its final and printed form this was modified and rendered into English: 'When the good news of the Kingdom of God and of Christ, and the unity of the faithful brethren in the Spirit was gradually organized into a religion, the Church acquired fixity and universality by means of the episcopate.' Söderblom, *Constr. Quarterly*, 1915, p. 285.

portant theological lecture of 1911, Söderblom had developed the theme of the extension of Revelation. This took place, he said, in a three-fold way, through the creative genius, in history itself, and through the renewal of the individual. On this foundation he went on:

God continually reveals himself. ... The Church is God's work and God's instrument. The religious significance of the Church is sometimes over-emphasized, but also often understated. God has given to the Church the divine privilege and the challenging duty in word and sacrament to *impart* God's grace. Our faith in an extended revelation in history compels us with greater care and veneration to appreciate the worth of men, means, and organizations which divine guidance has given unto our churches throughout history.[3]

In this sacred history the genius, the hero, the saint are all expressions of that renewed revelation, and certain individual personalities thereby acquire special importance in the economy of God.

Here was then the divine dynamic, the creative principle in and through the Church. But this Church, he always insisted, had a body and a soul. What did these terms imply?

The body first. From one point of view it was the outer shell of the Church; there were aspects of it which were 'purely external'. In 1915, he could, in one context, relegate the framework of the liturgy to this category.[4] In the same breath, by insisting that the Church 'acquired fixity and universality by means of the episcopate', he indicated that the episcopal ministry, too, so fundamental to him and his ecumenical outreach, could be regarded as something external; it gave 'continuity and authority' to the Church, but it was not, as such, part of the 'soul' of the Church.[5] With a somewhat sweeping gesture, he would say that dogmas and creeds pertain to the settled form or firm framework of a church.[6]

From one point of view this was part of the institution or organization, which constituted the body. Again and again he returned to the idea of the provisional character of the institution. In a sermon at Västerås in 1923, he put this view very succinctly:

The outer things which constitute the organization, the forms and the body of the Church, have no value in themselves. They have value only

---

[3] Söderblom, *Ett bidrag till den kristna uppenbarelsetrons tolkning* (1911), p. 20.
[4] *Constr. Quarterly*, 1915, p. 306.
[5] Söderblom, *Sv. Kyrkans kropp och själ* (1915), p. 12.
[6] *Constr. Quarterly*, 1915, p. 531. The Swedish term was *'fasta skepnad'* of the Church.

as a means and a channel for the saving truth of God. Nobody must imagine that the Church, its servants and institutions have dignity in themselves. The question is: do they serve the Gospel?[7]

This did not mean that one could discount the body. As a vehicle for the soul, the body was indispensable. From this standpoint he would, as a rule and up to a certain point, insist on tradition and order as enriching the Church. He did so in the little study from which we quoted, inspired in him by the consecration of the first Archbishop of Uppsala in Sens Cathedral in 1164, seven and a half centuries prior to his own consecration. With what love and veneration he wrote there of the rites and the insignia used in those early times!

Söderblom claimed that the two, body and soul, must be held in balance, that they were an 'organic unity', to borrow Sabatier's formula, but if there had to be a choice, Söderblom was, of course, all for the spirit. At the Faith and Order Conference in Lausanne in 1927, he put this neatly: 'If I am bound to choose between Institutionalism and Spiritualism I prefer the latter. We must worship God in spirit and truth.'[8]

Understood in the widest context and in a long perspective, this motif in Söderblom was part of his Pietistic inheritance, if it be remembered that the salient idea in that tradition was the 'secret of life' as the connexion between revival and mysticism.[9] The idea of the spirit as part of an antinomy, body-spirit, was taken over by Söderblom from Sabatier.

The French *maître* knew of a 'substantial foundation' of the dogmas and the symbols 'which is the religious reality itself, the *vital process,* infinite and eternal, which the Spirit creates',[1] and the young Söderblom had especially underlined those words in his well-worn copy of Sabatier's book. From this there is a straight line via Bergson's *élan vital* to his own formula 'existence as life', combined with his reading of the prophetic tradition in Holy Scripture.

We have, of course, not exhausted the theme with these few indications, there were also other factors. One at least must be mentioned here. Söderblom the Archbishop was also the scholar of the history of religions. In the year 1914, when he conceived the idea of

---

[7] Söderblom, *Svenskars fromhet,* p. 34.
[8] *Faith and Order, Lausanne, 1927,* p. 324.
[9] Cf. M. Schmidt, *Theolog. Lit.ztg,* 1949, p. 18.
[1] A. Sabatier, *Esquisse d'une Philosophie de la Religion,* 1897, p. 404.

the relation Body–Soul in the Church, he also published one of his most important books *The Origin of the Belief in God*. There cannot be much doubt that he felt that one of his most important theses in that book was his interpretation of animism, and of Moses's Jahveh as appearing 'in the cover of an animistic deity'.[2] We must not overemphazise this particular connexion; if challenged, Söderblom would probably have eschewed it, but it should be kept in mind.

The terrible experience of war tore asunder much of his frame of reference, *Religionsgeschichte;* but to him, this experience underlined the reality of the Spirit. 'Here religion is forced to its centre. What is the centre of Christianity, if not God? God is not a dogma or a thought, but a living spirit, nearer to us than anything else.' In this very context he felt he could approach the reconciliation of the peoples. How was that to be achieved? The Spirit was the answer. He then continued in these words: 'The Christian Church should, apart from confessions, and as far as it is animated by the Spirit of Christ, come to an understanding about common teaching, proclamation, and a common endeavour in brotherhood. Catholicity has received an international task which it has neglected, but which, with the seriousness of judgement forces itself upon us.'[3]

From this, there was for Söderblom only a very short step to the political programme of an emerging Life and Work movement, the connexion with the League of Nations and the establishing of international law. He even introduces his term catholicity in this broad context: 'The new catholicity which we now consider as the foundation for supranational order of law and supranatural continuity of law.'[4]

In defining the relation between the body and the soul of the Church, Söderblom attempted to neutralize or ward off such spiritualistic consequences as his concept necessarily carried. He was aware of these consequences. 'With full intention, I do not differentiate between invisible and visible Church,' he would say.[5]

He did not however find a solution in incarnation. To be sure later at Lausanne, 1927, he insisted that the unity of 'body' and

---

[2] Söderblom, *Gudstrons uppkomst*, pp. 366 and 28. One of his references in this connexion is to William McDougall's, *Body and mind*, 1911.

[3] Söderblom and others, *Enig Kristendom* (1919), p. 105.

[4] Ibid., p. 110.

[5] Söderblom, *Body and Soul of the Swedish Church*, p. 85.

'soul' which he attempted should be termed 'incarnationalism'.[6] This, perhaps, was largely a subsequent rationalization or accomodation.

In his Lausanne address, August 15, 1927, Söderblom made the point that unity in faith and order could be achieved by three different methods: Institutionalism, Spiritualism, and Incarnationalism. All he says about the last, apart from a reference to the concentration of revelation in the Logos, is in fact part of what he calls the second alternative. These were his words:

This third group emphasizes, as against the first, that religion is not essentially a body, a fixed form, a doctrine, a hierarchy, but primarily a soul, a spirit. It emphasizes as against the second group that for us, in this earthly existence, every spirit must receive bodily form, be incarnated in words, in deeds, men, institutions, doctrines, and forms of service, in order to become active and lasting.[7]

His instinct was to be somewhat apprehensive of incarnational theology as such, particularly in its Anglican form, and there is no doubt that his struggle at Lausanne, 1927, was really over this issue.

He would confide his misgivings to his diary. After a visit to Archbishop Davidson in April, 1921, he wrote:

It is a good thing that St. Augustine had not studied Greek, for [if he had,] he might, as some Anglicans have, been caught, with the Greek Fathers, in Incarnation, and not have proceeded to *redemptio* and salvation and the Cross.[8]

Once only—as far as we can judge—did he put this into print, namely in a collection of articles on the Nordic Churches in the same year, 1921.[9]

His 'spiritual' and experiential approach made it natural for him to meet other churches with an attitude of generous, large-hearted comprehensiveness. Contacts with the rich variety of the Church which he had in April, 1914, in that month full of great anticipations, gave him an ecumenical experience on the deepest level. In a matter of a few days, he then visited a number of churches in Europe; later he referred to these visits in his diary.

[6] Söderblom, *Christliche Einheit!*, 1928. At this time Söderblom felt a need to defend his standpoint over against accusations from Roman Catholics.

[7] H. N. Bate, ed. *Faith and Order*, Lausanne, 1927, pp. 324 and 327.

[8] Diary, 'England etc. 1928', p. 34.

[9] Söderblom, in A. Th. Jörgensen (ed.), *Nordens kirker*, 1921, p. 18.

In Sens [at the time mentioned] nominated to the archiepiscopal see; in front at the High Altar, alone, perhaps [together with] some astonished fellow visitor; prayer for the unity of the Church. In a stall of a minor canon in Westminster Abbey. In Thomas Church in Leipzig. Standing reading, and singing in a church in Athens in Holy Week. Why must there be separation from these devout [people]? Why should our different views, which I on no account could modify or give up, why should they hinder us from feeling united in one Church?[1]

As far as he attempted to establish 'organic unity' of the Church's body and soul, he found this in the concrete reality of the actual functioning Church, which in his case meant the Swedish Church. Faced with the challenge, 'at last to say a word about what we mean by the Church,' he said, 'a definition in fact is not needed. Because the Church lives and appears, and is to be found in our midst both for those who wish, and those who do not wish, to see her. I mean by the Church, quite simply, our State Church, but understood so deeply and so widely as its nature requires. Revelation, or if you like, the faith, the individuals, and the institutions (the ministry and all other ordinances), these three constitute the Church. Together they form an historic entity, an organism. .. Above all, the Church means ... Sweden as a part of Christendom on earth.'[2]

In these latter formulations, Söderblom was influenced by the 'discovery of the Church' in the Uppsala 'Young Church' revival of 1908–1909, and the ideas of the Uppsala S.C.M. expressed by Eklund, E. Billing, and Björkquist. Yet, there is always a certain oscillation in Söderblom with regard to these ideas. The compass needle was pointing in one direction, but there were still these constant oscillations. As Söderblom published his lectures on the Body and Soul of the Swedish Church in its Swedish form, in December, 1915, he wrote a preface with a warning in it to his 'Young Church' friends, in Uppsala and Sweden generally. In latter years, the Church had been so definitely discovered, he thought, that he had to abstain from saying any more about the matter. 'I do not say that the discovery has always concerned the Church in her mysterious life. ... People seem to feel comfortable in the 'Church renaissance', and are in danger of talking the thing to death.'

With this geographical and national concreteness of his Church,

---

[1] The date of the diary note is Jan. 16, 1918, the day after his birthday. He recalls his experience from April 1914.

[2] Söderblom, *Den enskilde och kyrkan*, 1909.

he naturally connected the Church of the ancient creeds. Speaking to his Lutheran brethren at the Philadelphia Seminary in 1923, he took his stand with the Nicene Fathers and Dr. Luther's Catechism:

When we confess our belief in the Holy Catholic Church, or according to the Nicene Creed, in the 'One, Holy, Catholic and Apostolic Church', we do not think of any special organized section of the Church, but of the Church as a whole. ... In order to avoid any particularist misunderstanding and to emphasize the Catholicity or Universality of the Church, Martin Luther speaks of 'The whole of Christendom on earth.' ... Therefore he finds that the very best and clearest rendering is 'Eine heilige Christenheit', that is One Holy Christendom on earth. ...

In the Third article of the Creed itself the unity and the catholicity of the Church is regarded as an object of faith. Not as if the Church was only invisible. The Church is apparent and visible in manifold ways. ...

The Unity and Catholicity of the Church is not something to be achieved by men. It exists through God's creation. In speaking of the Unity and Catholicity of the Church, we do not speak of an ideal to be accomplished by our efforts. No, we confess our faith strengthened by experience. We state the existence of the One Holy Catholic and Apostolic Church which includes all true believers in heaven and on earth.[3]

Evangelical Catholicity

The Church he served was Protestant and Lutheran; kindled to new life by sixteenth century Reformation, solidified—some would have said petrified—by seventeenth century Orthodoxy, shaken by nineteenth century revivals. This Archbishop, returning from Europe to his native Swedish land, and to his own Uppsala, was soon using new, bold and startling words for this Church as he visualized it and its task in the world. His programmatic term was 'Evangelical Catholicity'.

One can approach this concept of Söderblom's by way of confrontation with other forms of Catholicity. As first conceived by Söderblom, the idea had a sharp, almost jarring, accent of anti-Roman sentiment. 'Evangelical Catholicity', in that context, at first meant an alternative to Roman Catholicism. It was the 'spiritual' alternative to the infallible papal institution of Rome. This must be understood in its historical setting; the time was not that of John XXIII but of the system of Vatican I, and its representative, Pius X. There were very few Protestant scholars who sympathized as deeply with,

---

[3] *The Lutheran*, Philadelphia, 1923, p. 11.

and were as informed about, the revolt of Modernism against this system, as Nathan Söderblom, and he admired their courageous stand against the coercion of the Church. He knew Loisy and Tyrrell, and his great book *Religionsproblemet* of 1910 was mainly devoted to their struggle; he felt that they were out for an 'ecumenical, non-Roman Catholicity'.[1] They were as gripped by ideas of movement and life, as distinct from rigid systems of institutions, as he was.

After the war, as he consciously developed his idea of an Evangelical Catholicity, he did so against the background of the Roman system. All the harsh rigidity and inflexibility which he subsumed under the term 'body', was there incarnate; was 'a prison which encloses and chokes the spirit'.[2] Rome, he thought, wanted to enforce obedience by organization, institution, the religion of law. Here an intransigent religious system stifled human freedom and the personal respect for truth. This was all part of the 'Yoke of Rome', and Rome was therefore more of a sect than any other part of the Church. Worst, in Rome was the Jesuit order, 'the caricature of real Catholicity', for this system tended 'to make men into obedient machines'.

As for its vision of unity, Rome stood for the method of absorption and was, as such, the sad and bad alternative with which he compared his own 'method of love'. As compared with Roman Catholicism, understood in these terms (which today we can hardly fail to recognize as an unconscious caricature) Söderblom's own Evangelical Catholicity was seen as the defence of the freedom of the true Evangelical faith.[3]

The other 'Catholic' alternative, *Liberal Catholicism*, he hardly recognized as such, just as his own 'Evangelical' Catholicity, for various reasons, was never taken very seriously by the Anglo–Catholics. This was so mainly for semantic reasons. The greatly overworked term 'Evangelical' hardly conveyed the meaning in English that Söderblom was out for. The overtone of narrow pietism is the very opposite of the rich and generous, joyful and liberating note which Söderblom wanted to convey.

He attempted, it seems, to obviate this semantic difficulty by using the adjective 'Evangelic'. Somebody, possibly Brilioth, had

---

[1] Söderblom, *Religionsproblemet*, p. 210.
[2] Söderblom, *Christian Fellowship*, 1923, p. 66.
[3] Söderblom, *Body and Soul of the Swedish Church*, 1915, pp. 157–159. *Evangelical Catholicity* (1919), pp. 86–97. *Christian Fellowship*, 1923, p. 121.

persuaded him to use this term for English consumption, and this was the expression that he used in English from 1919—Evangelic Catholicity.

However, Söderblom on his side hardly paused to consider the message of Liberal Catholicism. Here again semantics played their part. 'Liberal theology' was a bad term in Sweden, and no Swedish Archbishop, it seems, could very well accept being known in that sense as 'Liberal'.

In his book, *Gore, A Study in Liberal Catholic Thought*, J. Carpenter has clearly brought out the various marks of Liberal Catholicism—scriptural, historical, rational, constitutional, and comprehensive.[4] For his own programme, Söderblom accepted all these, except possibly the appeal to *ratio*, which, to him, always conveyed more of Erasmus than of Luther, and was for *that* reason, less appealing to him. Yet, while accepting these other marks, he did not necessarily do so for the same reasons as Gore and others had done. Particularly, the appeal to history understood as antiquity is absent in Söderblom's concept, there is no reference to *Patres* in his arguments for his own view. Neither is real anchorage in Holy Scripture his main concern, chiefly perhaps because he took it for granted. There was little indication in his own books and articles on the subject that he was particularly anxious to relate the 'Evangelic' to Scriptural authority, apart from general references to unity as 'Christ's plain commandment'.[5]

As for the marks of constitutionalism and comprehensiveness, Söderblom did not often use those actual terms, but the ideas as such were those for which he fought.

It is now time to define Evangelic Catholicity in positive terms.[6] Catholicity meant universality, and this was its chief characteristic:

---

[4] Carpenter, *Gore, A Study in Liberal Catholic Thought* (1960).

[5] Söderblom, *Christian Fellowship*, p. 18.

[6] We cannot make place here for a year-by-year presentation of the development of his idea of Evangelic Catholicity from about 1906, cf. N. Karlström, op. cit., pp. 240–243. We note however that as early as 1911, he took cognizance of Newman Smyth's book *Passing Protestantism and Coming Catholicism*. He did so the more readily as he recognized in the author an old friend from Hartford, Conn., 1890. In 1923 the met Newman Smyth again, and he notes in his diary that he told his friend how much his ideas had meant to him. This must not be overrated. But neither should the reference to Newman Smyth be overlooked. It was only in the early 1920's that Söderblom discovered that the Lutheran Orthodox teacher Joh. Gerhard (d. 1637) had used the term Evangelic Catholicity. Cf. Söderblom, 'Evangelical Catholicity', *The Lutheran Church Review*. Vol. 43, 1924, p. 4 ff.

a universal church, a universal society. To a certain extent this had already been realized once, in and through medieval society, of which Evangelic Catholicity was as much the inheritor as the post-Reformation Roman section of the Church. At that time the Church formed a 'magnificent universal society', and in the long run, mankind could not do without something like it.[7] The hallmark of this universal Church however, was unity, *not* uniformity; there must be room for the characteristic, the concrete and the practical, as well as for personal involvement with a prophetic note.

To Friedrich Heiler, his enthusiastic disciple in Germany, he could therefore write: 'It is clear that in *Evangelisch-katholisch*, I emphasize more the Evangelisch, you the katholisch. For me Evangelic Catholicity signifies that only the message of salvation of the Gospel, which does not bind in statutes but liberates to unconditional service of Almighty God, can achieve real Catholicity.'[8]

This prophetic Evangelic Catholicity, 'this new Catholicity towards which we are striving', could not but have consequences for the political involvement of the Church. A Christian Church which took its universality seriously had to be supranational, and therefore must be involved in the political problems of its time and generation. In this perspective the League of Nations, and similar international organizations, were not excluded from the ecumenical programme. On the contrary, 'as the League of Nations must become religion', to use Söderblom's quaint phrase, there was a close connexion between the League and the practical programme of the ecumenical Church.

Universal, yes, but this universality must be expressed in concrete terms and forms. This to the Archbishop meant that it had to be anchored in a particular church, the Swedish Church, 'Uppsala'. Here, in worship and witness and service, he could do more than try to define an ecclesiastical position by way of theological argument. He could act out his ecclesiology in the living drama of the Church; the pattern of its sacred year; the lofty words of its ancient ritual; but also its prophetic task on the national scene; and its bridge-building, ecumenical adventure with regard to other churches. It was in this context, and through Söderblom, that the Swedish episcopal tradition suddenly, without previous warning, acquired a key function. He felt he had the assurance of its historic succession from

---

[7] Söderblom and others, *Enig Kristendom* (1919), pp. 107–8.
[8] Söderblom, August 4, 1926, to F. Heiler.

the times of the Apostles, and from past dynamic and expansive periods in Swedish history, when the great Evangelical king, Gustavus Adolphus, saw his vision of a *corpus evangelicorum*. He had made these claims in the conversations with the Anglicans in 1908–1909. They were strongly and vividly emphasized in the Archbishop's programmatic book *The Body and Soul of the Swedish Church*, of 1915. And again, the idea and claim were reiterated in his book, of 1923, *Christian Fellowship*, which is one of his most significant, representative ecumenical pronouncements. In *Christian Fellowship* he repeated the claim of his great sixteenth century predecessor, Archbishop Laurentius Petri of Uppsala (d. 1573), who in his Church Ordinance had said of the Swedish episcopate that it was universally accepted and approved over the whole of Christendom. Söderblom would often quote Laurentius Petri to this effect and he went on to say: 'There is in our section of the Church no room for the slightest doubt about the unbroken continuity of what has been called apostolic succession. The bishop therefore did not belong to only the one nation or the other, to the one religious body or the other: he represented 'the bond with the universal church', he was 'a responsible servant in the Church as a whole'. Understood in these terms, episcopacy also stood for the independence of the Church over against any Erastian encroachment on the part of the State: this was a point to which Söderblom often returned in his interpretations of episcopacy in his own country and in connexion with the consecrations which he was to take abroad.

Yet, with all this Söderblom also held as a Lutheran who in the last resort felt that the 'soul' was preeminent compared with the 'body': 'No thought is here implied of a divine and unconditional law'; no fundamental difference existed according to Laurentius Petri or his disciple Söderblom 'between the essence of a bishop's office and that of a priest'.[9]

In the Europe that had been through the fire of world war, the Swedish Church had a unique calling of 'tying together' what had been broken.[10] It was in line with his idea on the role, in history and in the extended revelation, of the hero and the genius that, together with Martin Luther, Gustavus Adolphus was to loom large in his programme of Evangelical Catholicity. Some theologians, neat

---

[9] Söderblom, *Christian Fellowship* (1923), p. 126–128.

[10] 'Sammanbindande uppgift', a task of tying together, in Christendom, was the term he used when summing up his study, *The Body and Soul of the Swedish Church*, 1915, p. 59.

and nimble classifiers of ideas, insisted that all these concepts did not fit together. Söderblom was not perturbed; the scene was widened beyond the national boundaries; he looked to Europe and the world. At this point it may be worth giving an illustration of how Söderblom saw his ideas in practical relation to one another, and to the movement for Faith and Order as conceived by the Americans.

Faith and Order, Uppsala, 1919

Throughout the war, the untiring Robert Gardiner, lawyer and lay secretary of the American Faith and Order movement, had kept Söderblom informed about his plans; about exciting contacts with the Vatican in 1915, and about their common hope of seeing a speedy end to the War. As far as the plans of the Faith and Order movement were concerned, he told Söderblom that rapid results could not be looked for: 'That will require a great deal of correspondence and consequent delay, but of course it is very much wiser to take years, if need be, to find out what is the right thing to do, rather than to rush ahead and make mistakes which might be serious.'[1]

With his lead pencil, Söderblom made a mark in the margin by those few lines. It was April, 1915, Europe was involved in war, and Söderblom's concept of time was quite opposite to that equipoised attitude of Gardiner's. He would return to that category of time: 'time, [the] one commodity the international movement could not command.'[2]

Soon after the War, an American Faith and Order deputation went to Europe and the East, in order to establish contacts and explain the plans and programme of the movement. Part of the group visited Uppsala and Stavanger at the beginning of June, 1919. They included Bishop C. P. Anderson of Chicago, who had been a member of the Anglican deputation to Uppsala in September, 1909, Bishop B. Vincent of Southern Ohio, Dr. E. L. Parsons, and Dr. B. T. Rogers. The meeting in Uppsala took place in June, 1919.

Uppsala, 1919, seemed almost to be a repeat, after a ten years interval, of Uppsala, 1909, when the Anglican deputation had paid

---

[1] R. Gardiner, April 9, 1915, to Söderblom. Faith and Order-file. Söderblom papers.
[2] F. S. L. Lyons, *Internationalism in Europe, 1815–1914* (1963), p. 204, Dr. Lyon's comment referred to a Leipzig professor, W. Ostwald and his 'Die Brücke'-movement.

its memorable visit. This was another Anglican deputation to Uppsala, meeting now, as then, in the same chapter room in the shadow of the Cathedral; here was now, as then, the Swedish Archbishop with his chapter of theological professors; and now, as then, the most active members on the Swedish side were Söderblom and Einar Billing. There was also a difference, of course: The Archbishop was now Söderblom himself.

Söderblom, in his eloquent speech of welcome, could refer to the fact that Bishop Anderson, now chairman of the deputation, had been a member of 'the weighty ecclesiastical assembly' in 1909. As Söderblom went on to stress the fellowship of the Swedish Church with the Augustana Synod, 'our daughter community in the United States, and by far our nearest relation', Bishop Anderson must have recalled somewhat uneasily, how ten years earlier, he had heard those very words from the same person.[3]

Everything seemed so similar, and yet so different. For this was June, 1919; they were assembled, the Swedish Archbishop said, 'in this crisis and time of cruel martyrdom of mankind,' to consider the question of the Church's unity. What was the line to take, in *that* kind of situation, to bring about the unity of Christians? Old Bishop Vincent of Cincinnati, seventy-five years of age but full of vigour, had been given the charge of exercising that faithful hobby-horse of ecumenical parlance: 'not compromise but comprehensiveness; not uniformity but unity,' while Bishop Anderson set out to show that the two emerging movements, the American Faith and Order and the Scandinavian International Conference 'might advantageously combine our forces'.[4] This was a point on which he had written to Söderblom six months earlier. Westman, on Söderblom's behalf, had answered that this idea, while valuable, required careful and thorough consideration for there were obvious differences of scope and purpose between the two.[5]

In the conference, Professor Billing presented the Lutheran position with regard to orders: the ministry was not of necessity tied to any particular form of order but had its authority through the Word and the Sacraments. Söderblom joined in with this; he had

---

[3] Söderblom, draft of his speech of welcome on 'Faith and Order, Uppsala 1919'.
[4] *Upsala* (newspaper), June 5, 1919 and Bishop Anderson, January 28, 1919 to Söderblom.
[5] K. B. Westman, draft of letter to Bishop Chs. P. Anderson, no date, March (?), 1919.

only had time to jot down on a piece of paper, among names of speakers on the American and Swedish sides:

'Difficulty of this conference
Personal Religion
Institutional Religion
N. S. Else Divided impossible[6]

He did not need any more of course, as a support for his memory, for this was his favourite theme, and he now applied it to the relation between the two movements 'in process of formation', represented at the table. It was an historic moment, for this was the very first confrontation between Faith-and-Order and Life-and-Work.

The difficulty with the plans for the unity of the Church consisted in the opposition between personal and institutional religion, Söderblom said. This is as much as we can learn from the available sources. Whether in that atmosphere, in that room, he felt he could go any further than that, we do not know. He may have left it with those broad generalizations, for he was after all, the host of the party.

In an article on Evangelical Catholicity, published about that very time, he had developed the theme to which he alluded in broad terms when meeting 'the Americans'. In it he interpreted what the Americans were after: 'Catholicity, to a certain degree, and after the institutional method'. But further, in that connexion, he expressed satisfaction that Faith and Order, too, understood 'the evangelic principle of personal experience and conviction as indispensable conditions for fellowship; but added the warning: 'As soon as the institution is given precedence over the individual souls and their fellowship with God, then it is impossible for an Evangelical position to be taken', and felt he was a good Lutheran when he tacked on, in Latin, § VII of the Augsburg Confession.[7] 'For the true unity of the Church it is sufficient, *satis consentire de doctrina evangelii et administratione sacramentorum.*'

From these presuppositions he drew the line. It would be better if 'our conference' and the great American Conference would continue on parallel lines, particularly as the Scandinavian Conference seemed to be close to reaching practical goals.[8] Söderblom's own

---

[6] Söderblom had the habit, when referring to a point of view with which he identified himself, of writing his initials. He developed his ideas in interviews in *Upsala* (newspaper) the following day, June 7, 1919.

[7] Nathan Söderblom, *Enig kristendom*, 1919, pp. 101–102.

'Ecumenical Conference', as he now said, had another, more practical and immediate aim. They had special tasks, and could not wait for uniformity with regard to the constitutions between different churches. He rounded this off on a persuasive note; for the total effort it would be valuable if the smaller Scandinavian Conference could act as a forerunner to the World Conference which the representatives of Faith and Order had in mind.

The following day, June 5, Westman, before leaving for his Swedish summer holiday at Lake Siljan in Dalecarlia, went over the result in a letter to Söderblom:

It was fun to see how Chicago retired immediately on being duly informed about our conference. It was obvious too that the Americans appreciated the idea of being linked with an Evangelic-Orthodox connection until the day when Rome comes along and wants to participate.[9]

In a letter to Gardiner, Söderblom summed up his attitude: 'It is noteworthy that we fully agreed upon the necessity that our Oecumenical Conference must have its own way with its practical aim, imposed by the War and by the revolutionary state of things, and that it will thus serve as an excellent preparation for the "World Conference on Faith and Order".

Another aspect meant a great deal to him: This was the Communion of the disciples of Jesus Christ in the Eucharist. If there was, as we have attempted to suggest, an alternative 'Faith and Order' movement which was his very own, then it had to include Service and Intercommunion as vital elements. The encounter at Uppsala, 1919, with the American delegation made him visualize all the more clearly his own approach. He was to be interested in, yet constructively critical of, the 'American' approach but increasingly aware of a programme of his own, also in matters of Church order.

In the meantime however, Söderblom took as active a part in 'Faith and Order' as he could afford. It was Söderblom who, on the first day of the Faith and Order meeting in Geneva, August, 1920, proposed Gardiner's name as secretary of the movement, and Söderblom's friendship with Bishop Brent was deepened through the years. The real personal involvement of Brent in the life and work

---

[8] A few weeks earlier, Professor A. Kolmodin received a letter from Constantinople: 'Dear Daddy! ... Constantinople, Canterbury, Upsala is of course rather a beautiful combination which deserves to be furthered! Greet the Archbishop!' J. Kolmodin, February 11, 1919, to A. Kolmodin; UUB.

[9] K. B. Westman, June 5, 1919, to Söderblom.

of the Stockholm Conference, and the great loyalty he showed to the leader of that meeting, was something which Söderblom greatly appreciated.

Against this background, Söderblom would also occasionally sketch that united Church of the future, but he did so only sparingly, and then in broad generalizations. He did not allow himself to be tied to any of the current theories on the subject—the Federated Church, a 'branch' theory etc. He knew about them of course, and he could use them as the occasion offered itself; then the image grew before his eyes, and he could develop it with charming concreteness.

The 'branch' theory was a case in point. Generally he would only allude to it in his three branches of Catholicity: Roman, Orthodox, and Evangelical. But in his article for Deissmann's *Festschrift,* published in 1926, he suddenly *saw* the image, and the tree was there; not a pine tree, but an oak with mighty branches. 'The root was the biblical revelation', and in the trunk there were 'different kinds of sap and power and energy'. The revelation-mysticism of Paulinism and Augustinianism were continued in Luther and Calvin, while the Roman World Church, under the Pope, retained the hierarchy, with a rich variety of institutions and cults and types of piety.[1]

He had some of these images in mind as he visualized that Church-to-be. We shall find in this study how he saw certain grand ecumenical lines of connexion, where 'Uppsala and the North' and 'Uppsala-Constantinople', together with other combinations, played their part. It is possible that in the extension of these ideas, there was a concept of a Confederation of patriarchates, as we would say today, but Söderblom did not, *expressis verbis,* say so.

As compared with Rome, the Orthodox, he felt, placed the Gospel in the centre.[2] From his personal contacts with Orthodox theologians, such as Germanos and Glubokovski, he knew that the Orthodox were 'spiritual'.

The image, the 'incomparable image', as he said, to which he returned with almost surprising faithfulness, was one which he had heard from his friend Professor Glubokovski, when the Russian gave his Olaus Petri lectures at the University of Uppsala, October, 1919. Söderblom developed this in these words:

---

[1] Söderblom, 'Evang. Katholizität', *Festgabe für Ad. Deissmann,* 1927, p. 330.

[2] 'Common to the Orthodox and us is that we place the Gospel above everything else.' Söderblom, January 14, 1927, to F. Heiler.

'The unity that our Saviour loves and ordains cannot be brought about by means of mutual propaganda and conquest. It must be sought in the heights or in the depths of the communion's spiritual being. He took the image from his native country. A Russian house may be divided into several rooms by low walls; up above there are no dividing walls, down below the people live in separate rooms. Is unity to be gained by thrusting the walls aside, so that those who live in the other rooms must either be crushed to death or leave their dwellings and enter the one that is taking possession of more and more floor space? Or must they be crowded and quarrel about the space? Glubokovski indicated another way out of the difficulty. Let the walls remain. Each individual thrives best in his spiritual home. . . . Do not move the walls. But let us all grow in faith, hope, and love, so that we reach above the divisions and see and show our membership of the same Church and congregation of Christ.'[3]

This image greatly appealed to Söderblom; he could *see* that Russian *chata* with the smoke rising above the endless snow-fields, and he could hear laughter and the deep singing voices from those rooms, inside those walls. It must have reminded him of some peasants' houses in the province of Hälsingland, no, in that village Trönö. In 1919, as he first listened to Glubokovski, the image appealed to him also because it was presented by an Orthodox. Also he liked the concept because it was that of 'dear old Glubo', striving to convey what he wanted to say in that daring mixture of various European languages; 'the greatest Orthodox theologian of our generation', as Söderblom would exclaim with his exuberant sweep of appreciation.

Apart from these more personal considerations, there was this fundamentally federal and Church union concept, which, at that particular time, he felt should be striven for and could be realised. It was at about this time that he came upon Bishop Talbot's 'as if'-phrase, which we have quoted already: that all Christians should begin at once to act *as if* they were one body, in one visible fellowship.[4]

In his programmatic book, *Christian Fellowship*, Söderblom therefore quoted Bishop Talbot. Once again, as with the architectural image of Glubokovski's, so in the case of Talbot's vision, the Church and the man were important. The quotation was from an Anglican report, addressed to the Archbishop of Canterbury, but Talbot was to Söderblom that same Talbot who, in the midst of

---

[3] Nathan Söderblom, *Christian Fellowship*, p. 31.   [4] Ibid., pp. 210–211.

In the study, Archbishop's House, Uppsala.

My dear Dr Macfarland,

In thanking you for the valuable Telegram in behalf of the neutral conference I have the honour to express, in the name of the three inviting Scandinavian Bishops, our hope, that the Federal Council or, if this is more advisable, you and those whom you consult, will appoint at least 4 delegates to the ecumenical conference and that you may be one of these.

Believe me with the kindest regards sincerely yours

Nathan Söderblom

Letter to Dr. Charles Macfarland, January 4, 1918.

Cardinal Mercier, ^m
Malines

(Belgium)

Admirant votre persévérance
chrétienne je je <del>témoigne</del>
prie
d'agréer
votre Eminence l'un profonde
sympathie à cause de la déli-
vrance du pays martyre. glorieux

27 XI
1918

Archevêque Söderblom

Telegram to Cardinal Mercier, Malines.

Im Namen ..... Dieva tā tēva, tā dēla un tā svētā gara

vārdā. Āmen.

Lasset uns beten .... Lūgsim Dievu!

Allmächtiger .... Visuvarenais, mūžīgais Dievs, mūsu

Kunga Jēzus Kristus tēvs! Tu pats mums esi pavēlejis, lai

strādniekus izlūdzamies tavam pļaujamam. Esi žēlīgs|un

sūti derīgus mācītājus|un liec tavu svēto pestīšanas vārdu

viņu sirdīs|un uz viņu lūpām. Tava žēlastība lai uztur

viņus\nomodā par sevi pašiem\un par sludinamo mācību|un

dod viņiem spēku|pareizi izpildit tavas pavēles. Dāvini

mums, ak Kungs, tavu svēto garu, ka tavs vārds vienmēr pie

mums paliek,|aug|un nes bagātus augļus, un tavi kalpi ar

prieka pilnām sirdīm tevi, kā pienākas, apliecina|un tavu

svēto, kristīgo draudzi uztaisa\un tev kalpo pastāvīgā

ticībā|un pieaug patiesības atziśanā, \ caur Jēzu Kristu,

mūsu Kungu, āmen.

Die vom Kirchenregiment ...... Uzklausīsimies Baznīcas

Virsvaldes izdoto rakstu(par Latvijas evaņģeliskās baznicas

bīskapa ievelēšanu:

Nach erhaltener Berufung .... No Zinodes ievēlēts par

Latvijas evanģeliskās luteriskās baznicas\bīskapu, tu stāvi

pie tā Kunga altara, lai tevi śī amatā ievestu.

Gott der allmächtige stärke ...... Visuvarenais Dievs lai

tevi stiprina(un tev palīdz šos solijumus turēt. - Izpildīdams

uzdevumu, kas man šī lietā uzticēts, es tev\ .... bīskapa

amatā par Latvijas evanģelis.... luteriskā.. baznīc.. ...

Dieva tā Tēva, tā Dēla un tā Svētā|Gara vārdā, Āmen.

For the consecration of Bishop Irbe, Riga, 1922, Söderblom took the service in Latvian. The manuscript was well prepared, in Latvian, with Swedish translation underneath each word, and occasional words in German. At the bottom, reminder in Swedish of order in which should be handed over, the Letter of Appointment, the pectoral cross, the cope and the crozier.

war, had written those conciliatory words about the relations of Britain and Germany, Talbot, in his gaiters and with his beard and his pectoral cross, meeting the German delegates at Oud Wassenaar in 1919, and stretching out his arms, taking them to his heart.

Sentimental? Should not be quoted in a supposedly theological context? But this book deals with Nathan Söderblom, and to him these things mattered and belonged together. Personality, Church, theology, these were not different departments but one united whole. Hence, as he accepted Talbot's 'as if'-formula, and propagated it, sometimes of course much further than Talbot himself would ever have wanted or allowed, he did so because he felt that at that particular period in ecumenical relationships, this pragmatic approach was the one most promising of results.

But he also looked beyond the visions of the Talbots and the Glubokovskis:

When the Spirit of the Lord pervades our sundered, materialized, and crippled Christendom, then the dividing walls which have arisen in the course of time, will hold no longer. They shall be torn asunder, not by well-meaning strivings for unity, but by the Lord's own might. And in its single great flow, the flood of God's love shall unite us all who are moved by the Spirit of our Lord.[5]

Archbishop Söderblom's own Faith-and-Order approach emerged as a result of theological reflexion, but even more through his contacts with actual Church situations which he was invited to enter. In the first years of the nineteen-twenties, in a surprising outburst of altogether unprecedented activity, he made Uppsala the focal point for this programme. Going beyond the borders of Scandinavia he managed in those few years

→ to perform four, if not five, episcopal consecrations: Reval 1921, Riga 1922 (two bishops), Modra, Slovakia 1928;
→ to promote in a decisive manner the consecration of the first bishop of Tranquebar, South India;
→ to bring the issue of Evangelical Catholicity before churches in the United States and Germany;
→ to strengthen the new relationships between the Church of Sweden and the Anglican Communion, from that time implying mutual participation in consecrations;
→ to visualize a *synaxis* Uppsala–Constantinople and to help promote the *eisodos* of the Orthodox into the modern ecumenical movement.

---

[5] Ibid., p. 212.

II.

Uppsala–Riga

Söderblom's mission to the Baltic churches was no ordinary incident in the busy life of the Swedish Archbishop. He became engaged in this Baltic endeavour more perhaps than in any other of his international or ecumenical undertakings. His involvement in the Baltic church situation brings out his total attitude toward church and people. His sense of history was stirred by the new lease of life grasped so hopefully by the little Baltic nations. He admired their liberation movement; he enjoyed discovering their national and provincial peculiarities and attempted to speak their languages. The role which the Church played in the austere folk-life of the Balts greatly appealed to Söderblom the Swede. The invitation from Reval (now called Tallin) and Riga gave Söderblom the Archbishop an opportunity to express in concrete form his programme of Evangelical Catholicity, and to consecrate three bishops in 1921 and 1922, thus serving the ecumenical cause on a deeper level. Here was more than conferences!

The Baltic countries—Esthonia, Latvia, Lithuania—long under Russian rule, freed themselves in the tumultuous years around 1916 to 1920. They became independent states, and for a brief space of some twenty years, played their role on the stage of world history, only to revert again at the end of this short period, alas, to 'the forgotten republics'. These sturdy peoples, whose leaders had spent the best part of their lives in Russian prisons or Siberian camps and colonies, attending to the physical and spiritual needs of their fellow countrymen, realized that they had a new and precious lease of life. The Latvian poet, J. Rainis, expressed in 1921 their courageous and fierce resolve in memorable yet pathetic words,

If this time is slept away,
we shall sleep, not hundreds
but thousands of years.

It was providential that in those few, decisive years, the contact with Archbishop Söderblom became a bond of incomparable strength. His words and his visits were to be a source of inspiration to the Baltic peoples, and brought them closer to the Nordic family of churches.

During World War I, various Baltic leaders escaped to Scandinavia. In Stockholm some acted as propaganda agents for the liberation movement. By far the most remarkable of these Esthonian underground fighters was Alexander Keskula (1882–1965), who later on in life claimed with some justification 'Lenin was my protégé'.[1] He was a man of daring visions with a propensity for geo-political argumentation. In Sweden he propagated his idea of a Swedish-Finnish-Esthonian federation as a bulwark against Russia.

Swedes of all political parties observed these dramatic developments with keen sympathy. But no one, perhaps, could have followed the events of the revolutionary scene on the Eastern shores of the Baltic with more active and informed an interest than Söderblom. And Keskula was more impressed by the Swedish Archbishop than by the Swedish government and wrote to his friend Kolmodin in Constantinople: 'I am glad that in Sweden there is at least one person who is engaged in active foreign politics—the more pity it is that it does not occur to the Swedish Government to act on behalf of the country as that man does on behalf of the Church'.

Throughout the vicissitudes of the war Söderblom followed, as well as he could from Sweden, the Baltic liberation movement. Prior to the opening of the first Esthonian *Landtag* (July 14, 1917), Söderblom had taken steps to send his first ecclesiastical *ad hoc* ambassador, Carl Edquist, (a Swedish pastor conversant with Finnish) to the Church in Esthonia. Plans were already well advanced in the autumn of 1917 but the German invasion of Esthonia made further attempts abortive at that time.

Söderblom was kept informed about developments not only by Keskula in Stockholm, but also by Kolmodin in Constantinople. In Constantinople, Kolmodin was seemingly far removed from Baltic affairs, but in April, 1918, he reported to Söderblom that Professor F. Rendtorff of Leipzig—a former university colleague of Söderblom—had visited Constantinople. According to Kolmodin, Rendtorff had pleaded for an immigration of Germans into the Baltic countries so as to absorb the Esthonians. Kolmodin warned Söderblom about these plans. He suggested that the Archbishop 'establish a *fait accompli* regarding the orientation of the Esthonian Church', thus strengthening the Nordic–Baltic group of churches over against what he regarded as German pressure.[2]

---

[1] M. Futrell, *Northern Underground*, 1963, p. 18 and pp. 119–151.
[2] J. Kolmodin, April 4, 1918, to Söderblom.

Kolmodin's letter stimulated Söderblom's keen interest in Esthonian church matters, particularly as Kolmodin suggested an important historical frame of reference for Swedish activity in Esthonia. Kolmodin wrote: 'I am glad to learn that the ecclesiastical contacts with Esthonia are followed up. This matter is the more important as there are many signs of the formation of an Esthonian–Latvian–Lithuanian bloc to counter-balance Poland–Ukraine–Finland. One must take interest in this development, particularly—at least in the first instance—as a point of support for Protestantism south of the Gulf of Finland. Here is to be found a task which Finland with its present orientation cannot undertake!' Kolmodin, who was critical of the little-Sweden attitude of the Swedish government goes on to say: 'Here is the way in which the Swedish Realm (*Riks-Sverige*) can regain leadership within the world of "Swedish thought"—about which you should not inform their Excellencies. It might frighten them.'[3]

The pattern, or rather, palimpsest of visions and ideas behind these arguments expressed by Keskula and Kolmodin, was the *Dominium maris Baltici,* the seventeenth century dream of political, cultural and ecclesiastical unity between peoples and countries on both sides of the Baltic, a unity under Swedish hegemony.

We are not suggesting that Söderblom himself shared the somewhat extravagant political ambitions expressed by Kolmodin and Keskula. Nonetheless, he was well aware of the underlying signs of history. Some of his advisers may have seen nothing but ancient political patterns seeking renewed expression in a cataclysmic period of revolution and the aftermath of war. Söderblom transposed just these patterns into ecclesiastical design as part of his programme of Evangelical Catholicity, and this adds particular interest to his contribution to the churches in the Baltic. He never tired of referring to the Baltic sea as 'the water which does not separate but unites' the nations and churches around its shores. Of course, it was the obvious thing to say, but with Söderblom there was more to it than that. With him, geography and history were entwined in a way which reveals how much the insights of Harald Hjärne, the Swedish historian who had emphasized Sweden's historical horizon to the East, meant to him. To put it tersely, through Söderblom's visits to Esthonia and Latvia in 1921–1922 (and in 1928) Harald Hjärne's vision was transposed into practical, ecclesiastical action.

---

[3] J. Kolmodin, May 21, 1920, to Söderblom.

For the water that united Sweden with Esthonia and Latvia was the same on which Gustavus Adolphus Charles X Gustaf and Charles XII had sailed in their battle ships as on a Swedish lake. Söderblom's Baltic hosts would generously refer to the Swedish era in their history as 'the good old Swedish times', characterized by personal freedom and cultural expansion. Söderblom took this up and developed the theme. In his 'Record of the Consecration in Riga, 1922', he proved to himself that as Archbishop of Uppsala he did in fact not come as a foreigner. There are certain distinct overtones in his argument. To Söderblom they added a dimension of excitement and drama to his visit. He wrote:

I had not applied for leave of absence [for the visit to Riga] as the invitation extended by our sister church in Latvia did not concern this or that individual, but the Archbishop of Uppsala. This, because of the unity in Evangelical faith among the countries around the Baltic and more particularly with regard to the old Swedish-Latvian connexions still alive in fresh and blessed memory.

He never tired of varying this theme or of focusing this vision. While the North was the core of Lutheranism, the Baltic was 'a Lutheran inland sea';[4] 'Riga was to be the Evangelical centre of Eastern Europe'.[5] When he had concluded his work of consecrating the three bishops in the Baltic, he reported to his friend F. Heiler: 'The Lutheran ring established around the Baltic, *mare Lutheranum*'.[6] We have pointed to Harald Hjärne, and the Swedish historians as Söderblom's starting point for these ideas. Sometimes one feels that the Baltic peoples and churches meant something very personal to him and that he felt a particular affinity with them. I am even going to suggest that at a deep level of his personality there were memories from his schoolboy days in Hudiksvall, when at the age of ten or twelve, he would climb on to those mighty ships bound for Riga or Reval. And memories even earlier than that—the little boy looking at that fascinating white votive ship in the choir of the church at Trönö, the ship that had to be launched in the waters of the Baltic! We realize that in making these suggestions we have entered the realms of fancy rather than fact, but some such idea as this is necessary in order to explain his deep personal attachment to the Baltic peoples.

---

[4] Söderblom, *Evangelisk Katolicitet* (1919), p. 123; and idem, *American Scandinavian Review*, August 1920.
[5] Söderblom, July 18, 1922, to K. B. Westman.
[6] Söderblom, July 25, 1922, to F. Heiler.

The Baltic churches invited Söderblom to be the consecrator. Why did they turn to him? Why did they not invite a German church leader instead, or the Archbishop of Finland? A German solution was out of the question for political reasons and, at least in the case of Bishop Irbe, because of ecclesiology. The long era of German hegemony over the Baltic countries came to an end in 1918, but there were still serious tensions between the German minority and the Esthonian–Latvian majorities in the churches. Sweden on the other hand, was a favoured nation with the Balts at this time. As we shall see, both Irbe, and, more surprising perhaps, the German pastor, Poelchau, interpreted episcopal consecration in terms that reminded Söderblom of his own 'Evangelical Catholicity'. The question of the degree of Söderblom's 'Lutheranism' never seemed to worry the Baltic bishops. The Baltic leaders must have known, that he was suspect on this score in certain quarters, but 'Alt-Lutherisch' as they wanted to be and appear, they were unperturbed by this criticism. Here we must surmise that the power of Söderblom's personality was stronger than his supposed lack of a guaranteed Lutheran theology.

To the reasons of politics and theology that may have entered in, we must thus add the category of personality—the capacity for personal initiative. This becomes obvious in comparison with Archbishop Johansson, the Finnish Church leader. Söderblom had built up personal contacts throughout the war years. His great initiative with regard to the Uppsala Conference of 1917 was well known, and, unmistakably, there was also a certain urge in him to extend the frontiers of the influence of 'Uppsala'.

At the beginning of 1921, both Esthonia and Latvia approached Söderblom about episcopacy. Already in April, 1920, Söderblom had planned to invite the Esthonian bishop, J. Kukk, to take part in the first Nordic episcopal conference.[7] When in March, 1921, a conference on Polish church affairs was convened at Uppsala, Söderblom persuaded Kukk to attend. On that occasion he found time to discuss Baltic church problems too, and stated that it was then that 'Electus Jacob Kukk' invited him, in the name of the Evangelical Consistory in Reval, to 'install' Kukk as a bishop. However, Kukk had to act rather cautiously, for in a Church Assembly meeting in June, 1921, after his return to Reval, German members of the As-

---

[7] Cf. Söderblom, April 17, 1920, to J. Kolmodin.

sembly opposed what Söderblom described as 'the return of the Esthonian Church from the German order of Superintendents to Nordic bishops'. This matter was brought to a vote: there were 106 votes favouring the episcopacy and 62 against, thereby demonstrating the existence of a fairly resolute German minority in the Assembly. The more German opposition there was, the more enthusiastic the Esthonian majority members were over 'this return or development', to use Söderblom's words in his record of the Reval consecration.

Söderblom was, of course, well aware of the tensions between the German element and the Esthonian/Latvian populations. This tension was unavoidably present in the Reval consecration, and on that account Söderblom felt that the participation of the Finnish Bishop then of the diocese of Borgå, J. Gummerus, with his close personal contacts on both sides of the divide, would be particularly helpful. And so it proved.

The fifth of June, 1921, was a great day in the history of the Church in *Esthonia*. Some 20,000 saw the ecclesiastical procession slowly winding its way into the pro-cathedral. The procession went to the Karlskyrka, built—as Söderblom was sure to notice—in the times of the Swedish King Charles XI.

In the procession there were two bishops, Söderblom and Bishop Jaakko Gummerus. Assisting in the service were twelve pastors representing the Esthonian and German congregations as well as the churches in Latvia and Ingermanland. The Theological Faculty at Tartu was represented by Professor Rahamägi who later, in 1934, became Bishop Kukk's successor. Professor Rahamägi carried the Bible which was to be presented to the new Bishop. Söderblom says: 'of my own accord I had made the alteration [as compared with the Swedish rite] that instead of placing on [the new bishop] a mitre, I handed over a Bible—following the rule in England and Finland'.

After the procession reached the altar, Söderblom gave the consecration address. Such an address is an important part of a Swedish episcopal consecration, as it is often the occasion for significant statements on the calling of the Church and its ministry. Preaching in German—his address was afterwards read in Esthonian by Professor Rahamägi—Söderblom gave a characteristic interpretation of 'a Bishop's ministry' and of the place and role of the Baltic churches in the wider Northern European setting. A few relevant passages are quoted here:

... What my father gave me as his will, I also want to give to you, dear brother and fellow worker in Christ's Church in this hour of consecration, as a guideline for an evangelical bishop and minister of the faithful. Just a few hours before my father's heart ardently burning with pastoral care stood still in death—he said, 'neither as being lords over those in your charge, but as helpers of your joy'.

Not lords but shepherds. We do not form an hierarchy or bureaucratic class of civil servants. On the contrary, the evangelical episcopate has as its spiritual purpose the care of souls. Our authority is not ours, nor is the outward power. If we are capable of doing anything it shall only be derived from the Word of God and the power of our Saviour and therefore it belongs not to us but to our Lord. We are not dignitaries. We do not have any dignity, but are unworthy channels of the good news to mankind. We are not priests of mystery, but fellow-workers to give joy to the congregation.

According to our belief, God has given to every people a special task in that peaceful fellowship formed by the Church of Christ, a task that no other people could fulfill. And we know that Pentecost's Holy Spirit speaks every human language. Therefore we must give thanks and praise and have confidence in God that he has here let the freedom and independent development of the Esthonian nation find an open door which no one can close.

But if we let our eyes rest here upon the altar of the Lord where we have gathered from Esthonia, from Finland and from Latvia together with German brothers, and, further still, from Sweden—across the sea that does not separate but unites—our thoughts go more than two hundred years back to that time when we in Esthonia, Finland, Latvia and Sweden still belonged to only one State which according to its means honestly tried to create freedom through order, safety through justice and piety through the gospel.

Not only to our fathers has the Lord performed miracles. Do we dream, or are we awake? Here we are again together as in old days, from Upsala, Borgå, Reval and Riga, not united in the political sense, but joined together for ever in a far more sincere community. ...

Having given this address, Söderblom proceeded to read the Consecration Service in Esthonian. He then invited Bishop Gummerus to speak in Esthonian and then the assistants read set Bible passages, and Kukk recited the Apostles' Creed and answered the searching questions according to the Swedish rite.

The moment then came when the Archbishop, in the name of the Triune God, handed over the episcopal office to his Esthonian brother. He now took a pectoral cross from his own neck and placed it on Bishop Kukk. This too was an innovation of Söderblom's. (In a normal Swedish consecration, the pectoral cross is held by one of the assistants during the first part of the ceremony and handed to the Archbishop at the appointed time.) In June, 1921, the Church in Reval still cherished a sacred memory of the martyrdom of January 14, 1919, when a great number of Orthodox and Lutheran priests, including Orthodox Bishop Platon, were murdered by the Reds two hours before the city was liberated by the Esthonian Army. Bishop Platon's dead body was found, with his pectoral cross surprisingly still on. This was given to his successor to wear. There cannot be much doubt that Söderblom was aware of these overtones when he handed Bishop Kukk his cross. Neither was Söderblom a mere reporter when in his Swedish Record of the Reval consecration he quotes a simple Esthonian peasant who was heard making his interpretation of what had happened in the consecration: 'Today our Bishop has received the Holy Spirit.'

At Kukk's consecration one of the assistants was Professor Edward Tennmann. He taught 'Comparative Theology' at Dorpat from 1919 until 1936, the year of his death, and was one of the Baltic theologians influenced by Söderblom. In 1922 he was even commissioned by Kukk to accompany Söderblom to the Swedish congregations on the Esthonian islands. His name should not be forgotten. In order to show how much Söderblom's ideas of 'Evangelical Catholicity' were appreciated in the Baltic Churches we quote this important if unrecognized Esthonian theologian. In April 1922 he wrote to Söderblom's co-worker, K. B. Westman:

My colleagues and I here are particularly interested in the question of the leadership of the evangelical ecumenical Church, both in the personal and collegial sense. We are not at all averse to the idea of an Evangelical 'Pope', albeit without the doctrine of infallibility etc., but supported by a 'college of cardinals', the leaders of all evangelical churches acting in the interest of peace. These should establish practical-political contacts with the two Catholic Churches.

Tennmann suggested that one approach to this end would be a Church federation including Scandinavia, Finland, Esthonia, Latvia, 'and the Methodists', possibly with the American Federal Council. Perhaps also Hungary and Switzerland'. He also thought his plan would be furthered by introducing episcopal order in certain German churches, such as Saxony and Würtemberg. But he was sure where the initiative must be: 'Our sympathies belong to you in Sweden. We also believe that there are the leaders needed for this.'

He went on: 'The matter is of course of such delicate and fragile nature, as of glass. And yet terribly much is at stake. If one does not act now on behalf of the churches, the time can be too late forever.'

In the case of Esthonia there was tension between the national and the German elements in the Lutheran Church. In *Latvia,* similar tension existed between Latvians and Germans. The Latvian leader was an outstanding churchman, Kārlis Irbe. Born in 1861, and thus five years older than Söderblom, he had as a pastor served Latvian refugee groups in Russia and Siberia in the 1880's, in the last years (1917–20) as General Superintendent. In October, 1920, he was allowed to move from Moscow to his home country, and there he was promptly entrusted with the task of drawing up a new constitution for the Lutheran Church of Latvia. It was in this connexion that he contacted Söderblom; Irbe felt that Söderblom, more than anyone else, could advise his church.

Irbe's theological standpoint as expressed in his letter to Söderblom in February, 1921, is interesting. The doctrine of his church had to remain 'alt-Lutherisch', claimed Irbe, but his years in Orthodox Russia had left their mark. He wrote to Söderblom:

In an Evangelical Lutheran church, questions of church order are of course not of fundamental importance. Nevertheless they are important enough for the shaping of sound church life. My studies and observations hitherto have led me to this conviction ... we can win back that ecumenicity which Protestantism abandoned in principle in 1520 only so far as Protestant national churches place themselves on the ground—which unfortunately often was lost—of an episcopal, or a synodical-episcopal constitution.

A bishop, Irbe felt, should be allowed real influence. Otherwise he would become merely a superfluous decoration.

Söderblom welcomed Irbe's interpretation, and recognized in it his own programme of Evangelical Catholicity.

The recapturing of lost ecumenicity, the importance of episcopacy and the independence of the Church I have officially and privately recommended in the last two decades, and these thoughts are now confirmed by your own great and mature experience.[8]

Söderblom thought there could be established two types of Nordic church government:

---

[8] Söderblom, March 5, 1921, to K. Irbe.

1. The Danish and Norwegian summus episcopus system according to the German pattern, where the Crown appoints bishops and pastors.
2. The Swedish–Finnish system which is episcopal-democratic.

On one point Söderblom challenged the Riga church authorities. Irbe had suggested, possibly as a result of discussions with the church membership in Riga, that 'if the worse comes to the worst, the Bishop could be elected not for life, but for a term'. This Söderblom could not accept. A bishop ought to be elected to serve for life: 'This belongs to the idea of the servant ministry in the Church of Christ.' Söderblom summed up his view in two observations: 'A bishop should be regarded as a *Seelsorger,* preacher and spiritual worker in the widest sense, not as part of the Establishment. Thereby he does in fact win the greatest influence. Further, the episcopal office as such gives to its occupant and [his] church an ecumenical position.' To the Synod at Riga a year later he was to explain the benefits of episcopacy in these three key words: '1. Unity, 2. Independence [over against the State], and 3. Catholicity.'

In Söderblom's own programme of Evangelical Catholicity there was, as we have seen, an emphasis on the national and cultural heritage; for him, catholicity and universality had to be anchored in Swedish tradition. In Latvia, Irbe was groping towards a similar interpretation of Catholicity, and he had to do this in a situation marred by strong tension between the two national groups, the Latvian majority and the tiny German minority. Irbe suggested a solution which on the one hand eased this tension, but on the other, emphasized the existence of the problem. He proposed that the German section should elect their own 'Bishop of the German-speaking congregations in Latvia'. This he proposed in the Synod immediately after his own election. It was decided there and then, and P. H. Poelchau became Bishop of the German congregations.

Poelchau had since written to Söderblom in terms which proved the extent to which he shared Söderblom's and Irbe's intentions. In May, 1922, he asked Söderblom to 'instal me in the episcopal office, because it is indeed a matter of an episcopal office likewise for our German congregations, not just a question of giving the title of bishop to their leader'.

Söderblom tried, but not very hard, perhaps, to persuade the two parties to accept a common consecration service. In his letter to Bishop Poelchau he wrote: 'The most beautiful solution would, of course, be a common consecration of the two bishops.'[9] If however, a common consecration was impossible, he suggested various alternatives. In a situation where the wounds of national pride were still open, the outcome was that there had to be two different consecrations in the same city on the same day; the one for the Latvian Lutheran Bishop in the morning in St. Jacobi Church, and the other for the German Lutheran Bishop in the evening in St. Peter's.

As in Esthonia Söderblom had been assisted by the Finnish bishop, so now in Riga he was assisted by Bishop Kukk of Reval. Also participating were no less than seventeen leading pastors from the Baltic and the adjoining countries. These included a General Superintendent from Berlin, a theological professor from Helsinki, and the senior pastor of the Lutheran Church in Lithuania.

To the ecclesiastical solemnity of the occasion was added an extra touch of festivity by the visit of the Swedish 1st Torpedo Boat Flotilla. Light torpedo boats rode at anchor near the castle of Duna, and mariners in Swedish blue walked in the church procession from St. John's where the church service began, to St. Jacobi where Dr. Irbe was consecrated.[1]

Söderblom's consecration address in Riga was anything but conventional. He was aware of history, of the common past, three centuries earlier, of the Swedish and Latvian peoples, and this made him stress the role of the Swedish king, Gustavus Adolphus. He hardly paused to quote his Biblical text and refer to Latvia's newly won independence, before he went on to say:

As a Swedish citizen I may perhaps be permitted to express the joy which was felt by us on the other side of the water, like a warm beat of the pulse. With the permission of those in charge of this revered temple and on behalf of an anonymous Swedish worshipper of the hero King—who himself once prayed in this church—I take the liberty to present to this Evangelical church of St. Jacobi a copy of the best contemporaneous portrait of Gustavus Adolphus.

The evening before the consecration Söderblom had arranged to have the impressive picture hung on the North wall of the Church, near the altar.

---

[9] Söderblom, May 10, 1922, to P. H. Poelchau.
[1] There seems to have been nothing but coincidence between the two Swedish visits to Riga on the same day, but it exemplifies the keen Swedish interest in contacts between the two countries.

He did not care to mention—what everyone knew— that this was also a move in the tense struggle between the confessions over the fate and future of that particular Riga Church, St. Jacobi. Even churches can become pawns in the political game. As a reward to the Roman Catholic population of Latgale, a part of new Latvia, who had fought courageously for the liberation of their country, the Latvian Government were prepared to hand over the Jacobi Church to the Roman Catholics. This had caused much concern in the Baltic as well as in Germany, Scandinavia, and in Lutheran and other Protestant circles in the United States. In 1921, the German leader of the Gustavus Adolphus association, Professor Rendtorff, had pleaded with Söderblom 'as the most influential representative of the international concern of Lutheranism',[2] to use his influence against this threat to the Lutheran Church, and Irbe had in strong terms called upon Söderblom and fellow-believers in other countries to join in protest. On the occasion of the consecration in that same Jacobi Church, in July, 1922, Söderblom and his many listeners must have been well aware of the stakes involved.

The Prime Minister and the Minister of Foreign Affairs of Latvia were among the honoured guests in the St. Jacobi congregation that morning. Being Ministers of State, and Latvians at that, they listened in silence, but as they listened they may have conceived counter-plans of their own. Söderblom could not prevent what happened a year later when the Church of St. Jacobi was finally handed over to the Roman Catholics. The picture of the 'Swedish hero king' was then taken down from the wall and handed over to the Lutheran Synodical Council.

No sooner had Söderblom made the reference to the Gustavus Adolphus picture, than he made another—possibly improvised— suggestion. He was greatly impressed by Irbe and wished to emphasize that he was obviously going to be the leading Evangelical bishop in the Baltic. He was aware of the fact that Irbe himself had generously suggested that his colleague Poelchau be made bishop, but Söderblom felt that in comparison with the German immigrant, the national church leader should be given preference, and that this had to be expressed in tangible terms. He connected this with the important position of Riga: 'For a hundred years the biggest city in the Swedish realm; it long remained the greatest city in the Baltic, and is now the greatest Protestant city of Eastern Europe.'

---

[2] C. Rendtorff, June 28, 1921 to Söderblom.

From these considerations he drew a conclusion which he summarized in his Record in the following characteristic manner:

Because of this dominant position of Riga I suggested in my consecration address, without having asked anybody's advice, that Latvia's bishop ought to be referred to as archbishop. This naturally did not imply any hierarchical tendencies, opposed to our Evangelical faith. It was a surprise to find out afterwards that this idea had already been raised and seriously discussed.

It is not too much to call this improvisation in the field of high ecclesiastical politics—in a country which, after all, was not his own—unconventional. In that situation, Söderblom's suggestion would only too easily be used to nationalistic ends. Irbe stubbornly refused to follow it as long as he was bishop. His successor, in 1932, however, was called Archbishop, and one of the arguments used for change of nomenclature was the proposal made in 1922 by Nathan Söderblom.

This was not his only venture into what were, for him, uncharted waters. Having once decided that nationality and language were unavoidable factors, he proceeded both at Reval and Riga to give dazzling performances of linguistic skill. Not understanding a word of either Esthonian or Latvian, he nevertheless managed to read with great aplomb the consecration service in each of these languages. Long before the event he had had the order of service translated into the local tongue and practised reading it with gusto. The final text with phonetic signs and symbols of emphasis, with the Swedish original placed under the Latvian words gave the impression of a medieval musical score.

In doing this he felt himself to be continuing a tradition from the 'good old Swedish times', and he argued in a way which showed the extent to which he felt himself heir of that seventeenth century Swedish realm, writing in his 'Record of the Riga Consecration of 1922':

The 17th century Swedish Church was anxious to give, according to Protestant principles, each and every people in the Swedish realm religious books and teaching in the mother tongue. Thus appeared the Bible translations and other religious literature in Lapp, Finnish, Esthonian, Latvian and Russian languages. When now as a Swedish Bishop I was entrusted with an ecclesiastical task in Latvia, I felt it my unavoidable duty to use the language of the country.

Not that Söderblom was without his critics. A relatively unknown German observer, W. von Rüdiger, could not be satisfied, whether it was German or Latvian. In the morning, the Archbishop's Latvian was 'totally impossible in pronunciation—altogether inappropriate for the occasion'. In the evening, Söderblom, who sincerely held that in the Baltic the German language was the vehicle for cultural contact with the West and said so, then went on to praise German culture. It was typical of his all embracing generosity; though, in a situation of sharp and harsh national conflicts, it might not be understood by all. von Rüdiger listened to Söderblom telling Poelchau: 'You speak the language of Martin Luther, Johann Sebastian Bach, and Immanuel Kant,' More than thirty years later, he resentfully reported: 'Söderblom spoke mainly about the richness of the language of Goethe (sic), Kant and Bach and how happy our bishop could be in being able to call this language his own. ... No, in Sweden's archbishop we [German] Balts had not won a friend.[3] It was perhaps true of von Rüdiger.

As in the case of Esthonia and Latvia, the *Lithuanian* situation also had its share of problems of nationalism, cultural affiliation and linguistic expression. In the Lutheran Church of Lithuania there was no dominating church leader of the stature of Bishop Irbe in adjacent Latvia. The Lithuanian W. Gaigalatis, a burly, canny, perhaps even cunning nationalist, was more of a partisan than a leader. Problems of nationality, culture and language were here interwoven with a complex Church situation, into which Söderblom's envoy, Paul Sandegren, entered. There was no question of episcopal consecration here as in Esthonia or in Latvia. The Lithuanian situation, to which we can only allude here, was one with which Söderblom was concerned mainly from 1926 to 1928.

The Baltic Churches may have appeared to be tucked away in a corner of the North, and their fate and problems of little concern to the outside world. To Söderblom they represented both the past and the future, allowing him to express and to develop his programme of Evangelical Catholicity. Thanks to Söderblom they were no longer neglected, but became an important bridgehead in an ecclesiastical structure, the centre of which was Uppsala.

---

[3] W. von Rüdiger. *Aus d. letzten Kapitel deutsch-baltischen Gesch. in Lettland* (1954), p. 20.

Uppsala and Church Minorities in Eastern Europe

In the tumultuous situation after the War, and Versailles, the political and the ecclesiastical map of Eastern Europe was radically altered. Ethnic, cultural, and religious frontiers, were criss-crossed by new political power lines. It is out of the question to go into detail in showing how this affected the situation of the Evangelical Churches. Söderblom was involved in these developments, struggles, and tensions, to a surprising degree. We must limit ourselves to a few indications of Uppsala's role in these situations.

There is a certain pattern in these relationships, even if the national and ecclesiastical situation in each case was different.

Söderblom's actions here were an expression of a desire on his part to extend to his brethren a helping hand from 'Uppsala'. In each case it was prompted by special invitation from responsible church leaders in the countries concerned. These invitations to Söderblom illustrate the role he had established already during the War. A case in point was the appeal in 1916 from Lithuanians to the Swedish Archbishop for a general church collection in all Swedish churches.[1] In this case, the Lithuanians could point to a similar gift from the Vatican, and the Lutherans, led by the Swedish Archbishop, were asked to follow this example. Bishop Raffay of Barany in Hungary, visited Uppsala in 1919 in order to establish contacts with Söderblom.[2] Bishop H. Geduly of Nyireghaza in Hungary, gave an Olaus Petri lecture in 1919 at Uppsala University on the Church situation in his country.[3]

In each case, Söderblom sent special Swedish ecclesiastical envoys who would report to him on the situation. In the case of the Church in Poland, F. Sjöberg and Baron and Baroness C. Lagerfelt visited the churches in 1920. Through E. Berggrav there had also been close co-operation with the Church of Norway over the Polish problem.

All the threads were held together in the Archbishop's house in Uppsala. Over the Polish question Söderblom arranged an impressive conference in Uppsala, March 3–5, 1921, patterned on the Scan-

---

[1] *Pro Lithuania, Bulletin du Bureau d'Information de Lithuania*, Lausanne, 1917, p. 4.

[2] Söderblom on that occasion was in Finland, and Dr. Widner of Stockholm, always ready to assist Söderblom in his international work, took care of the Hungarian guests.

[3] The lecture was published in Swedish translation in the same year. Söderblom, pro-Chancellor of the University, managed to get an Uppsala honorary doctorate for Geduly.

dinavian (or Neutral) Church Conference at Uppsala, December, 1917, but with a wider scope. This conference likewise, met in response to an invitation signed by the three Nordic Primates. There were altogether seven Polish representatives from two contending Lutheran Churches (Polish-speaking and German-speaking), and there were representatives from Denmark, Norway, Finland (Bishop Gummerus), Esthonia (Bishop Kukk), and from the United States— Bishop Irbe of Riga was unavoidably prevented from attending. From Sweden there were thirty-three delegates, including five bishops, members of the Uppsala chapter, and a host of Söderblom's ecumenical experts and envoys, including Brilioth, Fries, Widner, Major Sjöstedt, Birger Forell, and F. Palmgren; the two last named now had their first direct ecumenical experience. Present were also members of Söderblom's delegations to Poland and the Baltic countries. Two legal experts were called in to assist in the drawing up constitutional measures—Hjalmar Hammarskjöld, Governor of the Uppland Province, and G. Ribbing, Söderblom's close Uppsala friend.

In the pattern of Church relationships there were however not only similarities, but also variations and differences. In the case of Poland and Lithuania, two countries at that time dominated by Catholic majorities, there were tensions within the Lutheran groups between national and German sections, and Söderblom and his envoys had to show much tact in handling delicate group relationships, including those with the Gustavus Adolphus organization in Germany.

In the case of the two Lutheran Churches of Poland, the one Polish-speaking, the other German-speaking, the problem of cultural affiliation and linguistic expression of the Churches loomed large. Such concerns were of course far from excluded from Söderblom's programme of Evangelical Catholicity. In fact, as we have already tried to show, he emphasized the provincial and the universal aspects, and he applied this to the Polish case.

The Uppsala Conference on Polish Church Problems, 1921, tried to ease the national tensions by a formula of sensible compromise. The principle of preaching in the mother tongue was upheld—this was devised to assist the German section in this case. At the same time it was insisted that servants of the Church be proficient in the official language of the country of which they were citizens.[1]

---

[1] *Kyrkokonferensen, Upsala 3–5 Mars 1921,* Printed report, 12 pp.

In the case of Czechoslovakia and Hungary, too, nationality played a considerable part in the time immediately after Versailles, with regard to religious affiliation. From Söderblom's personal point of view, his task appeared, above all, as one where, by way of his 'Evangelical Catholic' programme, he might attempt to strengthen Lutheran churches in a Roman Catholic milieu.

Faced with a strong Roman Catholic majority in his country, the Evangelical Bishop in Hungary, Alexander Raffay, felt that Söderblom—'the only Lutheran Archbishop in the world whom we can equate with the Papal nuntius'—might strengthen their position in their own country. At the Faith and Order meeting in Geneva in 1920, he invited Söderblom to come to Hungary, and Söderblom, who was never tired of emphasizing heartily that the Lutheran Church in Hungary called itself, not Evangelical–Lutheran but Evangelical, responded by offering to consecrate Bishop Raffay. Raffay recognized that the Swedish Church had retained what he called 'Apostolic Succession', he knew that Söderblom was 'the sixtieth Archbishop of Christian Sweden', he felt however that he could not accept this offer, lest it be misunderstood in Hungary.[5]

The situation in Czechoslovakia was different. The leader, Georg Janoska had known Söderblom since the Lutheran Conference in Uppsala in 1911. Appointed 'interim Bishop' in 1918, he asked Söderblom, in 1922, to do for the Lutheran Church in Slovakia what he had done in Esthonia, and to consecrate himself and his colleague Bishop Zoch. Söderblom was prepared to do the consecrations but could not then find time for the journey. He did not forget however, and an opportunity seemed to offer itself in connexion with the Stockholm Conference of 1925.

On August 16, 1925 the consecration of a new Swedish Bishop of Lund, Dr. E. Rodhe, took place in Uppsala and many bishops participated in it, Dr. Janoska being among them. In the vestry prior to the consecration, and apparently without any previous warning, Söderblom made a suggestion to Bishop Janoska; when the new Swedish *electus* knelt to receive consecration or the 'blessing', Janoska was to kneel with him. Janoska accepted. When he later recalled the moment, he thought that he had replied: 'Of course, why, we can never have enough of that blessing which we always need.'[6]

In a brief reference to this incident in Söderblom's book about

---

[5] Alexander Raffay, in *Hågkomster*, XIV, p. 320.
[6] G. Janoska, July 13, 1925, to Söderblom.

the Stockholm Conference, it is skimmed over, perhaps a trifle too lightly. He wrote: [Bishop Janoska] 'participated in the consecration in Uppsala Cathedral on August 16, together with other Lutherans, and knelt during the laying on of hands. In the debate on [August] 27, it was of particular interest to listen to his genuinely Lutheran appreciation of teaching in the home, school, and at Church.'[7]

This was a quick, possibly too quick, way of doing these things, but the echo was resounding, and it reached Germany. The periodical *Die Wartburg*, made an attack on the 'high church' character of the Stockholm Conference and used Janoska's consecration as a weapon.[8] This in turn led to an attack on Janoska in a Magyar Church paper, and Janoska discussed his line of defence with Söderblom.

On the other hand, this did not prevent Janoska and Söderblom from making further explorations of the same nature. In 1928, Söderblom was invited to participate in the consecration of Bishop Zoch's successor, Dušan Fajnor of Modra. This time Söderblom managed to be present. The consecrator on this occasion was Bishop G. Janoska. But particular significance was attached to the role of the Swedish Archbishop. Söderblom followed this up by sending, *post festum,* two pectoral crosses to Janoska and Fajnor. Janoska expressed his gratitude in terms which Söderblom must have appreciated: 'We regard the [gift of the] episcopal cross as a proof of the close durable fellowship in spirit and in faith, between the Swedish and the Slovak Churches.'[9]

Uppsala–Wittenberg

Both in the World Alliance and in the incipient Life and Work movement Germany's problems in those post war years loomed large.

Yet while the immediate day to day problems were those of relief and of social and international justice, the very struggle of the Christian community with these problems raised fundamental questions about the nature of that community. There were tendencies in different directions. There was the issue between the old and new theology, though what had, until 1914, been regarded as new and modern was already dated. The Liberal stalwarts were now

---

[7] Nathan Söderblom, *Stockholm 1925*, p. 603.
[8] *Die Wartburg*, Deutsch-evang. Monatschrift (25), 1926, no. 1.
[9] G. Janoska, October 3, 1928, to Söderblom.

harshly challenged by Barthian thunder, but the nineteenth century tensions between 'Lutheran' and 'Union' were still live issues which might flare up at any moment.

Luther research experienced a renaissance with Karl Holl's book in 1921 introducing a new epoch. Here as in Barth there was an emphasis on the *Eigenart* of Christian revelation and on justification by faith.

From all sides in the *Götterdämmerung* of post-war times there was in Germany radical questioning of the very structure and nature of the Church. 'Did we really have Churches hitherto'—'Hatten wir bisher Kirchen?'—was a question which two of Nathan Söderblom's closest friends in Germany asked, and denied in a famous debate. They were Theodor Kaftan, the solid ex-General Superintendent in Schleswig, and Friedrich Siegmund-Schultze, the Christian prophet and social reformer. Discussing this problem in Siegmund-Schultze's *Die Eiche,* they differed in many things, but were agreed in concern for the international and supranational orientation of the Church if it was to be the Church.[3]

Karl Holl, too, put a new emphasis on the Church, and Otto Dibelius presaged 'the century of the Church'.

The organization of the German Evangelical *Kirchenbund* in 1921 was hailed as a great achievement, but left many Lutherans dissatisfied. In response to contacts with conservative Lutheran forces in the United States—which in 1918 had formed themselves into the National Lutheran Council—there were attempts at a closer organization of the strict Lutheran groups. The formation at Eisenach, in 1923, of the Lutheran World Convention, was seen as a victory for these tendencies.

It is fair to say, we believe, that few if any foreign Churchmen cared to be, or even dared to be, as personally involved in this situation as the Swedish Archbishop. In Germany, his voice, advice, and help were in some quarters recognized as those of a generous and sympathetic friend. In matters of relief this was very obvious, but in Germany his theological and ecumenical position made Söderblom, the Archbishop, something of a controversial personality—a stumbling block to some, and a support and even an ideal to others.

Söderblom approached this complicated German Church situation

---

[1] *Die Eiche,* 1921 pp. 308 ff. cf. also Theodor Kaftan, *Erlebnisse und Beobach-tungen,* 1924, pp. 389–398.

in two ways, through personalities and through organizations engaged in social and international questions. As a Lutheran, it was natural for him, during his many visits to Germany, to emphasize the importance of a common Lutheran heritage. Here his research on Luther before and during the war, stood him in good stead; he felt that he could lecture with authority on the German reformer. Whenever he spoke in Germany in these post-war years, he chose to emphasize Martin Luther's unique role. To a certain extent, this was part of his generous ministry of encouragement and consolation with regard to defeated Germany; he wished to inspire the German people to realize their spiritual calling anew: 'I must not hide my conviction', he said in Stuttgart in 1921, 'that *if* in our time God gives to the Church a new revival and spiritual strength, it will emerge out of the sufferings of Germany; this will deepen and spread the influence of the German disciple of Christ, Martin Luther.'

In 1921 at Stuttgart, 1922 at Wittenberg, and 1923 at Eisenach, he went so far as to maintain, in almost identical terms, the uniqueness of his great hero: After the Master nobody had influenced the history of the West so deeply, so widely, so durably, as this monk-professor who at Worms stood before Emperor and Diet. In the same somewhat exuberant terms, he would also witness to his personal relationship with his hero: 'In my life, barely a week has gone by since I became a priest, when I did not daily thank God that I was born and bred in the sphere of Luther.' He goes on to say again: 'After the New Testament, he is the greatest evangelist in the Church of Christ.'

His Luther addresses in Germany were, at least in a subsidiary way, designed to cement his contacts with the strong Lutheran section of the Church. He was aware of the criticism which from time to time was levelled against him, his theology and his ecumenical plans, by the influential *Allgemeine Evangelisch–Lutherische Kirchenzeitung*. He was also keenly aware of the significance and potential strength of the emerging Lutheran World confessional movement as a whole, and therefore arranged that he was appointed by his own 'Life and Work' movement to be its representative in the international Lutheran organizations.

All the more anxious was he to interpret his ecumenical programme in terms acceptable to his Lutheran co-religionists with a view to winning international Lutheranism for the ecumenical cause. He was in fact involved in trying to shape something of a Lutheran world strategy. It was because of this that in 1922 he wanted the Lutheran world conference to be held at Budapest, although he soon loyally consented to the German claim for Eisenach.

Söderblom was duly present at Eisenach in August, 1923, but the organizers did not find it convenient to allow his name to appear on the programme. There had obviously been great tensions among those in command of the Lutheran World Meeting as to whether Söderblom was to be included, or the door was to be shut to him. We are told by no less an authority than Dr. Brandelle, President of the Augustana Synod in the United States, that faced with this question, 'the American delegation made it known that [closing the door to Söderblom] would not be acceptable'.[2] Söderblom was undaunted by the opposition. He had belonged to those who for some years had prepared the pan-Lutheran Conference, and had corresponded with Bishop Ihmels of Saxony and other German leaders about this, from 1920. It was Ihmels, his friend from Leipzig days, who secured for Söderblom the opportunity to speak at Eisenach.

The acknowledged Lutheran leaders at the Eisenach Conference recognized of course that Söderblom's interpretation of Luther and his message was not the same as their own. He emphasized what he called Luther's 'universal significance'; the reformer belonged to the whole Church. In his characteristic way Söderblom went on to say: 'Lutheran universalism means less suspicion, less negation, less caution, less fear, and more real trust in God.'

At Wittenberg in 1922, he contrasted what he termed 'Method Rome' with 'Method Wittenberg'. Relying on his concept of the fundamental theological tension between institution and spirit, he claimed that the latter 'method', that of Wittenberg, represented the 'spirit' and should therefore be the foundation of Church Unity: 'Need I tell you', he added, 'that only this pure doctrine, only this "Method Wittenberg", can bring about unity in the faith of the Church.' Hardly had he however made this claim, so reassuring and soothing to a Lutheran, than he went on to show that there was in fact a third, and even more excellent, way than 'Method Rome' or 'Method Wittenberg': 'Method Love'. Here he made bold to claim Luther for this third approach which of course was none other than his own Evangelical Catholicity.

Most German Lutherans of strict orthodoxy were not convinced by this. We have however hinted at Söderblom's personal contact

---

[2] E. A. Brandelle, in *Hågkomster XV*, p. 359.

with Ihmels; if Söderblom in spite of much opposition, had an entrée into the world of stricter German Lutheranism, it was because of this personal connexion. Here Ihmels was his greatest prize. In spite of some doubt, Ihmels was won for Stockholm, 1925, and there became one of the most prominent speakers. The significance of this can be gauged by the negative observation that Ihmels and other confessional leaders opposed German participation in the Faith and Order movement and thus were not present at Lausanne in 1927, but perhaps the clearest proof comes by comparison with a disarming letter to Söderblom from von Schéele some years earlier. In the confessional world von Schéele was conscious of representing influence, power and utmost rectitude. Besides, he held a position. So, in the middle of world war he wrote a letter from Visby to his Archbishop, that spills over with the happy sense of an old man's power. He was 79 at the time, and still second Vice President of the General Evangelical Lutheran Conference, and had just returned from its meeting in Eisneach that August 1917. He wrote: 'They were very cautious about election to the *"Engere"* [i.e. the Restricted Committee]. ... The rule was laid down that nobody must be elected unless he has won his spurs as a fully trusted Lutheran *(voll bewährter Lutheraner)*. When I had been told this by Ihmels, I did not mention your name to anybody but simply proposed the name of Aurelius ... [Erik Aurelius, New Testament scholar, Lund university]. But Ihmels told me in confidence that he was convinced that you would be gratefully co-opted as soon your Lutheran standpoint had been established, which, I trust, might happen at the latest in 1921.'[3]

Also in Germany, Söderblom's intention was to win the Lutherans, not least his Confessionalist brethren, for Evangelical Catholicity. When Theodor Kaftan had put his melancholy question. 'Did we really have Churches hitherto?', though he was thereby questioning the State connexion of Landeskirchen, he was also stretching out towards the supranational and universal Catholic horizon to which Söderblom's idea pointed him.

Kaftan's contact with Söderblom, whose consecration in 1914 he had attended, was catalytic here. Kaftan was one of a small but significant group, or perhaps tendency, among German Churchmen,

---

[3] K. H. G. von Schéele, August 10, 1917, to Söderblom. 1921 was the year in which it was hoped to call a conference in Gothenburg, 'the capital of Lutheranism in Sweden'.

who in the post-war situation looked with expectation to Söderblom's programme of Evangelical Catholicity, and who, in this connexion, tried to introduce Episcopacy into the Church. The group was by no means uniform: there was Kaftan, who although not recognized as absolutely Lutheran, claimed for himself, in that delightful mixture of Danish and German which the former Schleswig leader loved to use: 'I am a Lutheran from *top* to *taa*' [head to food].[4] There was Professor Adolf Deissmann with his West German background and supposedly 'liberal theology'; and there were also in the group High Churchmen of various shades, among whom the most prominent, but definitely not all-powerful, was Heiler.

A bold move by Söderblom caught the imagination of some of these men. In 1917 Söderblom approached no less an authority than Kaiser Wilhelm II, suggesting that Evangelical episcopacy be 're-introduced'; by this fellowship in the ministry between the Germanic Churches north and south of the Baltic, Söderblom wished to establish a closer connexion between them, while keeping in mind their different historical and doctrinal development.[5] The Emperor's chaplain, Dr. Dryander, was also involved in this issue. He, like his young protégé Sigmund-Schultze, had a great respect for the Swedish Archbishop, and was probably in a position to discuss the benevolent Imperial answer sent to Söderblom.

After the war, Deissmann played a leading role in the Episcopacy debate, particularly at the important Prussian *Kirchenversammlung* in 1922. He was convener of the particular committee appointed to deal with the issue, and he reported to the Plenary Session of the *Church Assembly*. He summed up rather neatly the two sides of semantic warfare over the word 'episcopacy'. A Bishop, he made bold to state, was to a certain extent different from a General Superintendent, in fact he had a certain extra, a certain *plus,* as compared with that other title. What was this plus? The friends of the name, he said, look to what seemed the shining, ecumenical, genial, *volklich,* fatherly and loving in that word, while its opponents know it ad demonic, weakly romantic, un-German, hierachical, and Catholic.[6]

Deissmann was for Bishops—in fact he had himself been app-

---

[4] Th. Kaftan, 'Evang. Katholizität', *Die Eiche* 1925, p. 330.
[5] Peter Katz, *Nathan Söderblom*, 1925, p. 48.
[6] *Sitzungsbericht, Ausserordentl. Kirchenversammlung* (1922), publ. 1923, p. 1006. Deissmann had received valuable material for his study from Söderblom's co-worker, Prof. K. B. Westman. Ad. Deissman, February 20, 1922, to Söderblom.

roached by his native Nassau to become their first Bishop.[7] In that very interesting debate, the men with international experience from the first few 'Life and Work' committees, were those who advocated episcopacy. Dr. Spiecker, a leading layman in the Assembly, a former managing director of the Siemens Company, and President of the German Council of the World Alliance, told his, possibly provincial, fellow-Germans about experience from the Life and Work meeting in Hälsingborg, 1922. He felt it was necessary to establish a united front of the Evangelical Churches together with the Anglo-Saxons, over against Rome. For this pious purpose, Church leaders must be known as 'bishops', not 'General Superintendents'. With this title, we place them on a level with English Bishops, was the idea of this benign ecumenical layman.[1]

Deissmann the theologian, lifted the debate on to another level, that of personal spiritual leadership in the Church. This was in fact the real interest of the German Churchmen who advocated Episcopacy, and the more so as they shared and promoted Söderblom's programme of Evangelical Catholicity. However, Deissmann and his co-workers had to admit that they could not win the majority in the old Prussian Synod, but they did not give up hope. The question was brought up year after year, and attracted keen attention.

Dr. R. H. Wallau, who published the important book *Die Einigung der Kirche vom evangelischen Glauben aus,* in 1925, and who made Söderblom his central figure, brought out this aspect. He told Söderblom: 'Leadership through inspired personalitites was what was needed.'[2] This, he thought, was ideally expressed by Bishops, and Wallau pleaded for a renewal of the age-old episcopal ministry in the New Testament meaning of that word, and then went on to say: 'In the person of the Swedish Archbishop we find the most impressive illustration of the Evangelical concept of a Bishop.'

Wallau was, however, aware of a certain danger of Söderblom's being misunderstood in Germany by his most enthusiastic friends. More particularly Wallau warned against that interpretation of Söderblom's idea of Evangelical catholicity which was represented by Friedrich Heiler. Wallau complained to Siegmund-Schultze about this: 'As long as this *Tohuwabohu* [of Heiler's interpretation] is

---

[7] Deissmann, May 19, 1919, to Söderblom.
[1] *Sitzungsbericht,* p. 1077.
[2] 'Geist-erfüllte Persönlichkeiten', R. H. Wallau. September 26, 1924, to Söderblom.

not cleared up, Söderblom's great vision cannot find room in German opinion.'[3]

Söderblom liked to believe that his ecumenical programme was both Evangelical Catholic and Lutheran. He was challenged on this point in his many-sided contacts with German churches in those years. On the other hand, his contribution was itself a challenge to German churchmen, and had, as we have tried to show, a catalytic effect in the German situation.

The idea that there could be a more excellent way than 'method Wittenberg', or that of faith, was designed to raise Lutheran eyebrows and not only in Wittenberg. There were of course real theological differences here. Söderblom's interpretation of doctrine and of Luther was another than that of the confessionalists, and in the new theological climate of the nineteen-twenties this difference increased and tended to be emphasized. With his theological background of 'symbolism' and his pragmatic involvement in social and international problems Söderblom took a relativistic view of doctrine. His image of Luther, that of the hero and of the religious genius, was also different from that which now with Karl Holl emerged on the German scene. No wonder therefore that German Lutherans asked themselves whether Söderblom was sufficiently 'Lutheran' to be accepted as spokesman for Lutheranism in world-assemblies. Yet—if we may anticipate later developments—when confronted with other, non-Lutheran traditions as at Lausanne 1927 Söderblom himself could react as a defensor fidei of his own confession.

Our considerations of the German theological situation hitherto have pointed to the complications involved as Lutheran confessionalism was confronted with Söderblom's programme of Life and Work, and his emphasis on 'method love'. There was a psychological and cultural element in Söderblom's 'Evangelical Catholicity', and to this was due part of the complications thus experienced. But there was also a 'Catholic' component in his programme, and both Söderblom and his German followers were convinced that episcopacy was one of its expressions.

Uppsala–Rock Island

The last quarter of 1923 was spent by Söderblom on an extended tour of the United States, which was very exacting and much longer

---

[3] R. H. Wallau, November 16, 1924, to F. Siegmund-Schultze, Soest.

than any of his other journeys abroad that he had managed to undertake. He emphasized its importance by writing a book about it, in Swedish, called *From Uppsala to Rock Island,* Rock Island being the headquarters in Illinois of the Augustana Lutheran Synod. The American tour in fact resulted in two books since Anna Söderblom who, together with their son Jon Olof, accompanied the Archbishop, wrote her own volume. This was a charming and highly perceptive account called *En Amerikabok,* published in 1925. The bare outlines of the American tour are soon traced. It was designed to bring Söderblom in touch with 'all' of America. It took him, of course by train, from New York to San Francisco and Los Angeles; to the North and the Middle West, including Chicago, Minnesota and Rock Island, Illinois; to Pennsylvania and New England, including lectures at Harvard and Yale; with the final days in New York and Washington. He was given an exacting programme, speaking on some one hundred and twenty occasions, 'two months with voice, one without voice', as Söderblom, so conscious of voices, his own included, used to say afterwards. The press coverage was imposing, and the combined efforts of Dr. Atkinson and the Augustana Synod, helped to make Söderblom's visit one of the most notable events of the year.[1]

Less than a year after his return to Uppsala, Söderblom had a letter from Dr. Macfarland of the Federal Council; he wrote about Söderblom's tour:

It has been remarked here several times that you had little or no contact with the great denominational leaders who lead the co-operative movement. It has been further remarked that your time was spent with men hostile to co-operation or who knew or cared little or nothing about it. It was very unfortunate that your sponsors forced you to seem discourteous in appearing to decline to meet the Federal Council which had invited you to America, whose invitation you had accepted, which arranged a date with your committee officially to receive you, only to have your declination.

To tell you the truth I was to blame. I had heralded you as the great prophet of unity. Then when you came it looked as though you not only

---

[1] Söderblom, *Från Upsala till Rock Island* (1924). Söderblom's book has two parts: I. *Sermons and addresses* (in the Swedish original), 190 pp. There are about twenty of these altogether, including theological lectures on Martin Luther and on Faith and Science.

II. *Impressions and Remembrances,* 165 pp. (1) American idealism and religious life. (2) The calling of the Swedes. (3) Old Sweden in America. (4) The Church in Sweden and England and the daughter Churches in America.

repudiated the title but also repudiated myself. It was the subject of many jokes for some time.

That however is all past. It has had the effect, however, of creating the impression that you stood for exclusive Pan Lutheranism rather than for general co-operation. . . .[2]

These were harsh words, written to the pioneer and leader of 'Life and Work' by America's foremost promoter of 'Life and Work'. How do we explain this castigation? What had happened? The conflict of interests reflected in Macfarland's words draws attention in dramatic fashion to a problem inherent in Söderblom's total effort, the tension between the ecumenical and the confessional. This tension was by no means confined to the American scene. We have noticed it in regard to Söderblom's relations with the Churches in Germany. It was accentuated however by his American visit. An account of 'Uppsala–Rock Island' serves to bring out in sharper relief Söderblom's own particular approach to some of the ecclesiastical and ecumenical problems of the nineteen-twenties.

Söderblom's visit to the United States had been under discussion for quite some time but postponed for various reasons, including those of health. The years 1922 and 1923 had been of great importance to him and his Church. In 1922 there was the agreement with the Church of England; and for Söderblom, ever since 1909, his contacts with the Anglican Communion were always complicated by his concern for the Augustana Synod in America. In April, 1923, he met the Lutheran leaders at Eisenach, Germany, and this was both positively and negatively a challenge to him. After Eisenach, his Swiss co-worker Adolf Keller, who in 1922 had published a perceptive book on the American scene, wrote to Söderblom, asking him to use his influence to win the American Lutherans for a less confessional, more ecumenical position.

The two claims on Söderblom—ecumenical and confessional, or international and national, according to different emphases—were rooted in his own heart. It was Macfarland who had written in December, 1921, 'It is about time you returned some of our visits. Let me assure you, that when you do come we shall give you a *big* time'.[3] But it was Atkinson as General Secretary of the Church Peace Union and the World Alliance, with the backing of the Federal Council and of the American Scandinavian Foundation, who in July, 1921, con-

---

[2] Chs Macfarland, September 4, 1924, to Söderblom.
[3] Chs Macfarland, December 21, 1920, to Söderblom.

veyed in person to Söderblom the official invitation of these four bodies. That November, Söderblom felt prepared to accept. He saw tasks which he wished to accomplish: 'It is our sacred duty to promote the united Life and Work of Christendom.' 'My research', he added, when discussing the programme, 'has had two chief objects: 1. Comparative religion, and 2. the great genius of religion who is called Martin Luther.' It was in these interests that he had determined to lecture.[4]

On the same day, November 16, 1921, Söderblom wrote another letter to a friend in America, this time to Dr. L. G. Abrahamson, who was the editor of the *Augustana* and a prominent leader in the Augustana Synod. He had known Söderblom since 1897, and belonged to that select group of friends who had attended Söderblom's consecration in November, 1914. In 1916, Augustana invited Söderblom to visit America for the Reformation Jubilee of 1917. Abrahamson was joined by other Augustana leaders, including Gustav Andreen, President of Augustana College and Seminary, and what was always important to Söderblom, a Yale man; and Sven Youngert, Professor at Augustana and possibly Söderblom's oldest acquaintance among American pastors—they had been students together in Uppsala, 1883 to 1884.[5]

Thus when Abrahamson, of course quite independently of Dr. Atkinson, invited Söderblom to the Augustana, Söderblom could not but accept. He was prepared to come in order to improve the relations between Augustana and the Church of Sweden, to promote Lutheran unity in America, and to lecture on Martin Luther.

Dr. Atkinson now prepared an ambitious speaking and lecture programme, but knowing that at the end of 1922 Söderblom had had a severe heart attack and had been for months under doctor's orders, he tried not to press his guest too hard. He was surprised however, when he learned in June, 1923, that the Augustana were also arranging Söderblom's schedule, and he probably thought that he was being too generous when in writing to Abrahamson, he allowed Söderblom one week to be spent in Rock Island. The reply came promptly. On June 16, 1923, Dr. Abrahamson wrote: 'There must be some misunderstanding with regard to the pending visit of Archbishop Söderblom. He comes here, and will travel here, under

---

[4] Söderblom, November 16, 1921, to H. Atkinson.

[5] Youngert was an enthusiastic friend. When he travelled in Europe in 1919 on a war relief assignment for the National Lutheran Council, Söderblom included him among the Olaus Petri lecturers of 1919.

the auspices of the Lutheran Augustana Synod, he has been invited by the said Synod, accepted the invitation, and stated plainly that he comes: 'as the guest of the Augustana Synod. ... We have also renewed, on the suggestion of the Archbishop, a petition to King Gustav V, that he may commission the Archbishop to our Church and our Swedish Lutheran colonies this Fall. Hence we are laying out plan for the itinerary.'

There was a real clash of interests here, but the two Americans settled this embarrassing matter admirably and generously. The correspondence between them preserves—as one must expect—American exclamations about European lack of business methods. In the end, three of Atkinson's sponsors gave up. This left Atkinson's own Church Peace Union and the Augustana Synod to arrange the trip and to foot the bill.

In making generous promises in both directions Söderblom had not perhaps fully realized that America was a vast country. He had never been fully content with the trivial limitation of unilocality and would have liked to be able to have been in more than one place at a time. Faced with Atkinson's question about how to reconcile the claims from both sides, he wrote: 'The most important thing I shall try to do in America for our common sacred duty of unity—if it may be possible for me in some slight degree—is to increase in Augustana an interest and confidence in our Evangelical strivings ... but the kernel of American Lutheranism is to me the Augustana Synod. That is the Swedish Church in America. ... Now, I venture to send you the enclosed compromise'.[6] There may have been a certain amount of rationalisation in Söderblom's reply to Atkinson, yet the more he debated with himself about what he could do in the States, the more convinced he became that he had to win, if possible, the Lutherans of America for the ecumenical cause.

In making the issue one of confessionalism vs. ecumenicity, we have so far omitted one important factor. To Söderblom, Dr. Abrahamson and the Augustana Synod were not only Lutherans but also, and perhaps primarily, represented the Swedish Lutheran tradition in America.

The year 1923 was one of great significance for the Augustana Synod from the point of view of cultural policy. This was especially relevant to an Archbishop from Uppsala. The Lutheran Churches

---

[6] Söderblom, July 23, 1923, to H. Atkinson.

had moved with various speeds towards full integration into American society. Here the language question was crucial. In 1923 the Augustana Synod, in spite of a certain resistance from within, was prepared to conclude this process of Americanisation. In fact 1923 was the last 'Swedish' year in its existence. This was expressed by the fact that until then the Synod's minutes were published in the old language—Swedish. From 1924 Augustana like some other Lutheran Churches before it, had their official minutes published in English. Söderblom fortunately was more sensitive than most Swedish Churchmen at that time, and appreciated the importance of this, obviously belated, change. In spite of sentimental temptations to the contrary, he emphasized the necessity and importance of this reorientation. At the same time he agreed with Augustana leaders that there were certain values in the Swedish historical tradition which might well be incorporated in the culture of the New World.

Söderblom encouraged Augustana—if encouragement were at all needed—to see its place in this new world. 'America is a rejuvenated Europe', Harald Hjärne had written in 1902, and travelling in the States, Söderblom felt that what he saw fully corroborated this view of his great Uppsala authority. America fascinated him. Riding in his Pullman wagon he would jot down in his diary a few impressions: 'U.S.A.—our closest neighbour on the map of the heart and of imagination, not according to the usual geography. Air for the wings! The chest expanded!' (Söderblom had had his first serious heart attack a year earlier.)

To this concern for cultural integration there was added on Söderblom's part a particular personal interest in the Swedes. In her book, Anna Söderblom stated that in the last resort the purpose of the westward journey, 'what he really went to America for,' was to find out 'where the Swedes went.'[7] However official his visit may really have been, there was at the same time something very personal about it and it brought out something deep in his personality. He had noticed some of the problems of Swedish emigration to the United States from his own boyhood days, and at Rockford, Illinois, an eighty-year-old Swedish gentleman, Per Hedlund came up to him—he was Söderblom's godfather, and had emigrated from Hälsingland to the United States in 1888!

So, visiting the Swedes in America was for Söderblom to re-live his early youth. He met there again, in those who had emigrated, his

---

[7] Anna Söderblom, *En Amerikabok* (1925), p. 8.

native Hälsingland, its folk-culture and its pietism. At that time he often mentioned having heard Moody as a young man in 1890; but did not that fiery old preacher represent something deeper and closer to his heart—the image of the father, perhaps? Söderblom startled an American dinner audience by suddenly, in the middle of an address, breaking out into all five verses of: 'There were ninety and nine that safely lay in the shelter of the fold.' He spoke of the example of Moody and Sankey, but was it not the father, Jonas Söderblom, singing those songs of Zion?

It was a great personal sacrifice to Söderblom not to be able to visit Bishop Hill, Illinois, not far from Rock Island, the centre of a peculiar sect—the Eric Jansonists—of Swedish 'enthusiastic' revivalism. Instead Söderblom had to attend the 'Life and Work' and World Alliance meetings in Philadelphia, November 12 to 15, and it was Anna Söderblom who in his place represented the family at Bishop Hill. Here she met the son of Sven Svenson, an old member of the sect, hailing from Söderala, Hälsingland, himself a cousin of Jonas Söderblom, the father of the Archbishop. If only Dr. MacFarland had known the circumstances, he would have appreciated the sacrifice which the Archbishop made!

With the reference we have just made to the meetings of Life and Work and of the World Alliance, we have in fact indicated that of course, Söderblom was by no means exclusively concerned with the Lutherans, an impression one might have gathered from Dr. MacFarland's letter. He managed to give a considerable part of his crowded time in the United States to lectures, addresses and important personal contacts on behalf of his wider ecumenical endeavour. His lectures included themes such as 'the unity that is and the unity that is to be;' the reconstruction of Europe; world peace; and his own projected Stockholm Conference. In the Universities of Berkeley, Chicago, Harvard, Johns Hopkins, Pennsylvania and his beloved Yale, and in theological seminaries such as Union and Mount Airy, he gave lectures on certain fundamental issues in the History of Religion, as well as on Luther. Wherever he went, he took the opportunity of speaking on Luther in interdenominational groups, and on his ecumenical and Evangelical-Catholic view in Lutheran assemblies.

In his own programme of Evangelical Catholicity, episcopacy was an important issue, and while he was in America, Söderblom was far from unmindful of this issue. He had however to approach it with

Welcoming the world to his Stockholm Conference, 1925.

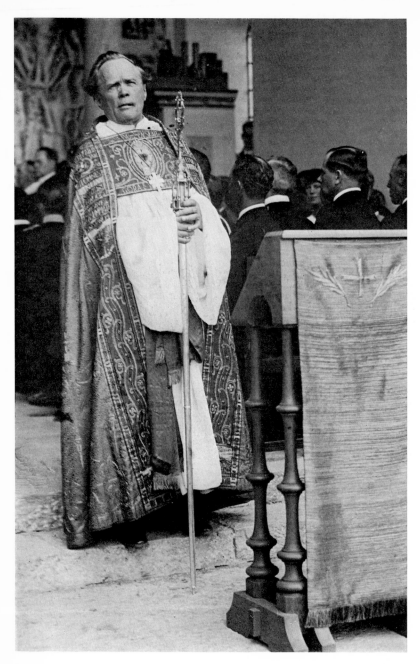

Dedicating the St. Ansgar Chapel, 1930.

Söderblom welcoming to Stockholm 1925, Patriarch Photios of Alexandria. In background Major A. Sjöstedt.

The square between the Cathedral and the Archbishop's House, Uppsala, was first called Odinslund, (Wotan's Grove.) In 1964 the civic authorities of Uppsala christened it Nathan Söderblom's plan. Even the streetlights have episcopal connotations.

great circumspection, and this he evidently managed to do. In order to understand Söderblom's attitude it is necessary to briefly allude to the history of this question within the Augustana Synod.

Episcopacy was a live if controversial issue in the Synod at that time, and had been for more than two decades. Bishop von Schéele of Visby had visited Augustana on three occasions—1893, 1901 and 1910—and the matter was raised then, in fact, the Bishop himself was approached in 1907 with a view to his exchanging Visby for Rock Island. He declined, and in terms which showed that it was probably a good thing that he did so: 'I have always rejected any suggestion of this kind. I strive to give unto my life as uniform a character as possible, and I could not at 63 accept this proposal.'[8] The debate within Augustana for some time centred round his name, the New England conference of the Synod being particularly concerned with the introduction of Episcopacy.

Soon after Söderblom's taking office, he was informed that his Augustana friends were pursuing the episcopacy issue. Dr. Gustav Andreen could tell him that the New England Conference of the Augustana had decided to accept episcopacy, on their own if need be, or with the consent of the Synod as a whole. The idea however was fatally bound up with 'Swedishness'. The protagonists of episcopacy thought of it in terms of a uniting link between the 'Swedish mother Church' and her 'daughter' in America. Plans were sufficiently advanced for this party to hope that the first Bishop could be consecrated in Uppsala Cathedral at the Reformation Jubilee in 1917, and Söderblom was duly informed about these plans, but the enthusiasts found that they could not cajole the tougher brethren of the Mid–West and so the matter was postponed. It is necessary to keep this discussion in mind in order to appreciate the delicacy of the situation in 1923, and the self-discipline which Söderblom imposed on himself. It was after all a matter of very personal concern to him; Reval and Riga of their own accord had asked Söderblom to consecrate. There, Söderblom as we have seen, used the situation to the full.

Rock Island was a very different proposition. The linking of Episcopacy with loyalty to the Old Country backfired; for 1923, as we have already indicated, was the decisive year for Americanisation in the history of Augustana. Söderblom trod warily. The problem followed him wherever he went, in meetings and at meals. At an offi-

---

[8] C. Norrby, *Knut Henning Gezelius von Schéele* (1925), pp. 177–8.

20 – 684363 *B. Sundkler*

cial dinner in Minneapolis, Preuss, the Governor of Minnesota and a good churchman of Scandinavian descent, gladdened the Archbishop's heart by telling him that he sang the *Gluntarna,* the famous Uppsala students' duets, but soon the Governor shot an incredulous question over the table: 'Do you still care about Apostolic ordination?'[9] Söderblom's reply is not known, he may have felt that on that festive occasion, so many centuries after the Apostles, he had better be diplomatic and stick to the *Gluntarna.*

Söderblom had to be satisfied with any positive evidence which he could find of interest in Episcopacy. He was particularly happy that leaders in some of the Lutheran Churches, such as Dr. F. P. Manhart of the United Lutheran Church, came forward in support of Episcopal leadership, and he discussed the matter with Episcopalian leaders in America. However with the Augustana men he avoided pressing the issue. Sometimes he felt that he could attempt to disarm criticism by a somewhat roundabout, pragmatic interpretation which appeared reasonable. He would present the matter in this way:

In the house of Lutheranism in America there are many mansions. They are solid, and the walls rise slowly but surely; but the Episcopalians have placed a flag-pole with a flag on their roof. Does it greatly matter if you live in a house with or without a flagpole? Would anybody consider moving on account of that flag? How do I know? But if it were so, that some people prefer to see a flag waving on their roof, it would be bad if because of this, he felt tempted to leave the great building of Lutheranism. If he ascribes unreasonable and almost magical importance to the flag, then the matter cannot be helped. But if it is a question of taste and style, of convenience and tradition, then nobody must accuse Lutheranism of callous stubbornness which abhors to place a flag on the house. Because to the essence of Lutheranism—if the name does not betray—belongs not to be afraid, not to be bound by forms, but to be free. The flag is Episcopacy![1]

In his book on America, the concluding pages are devoted to Episcopacy, but in the somewhat evasive way, which he felt—perhaps with a pang—was the only possible attitude in such a delicate situation. On a deeper level, he rested assured, he said, that the Lutherans would not take as long a time as the Episcopalians—one hundred and fifty years!—to get Bishops![2] Time was on his side and worked for his plans, he felt; he was in a hurry, but he could wait.

---

[9] Nathan Söderblom, *Diary,* October 28, 1923.

[1] Nathan Söderblom, *Från Upsala till Rock Island,* p. 367–368.

[2] Ibid. p. 373. Dean Rogers of Detroit had made this estimate, and Söderblom made it his own. (Rogers was an Episcopalian.)

He was content with muted suggestions from afar and of course there must have been some, to whom already this was much too loud. In 1930, together with the whole Swedish college of Bishops, Söderblom presented Dr. Brandelle, Augustana's President, with a pectoral cross. It was sent by post, and handed to him at Rock Island. There was some discussion in the Synod as to what to do with this gift, and eventually it was accepted, 'not as a badge of office, but as a symbol of friendship with Sweden.' To that extent, that piece of gold symbolised the tension between the universal and provinsial characteristics in the Church.

While in America, and under the auspices of the Augustana Synod, Söderblom thought it wise not to press this controversial problem too much. He lectured on his great hero Luther, and no doubt this helped to overcome much of the resistance in the Lutheran camp. This was particularly so in the United Lutheran Church, where the change of attitude with regard to Söderblom can be studied in the official periodical of that Church, *The Lutheran*. It had nine articles on Söderblom between September 6, 1923, and June 3, 1924, and shifted from a certain reserve to whole-hearted acceptance of the Swedish Archbishop. When Söderblom visited the headquarters of the Church he was shown round by a young man who later was to become one of the great leaders of the World Council of Churches, Dr. Franklin C. Fry.

In the last article, Söderblom's influence in the United States was ascribed to 'his genial manner, his broad scholarship, his keen reasoning, and his courageous defence of his own convictions'. This change of heart on the part of the United Lutheran Church was a great achievement. This Church sent to Stockholm 1925 four regularly appointed delegates and six observers.

Even more positive of course was the response of the Augustana Synod itself. The fact that Söderblom was a Swede, and the Archbishop of the Swedes was an important factor here. Söderblom's charm and magnetic personality were of particular value, but there can be no question that it was his central personal conviction expressed in his argument about 'Martin Luther's ecumenical significance' which contributed towards winning some of the American Lutherans for the ecumenical cause.

Uppsala–Tranquebar

Söderblom's programme of Evangelical Catholicity had an appeal in the Baltic states and in Germany. He also discussed it in the

United States and found response for it there. But 'Catholicity' implied a horizon beyond the limits of the Western world. By definition of the term it must be universal. South India and Asia provided that larger horizon.

Yet as he applied, in 1919 and the following years, his programme to the young Church in South India, Söderblom discovered that the problems were, almost paradoxically, an extension of the situation in Northern Europe. This was even more surprising as the year 1919 was the time of acute experience on the part of the Indian people, of the need for Swaraj and for independence from Western rule. 1919 was the year when Gandhi became the recognized leader of Indian aspirations. In that same year, when the Mahatma sensed in the Indian masses 'a passion for unity', a group of men from differing Church traditions (Anglicans, Presbyterians, Congregationalists) met at Tranquebar to bring about in the Church that unity for which India yearned. It was in that same year, that Söderblom suggested to the Lutheran Church in South India the introduction of episcopacy. He interpreted the work of a bishop in terms of 'unity'. One particular ministry, common to all congregations, was needed for the unity of the Church and for the care of souls. This ministry, he made bold to suggest, was episcopacy.

In South India, German and Swedish missionaries had been co-operating since the 1850's in Tamil country carrying forward traditions of Lutheran Pietism which once in 1706 had pioneered Protestant mission work at Tranquebar, the little coast village south of Madras. The co-operation between the two missions was not without tensions. The Leipzig Germans knew that they represented the genuine Lutheran tradition; while their Nordic partners tended towards something described as 'Swedish Liberalism' expressing itself in occasional intercommunion with other Churches.[1]

This tension was aggravated when the Swedes in 1906 led by C. J. Sandegren suggested that ordinations in the Lutheran Churches in India be performed by a bishop, common to all Lutheran Churches in India. Sandegren wrote to his Mission Board in Uppsala, asking them for guidance in this matter. Archbishop Ekman felt that the question should be settled by the Swedish Government and hoped to get his clue from the Swedish Minister for Ecclesiastical Affairs. The answer he got was evasive, as well it might have been.

---

[1] P. Fleisch, *Hundert Jahre luth. Mission* (1938), p. 221.

Söderblom often spoke of the official Church system as a heavy machinery. The Swedish Church only moved slowly. The Mission Board sent its enquiry to the Government in December 1906, and in March 1909 still no answer had been received! In the meantime, there was the interesting contact between the Swedish and the Anglican churches, in that Bishop Tottie visited the Lambeth Conference. On his return he had talks in Uppsala with the Mission Director, K. A. Ihrmark. On this occasion, the suggestion was made that ordinations in South India might be performed by an Anglican bishop and Ihrmark followed this up by mentioning the idea to Archbishop Ekman, who seemed to think it would be something of a solution. On March 30, 1909, Ihrmark wrote to Bishop Tottie for his official statement on this suggestion. Did he think that the English bishops would be prepared to ordain in South India if asked to do so? Ihrmark was sufficiently sure of Tottie's view that he, anxious to present at last a solution for the Lutheran Church in South India, wrote a letter to South India, *before* he had had an answer from Tottie. When Tottie's letter of April 9, 1909 did arrive he advised caution. He reminded Ihrmark of the Committee which the Archbishop of Canterbury had appointed to enquire into the proposed intercommunion with the Church of Sweden. It would be wise to await the report from this Committee. One should not at that stage anticipate the results of the enquiry. Any agreement on ritual, such as for ordination, should be made with that Committee. The Bishop of Madras had no authority outside his own Church. Tottie had met Bishop Whitehead of Madras and knew him as 'very High Church (in an Anglican sense)'; he might easily have misgivings against acting in accordance with the idea that Ihrmark had mentioned. Tottie's conclusion was definite: 'the best solution would be that we get our own missionary Bishop for the mission fields of our Church.'

When Ihrmark received this wise and well informed letter, his own impetuous proposal had already been sent to South India, in a letter to C. J. Sandegren dated April 5, 1909. He suggested that the ordination be taken by 'either the German Provost or one of the English bishops' and being Mission Director he knew that his Board in Uppsala was going to decide accordingly later in the same month. By these plans, he suggested, 'we stand on very firm ground'.

This geological hypothesis was not acceptable to Sandegren: 'Firm ground', he moaned. 'I rather believe that if this were tried, the ground would prove to be volcanic.' It would spell the ruin of the Swedish mission in India. And if the proposal for Anglican bishops were forced through, the Lutheran congregations would not accept pastors thus ordained.

The spectre of Anglican bishops hovering over that Lutheran sanctuary threatened Sandegren's efforts as much as it confirmed the very worst suspicions of his solid German colleagues. The Mission Board discussed Ihrmark's idea at the end of April, 1909 but cautiously left the Anglican bishops out of the picture, and focussed their attention on the German Provost, although one of the Board secretaries, G. Hogner, insisted that it was none other than Sandegren who should be asked to ordain, by direction of the Board. Four months later they found that the reaction from South India was too strong, and followed Hogner's advice, commissioning Sandegren to ordain.

This was the Indian church situation which Söderblom faced when he became Archbishop. It has been necessary to recall these tensions and frustrations in order to understand the measures taken by Söderblom. From Leipzig he had followed the development with interest and in March 1913 written an article in *Stockholms Dagblad* emphasizing the need for a Swedish missionary Bishop, an 'envoy of Swedish Christendom'. He was at the same time anxious to win his Leipzig brethren.

On his appointment as Archbishop he wrote to the 'College' of the Leipzig Mission:

None of the responsible tasks connected with the archepiscopate is closer to my heart than the sacred missionary duty of our Church which she pursues in blessed union with the Leipzig brethren who are of the same evangelical Lutheran faith. And I regard it as a special grace that in these last two years I have had the privilege to get to know the work of the Leipzig Mission better; its leaders and some of its activities.[2]

This was the obvious, friendly thing to say, writing, as he did, from Leipzig itself. There was no doubt, however, that Söderblom was genuinely interested in this particular work.

Söderblom was determined to settle the question of a missionary bishop, as soon as he himself had become Archbishop. In October, 1914, in his very first meeting with the Board, he proposed the appointment of a committee to deal with the matter. The nomination was characteristic. The members of the committee were, Söder-

---

[2] Söderblom (no date: Approx. June 1, 1914), to Leipzig Mission: Akten, Schweden, 1908–1915, Leipzig.

blom himself and Bishop Danell, together with a legal expert who was none other than Söderblom's old friend, H. Palmgren, now a high official in the Swedish *Regeringsrätt*. The committee emphasized the need for bishops, one for India, another for South Africa, in the interest of the building of the Younger Churches and more especially for the sake of ordinations.

But Söderblom took one further step. In October, 1914 he had changed the formula used for delegating the power of ordination to the leading missionary in the field. Until that time, such delegation had implied authority to ordain 'on behalf of the Swedish Mission Board'. From this time onwards the formula became 'on behalf of the Archbishop of Uppsala'. This was as far as he could go, in 1914, but he already looked beyond this interim measure to a time after the war when the matter could be settled.

The World War both furthered and complicated the matter. India was British India and therefore, for the duration of the war, the German mission an 'enemy mission'. The German missionaries had to leave the country. The neutral Swedes took over the responsibility for the mission work as a whole. Söderblom devoted a great deal of effort to this task. While the Germans in Leipzig worked on a Tamil church constitution which tended to refurbish earlier traditions in the mission, Söderblom visualized a constitution which through a Synodal Council assured a measure of continuity of the direction of the Church's affairs.

Söderblom contributed with characteristic energy to the work of a Constitution Committee with Bishop Danell and the new Mission Director, Brundin, which met regularly in the Archbishop's House in the summer of 1917. Here the blue-print for an independent Evangelical Church in South India emerged. As the World War came to an end, the Lutheran congregations constituted themselves on January 14, 1919, as the Tamil Evangelical Lutheran Church, but such was the strength of the traditional German influence that for its constitution the Church took the German outline and left the Uppsala blue-print aside.

This was of course an epoch when Western influence was still a real factor in Indian Church affairs, and in this particular case, even at its moment of independence, the traditional influence from the Leipzig fathers made itself strongly felt.

But the Swedes, too, had a word at that time, and, as it happened, an Archbishop who knew what he wanted.

So when the Indian Church asked the Board in Uppsala to confirm its decision, the answer was, 'in general, approved'. This tele-graphese meant, and the Indian leaders realized this, that the Swed-ish Board had some suggestions of their own to make.

In that tumultuous autumn of 1919 with the slogans of Gandhiji's Swaraj in the air, the Indian leaders and the Swedish missionaries in South India read the proposal from Uppsala: the constitution should have a Synodal Council and a President elected for life-time; this President to become Bishop.

Against the historic background which we have, however, briefly sketched, one can appreciate the confusion caused by this interven-tion from Uppsala.

Söderblom found it necessary to explain the constitutional propo-sals in an Episcopal Letter to the Synod of the Tamil Church. He maintained that it was the responsibility of the Board to scrutinize, and, if possible, to improve on the suggested wording of the consti-tution. 'When it is the case of a building to last for centuries, ought one not to examine the drawings particularly well?' The main bur-den of his Letter was an interpretation of episcopacy trying to per-suade those who might be suspicious of a type of ministry, rumoured to be authoritarian and dictatorial. The innocuity of Söderblom's argument could hardly be bettered. It might even be suggested that the Archbishop allowed himself to go rather far in his pedagogical concern not to offend anybody:

In addition to the common representation in the Synod and in addition to the ministers of the congregations and the Executive, we need, in order to unite the different parts of the Church, a ministry common to all its parishes to take care of the souls and welfare of the Church. This servant of the Church is called from the Greek word in the New Testament 'Bishop', in Latin 'Praepositus', or 'Superintendent', or by other names and is as a rule appointed for a lifetime. All the Evangelical Lutheran Churches in the world have had this ministry from the beginning or have had to introduce it later. Here in Sweden the Bishop is included in the Chapter or 'Consistory' as its President. This ministry was, as it were, pre-shadowed in our Tamil Mission by the Provost or 'Probst', the equivalent of the Latin 'Praepositus'. It would be a retrograde step to deprive the Church constitution of the strength which lies in this ministry.

Countermeasures against these Swedish attempts were taken both in India and in Leipzig. The German Mission sent its Director, C. Paul, an old acquaintance of Söderblom's from his Leipzig days, to Uppsala to warn against the introduction of episcopacy in the In-dian Church. But Söderblom was unmoved. In the discussion with

Paul, who could be expected to know his theology, he showed himself more definite with regard to the substance of the episcopate. He would not be told that a bishop was just another Inspector for the external administration of the Church. The episcopal ministry was that of 'a pastor of souls'.

In India in May 1920, the Church elected a Swedish missionary, Ernst Heuman, as President for life and the majority of the Church felt that by this the matter was settled. The man they had selected was no stranger to the Archbishop. He was an old friend from Söderblom's student days in Uppsala. Heuman had been a leading figure in the Student Missionary Association in Uppsala at that time. It was here that he felt the call to become a missionary to the Santals in North India, where he spent some ten years. After a decade he was, in 1896, personally faced with that same problem with which the Tamil Evangelical Lutheran Church was to struggle a generation later: the authority of ordination. Heuman was in fact one of a comparatively large company of Protestant missionaries who having started out in a Pietistic group of an 'alliance' type were led, by the situation of the Young Church, towards a more 'Catholic' position. Heuman decided for himself that, having been ordained by a mission pastor he should seek ordination also from a Bishop, and he was duly ordained in Sweden by the one Swedish bishop at that time with an international outlook, von Schéele of Visby. This made him *persona ingrata* in his old mission. He returned to India, but now to the South and to the Tamils.

Heuman was aware of the tensions over the episcopacy issue in 1919–1920 and did not wish to press the matter. Once again, the initiative was taken by Uppsala, no doubt by Söderblom himself who firmly held that personal contact and counsel were preferable to correspondence. He informed the Church that a commission of three 'fathers and brothers in Christ' was to be sent out, Bishop Danell, Professor K. B. Westman, and the Mission Director G. Brundin.

In South India, the Swedes seemed to act true to type. On May 1st, 1919, a handful of Anglicans, Presbyterians and Congregationalists met in a conference at Tranquebar: it proved to be immensely important for it was the decisive, initiatory meeting of what a generation later was to become C.S.I., the Church of South India. They met in Lutheran Tranquebar, and the young Swedish missionary, Paul Sandegren was there as their host. When the delegation from Uppsala arrived, even more dramatic things happened. Bishop Danell was regarded, by many in his home church, as the prototype of the Orthodox Lutheran: but what did he do when he came to South India? Apart from attending a number of Lutheran meetings he also participated in the Church Missionary Society Centenary at Palamcottah. He may even have felt that it was natural for him to do so. For it was with the C. M. S. at Palamcottah that Peter Fjellstedt, Swedish priest and the greatest Swedish missionary of the century had worked in the 1830's. However, Danell was not merely an interested onlooker at the meeting. Invited by Bishop Westcott, the Anglican Metropolitan, he was asked to assist in the distribution of Holy Communion. He did so and himself communicated on the occasion. In a report to the Board at Uppsala of April 4, 1921, he informed Sweden that he served in this capacity 'with the bishops of Tinnevelly, Travancore and Dornakal (the latter an Indian by name of Azariah)'.[3]

The three members of the Swedish delegation spent a large part of their time on theological lectures to various groups in the Church, on the ministry, more especially episcopacy. Nobody could have represented Söderblom and interpreted his programme of Evangelical Catholicity so well as Professor Westman, the Archbishop's co-worker, and Bishop Danell. The latter had been critical of Söderblom on many occasions in the past. In the South India situation he furthered Söderblom's programme with complete loyalty, as did Brundin, the Mission Director. At an extra Synod, March 1921, the Church decided to accept episcopacy and on the very day that this decision was taken, Heuman was consecrated by Bishop Danell. The Church decided that the bishop's designation was to be the 'Bishop of Tranquebar'. Johannes Sandegren and, after him, Rajah B. Manikam were to carry that title and by their work make it well known throughout the Churches in Asia and the world.

Without the Archbishop of Uppsala, his vision, perseverance and determination, this would, conceivably, never have happened.

Uppsala–Canterbury

To the family of Lutheran Churches in the world the Swedes seem somewhat different and therefore possibly difficult. This situation was conditioned by history and also by a new relationship with the

---

[3] For this section, see correspondence in Church of Sweden Mission archives, and L. Österlin, Det svenska biskopsämbetets införande i ... Sydindien, in [S. Kjöllerström], Kyrka Folk Stat (1967), pp. 159–181.

Anglican Communion which, on the Swedish side, was largely initiated by Söderblom. The orientation westwards was, as we have seen, part of a general trend in Swedish politics and culture of the nineteen–twenties. In this respect Söderblom was representative of an important change in his own people and country. Increasingly, and very particularly in his capacity as Archbishop, he emphasized the sense of tradition and continuity, and he loved to recognize this in the English people, and especially in the Church of England and in the British institutions such as the universities. Speaking in April 1920 to the Anglo–Swedish society in Stockholm he poured scorn on a certain modernist Swedish tendency to be heartily pleased when one has succeeded in abolishing something just for the pleasure of abolishing or changing something external'. He contrasted this with the English realism: 'The important thing is not new institutions, nor alterations, but renewal of man and the ability to put to use that which is given.'

It must be pointed out however that while Söderblom wanted this new relationship and valued it highly, he was not an uncritical admirer of the Anglican position, and while the 1922 agreement on intercommunion between the two churches seemed to strengthen Söderblom's programme of Evangelical Catholicity, it was a fact that this concept of his met with much less understanding among Anglicans than among some of the German Lutherans. The situation was therefore somewhat complicated.

The Anglicans took the initiative at Lambeth 1920. The Lambeth bishops had before them the recommendations of the Anglican Commission on relationships with the Church of Sweden; this commission had already produced its formal report in 1911 which said:

(1) That the succession of bishops has been maintained unbroken by the Church of Sweden, and that it has a true conception of the episcopal office ... and (2) that the office of priest is also rightly conceived as a divinely instituted instrument for the ministry of Word and Sacraments, and that it has been in intention handed on throughout the whole history of the Church of Sweden.

A precedent to which the Commission referred was, interestingly enough, the agreement of 1888 with the Old Catholics of Germany, Austria and Switzerland. As a parallel to this undertaking 'members of the National Church of Sweden, otherwise qualified to receive the Sacrament in their own Church, might be admitted to Communion in ours ...' Lambeth 1920 accepted the Commission's report on 'the unbroken succession of the Episcopate in Sweden, and on the conception of the office of priest held by that Church . . .'

We also hold that the time has come when, in the event of an invitation to an Anglican bishop or bishops to take part in the consecration of a Swedish bishop, it might properly be accepted . . . We think also that in the first instance, as an evident token of the restoration of close relations between the two Churches, it is desirable that more than one of our bishops should take part in the action.

The approach from Lambeth was thus a follow-up of the Uppsala conversations of 1909, yet the situation was different. In 1909, at a time of large-scale Swedish emigration to the United States, the relationships with Augustana had tended to overshadow the Anglo-Swedish talks. The focus in the early nineteen–twenties had shifted to the relationship between Sweden and England, while overseas it was other and new contacts which now demanded some measure of consideration. Swedish and Anglican interests in South Africa and South India—these issues were of real importance to some of the most vocal at Lambeth, for example Bishop Weston and Bishop Palmer.

To Söderblom the year 1920 was a year fraught with risks with regard to his contacts with the Church of England. His persuasive efforts seemed at that time to be lost on Archbishop Davidson who had decided to withold Anglican representation at the Life and Work meeting in Geneva, August 1920. To make up for this, Söderblom could take comfort from the fact that he had other friends among the English bishops. Hensley Henson was one, and Söderblom tended to take his cues on the Anglican position from his correspondence with the controversial Hensley Henson. In May 1920, prior to Lambeth, Söderblom had invited him to assist at a Swedish episcopal consecration to take place in September 1920. It seems that Söderblom sent this invitation direct to Hensley Henson without informing Davidson, a measure which did not make things any easier for Dr. Davidson; in fact Davidson was afraid lest the invitation to Hensley Henson should jeopardize the Swedish case before Lambeth. On the other hand Söderblom's invitation showed Lambeth that they dealt not with a theoretical proposition but with a practical issue demanding a solution there and then.

A characteristic compromise was found to solve the problem raised by Söderblom's invitation; Henson could go to Uppsala but not alone. Hensley Henson of course wrote of this in his *Retrospect*, putting it in his own inimitable terms: 'I have sometimes allowed myself to wonder whether, if I had not already guaranteed the presence of *one* Bishop [i.e. himself] at that great and significant ceremonial, the Lambeth Conference would have authorized that of *two*.'[1] For the whole development of the Life and Work movement under Söderblom's direction, it was providential that Theodore Woods, then of Peterborough, became that other bishop to take part in the Swedish consecrations. To Söderblom personally it was a special joy that on St Matthew's Day, 1920, he could invite Bishop Woods to celebrate Holy Communion at the altar of Holy Trinity in Uppsala—eleven years after that first memorable occasion.[2]

Woods was to succeed Ryle and Talbot at Winchester, and these three were Söderblom's dearest Anglican co-workers. To Söderblom the line 'Uppsala–Canterbury' was in fact a line 'Uppsala–Winchester'! There was Ryle from whom he had received Holy Communion at the altar of his own Holy Trinity Church in Uppsala in 1909; Ryle, 'the most modern of English Bishops', as Söderblom said. There was Talbot, a venerable patriarch in the Church of Christ, representing that combination of solid churchmanship and social awareness which Söderblom appreciated more than any other ecclesiastical position. The same could be said of Theodore Woods, who in the nineteen-twenties was to be one of his closest co-workers in the Ecumenical movement. To Söderblom this churchmanship was represented also by Bishop William Temple who had influenced him greatly during the War, and Bishop Burge of Oxford, who for a few years was to give Söderblom his support in the Life and Work movement.

To all this was added a direct and personal touch—that of Yngve Brilioth. In 1919 Brilioth left Uppsala for Oxford where he began his research into 'The Anglican Revival'. In England, Brilioth established for himself, but no less for his Archbishop and father-in-law, Anglican contacts representing different traditions and a wide variety of churchmanship. Both by his research and by the personal connexions which he managed to make, Brilioth became the Archbishop's personal envoy into a situation which was, strategically, particularly important.

We emphasize Söderblom's role here for two reasons. He was the Archbishop, and more than anybody else was instrumental in bring-

---

[1] H. Hensley Henson, *Retrospect of an Unimportant Life,* Vol. I, p. 321.

[2] Söderblom, Diary 1920. September 9, 1920.

ing about this new relationship. It was achieved not by sudden impulse, but as the result of a long term effort. On Söderblom's part it was a realization of what he had called an 'old dream'. In order to see things in perspective, some indication of the attitudes of the other Swedish bishops should be added, to the extent that they are known, with regard to this particular issue.

There was the old leader of the Schartau die-hards in the diocese of Gothenburg, Bishop E. H. Rodhe. He raised a warning finger to Söderblom. 'This friendliness to the Anglicans must be demonstrated with the utmost caution. In our time one cannot emphasize enough the importance of safe-guarding our Lutheran identity so that it will not in any way be effaced. ... The English do not understand Lutheranism and never admit that we have in it the truth in its greatest purity.'[3]

This was also a standpoint in the sense that one could not *move* from there, and the interesting point is that the old Bishop was almost the only one of the Swedish bishops to take this stand. His neighbour at Skara, Bishop Hjalmar Danell, generally regarded as the prototype of the solid and examplary Lutheran bishop, 'our best bishop' as Söderblom used to call him, is a case in point.

Bishop Rundgren of Visby was recognized as one of the great preachers in the fine tradition of Swedish 'Church pietism', nevertheless he could write to Söderblom from his island see: 'To me it appears that the Thirty-nine Articles allow an interpretation in Lutheran spirit. Through 'a quiet reformation', (he put this in German, '*die stille Reform*'), the view of the Swedish Church has been modified in the direction of England, and that of the English Church in Luther's direction, so that by this time they should be regarded as coincident (*sammanfalla*).'[4] If the Swedes were to be excommunicated, this bishop expected such condemnation from supporters of a radically right-wing Lutheran viewpoint, not from the Anglicans.

What has been said here of Danell and Rundgren could be claimed for the majority of the other bishops. Bishop Einar Billing who, as we shall see, played a special part with regard to the letter from the Swedish Bishops, was obviously all for intercommunion with the Anglicans as long as this did not endanger the fellowship with other Lutherans.

These episcopal opinions are produced at random to show that

---

[3] E. H. Rodhe, January 20, 1921, to Söderblom.
[4] V. Rundgren, February 23, 1923, to Söderblom.

while Söderblom had of course taken the initiative with regard to the Anglican policy, he certainly did not stand alone, for his point of view was at least to some extent shared by his episcopal colleagues. At least, one cannot show that Söderblom directed the course to Canterbury without taking into account 'the Church as a whole'.

The Letter from the Swedish Bishops to the Conference of Bishops in the Anglican Communion was dated April 21, 1922, and it was signed on behalf of the Swedish Bishops' Conference by Söderblom and Bishops Gottfrid Billing and Hjalmar Danell. It was actually written by a triumvirate consisting of Söderblom, Bishop Einar Billing and Professor K. B. Westman. These three were used to combining their resources; as we have already seen in an earlier context, the declaration on the doctrine of the ministry in the Swedish Church in 1909, in connexion with the Anglican conversations, had been drawn up by Söderblom and Einar Billing, then professorial colleagues in Uppsala. This earlier declaration formed a central part of the Letter of 1922, which was a characteristic variation on the usual Lutheran theme: the ministry as instituted *iure humano*, not *iure divino*. It is well-nigh impossible now to establish in detail the share of each of these three in preparing the new document.

We must pause here to consider Söderblom's colleague Einar Billing. One of his friends and disciples said of his international outlook that, even as Immanuel Kant is reputed never to have left Königsberg, so Einar Billing moved only between Uppsala and Västerås, a distance of some 50 miles. This however was not said in order to depreciate his orientation in the world of ideas. He was the leading Lutheran theologian on the episcopal bench in the nineteen-twenties; a scholar of deep insight and a churchman with great personal authority, he wielded great influence both in his diocese of Västerås where, in 1920 he had succeeded the practical Lövgren, and in the Swedish Church as a whole.

He was prone to bouts of neurosis, his 'vapours' as he called these constant attacks of anxiety and depression, and he had a disarming tendency to give the impression that he was generally incompetent. Thus, when Söderblom asked him to prepare a draft answer to Lambeth, Billing replied with the self-depreciation which had become almost a habit with him:

I should have answered immediately when you wrote about the answer to the decision of the Lambeth Conference about intercommunion, but as I was groping in total darkness as to the significance of this task, I dimly recalled that I had given a promise, rashly I am afraid, but with that my Latin was at an end, and I could not locate the Lambeth minutes in my papers.

I have now studied these documents a little, but all the same I feel very much at a loss as to the purport of the job and what ought to be said.[5]

He had hoped to be able to discuss the matter with Söderblom in person but this could not be arranged. He therefore suggested that Söderblom give the necessary instructions to Professor Westman. It would be best, he thought, if Westman, 'who knows not only England but also theology, could prepare the translation. You could scrutinize the draft before it was translated'. Westman's share in that document must have been much more than that of a recording secretary, but Billing's theological concepts gave the Letter its fundamental structure. It is safe to say that while the final text was probably, to a large extent, prepared after two sessions, one between Söderblom and Westman and the other between Billing and Westman, it was, broadly speaking, the result of the combined efforts of these three men.

The Letter is one of the great historical documents of the Swedish Church in this century. If the note of Lambeth 1920 was that of comprehensiveness, this was even more prominent in the document from the Swedish Bishops, for the Swedes, while glad to welcome the approach from Lambeth, were just as anxious not thereby to alienate other Churches, and more particularly their Lutheran sister churches to whom Sweden, traditionally and as a matter of course, was related. This point was stated in unmistakable terms.

Unity as something which had 'always existed and exists between all true disciples of Christ' was understood to be an accepted Lutheran standpoint, and it was felt to be particularly Lutheran to stress the supremacy of Holy Scripture. No other authority must be put directly or indirectly above (or, which amounts to the same thing), on a level with the prophetic and apostolic word in Holy Scripture. This general principle was underlined in the Letter by a sentence which judging from internal evidence is Söderblom's own. 'Both principles could be most simply combined in this: between God and the soul, or which is the same to us, between Christ and the faith, nothing, no third principle, no institution, no law, no proper works must intervene.'

Having said this Söderblom, as we see from his own notes, added the following:

---

[5] E. Billing, March 18, 1922, to Söderblom.

The same conception is retained in its outlines, so far as we have been able to see, partly in the sixth, partly in the eleventh, twelfth, and thirteenth of the Thirty-nine Articles.

We are convinced that between our branches of the Universal Church of Christ, notwithstanding the shades of opinion that may exist, there is an essential unity in that fundamental conception which we have now briefly indicated, and to which we unswervingly adhere. . .

He instructed Westman to insert the actual text of the Anglican Articles, but Westman must have felt that in a document addressed to Lambeth, this was something that could well be dispensed with.[6]

Another characteristic sentence introduced by Söderblom reads: 'In the Church and congregation of Christ, as in every living body, real concord is not characterized by uniformity, but by unity in diversity. . . .'

On the foundation of these general principles the Swedish Bishops recommended that the practice introduced in September 1920 by the participation of Anglican bishops in the consecration at Uppsala, should be reciprocated subject to the approval of the Archbishops of Uppsala and Canterbury. Swedish bishops should be invited to participate in Anglican consecrations.

The Swedish document also commented on certain desiderata raised by Lambeth, referring to the Diaconate, and to the laying on of hands in confirmation. The extant notes show that Söderblom himself had a considerable share in the phrasing of these paragraphs. He always held that the Swedish confirmation candidates (he may have thought of his own confirmation in 1881 and of his own catechetical teaching), received a more thorough instruction than was the case in the Anglican Church. This was actually said in the document, but Söderblom softened this by a conciliatory addendum:

. . . Against the admission to the Lord's Supper in our Church of persons confirmed in the Anglican Church, hesitation has earlier been expressed among us because of the duty of instruction laid on the Church in Matthew XXVIII. 20. Nevertheless this has not prevented admission to Holy Communion in our Church for those confirmed in the Anglican Church. We are of opinion that both Churches may have something to learn from

---

[6] In the Swedish text in *Kyrkohist. Årsskrift* (1923), p. 370 the reference is to Articles 11, 12, and 30, probably because of a trivial typing error, inserting the vowel 'i', *trettionde* instead of *trettonde*. Not that this mattered. Nobody, neither friend or foe of the document, noticed this then or at any other time. Insignificant as the point may be, it is all the same a nice reminder, by way of negative demonstration, that these important matters settle themselves not only on the level of theological encounter.

each other, both with the regard to the preparation for Confirmation, and to the act itself and its significance. Thus, what has been said about the instruction of the first communicants must be considered as a desideratum, but not as a condition for intercommunion.

In the twenties Söderblom pursued this idea. He tried repeatedly to persuade his Swedish colleagues to go to Canterbury in order that the Church of Sweden might reciprocate the Anglican participation of 1920, but it is a measure of the general provincial isolation of the Swedish Church at the time that he did not easily succeed. Language difficulties, old-age or illness were cited as excuses. Bishop Edvard Rodhe of Lund (from 1925) who now emerged, besides Söderblom, as the bishop with the widest connexions abroad, could not go. It was not until November 1, 1927, that Bishop E. Lönegren of Härnösand could be prevailed upon to participate. In this case it was at a consecration of Bishops for Mombasa, Hokkaido and Dover. Söderblom described this visit in the minutes of the Swedish Bishops' Meeting as a 'final act' (*slutakt*) in the agreement on intercommunion between the two Churches.[7] Similarly, bishop Edvard Rodhe's participation in the Lambeth Conference of 1930 corroborated the agreement.

In the Swedish Church, the Letter to Lambeth seems to have provoked hardly any comment at all, whether positive or negative, at the time. This was perhaps a measure of the relative isolation of the policy-makers from the rest of the Church at this juncture and of the lack of information and communication. The Letter, however, must have possessed some of the dynamic qualities of a time-fuse, for in the nineteen-sixties it has become the object of wise men's concern and criticism, stating that 'well-meant fraternal expressions of unity may sometimes prove obstacles to full church fellowship being attained'. To that extent this view is of course right that in 1922, the Swedish Bishop's Meeting acted in a situation where a national Lutheran Church felt it was autonomous and could make a move of this kind without referring it to superior confessional world organizations.[8]

The Letter reached Lambeth at a time of great expectation with regard to responses to the Appeal of 1920. In May 1922, a Joint Conference was held at Lambeth Palace between the Church of England

---

[7] *Biskopsmöte minutes*, October 8–9, 1928, p. 17.
[8] Cf. V. Vajta, [ed.] *Church in Fellowship* (1963), p. 248.

and the English Free Churches. Some of Söderblom's personal friends in the Life and Work movement were delegates, such as Archbishops Davidson and Lang, Bishops Talbot and Woods, and Dr. Headlam; from the Free Church side: A. E. Garvie, T. Nightingale, Alex Ramsay and J. A. Shakespeare.[9] The Anglican Church press was divided in its attitude to the Swedish Letter. The *Guardian* and the *Church Family Newspaper* welcomed the Swedish answer; while the Anglo Catholic *Church Times* was extremely doubtful about Swedish succession and sorry that the Swedes seemed so lax with regard to the rules for Confirmation. Their conclusion was strict: 'We do not think it possible that inter-communion with the Swedish Church can be accepted on this basis.'[1] English Free Church opinion as represented by *Evangelical Christendom* felt that the Swedes had shown a 'spirit of great frankness and adhesion to convictions'.[2]

Anticipating later developments we notice here that neither Davidson nor Temple attended Söderblom's Stockholm Conference in 1925. This was a disappointment to him. It was also a reminder of something he had known all along but found hard to accept or to explain, a certain difficulty in conveying and interpreting to Anglicans his own programme of Evangelical Catholicity. They preferred their own Liberal Catholicism which to them was both better theology and better English. While establishing and strengthening the contacts between Uppsala and Canterbury (or Winchester), Söderblom was also aware that there were differences between the two. The confrontation of his ecumenical vision with the far-reaching plans of the Anglican communion at this time helps to bring out Söderblom's own ecumenical position in sharper relief.

Uppsala–Constantinople

The Greek *eisodos* into the Life and Work movement at Geneva, August 1920, though brief, was dramatic and of great significance. The delegates in the conference most likely thought that it happened by coincidence. Far from it, there was a story behind it and Söderblom had been deeply involved in this for a considerable time. The Uppsala-Constantinople interchange in the years immediately preceding the Geneva conference is important for an understanding of

---

[9] G. K. A. Bell, *Documents on Christian Unity* (1924), p. 147.
[1] *The Guardian*, June 2 and 9; *Church Family Newspaper* June 9; *Church Times*, June 9; all 1922.
[2] *Evangelical Christendom*, London, July–August, 1922, p. 101.

the *entrée* of the Orthodox into the Ecumenical Movement. This also reflects particular aspects of Söderblom's programme of Evangelical Catholicity, where the Uppsala–Constantinople link, in Söderblom's view, was part of grand strategy in the ecumenical outreach of Uppsala.

Söderblom could never have succeeded if it had not been for a seemingly fortuitous appointment in 1917 of an extra functionary at the Swedish embassy in Constantinople. In that year, a young Swedish scholar from Uppsala, went to Constantinople in order to do research in Turkish language and history. Johannes Kolmodin was a specialist in Semitic languages. He was only 24 when he had his first experience of the Orient. He spent two years, 1908–1910, in Ethiopia studying the Tigrinja language, a field of study with which his father, professor Adolf Kolmodin, had been engaged while General Secretary of the Evangeliska Fosterlandsstiftelsen's mission work in Ethiopia.

At Uppsala, he had been under the personal influence of Harald Hjärne, and he decided to study history, particularly Swedish-Turkish relations in the times of Charles XII. In the years immediately before and after the outbreak of the World War he had been one of the spokesmen of a somewhat activistic Swedish nationalism. Kolmodin went to Constantinople as a scholar. His keen historical sense and general political orientation made him follow the rapidly changing scene in Constantinople and the East, as also in the Baltic, with well informed interest.

More than most Westerners at the time, he appreciated the precariousness of the Patriarchate in Turkish Istanbul.[1] As a matter of course, he established generous personal contacts with the Turkish government. Indeed there seems to have been a certain mutual affinity between Kolmodin and some of the young Turk intelligentsia and élite. When in August 1918 he managed to get his first audience to discuss Söderblom's plans with Halil Bey, the Turkish

---

[1] Kolmodin's own position was less than secure. He was not appointed first secretary to the Legation until 1928. He had strong views about the ordinary run of Swedish diplomats not excluding ambassadors, and extended his views of the Establishment to the Swedish Government of the day. The only Swedish strategist whom Kolmodin was willing to recognize as being of stature and size was the Archbishop. In 1920 he felt that he might lose his job with the Embassy. He would like to have printed on his visiting card, he told Söderblom, 'Délégué spécial du Monseigneur L'Archévêque d'Upsala auprès de sa Sainteté le Patriarche Ecuménique et Son Altesse le Cheikh ul-Islam (the latter should not be forgotten altogether.)' J. Kolmodin, March 3, 1920. to Söderblom.

Foreign Minister, his linguistic ability and solid scholarship were helpful. The two men entered a discussion about the possible co-operation of their two religions. Kolmodin mustered for the occasion what he could remember from Söderblom's teaching on 'religion revelation'—and perhaps a little more.

So it came about [Kolmodin reported to Söderblom] that in the greatest harmony we could envisage a possible future 'entente' between the two great Occidental religions (the word Occidental understood as opposed to the religions of the Far East) Christianity and Islam—on the foundation of their common idea of revelation.

Söderblom immediately wrote back to say that he was impressed by Kolmodin's 'magnificent and exact conception of the affinity of the religions of revelation'.[2] It is possible that Kolmodin's intervention was the cause of more generous reference to Islam in the new, fifth edition of the Tiele–Söderblom Handbook which the Archbishop was just at this time preparing for the press. Until this time, Söderblom had been adverse to the recognition of any revelational quality in the teaching of Muhammed.

The contacts which Kolmodin established with the Turkish authorities were to prove particularly valuable for the practical realization of Söderblom's ecumenical designs. The good-will which he was able to create in Government circles could make it that much easier for Orthodox dignitaries to be given visas for meetings in Sweden. This was particularly so as the diplomat Kolmodin tended to stress that the object of going to Uppsala was giving lectures in the University foundation of Olaus Petri rather than attending ecclesiastical conferences designed to establish a common Christian front. Söderblom was anxious to get an Orthodox bishop or two for the Uppsala meetings which he planned in September 1918 and he praised Kolmodin's 'extraordinary diplomatic skill. and energy' in securing the permits required. We have already in an earlier context noticed these efforts to bring the Orthodox to Uppsala. We are concerned here with the significance of these attempts for the ecumenical programme promoted by Söderblom and those, worked out by the ecclesiastical dignitaries at the Patriarch's headquarters at Phanar, Constantinople.

In February 1918 Kolmodin managed to get his first audience with the Patriarch himself. He reports to Söderblom:

I waited upon His Holiness the Ecumenical Patriarch in Phanarion [the headquarters of the Patriarchate in Constantinople]. Through mysterious

---

[2] Söderblom, August 20, 1918, to J. Kolmodin.

passages, up the stairs and down again, I was at first brought into a kind of ante-chamber where two popes recieved me. In very broken French they asked me about my errand. As I regarded it as very unwise to risk offending subordinates—this according to my experience from the Orient must be avoided all costs—I produced your letter [this was a Greek translation of Söderblom's invitation to a proposed ecumenical Conference in Uppsala] and gave it to them to read, while at the same time emphasizing that I intended to place it into the very hands of His Holiness himself.

From time to time I managed to put in a remark. On a map hanging on the wall I pointed out Sweden and Uppsala, and said some words about the veneration which we felt for the throne which according to the tradition had been that of the Apostle Andrew. The upshot was that they had no objection to my explaining the matter to His Holiness. The Patriarch in long grey beard and an ankle length cassock was seated at his desk. I presented my case as eloquently as I could. I mentioned that the Archbishop of Uppsala thought that in the old revered Oriental Church he would find real understanding for his thought that at this time, in the most pressing period of the World War, a great demonstration of the unity of Christendom was needed.

Then His Holiness wished to be informed about the position of the Archbishop of Uppsala. 'Is he independent?' he asked (probably he wanted to ascertain that there was no Papal intrigue behind the whole thing). As well as I could I explained the ecclesiastical situation in the North. It is possible that the Patriarch received a somewhat exaggerated idea of the archiepiscopal chair of Uppsala. He regards it probably as a kind of Nordic-Baltic patriarchate—and of course we have not come as far as that yet. Finally, the Patriach declared that he was deeply moved and attracted by the truly Christian idea of unity which the invitation expressed.[3]

Kolmodin was convinced that in the precarious ecclesiastical situation of Constantinople, Söderblom's approach was the one which held the promise of a future, and Söderblom himself was full of praise. One report from Kolmodin elicited the highest praise that Söderblom knew: 'Nobody could have done this as well as you have done—not even K. B. Westman!' The visits to Constantinople by certain Protestant officials from the World Alliance made Kolmodin nervous, and he felt he had to steer the course very carefully so as not to offend the Orthodox. The young Swedish scholar knew that where World Alliance secretaries could not penetrate, he himself was accepted and could feel perfectly at home.

E. W. Nasmyth, international organizer of the World Alliance, contemplated organizing a committee in Constantinople consisting

---

[3] J. Kolmodin, February 8, 1918, to Söderblom.

of Orthodox, Gregorians and certain Protestant teachers from the American schools. 'On this point I washed him clean rather carefully the first evening.' These circumstances strengthened Kolmodin's faith in Söderblom's cause and approach. He discussed this particularly with Bishop Germanos who was to be the Patriarch's international ambassador. Germanos even expressed a wish to learn Swedish in order the better to serve the cause. Kolmodin sent to Söderblom repeated requests for a Swedish phrase-book. For his projected ecumenical meeting in Uppsala, 1918, Söderblom was anxious to get Orthodox representatives. He was specific in his demands! As we recall, Söderblom had tried to secure Orthodox representation if possible by one or two bishops at Uppsala 1918, and Kolmodin gladdened Söderblom's heart by suggesting that the new Patriarch himself might turn up in Uppsala. Kolmodin's Greek friends were not slow to draw a historical parallel which must have appealed to Söderblom: that of Patriarch Cyrillos Lukaris' visit to the West in the seventeenth century! But of course there was not to be any Uppsala Conference in 1918.

We know now that the Patriarch's Encyclical Letter of January, 1920, was largely written by Germanos. When Kolmodin read the Letter he thought that he recognized arguments that he had himself brought forward. As one reads this remarkable document there may well be some of the following passages which he had in mind:

Seeing that it is now a question of a mere contact and understanding, the difficulties, in our mind, will in any case be less serious, and if there will be a good will and disposition, neither can they nor should they constitute an invincible and insuperable obstacle.

We therefore, on the establishment of the League of Nations, which has now been effected with good omen, consider the matter to be both feasible and more than ever timely. For the terrible World War which has just come to an end, as it has brought to light many unhealthy things in the life of Christian Nations, and revealed in many cases a great absence of respect for the very principle of justice and humanity, so, too, it has not only made old wounds worse, but, so to speak, opened new ones of a more practical character, and with regard to which great attention and care is naturally needed on the part of all Churches.

Finally, it is the duty of the Churches which adorn themselves with the sacred name of Christ not to forget and neglect any longer His new and great commandment of love, and still to fall piteously behind the political authorities, who, truly applying the spirit of the Gospel and of the Justice of Christ, have under happy auspices already instituted the League of Nations, for the defence of right and for the cultivation of love and harmony among the nations.

Kolmodin wrote in March, 1920, to Söderblom:

[The Letter] contains many judicious viewpoints which correspond fairly closely to your own leading thoughts. To a great extent I recognize what I presented to those concerned on various occasions, the last time New Year, 1920. In our case, as you will find, it is the spirit of World Alliance, rather than that of Faith and Order which dominates here.

Söderblom concurred. He found the ideas expressed in the Letter 'very attractive, intelligent and surprising in their realism'. And he encouraged Kolmodin in terms which say as much of Söderblom's own powers of persuasion. Kolmodin, he wrote, should feel the greatest and purest satisfaction that anybody could feel 'to recognize your own thoughts and ideas in others, after an influence imperceptible or unconscious to them'.

The comparison with Faith and Order, of course was not lost on Söderblom, particularly as he now tended to see his own approach to Constantinople as a part of what can fairly be interpreted as a grand strategy of ecumenical relationships. Söderblom did not formulate this strategy in official terms. However, in his correspondence with Kolmodin one can see it emerge with an unmistakably clear outline. In this strategy, the Uppsala–Constantinople bond became an effective alternative to what Söderblom at the time with some concern interpreted as an increasing Canterbury–Rome connexion.

It is from these presuppositions that he wrote in December, 1919, to Kolmodin in Constantinople: 'Just as convinced as I am that the church-political role of the Archbishop of Canterbury with regard to Rome (for the sake of his Romanising High Church party) is an illusion, just as clearly I see [my] task to bring together, as far as possible, Evangelical and Orthodox Christendom.'

Kolmodin was used to thinking in terms of strategy and geopolitics, and he was duly impressed by Söderblom's argument. While emphasizing in talks with the Patriarchate that as a layman he could not speak on Söderblom's behalf, he did, however, suggest that the Church of Sweden was definitely against Rome's ecclesiastical 'imperialism'—a suggestion 'which, it seems to me, did fall in good earth and which perhaps to a certain extent has increased the interest in contacts with us, also independent of the attitude of the Anglo-Saxons.'[4]

---

[4] J. Kolmodin, March 3, 1920, to Söderblom. He informed Söderblom that in accordance with Söderblom's letter to him he had pointed out that the Romanizing tendency of the Anglicans hindered them from real co-operation with 'us others'!

In 1920, the Patriarchate sent its delegation to the West, including Germanos, now Metropolitan of Seleucia, together with the Archbishop of Nubia and Professor C. Papadopoulos. As we recall, they first appeared on the ecumenical scene in the Life and Work Conference at Geneva, in August 1920. They were welcomed in modern Greek on Söderblom's behalf by H. Neander.

Even more important from Söderblom's point of view was the fact that Germanos extended his tour to Uppsala. In August, 1918, Söderblom had for the first time tried to get an Orthodox theologian for the Olavus Petri Foundation lectures in Uppsala. Kolmodin kept this in mind and, as the Orthodox delegation in March, 1920, prepared to leave for the West, he was able to extend an invitation from Söderblom also to Sweden and Uppsala. In September, 1920, Germanos arrived in Uppsala. This was the occasion when Söderblom had invited two Anglican bishops to participate in a Swedish episcopal consecration. To Söderblom it was probably even more significant—and a result of years of patient probing—that on that day Metropolitan Germanos of Seleucia also went in the episcopal procession to the High Altar in the Uppsala Cathedral, adding colour and dignity and great ecumenical significance to the occasion.

Söderblom liked Germanos, and as he followed from afar the changes of ecclesiastical politics in Phanar, he hoped that Germanos would indeed be elected Patriarch and as such repeat his visit to Uppsala. But alas, this was not to be. In January, 1924, Söderblom wrote to Kolmodin, once again hinting at the line of contact which appears as an important part of his grand strategy in the realm of ecumenical relationship: 'What a pity that Germanos in London cannot become Patriarch. We need for the Conference in Stockholm, August 1925, preferably the Patriarch from Constantinople himself in order truly to seal the co-operation of the Orthodox and Evangelical Christendom.'

With this we are now prepared again to take up the thread of the Life and Work movement leading to Söderblom's Stockholm Conference, 1925. As we turn to his efforts towards this end we now know that as he called the Churches to consider their social and international responsibility there was a deep sounding-board to his appeal. He had made 'Evangelical Catholicity' into an ecclesiological concept of some importance, serving the cause of the unity of the Church.

His Stockholm Conference

Peace and yet War

On the continent of Europe the nineteen-twenties were the decade between Versailles and Hitler, between post-war bankruptcy and the Great Depression, between Spengler's *Abendland* and Remarque's *Western Front*. That noble Frenchman, Wilfred Monod, said in 1923: 'There is no peace in the Ruhr, why, peace has not existed in Europe since 1914.' Later in the year of the Stockholm Conference, the Powers met for the Locarno Conference. Together, Briand, Austen Chamberlain and Field Marshal von Hindenburg, could bring about an unwonted measure of *détente*, a new sense of international security, and Chamberlain had reason to claim that the Locarno Pact of December 1925 marked the 'real dividing line between the years of war and the years of peace'. With the years of peace came bold initiatives towards disarmament, culminating in the Briand–Kellogg pact of 1928.[1]

An American Secretary of State, Kellogg, thus became involved, but the scene was Europe and the horizon was that of the continent of Europe. This was also the case with Söderblom. In one of his Peace addresses, given in connexion with his receiving the Nobel Peace Prize he says in a characteristic phrase: 'We must not overlook the threat hovering over this little European mankind, now squeezed between the armed threat from the East with the World revolution and the young dynamic universal state of America.'[2] He had noticed the French play *'Sous l'Arc de Triomphe'*: those who were concerned with this drama 'dared', he said, 'to face reality and unveil from the horror of war any protective disguise.' Such minds build 'the spiritual structure of the United States of Europe'. This quotation is from Söderblom's chapter on War and Peace in his book on

---

[1] Cf. G. N. Gathorne-Hardy, *A Short History of International Affairs, 1920–1934* (1934), p. 67.

[2] Nathan Söderblom, *Är fredstanken en illusion?* (1930), p. 5.

the Stockholm Conference. He ended his chapter by quoting without reservation, a prayer by Emanuel Linderholm, an Uppsala Professor of Church History. In this prayer addressed to Almighty God, the outline of Europe was drawn with unmistakable clarity: 'Particularly we praise Thee for that Thou hast entrusted Thy Gospel to our continent and its daughter-nations beyond the seas. Bestow now, O God, upon all these peoples who rule over most of the globe, to remember the greatness and responsibility of Thy calling.'[3]

Europe was the horizon, and therefore it is necessary here, in order to understand Söderblom's role with regard to the Stockholm Conference, to give, however briefly, a survey of the general political situation in Europe, 1920–1924, as understood by Söderblom.

Europe was the horizon and it was a continent of tensions and dangers. Söderblom was more aware of these political problems than most European Churchmen of his day. He had welcomed the formation of the League of Nations with high hopes and was all the more saddened and shocked by the failure of the world organization to act wisely, indeed to act at all. As he witnessed the chaos and misery of post-war Europe, he told a Danish journalist: 'Now we are really in hell. Yes, it seems to me that the present situation in the world, at least in Europe, cannot be compared to anything else.'[4] He gave the interview on the occasion of the important 1922 meeting of the World Alliance at Copenhagen. He had listened to Dr. Mott suggesting in his most optimistic vein that a world war had been a necessity in order to create, as a reaction, a renaissance movement all over the world. Söderblom challenged this: 'No, no, no! I know John Mott very well, but I cannot share his view on this subject. The world war was terrible, only terrible. It was disaster, only disaster!'

It was in this mood that Söderblom delivered his possibly most challenging political address. The World Alliance meeting at Copenhagen in August 1922, gave him the occasion in a setting that was characteristic, for it was in the framework of the World Alliance rather than in that of his own 'Life and Work' that he made his own most challenging statements and appeals for reconciliation and peace and the other great issues of the times. He was feeling the

---

[3] Söderblom, *Stockholm 1925*, p. 548. One should not be too severe perhaps with Söderblom for having inserted that prayer in his book. An ulterior motive for so doing may well have been the generous wish of the Archbishop to win Linderholm for his ecumenical cause.

[4] *Politiken*, Copenhagen, August 8, 1922.

tension between France and Germany as the particularly deep tragic note underlying the whole cacophony of European politics at this time. In a political situation fraught with grave dangers and threats, he pleaded for an alliance between Germany, France and Britain!

I have [he said] two things to say about the rebuilding of our ruined civilization. One thing from the realm of dreams and the other from the world of realities.

I beg your pardon. We dreamt of a real League of Nations, but still today it is scarcely anything more than an alliance. It must become more. It shall become more. The only remedy is to give to the commonwealth of nations a Christian soul, because without that soul it is a dead body and with a non-Christian soul it is a beast or a devil.

I venture to mention this self-evident solution even at the risk of being horribly naive. Is it a Utopia that the three, Sparta, Athens and world-embracing Macedonia, would go together? The prophet says: 'In that day shall Israel be the third with Egypt and with Assyria.'

The three today have other names. The only alliance that would intone in our hearts a Te Deum, consists of course of France, Germany and England. Germany, the nation of thinkers and of the music of sacred Passion; France, the nation of style and brilliance and energy; and the British Empire, the complex Commonwealth of accomplished insight and of mystics. These three linked in one alliance would let us sleep and awake in peace. It would do if only the two Continental Powers could settle their neighbourship. Such an alliance would threaten nobody; attract everyone. It would mean the restoration of European civilization.

I have now given free course to my mad love for all these three wonderful champions of Europe's glory. Our task as Christians ... constitutes the *conditio sine qua non,* the one thing needed; the very spirit that must animate any real reconciliation and any real building up. ... Our task as members of the Church of Christ is to realize a society of men under the absolute command of God's authority.

Apart from Söderblom's lecture, the most radical address on this occasion was that of an American Quaker, Dr. Wm. I. Hull, who as a 'Quaker boy was taught the horror and wickedness of war', and now presented the Copenhagen Conference with a memorandum on disarmament. He modified his resolution so as to ask for universal restriction of armaments and the adoption of methods of arbitration and mediation of international disputes. The Copenhagen Conference modified this again to emphasize the need for 'disarming of the spirits' and for general restriction of armaments while on the other hand accepting for the sake of national security, the necessity of armed forces. It was the Swedish Archbishop and the

American Quaker who together sounded what was thought to be a radical and prophetic note at Copenhagen. A telegram had been sent to the Copenhagen Conference by President Harding. Söderblom proposed that the Conference ask the President to work for the calling together of a conference on Europe, similar to that which had been held in Washington in 1922. In an interview he added: 'We cannot wait until the Spirit of Christ has permeated the Churches, we must create practical results, and even if churchmen cannot mingle directly in politics, I cannot but say that we need a political conference to do this.' Time and again Söderblom returned to this idea of an alliance between France and Germany. It was a daring concept; from his wording one can sense that Söderblom realized that it must strike his listeners at that time as almost impracticable. He felt that he had inherited that vision from his great French *maître,* Auguste Sabatier and already this fact gave him some of the courage he needed in raising this matter, in interpreting this 'mad dream of his'. In his Swedish addresses on the subject in these years (but not in those appearing in English, German or French) he mentioned Sabatier's role; for Sabatier had taught at the Strasbourg university prior to 1870 and would emphasize that this gave him a particular responsibility to work for French–German reconciliation.[5]

The Ruhr issue in 1923 was also a tragedy for Söderblom for it brought him into momentary conflict with some of his best French friends. He loved France and wished France to realize this. 'There is hardly anybody [in Sweden] who feels warmer gratitude towards France and its culture than I, towards the best in the French spirit, its great personalities or humble servants. ... It is a fact that in Sweden there is nobody whose heart beats faster at the sound of the most beautiful of all languages.'[6] He dreaded the thought of having to use that incomparable linguistic instrument to criticise France and its politics. Nevertheless, when French troops occupied the Ruhr, January 11, 1923, Söderblom felt that the Church had to speak. He contacted his colleagues, the Swedish bishops, and they signed Söderblom's appeal dated February 1, 1923. The message bore the unmistakable imprint of Söderblom's style, his conviction and his Christian compassion. It was definitely challenging:

---

[5] Söderblom: 'Tidens tecken', *För tanke och tro: Oscar Ekman festskrift* (1923), p. 19.
[6] Ibid.

We judge nobody [the Swedish bishops said] for our knowledge is in part. But we condemn the methods of violence. The curse which is sown will bear new, even more terrible wars. Conscience and hearts everywhere burn with the question, What can be done? We, the servants of the Church in Sweden, appeal to our fellow Christians in France and in all countries, to join with us to invoke from God clarity and strength for a heartening act.

The Swedish Bishops' protest was no isolated affair. The solidly pro-French, Swedish Prime Minister, Branting, made his protest, speaking in the Council of the League of Nations.[7] From Britain, the United States and Holland, to mention only representative instances, similar opinions were expressed in no uncertain terms. Manifestations came from the other Scandinavian countries. Söderblom's hand was strengthened by the report sent him by the Swedish authoress Elin Wägner, all the more significant as she was generally recognized as a life-long friend of France and French culture.

If the French text of the Swedish Archbishop's letter was worded in general and seemingly unobjectionable terms, there were definite infelicities in the presentation of the message. The letter was addressed to 'our fellow Christians in all countries and to the responsible statesmen, especially to President Harding'. The French may have felt that this reference to an American super-judge was uncalled for. The other addressees of the message were President Poincaré, Wilfred Monod, member of the commission of the French Protestant Federation, the Prime Minister of Great Britain and the Archbishop of Canterbury. By some unfortunate accident in the machinery of translation, two expressions included in the English text did not appear in the French version; the first suggesting that the occupation led to 'sexual degradation' and the second that troops had 'torn large pieces of territory from their unarmed neighbours'.

The French took Söderblom up on this point, and he could only declare that 'the translator, a well-known author, cannot explain this incomprehensible mistake'.[8]

French and Belgian opinion felt hurt by the Swedish intervention and their criticism was naturally turned against Söderblom. Söderblom wrote to Mme de Quirielle: 'Hardly anything in my life has caused so much worry, prayer and hard thought, day and night, as

[7] E. C. Bellquist, *Some Aspects of the Recent Foreign Policy of Sweden* (1929), p. 338.
Söderblom, in *Die Eiche* (1923), p. 200.

the Bishops' Appeal. ... With politics, I as a churchman have nothing to do.'[9]

This was just the point. The Swedish appeal, however objective it appeared from a Swedish point of view, could not divest itself of political overtones, since it referred to an explosive political situation. Poincaré and the Catholic Archbishop of Paris, Dubois, replied in a dignified manner. The French Protestants were placed in a difficult position. They did not wish, nor could they at this time very well afford, to appear disloyal to the politics of their own country. Söderblom had addressed one copy of the letter to W. Monod, possibly in his capacity as chairman of the French section of the World Alliance. Monod was not the President of the French Protestant Federation at this time, and he handed over the letter to the President of the Federation, E. Gruner, for him to write an official answer. Here it was claimed that it was not France's guilt if there was no peace, 'Germany continues the hidden war.' Monod as an old friend of Söderblom's found it difficult to answer. He published his reply as an interview with *Svenska Dagbladet* in Stockholm, February 8, 1923. He referred to his friendship with Söderblom. 'But I am astounded that by its formulae the Council in Stockholm gives the appearance of making itself an advocate of a German standpoint.' He knew, he said, that there was no peace, but declared, with forced optimism, 'the war of 1914–23 will take an end'. Söderblom received declarations from individual Frenchmen, such as J. Jézéquel, saying that they defended him and tried to explain that the Swedish archbishop was not an enemy of France, but it was taken for granted that such defence and explanation were needed.

Belgian Protestants associated themselves with the French reaction. From French-speaking Switzerland, Choisy wrote to Söderblom on the dangerous situation. He felt that the future of the planned Stockholm Conference was in jeopardy.

Even the very best, from the two camps, found difficulty in understanding each other. National pride and prejudice played its role. There were also problems of semantics. The Deissmann–Monod debate 1923–1924 showed this. They had met at Copenhagen and Hälsingborg in 1922. Visiting England in 1922 Deissmann was impressed and encouraged, by the critical British attitude towards the French occupation of the Ruhr and he wrote a letter on February 22, 1923, to Monod asking his French colleague to try to remedy the

[9] Söderblom, March 14, 1923, to B. de Quirielle.

situation. This was the time when Monod to his great grief and hurt surprise had received the letter from Söderblom and the Swedish bishops. Instead of answering Deissmann in Berlin, Monod sent his reply to Willoughby Dickinson in London and published it in French in the April issue of *Christianisme Social*. Deissmann felt that Monod was trying to make him suspect in the eyes of his English friends, even at a time when he, Deissmann, visited England. Being an academic himself he was not without a certain capacity for elaborate sarcasm. He referred to Monod's article in these words:

'In the nearly intolerable pose of the superior moral judge which Monod takes as soon as a demon has tempted him to go to print!'[1] Monod suggested about Deissmann: 'It is not difficult for him to win Anglo-Saxon sympathies; it would be more excellent, beautiful and useful if he were to acquire sympathies in France'. But the reconstruction of Europe depended on a French-German reconciliation. Deissmann in his Open Letter to Wilfred Monod of February 10, 1924, attempted to show that Monod had misinterpreted some of his German and Greek expressions, but wanted to conclude on a conciliatory note: 'The faith in our evangelical unity I do not give up.'[2]

This was an agitated and disturbing debate. Deissmann said that in the encounter with Monod he had expressed 'much which lies as leaden weights on my soul'. Söderblom followed their debate and the total French-German argument with anxiety, not least because his own conference plans were continually threatened by this struggle. On the other hand, the very fact of these tensions made the Stockholm Conference all the more desirable.

Nationalism as a problem for the Church to tackle was something that engrossed much of Söderblom's attention in these years. He raised it in various connexions. One was in the teaching of history in schools: eradication of nationalistic bias from school text-books became a hobby-horse of his. Söderblom tried to high-light and dramatize this issue. For years he devoted his interest to this matter. Wherever he went in Europe he was wont to pick up history text-books for the schools. He wanted to find out for himself what French school-children were taught to think about Bismarck and German school-children about Napoleon. He well understood, he said, the great Leopold von Ranke who had introduced a study on the Rise of

---

[1] *Die Eiche* (1923), p. 176. Deissmann, May 24, 1924, to Söderblom, UUB.
[2] *Die Eiche* (1924), p. 239.

Prussia with the happy exclamation: 'At last the Swedes had been driven out of Germany'. It was, as he always emphasized, Mrs Söderblom who had drawn his attention to the textbook problem on one of their visits to Denmark, a Scandinavian country which had been one of the historic 'enemies' of the Swedes. But it was characteristic of Söderblom that he did not take the easy path of only finding faults in these books. Wherever he found expressions of noble altruism, he lifted these up and quoted them. He had found a German textbook with this conclusion: 'Every peace movement must begin with ourselves'. Söderblom never tired of reminding his listeners of such statements.

This was a matter for the specialists and Söderblom found a team of three remarkable men for the purpose. They were Professor Otto Nordenskjöld, geography professor in Göteborg (as he was of a noble family, Söderblom insisted on referring to him as 'Sir Otto Nordenskjöld'), Dr. Wm. Carlgren, well-known history scholar and Dr. V. Söderberg, editor and historian. The members of this little team all happened to be Swedes: but more important was the fact that they were eminently competent and inspired by Söderblom's vision. They produced a challenging report to 'Stockholm' and also arranged an exhibition of textbooks, some of which were not attractive exponents of their countries of origin. 'Stockholm' had a special sub-commission dealing with this issue and decided to constitute the Swedish team of three as a Working Group on behalf of 'Life and Work' and the World Alliance.

In the latter organization, which was of course keenly interested in the matter, Nordenskjöld was one of the experts on this question. Söderblom also hoped that the Ecumenical Institute would devote special interest to it. 'It is necessary that the Church with its supernational authority stand behind the whole undertaking, lest it be neglected.'[3]

Preparing the Conference

The fact that the Bishop of Peterborough, Dr. Woods, welcomed the Life and Work meeting to Peterborough in 1921 was a source of personal satisfaction to Söderblom. In 1920 he had felt great anxiety over the Anglican refusal to participate in the Geneva conference. But the Orthodox presence at Geneva and the invitation to the

---

[3] Söderblom, *Stockholm 1925*, p. 618.

Roman Catholic Church had given Dr. Davidson the assurance he needed. These two factors were of importance for the *image* of the emerging Life and Work movement. It was not, as some feared, just another Pan-Protestant affair. It was in principle 'universal'.

Söderblom had personal contacts with Bishop Woods from September 1920, when as Bishop of Peterborough he had taken part in the consecration service in Uppsala. Bishop Woods and Bishop Burge of Oxford now emerged as Anglican spokesmen in the Life and Work movement; Woods with his experience as General Secretary at Lambeth, 1920, and Burge, a former schoolmaster, as much involved in social reform as Woods.

Söderblom had taken for granted that William Temple, then of Manchester, was going to play an important part in his movement. When preparing the Agenda for the Hälsingborg Executive meeting, 1922, Söderblom and Westman hopefully placed Temple's name on the programme. They wanted him to speak on the relationship between Faith-and-Order and Life-and-Work. Temple, however, could not attend any of the pre-Stockholm meetings outside Britain; neither did he manage to attend the Stockholm Conference itself.

In order to emphasize the Anglican role, Söderblom insisted that Woods take the chair at the meeting in Peterborough. This was a small committee meeting, but nonetheless of great importance. The Orthodox had arrived: a fourth, Orthodox 'group' or section was formed at Peterborough and Archbishop Germanos became a member of the Executive. An invitation was sent to Rome, albeit without great hopes.[1]

The name of the projected Conference was now defined as the Universal Christian Conference on Life and Work. Universality, on

---

[1] Söderblom's invitations to the Pope in Rome: on January 26, 1918, Söderblom commissioned H. Bildt to extend an invitation to the Uppsala conference planned for April 14, 1918; on March 11, 1918, the three Nordic Primates signed an invitation for a similar conference postponed until September 8, 1918; after the Geneva 1920 Meeting, the same three Primates, on behalf of the Life and Work Movement as a whole, on February 20, 1921, addressed his Holiness the Pope, inviting him to send delegates to the Universal Conference, then expected to take place in 1922 or 1923. There were brief acknowledgements addressed to 'Perillustres viri' by Cardinal Gasparri; the 1918 reply underlined that anything done for peace would pave the way for what the Gospel expressed in the words: 'that there may be one fold and one shepherd.' See N. Karlström, 'Rom und die Stockholmer Bewegung, ein chronologischer Beitrag', *Sv. Kyrkohist. Årsskrift*, 1931, pp. 100–112.

the other hand, also implied real anchorage in national or sectional organizations, and the principle was formulated that such national conferences would not conflict with, but prepare the way for, the Universal Conference. It was according to this principle that the British Copec meeting, at Birmingham 1924, was both a British affair and a preparation for 'Stockholm' the following year. There was already pressure for an increased number of themes to be included in the final programme. Söderblom had insisted, and in his fashion continued to insist, that only a limited number of subjects should be accepted for the agenda. Peterborough now added a theme to the three originally proposed by Söderblom: 'Social concerns' was divided into one on Industrial problems and the other on Family problems. Söderblom was soon to face that agenda problem again.

The meeting at Hälsingborg in August 1922 was even more impressive than Peterborough and constituted a major landmark between Geneva 1920 and Stockholm 1925. It had been immediately preceded by the World Alliance meeting at Copenhagen with over two hundred delegates from twenty-five countries, an occasion where, as we have seen, Söderblom played a leading role. This was followed by an expert conference on European Relief, where Dr. A. T. Jörgensen of Copenhagen and Dr. Keller of Zürich were the leaders. This was a matter of paramount concern for Söderblom. He told Jörgensen that one fifth of his time was devoted to relief work.

Söderblom dominated the Hälsingborg meeting to a perhaps greater extent than any other in the nineteen-twenties. He and Westman had prepared the agenda in detail and he chaired every session. He characteristically welcomed the delegates in five languages: English, German, French, Latin and Swedish. This was followed by prayers where the delegates addressed the Deity in five languages, Greek, English, German, French and Scandinavian. Another characteristic touch, anticipating Stockholm, was a brief address by the Swedish Crown Prince, in terms which showed affinity of thought and intent with those of Söderblom.

Though Söderblom so obviously held the reins at this meeting, this was also the occasion when this movement, hitherto mainly an extension of an expansive and communicative personality, was decentralised; from that moment the national organization, constitutionally empowered, could develop their own characteristics. In terms of Söderblom's personal influence it is fair to say that his movement could now increase extensively but no longer be as directly dependent on him as hitherto.

It was the American organizers headed by Dr. A. J. Brown who placed the movement on a firm regional basis by introducing an International Committee of some forty members, with executive power and the provision that this number may be increased at the discretion of the Executive Committee, by a number not to exceed eighteen. This latter provision made for a certain elasticity; in Söderblom's case it offered opportunities of shaping the Conference to some limited degree. There was a characteristic difference between this parliamentary approach represented by Dr. Brown and his colleagues from the American Federal Council and Söderblom's idea about joint-chairmen which preserved the traditional honour due to Constantinople and Canterbury.

Hälsingborg again loaded the agenda of the projected Conference. It was now increased from three to six themes: Söderblom would later insist that it had never been his intention to exceed the number of three.

The Hälsingborg meeting also served to define the Life and Work movement as compared with Faith and Order. There was a structural similarity between them, in that Life and Work, too, was a movement of the Churches. At Hälsingborg 1922, the principle was stated: 'all organized branches or communions of the Universal Church of Christ are invited to participate in [the Universal Conference]'. Yet, there were differences in approach. As Faith and Order in 1922 planned to hold its world Conference in 1925 at Washington, D.C., it invited its sister movement to hold the Universal meeting on Life and Work in the same place, immediately after that of the Faith and Order movement. In this way, Bishop Brent and Robert Gardiner suggested, the close affinity between the two bodies would be emphasized and the unity between them strengthened. The Hälsingborg meeting discussed this proposal. Dr. Kapler, a newcomer to the movement, vice-president in the newly formed Kirchenausschuss joined the discussion with fresh energy. Layman with a legal education, and representing the Prussian 'Union' standpoint in matters of church relationships, he took a pragmatic view of Christian co-operation subordinating faith and doctrine to Christian service. A phrase which he used in his address was, 'doctrine divides, service unites'. Söderblom often quoted it; it became one of the most memorable from the Hälsingborg meeting. The particular task of the Life and Work movement was to create a spirit of brotherhood. It might well be that this spirit would make it easier to reach and realize the aims which Faith and Order regarded as their concern. The answer to Faith and Order was formulated on these lines.

We have already hinted at the fact of a certain change in the nature and range of Söderblom's influence after Hälsingborg. Among the factors contributing to this change, two should be mentioned. His state of health was one. It was in October 1922 that he began to feel the first definite symptoms of his *angina pectoris*. There are suddenly a few disturbing lines in his diary October 1922. '1912–1922 wonderful strength for work. Now this autumn, particularly in Munich [early September] smarting pain in the chest and the right arm; cramp; groaning. Rheumatism? No, the nerves of the heart.' These symptoms were to enforce occasional sick leaves at the Nauheim Sanatorium, Germany. He worked seemingly with the same speed and determination as before, yet, he had had his warning, and he was to get many more.

The second factor concerned the secretariat. At Uppsala Söderblom had been assisted by Westman, who at Geneva in 1920 was provisionally elected as General Secretary for Europe. Westman had a firm grasp of the European situation. In October 1921, he went on tour to London, Paris, and Berlin. In London he addressed a Conference in Economic Recovery and World Peace together with J. M. Keynes, and he pleaded for reconciliation between Britain and Germany. He had important negotiations with the men and women who were to lead the national movements in Britain, France and Germany. His reports on this and similar visitations on Söderblom's behalf were of the highest quality. But in 1923, Westman left for China where he was going to work until 1927. In the Church of Sweden Mission Board, Söderblom voted against Westman's transfer to China but was outvoted by the majority. Söderblom's main reason—however interested he was in Christian education in China— was Westman's importance for the Stockholm preparations. In April 1924 Söderblom wrote to Westman: 'would it be possible for you, at the expense of the (Stockholm) Meeting, to come home and run the General Secretariat in Stockholm with a very large staff of co-workers, from March [May?] until September next year?' Westman declined on account of his commitments in China. To Söderblom this was something of a defeat. As late as January, 1925, Söderblom wrote to Westman, hoping against hope to persuade him to return to Uppsala: 'The most important thing is capacity for a total view of the whole and a sure judgement in all possible, large and small questions.'

At Hälsingborg, Dr. Atkinson was elected General Executive Secretary, with Thomas Nightingale, an English Methodist, and two Swiss, A. Keller and E. Choisy, as associate secretaries. Dr. Atkinson was efficient and capable and established wide contacts. His visit together with Herman Neander, in 1924, to the Eastern churches was a great success, paving the way for increased Orthodox representation in Stockholm. But Atkinson lived in New York and, at critical points in those years, correspondence with Uppsala seemed to be much too slow. The tug-of-war between Atkinson and Dr. Abrahamson over Söderblom's American tour was trying for all concerned. (We need scarcely underline here that this definitely was not the Americans' fault). As the great Stockholm meeting approached, Söderblom's load of work in Sweden and outside his country increased alarmingly, but he was able to set aside certain times when he gave his concentrated attention to the continued planning of his Conference. One such occasion was just before leaving for his long American tour when he sent Atkinson an important memorandum (of August 15, 1923). In connexion with the Copec conference 1924 he called his Executive to Birmingham and had days of intense preparation of the programme for Stockholm. He felt then he was particularly helped by E. Stange, the German secretary, and by Bishop Woods, and Dr. Kapler. It had been difficult for him to take that time off, yet, in retrospect he was glad that he had done so. 'Now I see, that my absence would have been betraying the flag', he wrote to Mrs Söderblom on April 13, 1924. During these months he felt that he had to carry an inordinately heavy burden. Brilioth, with a diplomatic choice of words describes the situation: 'The last few weeks prior to the [Stockholm] Conference, certain difficulty arose because the Archbishop found it necessary to hand over to the Swedish Secretariat a number of tasks which rightly belonged to the International Secretariat. It was necessary to draft a preliminary programme before the General Secretary arrived in Stockholm at the end of July [the meetings were to begin on August 10].'[2]

Fortunately, Söderblom could rely more and more on Brilioth, who came to carry a very considerable share of the load. Atkinson himself recognized Brilioth's role in the preparation for Stockholm. In a letter to Söderblom in July 1925 Atkinson set down on paper his thoughts for 'the future of the Conference'. Two of his main points were:

'Elect the Patriarch of Alexandria or Germanos as Chairman;

---

[2] Y. Brilioth, in *Nathan Söderblom in memoriam* (1931), p. 325.

elect Dr. Brilioth as General Secretary.' Brilioth was, however, doing Church History research and could not follow Atkinson's suggestion, and Söderblom needed somebody close at hand who could work full time—and who had the exceptional qualifications required.

Söderblom's uneasiness about the Secretariat, prior to Stockholm, suggests a more general problem. The 'Universal Conference' was by definition international in scope. Nobody understood this better than Söderblom, and as a matter of course he had welcomed the fact that an American was elected General Secretary in 1922. The problem arose mainly from the sheer intractable fact of geography. With Atkinson almost permanently in the United States, it was not easy for Söderblom to direct the movement as he wanted and often needed to do. And however international Söderblom was, he often felt the need of somebody with a real grasp of European problems, at a time when Europe was the main concern, who in free and unhampered discussion had an ear for the overtones of his message; somebody who could support and help him. He had relied very considerably on his Swedish co-workers until this time, and as far as possible he continued to do so.[3]

In the meantime, Söderblom gave his thoughts to those large and small questions to which he had referred in writing to Westman. One matter that attracted his attention, to an almost surprising degree, was that of international church statistics. He has explained the reason why in his book on Stockholm:

We must refer to a problem which may have eluded most people. Who were assembled at Stockholm? Americans, Negroes, English, Scots, Irish, French, Germans, Poles, Rumanians, Russians, Bulgarians, Serbs, Swiss, Dutch, Syrians, Hindus(!) Chinese, Japanese, etc. etc. They were Lutherans, Calvinists, Methodists, Ortodox, Baptists, Uniats, Anglicans, Quakers, etc. For many years, research had been undertaken in order to determine the wisest representation from these various languages and countries and confessions, not only according to a membership whose extent is often very difficult to ascertain, but also with regard to their spiritual position and importance within Christendom. It was likewise necessary to maintain

---

[3] The Scandinavians on the International Committe understood this problem and sympathized with Söderblom. This was shown in the election, 1923, of a secretary for the Continent of Europe, to succeed Westman. Erich Stange, secretary of the German Student movement, was elected. There were strong reasons for the highly competent German for this post. But there were dissentients: Hoffmeyer of Denmark wanted 'a Swede' to succeed Westman. Gleditsch of Trondhjem, Norway, suggested Stange 'or a Swede': 'Brilioth, S. von Engeström or some other Swede to be nominated by Söderblom'.

such proportions during to the Meeting. I dare say very few realize how delicate was the task which the Executive had to tackle in this respect.[4]

Söderblom had already raised this matter at Geneva in 1920, and
took it up again in 1921: this time he had his statistical formula so
that he could argue his case with assurance. It is characteristic that
Söderblom's statistical expert was part of what we have called his
'extended Uppsala family': Olof Quensel, son of Söderblom's close
friend and doctor, professor U. Quensel. Quensel argued in this way:
'A large church should have more representatives than a smaller one,
but a small church should have a relatively more numerous representation than a large one.' Quensel suggested a statistical formula:

$$r: 35 \left(e_{\log} \frac{m}{10} 7 \right) - 1$$

which gave a scale according to which a church with 100,000 to
400,000 members would get 1 representative and a church with 13
million members would get 30 representatives. Söderblom kept a
file—referred to in the Archbishop's House as 'Urkunden', or the
fundamental text—where he could juggle with these figures, in his
attempt to give to the churches as just a representation as possible.

Delegations to Stockholm

The representation to the Stockholm Conference was decided not by
Söderblom but by the 'groups'—the national and continental organizations. Constitutionally, the Hälsingborg 1922 meeting brought
about decentralization of decision-making and responsibility in this
important matter. Söderblom had therefore in principle very little
to do with the composition of the delegations. He was aware of the
fact that groups or individuals felt that they were locked out by certain political or theological tendencies within the particular continental or national organizations, and he was sometimes led to attempts to counteract such influences. There were, of course, ways
and means for Söderblom at least to modify the membership of the
Conference. He exercised his influence by correspondence with the
secretaries of the continental and national groups. He made full use
of the authority which at Hälsingborg 1922 had been granted to the
International committee, to co-opt a certain number of leading
people. This was supplemented by power extended by the Interna-

[4] Söderblom, Stockholm 1925, p. 706.

tional Committee to him personally, or to him in conjunction with Dr. Atkinson, the General Secretary, to invite such delegates as were regarded by them as of particular value for the work of the Conference. At Zürich 1923 and Birmingham 1924 the International Committee, mostly on Söderblom's personal recommendation, added other names of special importance. On certain rare occasions he even had to be brought in with a view to preventing the participation of too outspoken or non-conforming brethren: the German situation, requiring a certain measure of discipline, was to provide an example of this. On the other hand as he tried to make his influence felt in this matter, as well he might on the strength of his unchallenged leadership in the movement, it happened that he was firmly rebuffed. This is obviously not the place for a detailed list of the delegations. We are interested in the Conference as an expression and extension of Söderblom's personality, and therefore emphasize certain delegations, which were of special importance to Söderblom as he prepared for his conference.

The *German* delegation presented a problem of its own, and Söderblom followed developments here with special interest and indeed with personal involvement. Better than any other non-German churchman after the war, Söderblom understood the importance of negotiations for a Federal Committee of the German Evangelical Churches, a Kirchenausschuss.

There were strong tensions within the Ausschuss with regard to questions of official German representation in the Stockholm Conference. Söderblom kept in constant touch with those German leaders who in various ways shared his vision and ecumenical aims: above all, with F. Siegmund–Schultze who did more than anybody else to further Stockholm's ideas and interests. There were a good number of the leaders, well-informed and personally involved who with varying degrees of enthusiasm supported these endeavours: Reichsgerichtspresident Simons, A. Deissmann, M. Rade, Ad. von Harnack, A. W. Schreiber, Theodor Kaftan. Others again were hesitant whether Germany, at a time when the Damocles sword of the *Schuldfrage* still hung over their people, should at all be officially represented at Stockholm.

There was also hesitation on the part of the Lutheran confessionalists, and determined efforts were made by some of them to instruct their people not to attend. In this situation Söderblom's long-standing personal contacts with Bishop L. Ihmels proved to be of great value. Ihmels was persuaded by the argument that the Stockholm

Conference must not be left without a consciously Lutheran voice, and he decided to go himself. Not only did he attend, but once he had been engaged, he devoted himself to the work of the Conference with characteristic energy and with great personal loyalty to Söderblom.

In that connexion T. Kaftan's case should be mentioned. Söderblom had a real admiration for what he called the truly episcopal personality of Kaftan. Some of the German church leaders regarded Kaftan as umpredictable, and he had a tendency to speak his mind on such delicate matters as that of the *Schuldfrage*. Unluckily, Möller, the new German leader of the Kirchenausschuss, who had been won for the Life and Work movement in 1922, was something of an authoritarian, demanding that certain tiresome 'free-booters' as he called them, such as Kaftan and Siegmund-Schultze, should not be included in the German delegation. In the case of Siegmund–Schultze, Söderblom knew that he could handle that problem in his own way: he sent him a special personal invitation, one of the very few in the whole conference to be thus honoured. But Kaftan's case was different, he had to be sacrificed in the interest of official German participation at Stockholm. Siegmund-Schultze felt that this was a 'brusque' procedure with somebody who, after all, had been one of the leaders of 'Lutheran–ecumenical' work in Germany.[1]

Söderblom found a way also with the hesitant. The very influential Dr. Kapler belonged to this group. Certainly, Kapler and those who followed his lead were impressed by Söderblom. Söderblom's record on behalf of German interests in those tragic and terrible years was well-known: his whole-hearted involvement in and, indeed, sacrificial service to Germany, particularly on behalf of thousands of starving children after the war; his help to German university professors and students; his courageous and costly leadership on behalf of the Swedish Bishops' Meeting protesting in February, 1923, against the injustice of the Ruhr occupation; his daring and spectacular initiative in saving Hainstein for the German Evangelical Church. As Söderblom studied the German situation, he could notice about 1924 a definite change of attitude on the part of German churchmen to participation in international affairs. After the long years of war and isolation, there was now a new readiness to take part in ecumenical work.

On the other hand, the German delegation had its particular prob-

---

[1] F. Siegmund-Schultze, in *Die Eiche*, 1933, p. 357.

lem. As the Conference approached, and as rumours had it that the German delegation intended to take up the 'war guilt' issue at Stockholm, Siegmund-Schultze and his colleagues found it necessary to discuss this question at a special meeting in Stuttgart in 1924. There it was officially decided that so far as the German representatives were concerned, this problem would not be brought up at the Conference. Germany's international position was, however, regarded as so precarious and delicate that the German delegation as distinct from other groups applied a certain amount of group discipline, *Fraktionszwang*. With the Stockholm Meeting approaching Söderblom left for Berlin in order to win Kapler to give full assent to official German representation at his conference. Nobody but Söderblom could have conceived of the particular method of persuasion which was applied in Kapler's case. It proved effective. Söderblom happened to visit Germany on the occasion of the visit to Berlin of the Swedish Crown Prince. He suggested to the Swedish ambassador that it would be a good idea to invite Kapler and Siegmund-Schultze to be presented to the Swedish royal guests. After dinner, Söderblom and the Crown Prince took Kapler into the adjoining room where Söderblom argued his case for a good many hours. In the meantime Siegmund-Schultze valiantly entertained the Ambassador and the ladies. At long last Siegmund-Schultze felt a pat on his shoulder and heard a stage whisper 'Got him', the archbishop happily beaming.[2]

The German members of the International Committee had all a close personal relationship to Söderblom. The president of the group, Kapler, had a firm grasp of the theoretical and practical questions of the Life and Work movement. He saw the importance of the movement also for his own country. At Hälsingborg he had expressed a discovery showing the significance of the movement as a whole at this time: 'Although the work of the [Ecumenical] Conference reaches out to the whole world, its particular concern is Europe. The healing of Europe is the healing of the world.' This statement of Kapler's was representative of attitudes in the Life and Work movement in 1923–1924.

Another lawyer in the German delegation was Walter Simons, the Reichsgerichtspräsident for the whole of Germany (1922), at

---

[2] As Siegmund-Schultze has already published, in German, a brief reference to the ambassadorial dinner, the story is rendered here, supplemented by information from Siegmund-Schultze, interview November, 1966. Cf. F. Siegmund-Schultze, *Nathan Söderblom*, 1966, p. 78.

one time Minister for Foreign Affairs, and in 1925, deputy to the German Reichspräsident. W. Simons was one of Söderblom's great personal discoveries. The German has vividly recalled their first meeting: at the railway station in Basel in 1920 as Söderblom overheard his name and immediately contacted him: 'From that moment he won me for ever', Simons stated. Söderblom relied on Simons for the presentation at Stockholm of the case for Christian responsibility for international affairs. Some fifteen church presidents and higher church officials were among the strong German delegation of forty-five members. Among the professors, the New Testament scholar Deissmann was one of Söderblom's close friends.

As one studies the proceedings of the post-war ecumenical conferences, one finds that the leaders of *French* protestantism appear comparatively late in the day. It was only with some hesitation that some of the French leaders eventually joined the movement. When K. B. Westman visited Paris on Söderblom's behalf, in October, 1921, he was asked by one of the leading 'evangéliques' whether co-operation in the Life and Work movement really meant that they must meet Germans. 'To which I replied', wrote Westman, 'with an equally blunt, Yes'.

As a matter of fact, Söderblom's own position was a problem to the French. We have already seen how the Ruhr occupation and the Letter from the Swedish Bishops on the Ruhr in 1923 seemed tragically to endanger Söderblom's standing with France and the French. This made him all the more determined to win his French friends for the Stockholm cause. He was encouraged by such French leaders as Jézéquel who at the height of the Ruhr crisis wrote to Söderblom that he knew him to be *quand même* a friend of France. During his visit to the United States, at the end of 1923, Söderblom was informed that the French Protestants hoped to join the Life and Work movement during the following year.[3] In Sweden Söderblom took the initiative in 1924 to organize the Swedish Society for French Protestantism, in order to further ecclesiastical and cultural contacts and co-operation.

Söderblom's attempts to see to it that the French played a central role in the work of the Conference must be understood in a wider context than that of Söderblom's personal preference for French

---

[3] From F. Palmgren's letter and report on the Antwerp Committee meeting, dated Sept. 6, 1923, to Söderblom.

language and culture. He had noticed how difficult it was for those who could speak hardly any English to make themselves understood, or their case appreciated, in ecumenical conferences and committee meetings. There are a number of important references in the many letters from and to Söderblom in these years to this problem. Söderblom was more aware of it than any other ecumenical leader of his time. If he felt that he should give a special place of honour to the French language, this was for various reasons. He wanted to emphasize the role of the French-speaking minority in Protestant Europe; he also knew that some of the French leaders had a message of special importance for his movement; and he increasingly felt that what was called 'the European point of view' must be vindicated in the face of an ever increasing Anglo-American influence. He tried his best to allow the French langugage a special place in the programme of the Conference. He wrote on July 25, 1925, to Bishop Eklund in Karlstad: 'In spite of strong Anglo-Saxon resistance, I have, except on one point, succeeded in carrying through the programme based on 'the European viewpoint', which does in fact find support from some Americans and Britishers. And now in spite of resistance and veto and counterproposals, the programme stands expressed in the French language with German and English translations, as needed.'[4]

How far this effort on Söderblom's part was generally understood at the time is not known. Contemporary books and reports have no reference to it. It certainly made it that much easier for Söderblom himself to emphasize the role of the French delegation. And it was in this group that Söderblom found his choicest spirits and friends. Elie Gounelle, representing a minority within a minority, in that he came from a French Methodist background, published regularly his remarkable *Christianisme Social*, printed at that time on

---

[4] We are aware of the fact that this is said in a letter to J. A. Eklund and that their personal relationships were complicated. Söderblom, ever anxious to persuade, may appear to have overdone his 'European' attitude one extra degree with a view to win, or please, Eklund. He was personally moved by the fact that his old antagonist had consented to speak at his Stockholm conference and he tried to meet Eklund's hesitation on account of the linguistic problem. Eklund wrote on June 10, 1925: 'I would never dare to give my lecture in German or English. My weak pronunciation would destroy everything—above all my poor self-esteem! Thanks therefore for the promise that I am allowed to be βάρβαρος as I am.' One month later Eklund writes: 'My incapacity in using the ecumenical language' entails that I won't be of any use. Rather the opposite'.

poor paper but with rich and inspiring contents. Here was unmistakably a prophet, a man of strong Christian conviction on the pressing social problems of the day. He spoke like a prophet, and looked like one, *'tout feu, tout flamme'*. At Stockholm he was not dazed by all the 'Reverends': 'Sa *grandeur*, sa *Bèatitude*, sa *Magnificence*—and they have forgotten Ragaz! who ought to have been at Stockholm: how shortsighted our Churches can be.'[5] Söderblom had rediscovered Wilfred Monod through the Ecumenical Movement. They first met as young students at New Haven in 1890, then again in a meeting of the World Alliance at Copenhagen in 1922. After a distance of more than thirty years 'our souls melted together'.[6] And it was Monod who was going to make a lasting contribution to the Movement because of his work on the Message of the conference.

The *British* preparations for Stockholm were in a class of their own. From Söderblom's point of view these might well have appeared as a follow-up of the support which Britain had given to his plans in the midst of war. The leadership of the 'Copec' conference (on politics, economics and citizenship), Birmingham 1924, consisted of the same combination of Anglicans and Quakers which, in 1917, had sustained Söderblom's effort. Temple, Bishop Burge of Oxford, Raven, Ede, Hewlett Johnson, among the Anglicans, and the indefatigable secretary, Miss Lucy Gardner, of the Society of Friends, belonged to the foremost leaders of the Copec conference. Temple's leadership, the expert preparation of the proceedings and the role of worship at the Conference as a whole, all this appealed to Söderblom. The preparation for Copec itself had been exemplary. Through it, the concern of the Stockholm Conference was brought to the attention of the British public and of the churches. Ten commissions were established, study groups were organized all over the country, and twelve volumes of the Copec Report were prepared and published. Without any doubt, Copec was the most important of all the preparatory conferences preceding Stockholm. Söderblom himself managed to attend the Birmingham conference; it inspired him. In his letters to his wife one can follow his growing appreciation and admiration for Copec.

At the beginning he wrote: 'Now they discuss Education. I feel

---

[5] *Christianisme Social*, 1925, p. 947.
[6] *Hågkomster*, XIV, p. 379.

very small, a failure, incompetent. The one thing is my love to Him.' He was impressed by what he saw: 'Bishop Temple, broad with thin lips and with will-power, presiding. Raven spoke with spiritual power. Copec has been prepared with British thoroughness and common sense and a simple, straight-forward interpretation of Our Lord's Prayer without much theology.' At the end of the conference, Söderblom was tempted to meditate on the significance of the initials, Copec. This was not Esperanto, he said, but English and meant Conference obviously prepared with extraordinary care. It was a living thing, he suggested, with a father, Bishop of Manchester, a mother, Lucy Gardner, and a soul, Canon Raven. This flight of fancy inspired him to another play with the famous initials: 'The true interpretation: Christ ought to penetrate every compartment of life.' Much as Copec was a preparation for Stockholm, some of its leading men, Temple, Raven and others, to Söderblom's great disappointment failed to participate in the Stockholm conference, not, to be sure, by lack of interest, but because of the pressure of other duties. Loyal to his old friends in the movement, Söderblom in 1922 could not visualize an Executive Committee meeting without Bishop Talbot present. So when the list of British participants did not include this beloved name, Söderblom asked K. B. Westman to inform Miss Gardner that he would wish this addition to be made. This method, however, did not appeal to Lucy Gardner, and in a British turn of phrase she said so. 'We on our side are not prepared to do business unless the meeting is called with due regularity. ... The Bishop of Winchester, much as we love him, is as we all know too frail to undertake such expeditions. ... It also makes our work impossible if delegates are to be chosen by anybody excepting the duly accredited body in this country.'

Bishop Burge of Oxford had emerged as perhaps the most devoted Anglican leader in the Life and Work movement, prior to Stockholm; it is significant for that close co-operation of Anglicans and Friends which Söderblom witnessed that Burge had been drawn into the movement by Lord and Lady Parmoor.[7] It was therefore a great personal loss to Söderblom and to his movement as a whole when Bishop Burge died just two months prior to Stockholm. All the more Söderblom relied on Bishops Woods and Dean (later Bishop) Bell, both of whom were to play central roles at Stockholm.

The British delegation included some of those who in the 'Inter-

[7] Söderblom, *Stockholm 1925*, p. 35.

national Committee' of Life and Work had given much thought to the preparation of the conference. There was Dr. A. E. Garvie, Presbyterian and polyglot, wise, loyal and indefatigable; Sir Henry Lunn, the rich Methodist layman (as he was then), one of whose 'Mürren' Conferences Söderblom had attended. There were Congregationalist scholars such as V. Bartlet, and a solid representation from Scotland. Even in 1920 Archbishop Söderblom had pointed out that his movement had a new pillar, the Scots. Dr. McClymont of Edinburgh was a member of the International Committee and had served as chairman of the important preparatory Life and Work Committee meeting at Antwerp, in September 1923. Dr. J. D. MacGilp of Aberdeen gave his special contribution to the Stockholm proceedings.

More than anybody else, the Secretary of 'Copec', Lucy Gardner (1863–1944) was responsible for the effort of forming a representative British delegation. Canon Charles Raven, who worked with her, says of her: 'She possessed to an almost unique degree the contrasted qualities of ruthless efficiency and exquisite personal sensitiveness'.[8] She had very definite theological views and took a well-defined ecumenical standpoint. Herself a member of the Society of Friends, she would not be a party to any pan-Protestant union move. When in 1924 she had been, mistakenly, told that Söderblom was 'going to attempt at the Stockholm Conference to make an effort towards a union of Protestant churches', she strongly advised against any such possiblity: 'If therefore there is any idea that the Stockholm Conference will be used as a lever to promote a pan-Protestant Alliance, my duty is clear. I must entirely disassociate myself from it.'[9] Söderblom could of course reassure Miss Gardner on this point: he had fought that struggle through, four years earlier, at Geneva.

Söderblom relied on Lucy Gardner for a good deal of his contacts with Britain. He appreciated the significance of this great woman's contribution, at a time in the 1920's when only very few women were appointed by their churches as delegates to an International Conference. At Stockholm, Miss Gardner was to play a prominent role. Söderblom asked her to be the keeper of the chairman's bell: In the discussions the speakers were allowed only five minutes. To the awed astonishment, and sometimes agony, of Metropolitans, Bishops and more humble members, Miss Gardner's bell promptly and vigorously punctuated the discussion.

---

[8] *The Friend*, December 15, 1944.
[9] Lucy Gardner, October 15, 1924, to Söderblom.

As the Conference drew near, Söderblom was anxious to add certain significant names. With Miss Gardner he found no sympathy. Greatly impressed as he was by Lord and Lady Parmoor, he wanted both of them as speakers at his Conference and invited Lady Parmoor to speak at Stockholm. Miss Gardner retorted:

I am distressed to find you have invited Lady Parmoor to speak without any consultation with the Committee who are responsible for the programme, nor with me, the person responsible for inviting British speakers. It makes work almost impossible as I have had to say before, if you continue with no consultation, or even without telling me, to invite British speakers. I think the best thing for me to do is to hand the whole thing over to you, and to have nothing further to do with it. Would you prefer that?

Söderblom tried to temporize and assuage: 'Your severe letter', he wrote July 9, 1925, 'is due to a rash mistake ... every human being has the self-evident right to express its wish that such and such /a/ member of the Conference should ask for the word and use the right of saying a few words on one of the topics of the programe'. But in a few days Lucy Gardner replied (July 13, 1925): 'I am sorry I cannot agree that I made a rash mistake!! You may be quite sure that I should not have written in that way without adequate cause. ... Of course I shall be delighted if she speaks, it was the principle of adding speakers to an already overcrowded programme that I objected to.'

The *American* delegation at Geneva in 1920 had given its determined support to Söderblom's conference plans and the same men, leaders in the Federal Council, continued to do so until—and beyond—the conference. In 1920, Söderblom's emissary K. B. Westman established personal contacts in New York with the Federal Council leaders. Söderblom's own visit to the States in 1923 strengthened this contact and above all achieved what had been Söderblom's main concern: to rally the Lutherans for the ecumenical cause.

Whether Ad. Keller was right when he surmised that at this period the ecumenical cause in the U.S. was sponsored mainly by a numerically limited group, 'a kind of ecclesiastical *corps diplomatique* of fifty-sixty men'[1] is difficult to say. More interesting is the fact that among these men were to be found some of the most devoted servants of the movement. They prepared the six commission reports

---

[1] Ad. Keller, July 4, 1923, to Söderblom.

which, with summaries in French and German, were presented to Stockholm. The U.S. Commission on 'Methods of Co-operation etc'. where Dr. Robert Speer was chairman, and Macfarland the Secretary, discussed 'advanced steps' which they visualized as a goal toward which to aim. There they expressly brought forward the idea of 'an international council of national denominations'.

On one point, this highly organized American study process was to influence the Stockholm conference in a way which has not been sufficiently noticed in the literature. One of the themes suggested for Stockholm was 'The Purpose of God for Humanity and the Duty of the Church'. Söderblom was never satisfied with this as a conference theme included in the programme on a par with the other, more concrete subjects. In his book on Stockholm he referred to this theme with the words: 'a formulation which betrays its English origin'.[2] Instead of treating this theme as a theological problem with a possibly enervating academic debate to follow, Söderblom proposed to handle it in his characteristic way: Let it dominate the worship and the sermons on the first day of the Conference! Very early in the day, he must have had a presentiment of some of the theological tensions which might flare up in the midst of his conference, as a result of a possibly heated debate on this issue. In accordance with his view of the necessary interplay of worship and debate in an ecumenical conference he thus advocated that this great but difficult theme be the concern of prophetic utterance rather than an object of theoretical discussion. It is characteristic that it was Wilfred Monod who was invited to speak first on that subject on the first day of the Conference.[3]

He instructed his secretary F. Palmgren to present this idea to the Executive Committee meeting at Antwerp September 1923, himself being prevented from attending. Palmgren noted that Dr. A. J. Brown shared Söderblom's view on this matter, but he could not prevail upon the majority of the Committee at Antwerp who decided that the theme be placed as the first subject on a par with the others. After the event Palmgren reported to Söderblom: 'The decision was taken for church-political reasons. In America, a Committee is already at work with that theme. And it would be unpropitious for Life and Work if they were to dissolve this committee.'[4]

While consisting of a large number of churches, the American

---

[2] Söderblom, *Stockholm 1925*, p. 239.
[3] Söderblom, August 5, 1923, to H. Atkinson.
[4] F. Palmgren, September 6, 1923, to Söderblom.

delegation all the same presented more of a united front at Stockholm than most other delegations. This was because of the federative idea carried by a dynamic optimism of which A. J. Brown, and particularly Charles Macfarland, were exponents. A. J. Brown was—together with Söderblom, the Patriarch of Constantinople, and the Archbishop of Canterbury—president of the Conference. He was the ideal chairman of meetings, and served as such also at Stockholm in sessions which sometimes were far from easy to chair. In a world conference mainly concerned with Western problems, his unrivalled knowledge of missionary issues was a special asset. Charles Macfarland, the General Secretary of the Federal Council who during and after the war had visited Europe on a great many occasions and knew its problems so well, was the dynamic Christian statesman. The leading German periodical *Christliche Welt* after the conference wrote very highly of this American contribution: 'Without the optimism of these men the Church Conference in Stockholm would indeed not have been possible.'[5] Some of Söderblom's most powerful co-workers from the Federal Council were included, such as Henry Atkinson, the General secretary of the Life and Work movement; Peter Ainslie; Wm. A. Brown, F. Lynch and H. G. Leach. To these names we should add here that of Bishop Brent, a member of the International Committee of the Life and Work movement. It was highly significant that the leader of the Faith and Order movement not only attended Stockholm, but entered fully into its work. This American bishop did so with greater pacifist conviction than many an old pacifist could afford.

It was due to Söderblom's efforts that three of the Lutheran Churches in the United States were represented. To Söderblom's great satisfaction, the Augustana Synod sent their President, Dr. Brandelle, and the United Lutheran Church sent a strong delegation.

The most spectacular delegation at Stockholm was, as a matter of course, *the Orthodox*. The appearance of patriarchs and metropolitans came as a great and joyful surprise to the Swedish public, and their participation in a Church Conference in a Nordic country brought to people's attention the comprehensive and world-wide programme of the movement. To the participants generally the accession of the Orthodox to the movement brought increasing significance and hope to the striving for ecumenicity and Catholicity.

---

[5] H. Hermelink, in *Christliche Welt*, 1925, p. 931.

To the Orthodox Churches themselves this participation was a great advantage. As some of their leaders admitted it was not until Geneva, 1920, and the Copenhagen [World Alliance] meeting 1922 that they had begun to know one another as Orthodox churches in a way which had not until then been possible in their seclusion from each other. The role of Archbishop Germanos of Thyateira, from 1922 Exarch for Western Europe—he had attended the meetings in Geneva 1920, Hälsingborg 1922, Birmingham 1924, and visited Uppsala in 1920—was particularly important in this respect. Not only did Söderblom and his Western co-workers and colleagues meet the Orthodox with keen expectations, but there were also on the part of the Orthodox, very particularly Germanos, real expectation of a deepened sense of the Church's unity. He realized that it was through an approach of friendly visitation and practical co-operation that the way would be paved for deeper unity. He is quoted as stating: 'Where hearts are united, the resistance of the head will diminish. It was the looseness of the bonds of love which brought the divisions of Christianity.'[6]

For Söderblom Orthodox presence at Stockholm was a real achievement. He had tried so hard and for so long. Herman Neander and John Kolmodin had cultivated the contacts with the Orthodox and interpreted his program on the spot. The personal union between members of staff in Söderblom's movement and World Alliance also was a factor that furthered these contacts. This was clearly seen at the Sinaia Conference in Rumania, an important meeting for Balkan churchmen, where the World Alliance was represented by Sir Willoughby Dickinson, Dr. Atkinson and Alex. Ramsay. Neander came as Söderblom's personal emissary. Neander expressed Söderblom's invitation in a fashion to which Söderblom would have had no objections:

The abyss which formerly existed between the Protestant and Orthodox Churches is now in the process of being bridged over through a wonderful mystical unity. There does in fact exist only one Church, in the same way as there is one sun with many rays. It is regretted that for the time being the Roman–Catholic Church stays aloof, but it is hoped that at least some official observers from that Church will be present. The greater is the joy that the revered Church of the Orient, this Church of martyrs and of the great Doctors, is prepared to express that spiritual unity in action.[7]

---

[6] Cf. Rouse-Neill, *A History of the Ecumenical Movement*, 1954, p. 651.
[7] Cf. *Die Eiche*, 1925, p. 64.

Neander went on from Sinaia to the Greek Patriarchate in Alexandria. In the spring of 1925, Söderblom sent another Swedish emissary to Alexandria, Cairo and Jerusalem, Dr. S. Stadener. Stadener visited Patriarch Photios, the Coptic Archbishop Johannes in Alexandria, and in Jerusalem the Greek Patriarch Damianos and the Armenian Patriarch Elisee.[8] This, however, valuable though it was, turned out to be Stadener's last work for the movement.

About the same time, Dr. Ad. Keller also visited the Orient on behalf of the Stockholm movement. In Cairo Söderblom's close friend Harald Bildt was now Swedish minister and he kept the Swedish archbishop well informed about developments. The visit of Canon J. A. Douglas of the Church of England was of particular importance in that he invited prominent Orthodox ecclesiastics to celebrate the 1600th anniversary of the Council of Nicea at Westminster Abbey, June 29, 1925. On this great occasion the Patriarchs Photios of Alexandria and Damianos of Jerusalem were present. So was Archbishop Söderblom who now for the first time met Photios.

All these contacts and personal visitations were of importance for Orthodox participation at Stockholm. Söderblom eventually acquired a wide knowledge of affairs and leaders in the Orthodox world. Together with his friend Germanos he prepared the list of the Orthodox delegation, consisting of metropolitans, archimandrites and lesser clergy together with some occasional layman, from Greece, Bulgaria, Rumania and Yugoslavia, Alexandria and Nubia. Söderblom attended to every detail of the arrival of the great Orthodox dignitaries. When Patriarch Photios was expected in Sweden, Söderblom sent Neander to meet the great man at Sassnitz. But when Söderblom learned that Photios was to arrive by an earlier train than anticipated, Neander, travelling in his South-bound sleeper between Stockholm and Trelleborg, was in the middle of the night awakened by a telegram from Söderblom instructing him to change trains and board the north-bound train. When this arrived at Stockholm in the early morning hours, there was Söderblom who had travelled by train from Uppsala that morning in order to welcome His Beatitude the Patriarch of Alexandria to Stockholm. As the old patriarch appeared at the station door, he raised his hand and blessed the city of Stockholm. Söderblom took Photios to the nearby Church of Saint Clara: the Archbishop of the North and the Patriarch of the South knelt together at the altar. The venerable old

---

[8] Letter from S. Stadener, February 2, 1925, to Söderblom.

church father prayed in Greek. All of church history came alive to Söderblom in that moment.[9] His own Stockholm Conference had now begun, and begun as he had hoped and prayed that it would begin.

He had already, when meeting Photios in London in June 1925, suggested to him that on the last Sunday of the Conference, August 30, 1925, he recite the Nicene Creed in Greek at the High Altar of the Uppsala Cathedral. This was the great moment to which he was already looking forward. It was to be the climax to all his efforts, and an earnest of Orthodox contribution to the Ecumenical movement.

Not all gave a thought to those who were *absent* from Stockholm. It was regarded as natural and indeed creditable that the Church of Rome failed to attend or participate.

Söderblom did not accept the absence of Rome light-heartedly. Having tried in vain on a number of occasions to secure Rome's presence, he finally accepted their absence but as a tragic fact. One of the best remembered phrases from Stockholm was Söderblom's reference to the two or three gathered in Jesus' name.

Two men are here gathered together. John, the Apostle of tender love and contemplation, and Paul the greatest disciple of the Saviour ... [whose] faith worked by love. The third man, Peter, the spokesman of the disciples, still tarries. Christendom stands out as divided, but Christ is one.

In his typescript Söderblom had another attribute to St. Peter after the spokesman of the disciples: 'the master builder of the Church'. This latter expression was crossed out in lead pencil, possibly at the last minute. One can sense his struggle even as he spoke; on the one hand, his Christian generosity and fervent hope one day to see the whole of Christendom gathered together; and, on the other hand, the way of wisdom on that occasion which forbade him to go too far.

A refusal, the echo of which reverberated far in the chilly air of the North, was that of Archbishop Gustaf Johansson of Turku, Finland. A splendid delegation under the leadership of Bishop Gummerus of Tampere did attend, but they came without their Primate's blessing. The old Finnish archbishop had a mind of his own and a theology according to J. T. Beck, the nineteenth century German professor. Söderblom sent Johansson a hopeful letter of invita-

---

[9] Söderblom, *Stockholm*, 1925, p. 740.

tion, but Johansson informed his Swedish colleague that for him
'social, economic and political problems do not belong to the domain of the Church'. He also knew that 'Rationalists' would attend
the Stockholm Conference but 'it would not do to mix Rationalism
and Christianity. ... I cannot co-operate with those who deny the
deity of Christ, and such people are sure to participate in the meeting.' The Articles of the Lutheran Reformation knew nothing of a
world conference, and the Finnish archbishop was sure that Martin
Luther himself would not have attended Stockholm, the programme
of which he could not have accepted. In the end, that is at the
eschatological end, the Return of Christ, everything would in any
case be made new. Until then, all these human efforts were doomed
to failure.[1] The old Finnish archbishop broadcast his views on Stockholm to the world, and this was apparently taken quite seriously
by some of those continentals who were critical of the ecumenical
cause. Söderblom, who was prepared to go to any lenghts to win
his Finnish brother, took this outburst with good grace. But a few
years later when Johansson thought he had discovered that Söderblom *pro primo* was a Free Mason[2] and *pro secundo* did not believe
in the Resurrection, he on this ground excommunicated the ecumenical Swedish archbishop. Söderblom at long last was moved to one
of the very few sharp rejoinders in his life.

Folkets Dagblad Politiken, the Communist paper in Stockholm,
wished to draw the attention to what they liked to regard as one
prominent absentee from the Conference. They ran a fictive interview on August 11, 1925, with Our Lord himself, a solitary, poor
and totally forgotten individual whom they had discovered in the
crowd of delegates arriving at the Central Station in Stockholm. He
had not received any invitation, he said, he was not a delegate and
came only in his self-appointed capacity of observer representing
'true Christianity'! In his report on Stockholm Elie Gounelle, the
French social reformer refers to this article.[3]

Gounelle had a point and Söderblom knew it. He also knew that

---

[1] G. Johansson, December 10, 1924, to Söderblom.
[2] Söderblom, January 21, 1928, to G. Johansson. The Free Mason story cropped
up in various quarters in the 1920's. It was a popular point also in Roman
Catholic propaganda and in fact altogether without foundation. One of the reasons for the emergence of the Free Mason myth in connexion with Söderblom was
probably the fact that in Stockholm the house of the Free Masons adjoined the
Musical Academy, the headquarters of the Conference.
[3] *Christianisme Social,* 1925, p. 947.

as far as he was concerned he had made the greatest efforts to invite representatives of the Labour movement such as Ramsay MacDonald and he could point to vocal delegates like H. Hallén, the Swedish vicar and Labour MP. This complex of problems was in the meantime treated by those who were preparing the proposal for an Ecumenical Social Institute.

There was another group comprising some of the Liberals in Germany, such as Rudolf Otto, with his great interest in unity through the World Religions who felt that they had been hindered from attending rather than helped, by their own particular national organizations.

The delegates to Stockholm were the officially appointed representatives of their Churches. At this stage in ecumenical history this meant that one very important category within Churches tended to be forgotten: youth. As it happened the Y.M.C.A. had sent a young deputy for their delegate; what is more, this deputy, to the pleasant surprise of the old stalwarts, rose to speak in the debate. Bishop Woods, the Chairman of the session, spelled to himself the double name before him to be sure of the pronounciation and called out 'Mr. Visser t'Hooft, please'. The young man spoke on the problem of youth. 'We would like to bring together the youth of all nations into world wide friendship and brotherhood. It is the church which more than anybody else can keep us, because what we want is the centre of the Gospel which the Church preaches'. The speaker's few words, while dramatically reminding the Conference of the absence of a youth delegation, were an earnest of things to come.[4]

'Stockholm 1925' was impressive, not least because of the array of ecclesiastical dignitaries and civil servants who attended the Conference. The point is, however, that if Söderblom had had his way, the galaxy of personalities would have been even more dazzling. For years prior to the conference, he had had in mind inviting the following: The President of the United States, or failing that, the Secretary of State; the Prime Minister of Great Britain; the Reichskanzler of the German Republic; and the President of Czechoslovakia. Finally, he had to be content with substitutes or telegrams from these great men. The absence of these people from the Conference was not Söderblom's fault. He had really tried.

Take his efforts to ensure the presence of Dr. Masaryk, the President of Czechoslovakia. This is a study in persistence. Masaryk, the

---

[4] Cf. Ad. Deissmann, *Stockholm 1925*, p. 282.

champion of the small nations, interested Söderblom greatly. His famous 'Mémoire to Sir Edward Grey' of April 1915, had established the modern principle of nationality. There Masaryk placed special emphasis on 'language as the medium of common cultural life and effort as the main test of nationality', an argument which appealed to Söderblom and which he applied not least to the Baltic situation. At the beginning of 1922 Söderblom had already established the first personal contact with Masaryk, inquiring about religious life in new Czechoslovakia. On March 15, 1922, Masaryk himself replied suggesting that 'someone (in Sweden) could come and observe things on the spot'. He also referred Söderblom to Professor Zilka, a member of the Evangelical theological faculty in Prague. In the following months Söderblom tried through Zilka, and through the Czecho-Slovak minister in London to persuade Masaryk to become a member of the International Committee for 'Life and Work', on a par with the Ecumenical Patriarch and the Archbishop of Canterbury. At the Executive meeting of Life and Work, Birmingham, April 1924, Professor Zilka was present, and there can be little doubt that it was on Söderblom's suggestion that it was decided at this meeting to ask Dr. Atkinson and Dr. Zilka to convey an invitation to Masaryk. On May 18th, Söderblom wrote another personal letter to the President asking him 'to accept the respectful invitation of our Committee to be the special guest ... and to deliver the keynote address to the Conference on the importance of the Christian ideal for public life, or any kindred subject that will be agreeable to you'. But Masaryk's decision must have crossed Söderblom's letter, for on April 5th Masaryk wrote to say: 'I hesitated: but after thinking and re-thinking I ask you not to elect me.'

This did not prevent Söderblom from new efforts. There were also Czecho-Slovak interests that tried to prevail on him, finding various ways in influencing the President, after all, to attend. As late as May, 1925, Söderblom suggested to Masaryk that his presence 'would mean an inspiration and a guidance'. At this time, Söderblom had had to face the hard fact that some of his most cherished ambitions were not to be realized. All the same he was now in a position to place an impressive list of potential members before Masaryk:

Among the statesmen, the President of the United States will of course not be able to come himself, but he will send a messenger with a personal message from him. In Stockholm we expect, among others, Lord Parmoor, Lord Cecil, Mr. Ramsey MacDonald, von Karnebeek or Mr. Loudon, Monsieur André Weiss, Professor Sarrut, Hon. C. E. Hughes, Secretary of State, now in New York, perhaps also Mr. Herbert Hoover, President Lowell, former President Gustav Ador, Dr. Simons, Leipzig, Reichskanzler Luther, former Premier of Finland, Sir Hj. Hammarskjöld, sometimes Premier of Sweden etc.

As it worked out, out of this optimistic list of great names only Reichsgerichtspräsident Walter Simons, Söderblom's personal friend from 1920, and Hjalmar Hammarskjöld attended the conference. But it is in the light of this euphonic catalogue that one understands better the number of encouraging letters and telegrams which Söderblom had sent to these men during the years prior to Stockholm. After a political conference in London, August 1924, Söderblom wrote to Herbert Hoover congratulating him on 'the mighty contribution made by American goodwill and power to the conclusion of peace.' After his visit to Hoover in Washington in December 1923, Söderblom jotted down this impression from the three-quarters of an hour with the Secretary of Commerce:

... the most remarkable man I met in the United States. Face somewhat shrunken, hair dangling over forehead. Looks up from time to time; small, clear, narrow, bright eyes. Hoover complained of Ford and France in the interview. I [spoke] on Life and Work'. Hoover—unmistakable surprise and assent. Enquired, made a note of 'August 1925, Stockholm'. I developed the two points on the programme, social ethics and international relationships and the schoolbooks. Hoover became animated. I invited him to speak to us [at Stockholm] on Morals and Economics. Hoover: 'I am constantly struggling with this problem, my life's calling lies here, and the question is essential.' I seized on this. Unfortunately Wallenberg, [the Swedish envoy] had to take me away on account of the lecture, otherwise the interview might have continued. It went on for three-quarters of an hour, becoming more and more captivating. Not only an ecumenical mind, but a Christian soul in earnest. One of the few great men of our distressed time.

Söderblom also sent a message to Hughes, adding: 'As an uncrowned prince of peace, you went to the governments of our old Europe for the real welfare of the Old World was well as that of the New World'. There is no reason to doubt that the sentiments thus expressed were genuine on Söderblom's part. Neither can there be much doubt that one of his motives for expressing these noble sentiments was to pave the way for Hughes' participation in the conference at Stockholm.

Particularly he hoped that the President himself, at this time Calvin Coolidge, would attend. In December 1923, Söderblom had paid a brief visit to the White House in order to interpret his ecumenical plans. This was his impression of Coolidge:

Small, big nose, crouching man, thin lips. Friendly eyes, received [me] in a low one-storey wing of the noble White House. Known as taciturn. Well, he was communicative, speaking quietly, warily. [I expressed] my joy over [American] wheat to Germany. The misery. 'You are the creditors of all the world, call the debtors together.' He found the situation desperate. Spoke on 'Life and Work', and asked Coolidge to support Americans who devote themselves to this task.

Söderblom used diplomatic channels and persuaded the U.S. minister to Sweden, Dr. Plimpton, to write to the President. But the United States had 'returned to normalcy', and Coolidge wrote: 'As you know it is not expedient for me to go outside the country.'[5]

Söderblom also held high hopes with regard to the German Reichskanzler, Hans Luther. Here Söderblom's devoted friend and co-worker Siegmund-Schultze was the intermediary. Also in this case, Söderblom's idea was that the great man was to give a lecture to the Stockholm Conference. He suggested the theme, 'The supranational and supra-state character of the Church.' But Luther had to consider possible reactions from the Catholic party, and decided to stay in Berlin. He did, however, send the manuscript of a paper on 'The Influence of Modern Industrial Organization on the Religious Mind'; this was duly read to the conference.[6]

These efforts, albeit abortive, reflect Söderblom's vision not only for his own conference, but for the role of the Church in the world. That is why he invited this galaxy of statesmen. From his Strindberg he knew that in order to reach the edge of the wood you had to go by the stars. Above all, the presence of the leaders of the nations, great and small, at his Universal Conference was to remind Christians everywhere that the Church must live not unto itself, but as a witness to the world, involved, *engagée*.

Extension of a Personality

It was to his own Uppsala that Söderblom had wished to invite Christendom. But in the very hour, in August 1920, when this was accepted, even by those who felt that Sweden was too far away from the centre of things, he had to admit to himself and to his closest

---

[5] G. K. A. Bell, *The Stockholm Conference*, p. 119.
[6] Cf. F. Siegmund-Schultze, *Nathan Söderblom*, 1966, p. 85 ff. Bell. *The Stockholm Conference*, p. 421.

co-workers that the Uppsala plan was impracticable. A conference of that size could not very well be managed in the limited physical situation of a little town with twenty thousand inhabitants. So it had to be Stockholm instead, and yet, with a happy compromise: the overture and the finale of the conference were to be played at Uppsala. The overture was an episcopal consecration on the Sunday, August 16. Gottfrid Billings successor, Dr. Edv. Rodhe, was consecrated on that day. In the procession were the Swedish bishops and bishops from the other Scandinavian churches. An altogether unique feature was the part played by Photios, Patriarch and Pope of Alexandria. Preceded by Swedish and Orthodox chaplains and attendants, he ascended to the High Altar from which he gave the blessing. Siegmund–Schultze of Berlin gave his impression: 'It is not easy to imagine anything more solemn than this procession of bishops in full ornate. ... The old archiepiscopal town was the right place from which to proclaim, against the background of tradition, the Christian influence emerging in all spheres of life.'

And the finale sounded its last chord in Uppsala Cathedral. The Archbishop preached on 'Ephphatha'. In that solemn hour addressing the delegates of Christendom, he made a scarcely veiled reference to his own secret, that of the joy of service, of being used to the full: 'Words are cheap. We must give ourselves. The waste of life consists in the love we have *not* given, the powers we have *not* used'.

Between the overture and the finale lay the crowded days of the Conference at Stockholm. The Conference commissions had met for days in the secluded comfort of hospitable castles in central Sweden. At last, on August 19 the six hundred delegates from thirty-seven nations and thirty-one churches could convene for the Conference as such. The organization has unanimously been regarded as 'perfection itself'. Stockholm provided a beautiful setting. The fact that all of Stockholm and indeed all of Sweden seemed to be involved in assisting the Ecumenical Conference gave a special note to its life and work. On the other hand, the meeting place, the rambling Blasieholmen Church, was not very inspiring, a Swedish version of Spurgeon's Tabernacle.

A press representative from Norway (he did not attend as a delegate), Eyvind Berggrav, wrote: 'a more languid conference hall than the Blasieholmen Church one has yet to find: colourless and cold with a strangely disturbing influence on the mind'.[1] But the place had the advantage of being spacious, holding 3,000 people.

---

[1] E. Berggrav, *Ekumeniska Mötet*, 1925, p. 11.

The seating arrangements for the Conference were logic itself, but unfortunate; the delegations were placed according to nationality and language: all the German-speaking delegates seated on the right hand of the platform, all the French on the left and the English between. This was a practical principle not least because of the very considerable problems of language and interpretation. But these solid blocks of nationalities reacting by applause or chilly silence did not make for the most desirable ecumenical atmosphere. There were only a few polyglots like Garvie, 'who always sought a seat among the German members and talked to them in their mother tongue'.[2] Here the difficult problem of interpretation should be mentioned. This was, of course, before the days of simultaneous translation. Söderblom himself revelled in the happy multiplicity of languages, the more the better. During the preparation for Stockholm he would, very characteristically, write to Atkinson, the General Secretary:

'In devotion and worship we shall give each language and communion time and solemn places of worship at Stockholm, at least (!) in the following languages: a) Scandinavian, b) English; c) German; d) French; e) Russian; f) Finnish and Esthonian; g) Greek; h) Italian and Spanish.'

But not all shared this view. Söderblom had made a very great effort to have all the lectures printed in French, German, English and Scandinavian, but for the impromptu discussions, interpretation was necessary. On this point Söderblom said: 'Perhaps one ought to say that the Swiss were those who have done most for our Meeting.'[3] He referred particularly to the capacity of the incomparable interpreter, Pastor A. Koechlin from Basel. Attending as a deputy. Koechlin, with his wonderful command of German, French, English *and* theology, became the chief interpreter of the Conference and thereby did much to ensure its success.

The headquarters of the Conference were in the building of the Royal Academy of Music. Every room was occupied by committees, secretaries, translators and journalists. The Archbishop's secretary, Gerda Rodling, was awarded space for herself and her typewriter, in the comparative quiet of the dark end of a corridor. For the Archbishop a box-room had been found.

During the lunch breaks Söderblom met the Executive and the

---

[2] A. E. Garvie, *Memories and Meanings of My Life,* 1938, p. 195.
[3] Söderblom, *Stockholm 1925,* p. 135.

secretaries in the nearby Strand Hotel. These occasions served as staff meetings where an astonishing mass of business could be rapidly dealt with.

There is a sense in which Söderblom was the Stockholm Conference and the Conference an expression, almost an extension, of his personality. This is probably more true of Söderblom and Stockholm than of any other church conference in relation to its leader. However, although he dominated the scene, Söderblom was far from domineering. On the contrary, he hardly ever entered the debate and was reluctant to appear. He preached twice, at the opening and at the close of the Conference, and he gave one address (out of a total of one hundred and eighty). For this address, he chose to speak not on any of the central problems, but sursprisingly perhaps, on the somewhat subsidiary question of Alcohol, although it should be remembered that drink and total abstinence were highly controversial political issues in post-war Sweden.

For the remainder Söderblom was prepared to direct from behind the scenes, appearing only as he encouraged speakers and debaters, and after their performance, expressing his appreciation. As joint President he acted as chairman for a day, taking turns with Dr. A. J. Brown and Bishop Woods of Winchester, the latter a deputy for the Archbishop of Canterbury. In addition to these, Metropolitan Germanos should have acted as Chairman on the same terms as Bishop Woods; he seems however to have preferred to leave this task to his three colleagues. Söderblom promoted Bishop Wood's leadership to such an extent that some of the continental writers felt that they must complain. The writers of *Evangelisch-Lutherische Kirchenzeitung* in Leipzig noted that Söderblom preferred not to appear, but that they had to face Bishop Woods instead. To some extent unaware of the niceties of Anglo-Saxon hierarchical differences, they deplored the fact that delegates invariably had to rest their eyes on the face of the 'Archbishop of Westminister'.[4]

Interpreting the Conference as an extension of Söderblom's generous personality we should not omit one less desirable aspect of the Meeting. The programme was much too crowded. In the nine days devoted to business, the Conference was treated to some one hundred and fifteen prepared addresses, the text and translations of

---

[4] *Evang. Luth. Kirchenzeitung*, 1925, p. 709.

which had been distributed beforehand, and in the sessions these were followed by some one hundred and forty contributions to the discussions. Some of the latter were of the greatest weight and importance; in fact, it is not always easy to distinguish between the two categories. Added to this were some thirty-six sermons, forty speeches, and the reading of the Conference Message. This was too much of a good thing. The result was that not even Söderblom's enthusiasm and devotion were enough to keep the delegates in the Conference Hall. 'There was a danger in this. Many of us thought when, on the first evening, the pews were already terribly empty: This won't do, they will all go home' (Berggrav). Soon this tendency rectified itself, but Söderblom was worried over this absence, and later, in his book about the Meeting, mentioned a few, the (then) Crown prince included, who deserved special praise for regular attendance at the meetings. This was in the early period of the ecumenical movement, and later meetings could learn from Stockholm's mistake. In 1919 Söderblom had, as we have already seen, insisted that, following the example of Lambeth, the plenary session of the Conference should be called together only at the beginning and end of the Meeting. But somewhere along the road to Stockholm this vision was lost sight of. Even some of the occasions particularly devised as refreshing diversions tended to be over-loaded. An example was the 'Swedish evening' with four solid addresses by Prince Carl, Selma Lagerlöf, Elsa Brändström and Nathanael Beskow, interspersed by John Forsell's singing. This was of course the very best that Sweden could give, but perhaps again, too much of it for one late evening. There was a combination of Teutonic energy and ascetic will-power in the planning of such programmes, and not all the delegates were either Teutons or that kind of ascetics.

The last day the Conference was received for dinner in the Hall of Uppsala University. Söderblom had discussed every detail of the dinner with the Pro–Rector of the University, who was none other than Ulrik Quensel, Professor of Pathology, Söderblom's close friend and doctor. The letter in which he informs Quensel about this dinner, with its references to the Governor of the Uppland Province, Hjalmar Hammarskjöld, the Mayor von Bahr and the Rector of the University, Stavenow, is a document about Söderblom's extended family, his closest friends, all anxious to assist their 'Nathan'. One notices that the ecumenical Archbishop identifies himself with the University: it was the Pro-Chancellor who was to see his friends from afar at dinner in that University Hall.

Bureau on Life and Work

Musical Academy, Stockholm, August 21, 1925.

Dear Friend,
We have now written to the Stadshotellet and accepted their menu for Sw. Kr. 3.75 [4 sh.] per person according to the following proposal.

Butter, Cheese
Hot, or cold, Consommé with Cheese Straws
Cold Prague Ham with vegetables
'Napoleon' Cream Cake
Coffee,
Lager and Lemonade

We have looked into the printing of the cards. I believe the most convenient would be broad cards in Cabinet size.

Then we could have these printed according to my proposal so that we who represent the University would appear in a line flanked by the Governor and the Mayor.

We will print everything here in Stockholm and also distribute the cards from here.

As we will be in the University, I have asked Stavenow to welcome the guests and the Governor to speak, at the end of the dinner, to the Conference as such. Further. I intend to ask an American and somebody from Europe, and possibly the Patriarch or some other Oriental to speak at the end.

It would be convenient, wouldn't it, to circulate lists where gown and town could sign up for the dinner for Sw. Kr. 4: 25 (including service charges)

Yours ever,
(Nathan Söderblom).

Another feature was the role played by the Swedish Royal family The Conference was opened in the Royal Palace at Stockholm by His Majesty the King, Gustav V; it was attended by the Crown Prince, now King Gustav VI Adolf, who in fact was one of the most faithful listeners throughout the Conference. We have already mentioned the contribution of Prince Carl.

Prior to the Conference, members of the eleven Sub-committees of the five commissions were the guests in this or that castle or country house in central Sweden. This gave an opportunity for contact with the Swedish nobility, Swedish history, and Swedish folk-culture. In the same way, the rich bourgeoisie of Stockholm was engaged by Söderblom to serve as hosts for exotic, or merely exalted, ecclesiastical guests, and many a private landing-stage on the waters of Lake Mälar was the scene of a happy and quiet afternoon's fishing, as Eastern Metropolitans or Western Congregationalists angled for the humble roach. The organization of the day-to-day running of the Conference was entrusted to prominent practical men, among them General O. B. Malm and Major Sjöstedt.

The whole of Sweden seemed to be involved in the Conference. Indeed they were, as a people, the hosts for this universal Christian Conference on Life and Work. This could never have happened had it not been for Söderblom's magnetic personality, his ever resourceful ability to attract people of high or low estate for his cause, and not least those who had never before thought of themselves as in any way concerned with the Church.

Ever since the days of the war Söderblom had kept this idea in mind. He underlined the importance of the cultural, national setting of an ecumenical conference. Looking back on his meeting, he wrote:

Christian international conferences are not seldom held in air balloons. One meets for a few days in a delightful place and spends hours and days full of Christian contents. But the surrounding milieu knows hardly anything of what is going on. This appears to me as a contradiction. A Christian undertaking must appeal to all Christian people and this was the reason why we were anxious to keep the Meeting in Scandinavia, where we knew that it would be carried by a strong and wide spiritual support, and we did not deceive ourselves.[5]

Stockholm 1925 has sometimes been called the Nicea of Ethics. Without much difficulty one can imagine such a conference devoted to social and political problems, organized and run as a purely technical conference of experts. A number of good names from Söderblom's own generation spring to mind as one attempts to visualize a conference with this orientation. But because this meeting on Ethics and Politics was conceived, and to a large extent shaped, by Söderblom, it received an imprint all of its own. It is indeed significant that the most striking thing about this Life and Work Conference was the emphasis on worship and praise.

If the Conference can be called an extension of Söderblom's personality, this was particularly marked in this realm of worship and music; here was a characteristic Söderblom touch.

First, we must notice the role of the new ecumenical hymnbook,

---

[5] Söderblom, *Stockholm 1925*, p. 68.

'Communio in adorando et serviendo oecumenica'. A special hymn-book for the Conference was pre-eminently an example of the '*le superflu, chose si nécessaire*'. Söderblom had a keen sense of such matters. It is a truism to say that if the book had not appeared, this conference on Social Ethics and International Relations would obviously have had to do without it. Only a few perhaps might have noticed the lack of it. But by being used the Hymnbook proved necessary and vastly beneficial for the spiritual climate and inner unity of the Conference. It was eminently typical of Söderblom's total conception of the nature of ecumenical work, an expression of his joy and awe at the richness and the manifold wisdom of God.

The editor of the Hymnbook was himself a member of Söderblom's 'extended family'. Dr. Emil Liedgren had been one of Söderblom's most devoted students at Uppsala in the early years of the century, and was now Sweden's leading hymnologist.[6] From the treasure house of the whole tradition of the Church throughout the ages, he selected sixty hymns and songs, in Greek, Latin, German, English, French, Danish and Swedish, which all appeared in the original together with translations into three or four other languages. Söderblom himself gave a large part of his time to this endeavour. Even as late as July 1925, with all the anxiety and pressure of work over the last minute preparations for the Conference programme, Söderblom would enjoy snatching odd moments, as far as there were any, for translating hymns, ancient and modern. 'It took more work than anybody could ever imagine.' Söderblom remarked on the preparation of 'Communio'.[7] The united and hearty singing in the Conference of the great hymns of the Church of Christ was felt by many as something of a Pentecostal experience.

This was true also for the Church services, one of which was outstanding. Söderblom described it as 'the most intimate moment (*innerligaste*) of the Meeting.'[8] This was the High Mass in the Engelbrekt Church, Stockholm, with Holy Communion shared by the great majority of the delegates. Earlier efforts on Söderblom's part towards intercommunion, particularly with the Church of England, now found fulfilment. To many who came from distant lands

---

[6] E. Liedgren in 1931 wrote perhaps the most inspired interpretation of Söderblom's life: '*A Christian's Freedom*', in *N. Söderblom in memoriam*. It is a fugue in four parts: 1) Overture. Allegro Vivace. 2) Andante Pastorale. 3) Scherzando. 4) Finale.

[7] Nathan Söderblom, *Stockholm 1925*, p. 167.

[8] Ibid., p. 198.

and different traditions, this was a new and unique experience. To Söderblom, the 'march of brothers' towards that altar, called to mind for him the great multitude before the throne of the Lamb.[9] One of the communicants was Bishop E. J. Palmer of Bombay. In a Bach recital during the conference he had proved to be an original interpreter of the great composer and was by that token for all time, Söderblom's friend. Participating in the Communion service he expressed not only the new and closer relationship Uppsala–Canterbury, but also, and especially the concern of the Younger Churches for organic unity.[1]

But worship was closely related to service and solidarity. An opportunity for this necessary relation was a memorial service for Patriarch Tichon of All the Russias. The worship was led by Photios, Patriarch of Alexandria, and Germanos, Metropolitan of Thyateira; it gave the Conference an opportunity of expressing solidarity with the Church in Russia. To Söderblom, it was also part of his grand ecumenical strategy where the Uppsala–Constantinople brotherhood in aims should be supplemented by fellowship with the Russian Orthodox Church. The Metropolitan of Bukovina, Roumania, preached, and there was a note in his sermon of this great Church strategy which Söderblom sometimes liked to develop: Rome had declined to assist the Eastern Church; at last a helping hand had been stretched out from the West, in and through the Ecumenical Conference of Stockholm.[2]

We have already underlined the role of the two Church services in the Uppsala Cathedral. The finale of the whole Conference was held there. The climax of that service was when Photios, the Patriarch, at that altar said the Nicene Creed in Greek. This was felt by Söderblom to be one of the greatest moments of his life and a worthy fulfilment of dreams, visions and prayers. In his book on the Conference he quotes an observer of that great occasion: 'Here a bridge

---

[9] Ibid., p. 193.

[1] In a series of articles on Stockholm for the *Gospel Witness* in Madras, Paul Sandegren generously enumerated the names of some of the ecclesiastic communicants on that day. In good faith he included in the group Bishop Ihmels of Leipzig. Enquiries from anguished Lutherans in India followed upon this reference. The matter was looked into, and minds were quieted when Sandegren's, as it happened, erroneous statement was retracted. A name had been cleared.

[2] Nathan Söderblom, *Stockholm 1925*, p. 207. The Orthodox Metropolitan drew parallels between Nicea and Stockholm, and between Gustav Vasa and Stephen the Great of Roumania. Cf. Ad. Deissmann, *Stockholm 1925* (1926), p. 393.

was built from the Stockholm meeting on Life and Work to the coming conference on Faith and Order; the Nicene Creed, said in an Evangelical cathedral by a Greek Patriarch, is to me a prophecy about the doctrinal unification of Christendom.'[3] It happily expressed Söderblom's view of the necessary correspondence between Faith and Order and his own Life and Work.

But Stockholm, 1925, was not only hymns and praise. It was also hard and exacting work, and discussions of difficult and dangerous issues. The idea had been born in war and want, and the Conference was therefore necessarily related to seemingly intractable problems. Nobody knew this better and felt this more than Söderblom himself. Discussion in Plenary Session and in private revealed great tensions between individual and group interests. Söderblom, who loved the outspoken prophets in his movement and acknowledged them as the very soul of the enterprise, had himself as the leader to reconcile seemingly irreconcilable and opposing attitudes in order to bring the whole of the Conference to a positive conclusion. This was his dilemma at Stockholm. One is struck by his concern for keeping the Conference united. Dr. Garvie in his capacity as English secretary on Commission V, saw what happened behind the scenes:

There I witnessed Söderblom's never ceasing care and incessant activity without which the Conference could have become something very different from what it fortunately did become. That the war-guilt question was not brought out into the open and that the Conference was thereby saved from a fateful falling apart, was due to (Söderblom's) manoeuvering of the situation, requiring more of the wisdom of the serpent than the meekness of the dove.[4]

There were tensions in that Ecumenical Conference between nations recently at war with one another. There were also tensions between different confessions and churches. There were misunderstandings because of language, where words and overtones of words, took on very different meanings to different groups of people. There was, in that great company of six hundred delegates the difference between the many newcomers to the ecumenical movement and the group of the very few who were beginning to be recognized as ecumenical experts.

In this field charged with tensions, Söderblom moved with amaz-

---

[3] Ibid., p. 213.
[4] A. E. Garvie, in *Hågkomster* XIV, p. 440.

ing sureness of touch and tact. He was not ruffled by differences of opinion, but recognized them as an enriching personal experience. It is well known that political tensions were particularly acute in the German delegation. On August 25, 'the black Tuesday' of the Conference, Superintendent Klingemann had, in harsh-sounding words, made a declaration on the League of Nations according to which, 'in the present state of the League, we cannot find religious power or any communion with the Kingdom of God.'[5] After that, the measured and balanced view of the German Missions expert, Julius Richter, was bitterly criticised by his German compatriots, and Richter left the Conference and Sweden that same evening. Two days later, it was Dr. Siegmund-Schultze's turn to speak. Months beforehand he had been invited by Söderblom to prepare an address on the 'Church and Peace', but members of the German delegation, apprehensive of the effect of Siegmund-Schultze's well-known pacifist attitude, threatened to leave the Conference if their radical compatriot was to speak. Siegmund-Schultze went to Söderblom and told him that he had taken his decision: 'I abstain from my lecture.' Söderblom embraced him, saying: 'You have saved the Conference.'[6]

Söderblom later followed this up in a letter: 'We deeply regretted that you did not give [your lecture], but I did understand your reasons and have accepted your silence and admired the sureness of your judgement. So the World Conference had to take the narrow path.'[7]

In his chapter on the international problems, Söderblom, unlike Siegmund-Schultze, does not refer to that day of particularly bitter tension as 'Black Tuesday', but as the 'great day of the Conference',[8] and why? 'Victories were won, above all victory over self.' He says of the German delegation: 'Those who understood their inner difficulties, had to admire the self-restraint of the united conduct of the delegation and its strength.'

This of course was the point of view of somebody who, in spite of the tremendous tensions, *had* to keep the whole meeting together. Looking at that scene from a distance, from the relative safety of the scholar's study, one might even suggest that the unity thus dem-

---

[5] G. K. A. Bell, *The Stockholm Conference 1925*, p. 452.
[6] F. Siegmund-Schultze to the present writer in an interview, November 1966. Siegmund-Schultze, *Nathan Söderblom*, 1966, pp. 97 ff.
[7] Ibid., p. 99.
[8] Nathan Söderblom, *Stockholm 1925*, p. 445.

onstrated had been bought at a price; some might have said that the cost was too high, and that a Christian conference even when it is thus 'saved', runs the risk of being too accommodating.

However anxious Söderblom may have been to emphasize the spiritual approach and to strike the 'prophetic' note, it was unavoidable, perhaps, in a conference embracing such a variety of national and political attitudes and standpoints that the prophetic was toned down. Söderblom must have felt as a tragedy what he noticed happening to the report from the French delegation on the 'Church and Economic, Institutional, and Social Problems'. That report was written by one man, Elie Gounelle, and it gave, with the conviction of a prophetic personality, an irresistible challenge to the Church of its time. But at Stockholm, even Gounelles' message had to be processed through the machinery of a Commission report and it could not be avoided that in the process the very fire of the spirit was transposed to the miserable majority prose of a committee.

This was no less true of the final result with regard to the Church and international politics and particularly the problems of war and peace. We have already noticed that the German delegation with great self-restraint, had decided prior to the Conference not to raise the question of war-guilt, but this problem hung in the air like a thundercloud. During the Conference passionate expressions of a desire for disarmament were made. Söderblom was impressed by Bishop Brent's declaration.

What is now needed more than anything else is courage to try God's way ... or shall I say God's highway ... it is because I believe in the sanctity of the nation and the magnificence of patriotism ... that I reaffirm my belief that the Christian Church if it be so minded can, in the name of Christ, rule out war and rule in peace within a generation. I may be a fool, but if so I am God's fool.

But after all the preparations and declarations, some felt that the particular passage in the Conference Message on the Church's responsibility with reference to this all-important issue was too polished.

We summon the Churches to share with us our sense of the horror of war and of its futility as a means of settling international disputes, and to pray and work for the fulfilment of the promise that under the sceptre of the Prince of Peace ... righteousness and peace shall kiss each other.

The Conference did not attempt 'precise solutions', the Message said, but above all 'to state principles and to assert the ideal'. In fact some few delegates preferred to register their objection to the Message as a whole because of this passage. This little group included Söderblom's close friend Nathanael Beskow.

'Practical Christianity' was the purpose of Stockholm. 'Praktisches Christentum' was the official term in German. Theory and theology were therefore not primarily its concern. Here the Conference had its great surprise.

Söderblom himself wrote: 'The main issue of the Ecumenical Conference was not printed in the programme. ... In all the preparations it had hardly been mentioned'. Yet there was the theme which was to dominate the whole meeting.[9] Theology could not be relegated to the scholar's study. It claimed its rightful place, the first place, in the meeting. Dramatically the two addresses on the very first day, by Bishop Woods and Bishop Ihmels, brought up the fundamental issue and thus the relevance of theology in approaching the problem underlying the whole Conference: the interpretation of the idea of the Kingdom of God. Bishop Woods spoke English as he referred in his sermon, largely echoing *Copec,* to the establishment of the 'Kingdom of God on earth': 'To set up the Kingdom of God in this complicated civilization of the twentieth century is a colossal task.' Bishop Ihmels used German as he claimed: 'Nothing could be more disastrous than to suppose that we mortal men have to build God's Kingdom in the world.'

This issue was to challenge and disturb the theological and ecumenical debate for many years after Stockholm, but Stockholm, 1925 had to bear the brunt. This struggle between the 'social'—shading off into an attitude summed up as 'Social Gospel'—and the eschatological approach, came out into the open for the first time at Stockholm.

Söderblom had not been without warnings. Dr. Keller in particular followed the German theological debate—he refers especially to Bultmann and Carl Ludwig Schmidt—and had registered its importance for the issues at stake. On June 4, 1925, he advised Söderblom to consider this, 'if there is still time', otherwise, he felt, their efforts would be in vain. 'I hear already at the door the feet of those that would like to carry this [Conference] to the cemetery.' But theological debate could not be settled by any last minute administrative device, and this unresolved problem resulted in continual misunderstanding at Stockholm, as well as at later conferences.

---

[9] Ibid., p. 232.

An analysis of Söderblom's chapter on the 'Chief Issue of the Ecumenical Meeting', a hundred pages long, shows that as far as he was concerned, he would put his formula for a solution of the problem in the concept devised by Commission V, combining the inner life, rooted in the absolute and eternal, with the outward life in the relative and changing sphere.[1]

How he viewed the Meeting

The Swedish Church, Söderblom claimed, had a body and a soul. As we have brought out in many contexts, his ecclesiology as a whole must be understood in these terms. As an historic phenomenon the Church of Christ was body *and* soul, institution *and* spirit.

Söderblom interpreted in similar terms his ecumenical movement in the tragic post-war world of the nineteen-twenties. There was the League of Nations, the Body Politic as it were, conceived in idealism but in need of a counterpart of spirit and life. Together with many of his generation of European Churchmen, Söderblom saw 'Life and Work' as that movement of the Spirit, the Christian soul, of which the League was in need. In his book on the Stockholm meeting he compared Stockholm and Locarno and writes:

'The League of Nations needs a soul, a spirit, an attitude in the nations ... else it becomes a dead mechanism. Or rather a soul may creep into this newly created and strange organism, but if it be not a Christian soul, unconditionally subjecting itself to right and righteousness, the soul easily becomes a devil.'[2] He remembered the occasion when in Harald Hjärne's study, he interpreted his vision to his friend. As Söderblom was about to leave, Hjärne said: 'This may turn out to be of greater importance than the League of Nations.'

Söderblom saw his conference in these terms. Politicians could be experts in the art of compromise; in Stockholm, he liked to think, the world was faced with that strange phenomenon which is called an idea, something which could not be changed and modified.

In discussing the fundamental question of the Conference, the theological understanding of the Kingdom of God, Söderblom formulated a passage which sums up his vision:

The revival which has its united expression in the Universal Church Congress in Stockholm, is dominated by two fundamental principles: firstly

---

[1] Ibid., p. 289, where he quotes Commission V, in which he of course had a dominating influence.

[2] Ibid., pp. 546–547.

the inner life is the essential. Institutions and organizations, laws and decrees, however good and necessary they may be, remain impotent; they are empty shells, dead bodies without soul or life, if they are not animated by a spirit which prays and believes, loves and hopes. No calculations, however clever, can give peace to mankind, only a change of heart and renewal. Whatever the Meeting has achieved, it has done so through the spirit which animates the whole.

Secondly, Love is called to conquer the world. The inner life (*innerligheten*) must not make for itself a cosy corner from which to condemn the world to ruin, but it must be mobilised, and this not for its own sake. Inner peace cannot be won without the dedication of love.[2a]

Here the essential Söderblom speaks on his essential task. This was what he wanted his conference to be and to represent: a revival of the Spirit in a world of war, Mammonism and nationalism. It was this line of thought which Söderblom followed when in 1925 he addressed the Royal family of Sweden in the Swedish Royal Palace; so similar to what he had said in the same place, ten years earlier, but then on behalf of the Church of Sweden: 'Your Majesties, when the Spirit of God visits humanity, the same flame is kindled in human hearts though land and water separate them. Such is the origin of this meeting of Christendom.'[3]

This is also expressed in the introductory principles of the Commission of the Stockholm Conference that dealt with 'Methods of Co-operative and Federative Efforts' and there cannot be much doubt that it was Söderblom as a member of this Commission who had formulated these words: The Movement must 'spring from the innermost life of the Spirit'.[4]

This theme recurred in many of the Stockholm addresses. Söderblom must have recognized the echo of many evening discussions at Uppsala in his own house and in the Governor's Castle, as Hjalmar Hammarskjöld said: 'The Conference has devoted great attention to international relations; here again it is the Spirit that is most important.'[5]

It was in the Frenchmen, such as Wilfred Monod and Elie Gounelle, that Söderblom experienced a spiritual communion which he appreciated greatly. On August 20, the second day of the Stockholm meeting, Söderblom said to Monod 'Let us have dinner together tonight on a terrace where we can see the lights being lit along the

---

[2a] Ibid., pp. 267–268.
[3] G. K. A. Bell, *The Stockholm Conference*, p. 45.
[4] Commission Report V, p. 10.
[5] G. K. A. Bell, op. cit., p. 748. W. Monod, in *Hågkomster*, XIV, p. 380.

shore, and see the stars mirrored in the water.' Monod later recalled
his impression of this meeting:

The whole time we stayed on spiritual ground; in my pocket I had a
little hand-written breviary which as a young pastor I had once prepared
for my wife. She had supplemented it with quotations in different languages and the whole was a spiritually invigorating collection. Söderblom's
face lit up as he turned over the pages, and he forgot to eat. Faced with
those passages in French, English, German, Latin and Greek, he would
give a cry of delight or sincere reflection.

There was a sequel, and an important and characteristic one, to
this meeting of minds, this communion of spirits. Wilfred Monod
recalled it in this way:

I was so moved by this time together, that I copied for Söderblom's benefit
some of the passages that had impressed him most. I collected this into a
little volume with the title, 'Help for the refreshment of your soul during the Council.' The following morning, I slipped towards Söderblom at
the Chairman's table from behind and handed this little volume to him.
He looked through it at once, gripped my hand warmly and whispered to
me: 'Write a message to mankind!' (He took care not to mention to me
that a special committee for this purpose had already been appointed.)

This is how Söderblom experienced his conference. Sometimes as
he looked around in the Commission on which he served, or in the
Conference as a whole, he would ask himself if this was only a
dream, a mirage. But no, it was true; their common enterprise was
moving forward, driven by an inner power. 'Now we are all incorporated whether we like it or not, into a movement, an irresistible "forward". They have been gripped by the mission of the Kingdom in our churches and in our so-called Christendom.'[6]

Beyond Stockholm

Söderblom could never regard the Conference as an end in itself. He
had called the leaders of Christendom to Stockholm in order to
propose certain definite and practical measures to be taken. In the
organization of the Conference Commissions he had this aim in view.
    In selecting the members of Commission V which had to dis-
cuss 'Methods of Co-operative Efforts by the Christian Communions', Söderblom did in fact appoint the General Staff of the Con-

---

[6] Söderblom, *Stockholm 1925*, p. 124.

ference and also shaped the group which was to carry on with the continuation work after Stockholm. He said of this Commission that it had been entrusted with the 'question which to Christendom, and public opinion in general was the most important task of the Conference'.[1]

The real issue was whether Stockholm should be followed up by a loosely organized committee or by a permanent Council. Commission V, after discussion of the nature of Church unity, was led to suggest that the Continuation Committee should not be any 'authoritative or permanent organization', it was to be a Continuation Committee 'to perpetuate and strengthen the spirit of fellowship which [Stockholm 1925] . . . exemplifies'.

As we have seen, Söderblom, in his very first appeal for an ecumenical conference, had pointed to the forming of a council as the real concrete task of the great conference.[2] Söderblom maintained his standpoint as he discussed the matter with Bell. Bell debated this issue with Söderblom and Brilioth in the months prior to Stockholm. The earlier records in Bell's journal show that he had looked upon Söderblom's plan with certain misgivings.

A Continuation Committee was what he also had had in mind at first, possibly on the lines of the follow-up of Edinburgh, 1910, but when he met Söderblom and Brilioth in London in June, 1925, he was convinced by them and changed his mind.[3] His contribution to the debate at Stockholm proved decisive; the Conference, following the proposal from Commission V, decided to form a Continuation Committee. At the same time, Bell, in accepting the Commission's report, stressed that the new body must envisage 'the possibilities of the formation of an international council'. This could not be reached at once. Such an important step needed time.

By this decision on the last day of the Stockholm Conference, Söderblom had not achieved all he wanted or hoped for, but he bided his time, until five years later the opportunity did arrive. In the meantime he kept his own aim steadily in view, and in anticipation of what had to come, he boldly declared the result of Stockholm, 1925:

'Thus the beginning is made for an Ecumenical Church Council, however one would prefer to name such a common organ for Chris-

---

[1] Ibid., p. 112.

[2] Cf.

[3] Bell mentioned the Edinburgh Continuation Committee in his address at Stockholm. G. K. A. Bell, *The Stockholm Conference*, p. 684.

tendom, empowered with purely spiritual authority, but capable of speaking and acting whenever needed.'[4]

He also felt that the decision to consider the formation of an ecumenical Institute was to strengthen his hand in achieving what he had set out to do.

The nineteen-twenties were of course a period when a number of international institutes for various cultural and social purposes were formed. It was the aftermath of war and Europe was looking for reconstruction and reconciliation. Institutes seemed to provide tools for this endeavour and one example, often quoted as a model, was the International Labour Office, founded in 1919. The idea of an Ecumenical Institute was raised in different countries by some of those most deeply involved in the ecumenical movement, all of them close personal friends of Söderblom. Its aim was to stimulate thought among churchmen who strongly felt their social and political responsibility.

One of the most interesting among these, and virtually unknown, was Edward Tennmann, the Docent in the small and remote theological faculty at Dorpat, Esthonia. 'Remote' is a relative concept and Tennmann might well have seen that he was centrally placed: on the threshold to Russia, with such contacts as were then possible in that direction, and with constant communication with the World Alliance; we have already seen how his friendship with Söderblom and K. B. Westman, from 1921, stimulated his ecumenical vision. It was at a World Alliance meeting in Oxford in April, 1924, that in the name of his Esthonian Council within the Alliance, he suggested the formation of a special Academy 'for the study, from a Christian standpoint, of all problems existing in political, social, and economic life, with all possible scientific means'.[5]

He found a great deal of interest in his ideas among that group of experts. Together with Professor Choisy, he was himself asked to prepare a detailed plan and he corresponded with Choisy, Willoughby Dickinson and Söderblom on the subject.[6] It was particularly important that Siegmund-Schultze took an interest in Tennmann's idea; he invited the Esthonian to publish his views on the subject in *Die Eiche,* and Tennmann's article *Friedens–Akademie* appeared in the October issue, 1924.

---

[4] Söderblom, *Stockholm 1925*, p. 888.
[5] World Alliance Minutes, Oxford, April 2–7, 1924. No. 35.
[6] E. Tennmann sent copies to Söderblom of his letters about the Academy to E. Choisy and W. Dickinson. September 16, 1924.

It was the peace problem that dominated his programme for an Institute: War brings shame on the Christian civilization. ... The Church ... must do everything to make war impossible.' To this end the Churches needed an 'analogy to the League of Nations', this he felt was the aim that Söderblom had in view. An academy must be created for the exchange of information and views and also for a bibliographic study, of the presentation of history in school textbooks. 'And what about the many economical and social problems? Can we not consider penetrating spiritual problems with the same consequence that pure technique uses!' Knowing Tennmann's wide horizon we are not surprised that he should add an important ecumenical provision. In order to approach all these problems, the Academy also needed contact with the Roman Catholic Church; this must 'not only be forbidden, but directly ordered.'

When Söderblom spoke of the beginnings of the Institute he claimed that it was first suggested by Bishop Einar Billing of Västerås. We have already met Einar Billing's name in other contexts; as a professor of Christian Ethics he had taken a keen interest in labour organization and similar problems, and in 1924 he became a member of the Swedish Commission on Social Affairs, preparatory to Stockholm. This was an interesting goup; it included men like Dr. Nathanael Beskow, Jonas Lindskog, Harald Hallén, and a leading journalist, Dr. Erik B. Rinman of Stockholms-Tidningen. They prepared highly competent memoranda on the Church and economic life. Billing's paper culminated in a direct proposal for the formation of an international research institute on concrete social and economic problems.[7]

In July, Söderblom received the French memoranda, brilliantly prepared by Gounelle. Here there was a more general reference to the need for the Church to establish contact with the research work

---

[7] It is characteristic of E. Billing's personality that he later could state that he had come upon the idea by coincidence. In a letter to Söderblom, December 27, 1926, he spoke of 'the contribution to the ecumenical movement which I came upon almost unintentionally through the idea of the Research Institute. I vividly remember how I first put it forward as a perhaps whimsical idea, in a little talk I had here in Västerås with [A.] Runestam and Bolling [the latter a priest the Västerås diocese], to consider the statement of the Swedish social commission, or whatever it was called, and with that hesitation I later proposed this for the Commission. In a way it was an old thought which lay behind, and in this matter my faith has been, and is, very definite, and I am really glad to have played a part in bringing it about'.

done by the International Labour Office.[8] Söderblom regarded this happy confluence of ideas as a promising omen for the Conference, and encouraged both Billing and Gounelle to develop the idea in detail.[9] Both were made members of the same sub-committee which discussed the Church and Economics prior to the Conference, in the comparatively affluent atmosphere of Brandalsund manor. Both pleaded, in the plenary session of the Conference, for the formation of an institute but with a characteristic difference.

The Swedish Bishop emphasized 'very strongly the scientific character of the institute';[1] the French social prophet suggested that there was a need for an international office which could be to the Church what the International Labour Office was to labour. This, he thought, was one way of recapturing the heart of the proletariat of the world. He saw visions: 'the masses may once again crowd into our cathedrals and our churches, making the Houses of God once more the true houses of the people'.[2] And once again varying that image which 'the men of Stockholm' never tired of evoking, he asked: 'Why should not 'Life and Work' aspire to become the soul of the International Labour Bureau, just as the World Alliance ... aims at endowing the League of Nations with a Christian soul.'

It was left to the Continuation Committee to follow this up. The idea had been launched and accepted by Stockholm. It was a great and responsible task for Life and Work to translate it into reality.

Wherever Söderblom was to move after August, 1925, he met the name of Stockholm. There were references to 'the spirit of Stockholm': and Söderblom found that he was regarded as one of 'the men of Stockholm'. At the end of his conference he saw them all leave, returning to their various countries and churches.

In his great book on the Ecumenical Meeting, Söderblom gave a thought to what might have been: 'They have accepted the expression. What they talked about was called in brief "Stockholm". And I am thinking, if only it had been Uppsala ...'[3]

---

[8] E. Gounelle, *L'Eglise et les problèmes économiques.* Paris, 1925, p. 49.
[9] Söderblom, July 16, 1925, to E. Billing.
[1] G. K. A. Bell, *The Stockholm Conference*, p. 197.
[2] Ibid., p, 702, cf. p. 172.
[3] Söderblom, *Stockholm 1925*, p. 903.

Great European

Söderblom would sometimes mockingly refer to some ambitious compatriot as 'world-renowned in Stockholm', or, and this was worse, 'world-renowned in Uppsala'. Yet if Söderblom came to belong to that necessarily restricted group of men and women who by reason of moral stature, and humanitarian achievement of Continental reach, deserve the name of 'Great Europeans', it was not because he scorned provincial roots. How could he, the devoted son of Hälsingland? In considering the relation between the universal and the provincial in the make-up of the true European, Willi Schmid, writing of another great figure, Pablo Casals, says with sure insight: 'Because he is a Spaniard and, more particularly, Catalan, he is at the same time the better European.'[1] This was eminently true of Söderblom. But, whereas Casals, Latin and Catholic as he was, might aspire as of right to the title of 'Great European', Söderblom, Teuton and Evangelic Catholic, had to establish a case. His international role and achievements represent his credentials. He is perhaps the only Swede since St. Birgitta and Linnaeus to join the select group.

In his mind and in his deeds, it was in a European arena that he moved. Others recognized this, saw his European stature and called on him to assume a European role. It was he, for instance, who was called on to write an Appeal to Europe (Mahnung an Europa).[2] A former German Reichskanzler, W. Cuno, head of the Hamburg–America Line, engaged Söderblom to speak at a Hamburg overseas week on the European situation.[3] He dealt with the need for real spiritual authority. His voice was heard all over the continent and there were reactions, positive or negative, to what he said.

About that time Söderblom also took great initiatives on behalf of Germany, and this was widely noticed on the Continent. He had been tireless and infinitely resourceful in his efforts to bring relief

---

[1] W. Schmid, 'Pablo Casals', *Stimmen der Zeit*, 1931, p. 98.
[2] *Hamburger Monatschrift f. Ausw. Politik*, 1923, No. 1, pp. 9–10.
[3] See letters from Cuno to Söderblom, June 18, 1922, July 28, 1923, and May 4, 1925.

to the needy in post-war Germany and Austria. During 1924, in a matter of days and by highly dramatic negotiations, he saved Hainstein for the Protestant Church, a renowned country house, formerly a sanatorium, opposite Luther's Wartburg. Without Söderblom's determined intervention, this centre would have been taken over by interests, which at that time were reported as far from friendly to the Evangelical cause.[4]

As we have already seen in another context, Söderblom had had to speak out in 1923 against his beloved France and this earned him sharp disapproval by the French. One can imagine how he longed for the day when he could redress this grievance. We suppose that the predominating French accent in the Olaus Petri Lectures programme for 1924 must be read in this light. There were not less than three prominent French Olaus Petri lecturers at Uppsala that year, E. de Faye, on Origen, A. Meiller, on Avesta, and H. Monnier, on Redemption; a total of seventeen lectures. It was also in 1924 that he formed the Swedish Association for French Protestantism. Above all he was anxious to write a word of gratitude or praise to a French Prime Minister. Locarno, 1925, gave him that opportunity, and Söderblom promptly sent a generous note to Briand: 'Locarno seems to us like the hearing of ardent prayers.'[5]

In 1926, Söderblom preached in Geneva at the opening of the seventh assembly of the League of Nations; this was the memorable occasion when, through the efforts of Stresemann and Briand, Germany was received into the League. In the same year to his great joy, Söderblom was invited to lecture at the Sorbonne. He chose to speak on 'the Church of Sweden, and France'.[6] Again, in 1928, at

---

[4] There is a voluminous file on Hainstein in UUB. In a matter of days, Söderblom had to find DM 650,000 in Sweden and Germany, or Hainstein would become the property of the Jesuits. September, 1924, was particularly dramatic; on September 12, Söderblom concluded a letter to Oberbürgermeister Janson in Eisenach: 'The Luther castle must be saved'. In the negotiations Söderblom, as always, was greatly assisted by the Swedish financier Dr. A. Ekström. Cf. *Hågkomster*, XIV, p. 401.

[5] Söderblom's letter and Briand's reply are quoted in full in *Christianisme Social*, 1925, pp. 1176–1177.

[6] The Swedish Embassy Rector in Paris, B. Bjurström, told me, in 1932, of the infinite care which Söderblom devoted to this lecture. When he arrived in Paris, a few days prior to the Sorbonne occasion, he had the lecture already typed out in French. He did not rely on the fact that French was his best foreign language, but instructed Bjurström to find a specialist of French, and he read his lecture to this person a great number of times. Then he was ready for the Sorbonne, to give an—improvised lecture!

the first international Christian Press Conference in Cologne, Söderblom was there speaking on the Apostolate of the Press.

Söderblom, as Inspector of the Swedish University Foundation of Olaus Petri, welcomed the opportunity of lecturing when so invited by comparable university foundations. He thus gave the Donellan lectures, at Dublin, in June 1926 and the Burge lectures (the Church and Peace) at Oxford in May, 1928. His position as the Pro–Chancellor of the University of Uppsala gave him similar opportunities for international contacts, thus he spoke in 1926 to the twelfth international Physiology Congress (on Science). On occasions like these he scintillated and captivated people's imagination.

Europe was his concern. This was not for lack of global perspective. Ever since his visit to the gate of Asia, in Constantinople. 1911, he had realized that the days of European hegemony were numbered. He emphasized this repeatedly after the war.

A remark in 1926 proves this: 'After the death of Lenin, Gandhi in India seems to me to be the most remarkable amongst our contemporaries.'[7] In the same way he, like Heiler in Germany and Streeter in England, showed a particular interest in, and became a determined advocate of, the Indian Christian mystic Sadhu Sundar Singh. Through his personal contacts with Haile Selassie, he was also to show interest in Africa. He had the great satisfaction of seeing 'his man in Constantinople', Johannes Kolmodin become political adviser to the Emperor in Addis Ababa.

But he felt that in his day, his task was Europe. In an after-lunch speech at the Harvard Club in Boston, November 1923, he said some regarded old Europe as hell, and America as heaven. But despite this he insisted: 'I am a whole-hearted citizen of sinful wretched Europe.'[8] This had for many years been his concern. In a lecture of 1912 he had stated that 'the need of a United States of Europe was felt stronger than ever'.[9]

Before 1925, there was already a tendency to build Söderblom up as the one great ecclesiastical leader of his time, and there emerged something of a Söderblom myth. Some dreamed of making Eisenach–Wartburg into 'an Evangelical Rome with Söderblom as an Evangelical Pope'.[1] In Jerusalem there were plans, or perhaps only

[7] Söderblom, 'Echo of Stockholm', *The Review of the Churches*, 1926, p. 352.

[8] Söderblom, Diary, November 28, 1923.

[9] Söderblom, Svenska kyrkans kropp och själ (ed. 1915), p. 157.

[1] Oberbürgermeister Janson, Eisenach, in *Hågkomster* XIV, p. 405.

rumours, among German and English groups, that Söderblom was
to be made 'Lutheran Pope in Jerusalem'.[2]

At the beginning of 1925, the year of the Stockholm Conference,
an interesting proposal was made by the German Paul Helbech. He
called for 'the de-poisoning of the European political atmosphere;
a task for the Christian Churches'.[3] The road to peace for Germany
and Europe, he suggested, could only go through the recognition of
common guilt leading to mutual reconciliation. To this end he
wanted to see an international conference of reconciliation in the
Hague, with representatives from both the victorious and the van-
quished powers. Three chairmen would lead the meeting, the Archbishop of Uppsala, the Vice Chancellor of the University of Basel
and one to be appointed by the Papal See.

This Utopian proposal did not lead to tangible results; but the
idea, and the fact that it was thought important enough to deserve
a place in Siegmund–Schultze's sober *Die Eiche,* reflects something of
the role which Nathan Söderblom had acquired, and the pre-emin-
ence, which through him, was accorded to the See of Uppsala.

Peace

It was this Archbishop, dynamic, winning, radiant and yet knowing
from personal experience the fears and worries of the human heart,
who in the last few years of his life devoted himself to the question
of peace.

At Stockholm, 1925, the Message on Peace to all followers of
Christ, was not very challenging, and some of the chief participants
in the ecumenical movement found it disappointingly vague and insipid. Söderblom no doubt shared in this, but his loyalty to his
movement and to his co-workers in the movement prevented him
from admitting any such criticism. At Stockholm he had had to try
to balance and harmonize tensions and differences. The leader of
the Conference had to be accommodating in order to steer Ecumene's
ship past the sunken rocks.

His attitude to peace in the post-war world cannot in fact be reduced to a neat and simple formula. This of course is true of Söderblom's attitude to most problems; he knew what some tended to
overlook, that every problem has more than one side. On the peace

---

[2] *Svenska Morgonbladet,* May 3, 1924. 'A fantastic plan: Sweden's Archbishop
Lutheran Pope in Jerusalem.'
[3] *Die Eiche,* 1925, p. 5.

issue his sympathies undoubtedly lay with the radicals. He recognized that the conscientious objectors were 'the salt of Christendom ... they had furthered the cause of true peace'.[1] Among admired friends were Quakers such as Dr. H. Hodgkin or Lady Parmoor, leaders like Siegmund-Schultze of Berlin and Elie Gounelle of Paris.

Yet he could not at first go the whole way. In an analysis dating from 1925, when he spoke of 'four attitudes to the peace problem', he tended to side with those who took a more circumspect position. He summed it up in an involved definition: 'The defence question must be treated in such a way that in the place of armaments there will be established a well-balanced system, common to all peoples and nations, of a reassuring guard for national values and for peace between the nations', and with his usual charm he added: 'So entangled is our human existence'.[2]

Yet increasingly in those later years of the nineteen–twenties he shifted from this accommodating position to a determined stand for disarmament. This may well, and here we can only guess, have been related to a certain dissatisfaction, deep down in his heart and mind, with the stand taken on peace by his own Conference. That Conference had been conceived as a meeting of the Spirit, but the 'body', the intractable facts of political necessity, made the words of the message less prophetic than he had at one time hoped for. It was perhaps this dissatisfaction with his own proudest achievement which in his remaining years moved him to a much more radical position on the peace issue.[3]

Söderblom himself, who had felt that Stockholm, largely against his will, had had to deal with too many issues, now turned with renewed concentration to the one important thing, the promotion of peace.

Increasingly his heart condition caused anxiety. There was now no journey abroad or outside Uppsala when a dose of nitroglycerine did not prove necessary: the attacks alarmed his family and closest co-workers; others fortunately knew nothing of these frailties of his. The more Söderblom realized that his days were numbered, the

---

[1] Nathan Söderblom, *Stockholm 1925*, p. 533.

[2] Ibid., pp. 529 and 533.

[3] In his Burge lectures of 1928, on the 'Church and Peace', Söderblom referred to the Stockholm resolution: 'The Stockholm meeting *attempted* in 1925 to express what would be a programme for all Christians.' *Kyrkan och Freden*, p. 23 (our italics).

more he told himself that he must give his strength to the one issue of paramount importance, to Europe and world peace.

We have noticed that Söderblom's view of the peace problem was not distinct from, but necessarily integrated with his view of Evangelical Catholicity. In devoting his time to this question, he did not therefore abandon his concern for the Church. It was as a Churchman and, thus, as deeply involved in the anxieties of the world that he concentrated on the problem.

He followed with keen interest the political debate in the world at large and in Sweden. The Locarno Pact of 1925, itself the result of a remarkable interplay of political considerations and idealistic and religious convictions, was the start of many movements towards peace. The 'Outlawry of War' movement on the one hand, initiated by S. O. Levinson, and Dr. James T. Shotwell's endeavours on the other, were sustained by encouragement from Church leaders such as Dr. C. C. Morrison of the *Christian Century*. Dr. Shotwell's aim was to stamp the institution of war as 'substantially an international crime', and he found both Briand in Paris, and Kellogg in Washington, ready to listen to this argument and to act accordingly; neither should Stresemann in Berlin be forgotten. Briand and Kellogg concurred in renouncing war as an instrument of policy between their two nations; by a 'General Act' this was, in principle, extended to some sixty nations. The Pact was signed in Paris on August 27, 1928. The nations, it seemed, were ready for disarmament.

Disarmament was the one great political issue in Sweden about the middle twenties. The Riksdag of 1925 decided to reduce armaments; a small but determined group of Social Democrats propagated unilateral Swedish disarmament. Towards the end of the nineteen–twenties their numbers increased. Efforts were also made in the Progressive Party for a policy of absolute disarmament. The Conservative Party fought with almost desperate energy against these moves.[4] The issue even affected the list of speakers for Söderblom's Stockholm Conference. In his array of great statesmen to be enlisted for the conference, he had determined to include Hjalmar Hammarskjöld, ex-Premier and now Governor of Uppland. Hammarskjöld delayed his answer, but wrote on July 2, 1925 to say:

From the beginning I had the strongest misgivings caused by doubts, only too well founded, as to my suitability, ability and availability (for the

---

[4] See H. Tingsten, *The Debate on the Foreign Policy of Sweden, 1918–1939* (1966). H. Wieslander, *I nedrustningens tecken* (1966).

task). To these misgivings, which in themselves ought to be decisive, is now added another hindrance. Under the impression of the unfortunate 'solution' of the defence question, and with my own special obligations in this matter, I cannot force myself to be actively associated with a meeting which is looked upon by many as pacifist.[5]

Against this political background of international and Swedish debates on peace we must now place Söderblom's activities in the same field. On the final day of the Stockholm Conference the German delegation had handed over a memorandum to the Continuation Committee pleading for a settlement of the vexing war-guilt problem by that Committee. It was now the difficult and exacting duty of the Committee to deal with the matter, and if possible to find a solution. From Uppsala, Söderblom, by a spate of letters in all directions, cajoled and encouraged German, French, and British, to find a common solution. It was a difficult process. Once again German-French relations within the movement were strained, and the whole issue was sometimes treated as if it were exclusively a French-German problem. Dr. Garvie, 'that canny and Christian Scot', together with Jézéquel and Kapler, worked over the wording of a statement in the early months of 1926. The memorandum, prepared for a meeting of the Continuation Committee at Berne in August 1926, did not pronounce any judgement on war-guilt, but simply stated that an adverse moral judgement was inappropriate to a peace treaty, that the conditions under which the treaty was drawn up were such as to preclude any final, impartial judgement, that the data for such a judgement were not yet available, and that Christian fellowship transcended all national differences.

With a reasoning which may strike the reader today as surprising, the Berne Conference added to these formulae, paragraphs underlining that the Continuation Committee had no claims 'to deal with any political problem', and that its declaration, 'void of any political motive' had a purely moral and totally religious character. In this, the Committee felt that they followed Christ's own example.

By Söderblom and his Movement, this settlement, after years of anxiety, was considered a great victory, and Söderblom felt that he had reason to call it 'one of the greatest moments in the history of our fellowship'. In thanking Wilfred Monod for his share in the resolution he wrote: 'The document on war-guilt is a marvellous thing, I would say a miracle', and quoting a journalist's reference to this problem he said: 'The corpse (the question of war-guilt)

---

[5] Hj. Hammarskjöld, July 2, 1925, to Söderblom.

had to be thrown overboard.' From that point of view at least, he knew that the sailing was going to be easier than in the first years.[6]

The next great step forward on the peace issue was taken at Prague in 1928. This was within the framework of the World Alliance. On that same day as the world's politicians met in Paris, August 27, 1928, Söderblom and other Church leaders met in Prague for the most important World Alliance conference of the twenties. What had the Churches been doing in this matter of peace and war? When the leaders of the nations spoke in the terms of the Briand–Kellogg pact, had they tended to become a mere echo instead of setting the pace? The least the churchmen could do, was to echo and respond. At Prague, Söderblom found some of the great leaders whom in vain he had tried to persuade to come to Stockholm, statesmen such as Hans Luther, Edward Benes, and Albert Thomas. There were also radical churchmen and theologians like Martin Rade of Germany and Marc Sangnier of France.

The general political climate was changed by the Briand–Kellogg pact, and against this background Sir Willoughby Dickinson did not need to labour the point, when at Prague he insisted that the Churches should see disarmament as their moral obligation.[7] The 'Men of Stockholm', Simons, Gounelle, and Monod, supported this from different points of view, and Söderblom himself attempted to convey something of this message in the final sermon of the Prague Conference on 'Sanctification for the Cause of Peace'.[8]

The resolution of the Conference pledged the Churches to work for reduction and limitation of the armed forces, and for a universal system 'whereby disputes shall be settled by peaceful, judicial methods in lieu of war'.[9]

From Prague, 1928, it was but a short step to Eisenach, 1929, the first occasion when an international Life and Work Conference met on German soil. Söderblom himself, ailing, and busy with his prepa-

---

[6] Nathan Söderblom, *Stockholm 1925*, p. 922. Siegmund-Schultze did not share the jubilation over the results at Berne; and as to the corpse having been thrown overboard, he pointed out the geographical fact that 'in truth there is no ocean at Berne, and in truth the corpse is not dead'. *Die Eiche*, 1926, p. 400.

[7] Dickinson, 'Disarmament, A Moral Obligation' in *Stockholm, International Review*, 1929, p. 251.

[8] The report in *Die Eiche* 1928, p. 485, was critical of Söderblom's address. 'Unfortunately this very well attended service lacked solemnity and real religious dignity. ... There was a lack of inspiring *engagement* for a cause which the World Alliance regarded as the calling of Christ to Christendom'.

[9] Cf. *Stockholm, Internat. Review*, 1929, p. 253.

rations for the Gifford Lectures, was absent, but his emissary, Paul Sandegren, kept him informed. In May 1928, Söderblom had given his Burge Lectures on 'The Church and Peace' at Oxford, which were to a large extent variations on the theme of the Briand–Kellogg Pact. In connexion with his Burge lectures he had an opportunity to discuss the peace problem with Bishop Bell. Bell confided to Söderblom that at Eisenach he wanted to go much further than the Prague Conference, and Söderblom, who greatly admired Bell, heartily agreed. Supported by Simons, the German jurist, and by the Frenchman Monod, Bishop Bell presented his famous Eisenach resolution. This in four crisp paragraphs urged the Churches to draw the pacifist conclusion from the Kellogg Pact's renunciation of war as an instrument of national policy. Here the Churches declared war 'as an instrument for the settling of international disputes, [to be] incompatible with the mind and method of Christ and therefore with the mind and method of his Church'. Disputes should be settled by arbitration.

In paragraph four, Bell said:

We earnestly appeal to the respective authorities of all Christian Communions to declare, in unconditional terms, that they will not countenance, nor assist in any way, any war with regard to which the Government of their country has refused a bona fide offer to submit the dispute to arbitration.

Söderblom had no opportunity internationally to support the Eisenach thesis, but identified himself all the more in Sweden with this radical theme. He brought the Eisenach message to the solemn assembly of the General Swedish Church Meeting thereby provoking a sharp debate. Söderblom felt that Eisenach represented a higher duty, an evolving supra-national order of law. He defended against criticism the controversial Point IV of the Eisenach resolution: 'The Church must show loyalty to international order and obligations. ... It must say unequivocally that it is the Church's duty, even in a case or serious conflict, to be loyal towards the law which makes for peace.'[1]

Since, to Söderblom, Great European, peace became the dominant issue in his last years, it was fitting that his achievement as pioneer of the ecumenical movement and in the cause of peace, should be crowned by the Nobel Peace Prize. The possibility of his being awarded this recognition was mentioned in the Scandinavian

[1] Söderblom, in *Kristus i Folkens Samliv*, 1931, pp. 12–13.

and international press in those years. A group of some sixty Swedish members of parliament, headed by Professor K. G. Westman, the same man who, as a young Minister for Ecclesiastical Affairs, had appointed Söderblom as Archbishop, made a formal proposal to the Nobel Committee of the Norwegian *Storting*.

When the announcement was made, in September, 1930, it brought together in Söderblom's mind the beginning and the end. He recalled his first years as a young pastor, when Alfred Nobel was his parishioner in the Swedish Congregation in Paris, and he compared this with those autumn months of 1930, when he and Mrs. Söderblom sometimes looked towards retirement in a little flat in Paris, near the Bibliothèque Nationale. Of all the winners of that great prize, Söderblom was the only one to have known Nobel personally, who had indeed won his confidence.

When he received the Prize at Oslo, he spoke of his friendship with Nobel, and interpreted Nobel's ideas on peace and war, and his visions for an international Court of Arbitration. This, according to Söderblom, was an anticipation of the League of Nations, but he also hinted at his own anxiety over the efficacy of the League.[2] It gave him an opportunity of varying his most cherished metaphor: 'The peoples are members of an organism, but a body must have a soul, else it becomes at best a dead mechanism. This soul will be the love and righteousness of the Gospel and not the devil of selfishness. Thus the work of peace must begin in one's own heart.'[3] He knew, in common with Alfred Nobel, the threats from the powers of evil. In that dark December of 1930, how far could he pierce into the future when he quoted Nobel's own words? He showed how, in the eighteen–nineties, Nobel considered disarmament as too risky. 'I do not know', Nobel had said, 'whether at present this would be desirable. A new tyranny, out of the deep, is lurking in the dark, and one can as it were, hear its distant rumblings'.[4]

The festal assembly in the Nobel Institute at Oslo, on that December day in the first year of the nineteen–thirties, could not imagine that Nobel's words, quoted now by Söderblom's sonorous voice, were an omen.

---

[2] *Les Prix Nobel en 1930,* First Part; Stockholm, 1931, p. 73.
[3] Ibid., Second Part; p. 20.
[4] Ibid., First Part; p. 73.

Ecumenical Institute

To Söderblom the Stockholm Conference was not the end but a beginning pointing beyond itself to wider horizons and even greater tasks. Even five years earlier Söderblom had visualized the chief function of his World Conference to be the creation of an ecumenical council. Unavoidably his concept changed somewhat in the meantime, but fundamentally he retained the same idea during and beyond 'Stockholm'.

As he had planned the composition of the Continuation Committee and its future task, he had also had in mind to try to decide where the headquarters would be. Until that time of course, the ecumenical headquarters had been Uppsala, or rather the Archbishop's house in Uppsala. It was probably true to say that at no other place was there at this time so much knowledge of the wide ecumenical movement as at Uppsala. Söderblom was too identified with his movement seriously to entertain at first the idea of any other locality. It had to be Uppsala (or Stockholm) in order to allow him to keep in effective contact with the further development of the Movement. This also implied the problem of staff, and time and again Söderblom returned to the name of K. B. Westman, hoping against hope to bring him back from China to Uppsala.

At Stockholm he confided his plan to the American leader, Macfarland. He had written a memorandum in which he developed this plan; Sweden was to provide the place for a permanent ecumenical headquarters. We do not know how far he had thought that he could persuade his American friend, but later Macfarland recalled the scene: 'I bluntly declared that I was convinced that the Commission [No. V, dealing with post-Stockholm planning] would prefer a more central and get-at-able place, e.g. Geneva. After a brief argument and with a smile, Söderblom put his papers together and never more referred to this proposal.'[1]

The episode is more important than it appears. It allows an insight into that combination of perseverance *and* flexibility which was characteristic of Söderblom. As a matter of course he was more committed to this great endeavour than anybody else. He knew what he wanted, and also felt that he understood how the cause was to be furthered after Stockholm. Yet, totally involved and committed as he was, at the same time he was free and prepared to let others

---

[1] Macfarland in *Hågkomster* XIV (1932), p. 135.

take over as the focus of the day-to-day activities of the Movement passed from Uppsala to some other centre.

Macfarland had suggested Geneva, and his American colleagues agreed with him that the centre of 'Life and Work' should be locally related to the headquarters of some of the great international movements, at Geneva. This was a logical consequence of the connexion between the League and ecumenism. Using a similar argument, the Hague too was a possibility, and the Hague was mentioned in the discussions of Commission V at Stockholm (with its associations with Oud Wassenaar of 1919).

Geneva as a centre was not universally popular among the 'men of Stockholm'. The Germans in particular were opposed to Geneva as it seemed too closely linked with the League, but also for linguistic reasons; if it had to be Switzerland, a German-speaking town was preferable.

While the Germans were reluctant about the Geneva idea for political reasons, there was a certain apprehension among the Continentals and Scandinavians that the Institute would be swamped by the big international institutions at Geneva, and Dr. W. Simons of Germany stated that he would have preferred the Institute to remain and get its initial strength in Zürich, before being exposed to the challenge of Geneva.

There was also a certain fear that the young ecumenical movement itself might develop into an impersonal machine, swamping the genuine interests of the smaller nations and Churches. Bishop Ostenfeld in Copenhagen, in an important letter to Söderblom, represented this standpoint.[2] While the leadership was at Uppsala and in Söderblom's hands, the smaller nations, he felt, had always been assured of a ready hearing and generous interest. Ostenfeld was anxious lest the big nations—he mentioned in particular the United States and Germany—should altogether take command. He had noticed that they had regular national meetings of their own. At Berne, 1926, he had seen how the Dutch, the Swiss, and the Scandinavians, were of one mind, and he pleaded with Söderblom to take the lead: 'you must, as a matter of course be the leader', in order to develop and cultivate the unity of this group of small nations for the good of the whole. Obviously such a group would be in a position to make its point of view heard.

---

[2] Ostenfeld, [early part of] Sept. 1926, to Söderblom. UUB. No date—'answered Sept. 11, 1926'.

If it had to be Switzerland for the sake of ecumenical interests in Europe, Söderblom soon found reason to support an alternative to Geneva, but with an argument that was characteristically his own. In the autumn of 1925, Archbishop Germanos visited him and the two men discussed the matter. Germanos proposed Berne, for a reason which commended itself to Söderblom. Berne was an 'Old Catholic' centre with a Cathedral and a rich liturgical life.[3] There cannot be any doubt that it was this consideration which made the Berne alternative preferable to Söderblom. He lost no opportunity of propagating the idea. But he used different arguments to different people, and in fact his correspondence on this point is a study in persuasion.

With Heiler, Söderblom was more candid than perhaps with any other non-Scandinavian. He explained to him that Berne was preferable to Geneva with its 'one-sidedly Reformed worship'.[4] When writing to Atkinson, the American Congregationalist with Quaker sympathies, he had to approach the matter in a more circumspect manner.[5] He took Atkinson into his confidence with regard to his concern for what in other contexts he called 'the European viewpoint'; and used this argument against the Geneva alternative. But to this was wedded his own chief concern for the milieu of ecumenical encounter: it must take place related to a centre of worship that allowed for a rich, 'Catholic', sacramental life.

... The great question is the situation of the Institute. As far as I can see, it is the following:

1: There is much criticism everywhere, at least outside Great Britain, of the idea that the Life and Work Institute should become at Geneva a kind of succursal or servant-maid to the League of Nations. The Hague was therefore, as you remember, proposed from different quarters. But at the Hague [just as in Copenhagen] the country does not speak an international language and, being near to the Court of Justice, we should be far from the League of Nations and its assembly.

2: Geneva is crowded by international institutions and Life and Work may disappear in the midst of them.

3: Our principle is to have the closest possible contact with the living faith and work in the Church where we gather. Geneva is of course the great historic place of the great Calvin, and Life and Work continues authentically his work, perhaps more than any one else among the re-

---

[3] Söderblom, October 6, 1925, to F. Heiler.
[4] Ibid.
[5] Söderblom, May 25, 1926, to H. Atkinson.

formers. But the capital of Switzerland is Berne, much more central from the point of view of Swiss Christendom.

4: Berne is near to Geneva without being identified with it.

5: We must take into account our Orthodox brethren. I have just re-cieved a most important letter from the Patriarch of Bucarest, who is strongly in favour of an approachment between Evangelical and Orthodox Christendom. There is probably an Orthodox chapel at Geneva, I do not know. But Berne is a centre of the Old Catholic Church that has a sanctuary and a faculty there. When, after much deliberation, I came to the idea that the Old Catholics in Berne could at least find a historical task in serving as intermediaries between us and the Orthodox brethren, it struck me that it is providential. In the Old Catholic Church, Orthodox service and Anglican service can be held easily. And don't you think that we must give the character of devotion to our whole work in our Confer-ence as well as in the Central Institute?

The Continuation Committee met at Berne in August, 1926. If ever there was, after Uppsala 1917 and Geneva 1920, an ecumenical meeting dominated by the radiant personality of Söderblom, that was Berne 1926. He was determined to make all his international group of co-workers realize the advantage of selecting Berne as the centre of the movement. There was the beautiful Berne Münster and the atmosphere of worship.[6] The whole Conference of some eighty delegates were all his closest friends and co-workers, and he was happy to work with them again.[7] There was also his contact with the *folk*-culture of the Berne Hinterland which must have reminded him of his own Hälsingland. A Berne Church choir appeared in provincial costumes, and Söderblom in his Swedish clerical coat with pectoral cross, broadly smiling, joined the choir. Solid members of the Continuation Committee were as impressed as the natives of the place when the Archbishop from the North sang with gusto: 'Vo Luzern uf Wäggiszue'.[8] Berne, provincial, yet international, was part

---

[6] Söderblom particularly commended 'the strong and hard tone of the organ', which gave him a chance to chide 'the usually much too muffled tone which (in Sweden) is *à la mode*'. Söderblom, *Stockholm 1925*, p. 892. Two years later he gave Kapler, his successor as President of the European section of the move-ment, advice as to the kind of place needed for an ecumenical conference in Germany: 'A town where the Evangelicals have a Cathedral or any other wonder-ful, great and beautiful church where the worship can develop the firm order and the rich solemnity of the evangelical Lutheran ritual.' Söderblom, Novem-ber 8, 1928, to W. Kapler.

[7] Söderblom invited the whole Conference to a dinner, and took endless care over the seating of his guests, as can be seen from the draft of a placing list. UUB.

[8] A. Keller, *Von Geist und Liebe* (1933), p. 202.

of Switzerland: 'Is not this small country, with its German, French, and Italian population, a prophecy of a United States of Europe.'[9] A Swiss journalist drew impressionistic sketches of the leaders, as they appeared in the pulpit of the Berne Münster: Monod of Paris 'slightly bent, an expression of visionary elation'; Arthur Brown of New York, calm and fully integrated; Woods of Winchester with his mighty head, a real personality; Deissmann of Berlin speaking 'with an exquisite German'.

And at last, as a storm roaring, the Swedish Archbishop Söderblom. The strong square man with his flowing blonde hair can hardly wait; he follows immediately after the interpreter of the English Bishop, and hardly has he climbed the pulpit than he starts mightily, speaking in a completely free manner in German, although this is after all to him a foreign language. One hardly feels it as foreign, because he masters the Biblical word better than most Allemands. The voice is light yet strong and allowing for variations of nuances. It can beat against the pillar opposite with a mighty roar, and change into the finest piano, without one word being incomprehensible. This man has the inner fire of a leader and commands supremely all means of rhetorical art. The climax he forms according to his will almost imperiously.

'We shall now sing the Luther lied'—and then with a threatening movement in the direction of the organ—'but straight away, without prelude, please!' One understands what he wants. The whole congregation rises and sings standing, as if by an inner inspiration, the great Reformer's mighty hymn of trust.[1]

Apart from Berne there were however, at least two other places in Switzerland to be considered: Dr. Keller, himself of Zürich, had for many years carried on from his home his remarkable organization of relief work, and he argued for his own town. But Söderblom, ever ready to consider and reconsider, was, even at Berne, prepared to listen to arguments in favour of Geneva, and he must have felt that the Anglo-Saxons being supported by the French-speaking members of the Continuation Committee, would in the end, insist on Geneva. He therefore characteristically anticipated this decision when writing his account of the Berne meeting: 'If one has been in Geneva, the city on the mountain, this gallant outpost of Evangelical faith, self-government and relief work, and seen the numbers of in-

---

[9] Söderblom, *Stockholm 1925* (1926), p. 896.
[1] *Der Bund* (Berne), August 29, 1926. From other sources we know that the first hymns of the evening in that Münster had given opportunities for displays of unending preludes!

ternational institutions with their headquarters there, he becomes almost converted ... The [International] Labour Office has shown strong inclination that the ecumenical Social Institute should work in immediate neighbourhood with what is already being done at Geneva.'[2]

At the meeting of the Continuation Committee at Winchester 1927, Söderblom was fully prepared to concur with the majority deciding that the headquarters should, as from 1928, be at Geneva. It was also on this occasion decided that the Institute should edit a trilingual review to be called *Stockholm*.

Totally committed as Söderblom was to his cause, he was however quite prepared to give up as soon as possible any administrative responsibility that he carried, satisfied to provide new ideas and constructive proposals instead of simply wielding the chairman's gavel. Health reasons increasingly forced him to hand over to others some of his administrative tasks in the growing organization; another reason was his literary commitments. The rub was—time. Even for Söderblom, time became an increasingly scarce commodity. After 1925, he would still gallantly exclaim: 'Time is elastic, almost anything can be fitted into it!' But as the months and years went by, he increasingly found it difficult to attend the Executive meetings. He had to rely on his Scandinavian co-workers—Bishop Ammundsen, Pastor Paul Sandegren, and Professor Runestam—to represent him. In Prague, 1928, he handed over the chairmanship to Dr. Kapler of Germany. It was not until 1930 at Chêxbres that he could again attend a 'Life and Work' executive meeting. The movement had increasingly extended its influence in Germany, and he may well have felt that it was immensely important that at this time, the end of the 1920's, this should be recognized through the transfer of leadership to his loyal and capable supporter, Dr. Kapler. Söderblom himself was on the same occasion elected Honorary Chairman.

Staff questions of the new Institute interested him. The Institute at first consisted of two parts, Dr. Keller's central bureau for Relief of the Evangelical Churches of Europe, *and* the Institute. With the new ecumenical headquarters placed in Switzerland, Söderblom entertained the hope that at least one Swedish co-worker of his would serve on the emerging secretariat. Before going to the meeting at Berne in 1926, he approached Dr. Kapler with a plan by which Dr. Keller's Central Bureau at Zürich would be supplemented by a

---

[2] Söderblom, *Stockholm, 1925*, pp. 907–908.

triumvirate for the Ecumenical Institute, with a German, an English-
man, and a Swede, on the staff.[3]

We must pause here to consider Söderblom's Swedish staff for his
international work from about 1925 onwards. We underline the
adjective 'Swedish', as we cannot in this connexion do more than
allude to the ever increasing network of contacts abroad, with A.
Keller in Geneva, E. Stange in Leipzig, H. Atkinson in New York,
and others. For the Stockholm conference we stressed Brilioth's
role, both for the British contacts and with regard to general planning. But in 1925 Brilioth moved to Turku (Åbo) in Finland as a
professor of Church History. Of course Söderblom's contacts with his
son-in-law were still very effective, particularly as Brilioth was appointed to the Swedish delegation for Lausanne.

Yet, for the day-to-day work Söderblom had now to rely on other
Swedes. Paul Sandegren became closely associated with Söderblom as
from the Stockholm Meeting. A former missionary to South India he
had a wide international horizon. He was sent by Söderblom on two
missions in 1926 and 1927 to the Churches in Lithuania, a difficult
task handled with competence. Paul Sandegren's Asia background
made him a spokesman for the formation of a Section V in the
Life and Work organization devoted to the Younger Churches. Sandegren was Söderblom's personal envoy to Jerusalem 1928 and to
Eisenach 1929. Söderblom persistently attempted to find a Swede as a
General Secretary of his movement, and Sandegren now seemed the
obvious name. Through Sandegren Söderblom hoped to secure a
closer link between Uppsala and his ever more internationalized
movement. He tried to persuade Sandegren to take over this work.
Nothing came of it, however; Sandegren had a rule never to accept
an offered task unless the offer was repeated twice; and Söderblom
did not try again.

In the Berne Conference, 1926, Söderblom was accompanied by C.
Bergendoff of the Augustana Synod. An American of Swedish descent, he spoke Swedish fluently and was in the Berne minutes described as a 'Swedish secretary'. A competent systematic theologian
with particular interest in the emerging Swedish theology of Lund,
Bergendoff assisted Söderblom 1925–1926. This contribution had the
extra value to Söderblom that Bergendoff was an Augustana man
and thus represented his never ceasing efforts to establish and
strengthen the contacts with the Lutheran Church in America.

---

[3] Söderblom, July 31, 1926, to H. Kapler.

We referred in another context to the role of the legation pastors as Söderblom's assistants. In the nineteen twenties Söderblom established special contact with Birger Forell, a young Swede who had become Rudolf Otto's devoted student and friend, in matters of Religionsgeschichte. It was a special satisfaction to Söderblom that in 1930 he could induct Forell as Swedish pastor in Berlin. Forell had already at this time a wide and strong net of contacts with progressive and radical-social elements in Germany. In the perspective of later history it proved to be significant that Söderblom in 1930 could place Forell in the German capital. Long after Söderblom's death Birger Forell demonstrated that practical Christianity in the most difficult and sometimes dangerous situations, in war and in prisoners of war camps, which seemed so consonant with Söderblom's own intentions.

Through his son-in-law, Professor of Ethics Runestam, Söderblom had come into contact with a promising young Uppsala theologian, Nils Ehrenström. He persuaded him to become assistant in the Ecumenical Institute in Geneva from 1930, and Söderblom had thus found his Swedish link with the Institute. To his regular work at Uppsala Söderblom could in 1923 call a young Swedish pastor Folke Palmgren as private Secretary. Palmgren had come into international work through connexions with Hellerström in London. In 1926, Palmgren was succeeded by Nils Karlström, later to become an acknowledged authority on the history of the ecumenical movement. These were all young men, devoted to Söderblom, inspired by him to great efforts on behalf of his cause.

A Swedish layman who gave Söderblom and his cause outstanding assistance throughout the twenties was Major Anders Sjöstedt. He was the enthusiast who had generously suggested to pay for the Conference if it were held in Uppsala or Stockholm. In the circumstances, he failed to do so, but he gave what he had: his time, his practical determination, his unlimited devotion to Söderblom.

Rome and Ecumene

If ever Söderblom's programme of Evangelic Catholicity was challenged and refuted, this was done by Rome, in newspaper articles, learned books and, finally, in Pope Pius XI's encyclical *Mortalium Animos,* of 1928. This reaction was not surprising in view of the fact that Söderblom's concept, Evangelic Catholicity, had to some extent been framed as an Evangelical alternative to the system of Rome. The operative word here is 'system'. The Rome Söderblom knew was one which had muted or cast out some of her best sons. His book 'Religionsproblemet' of 1910 was devoted to the cause and claims of that which Rome in those days condemned. Söderblom's attitude to Rome must be understood against the background of the role of the Roman Catholic Church in Western Europe in the times of Pius X, Benedict XV and Pius XI; a Church engaged in a relentless struggle against the threat of Modernism.

As Archbishop in Sweden he was sometimes confronted with less pleasing aspects of Roman propaganda. In 1923, Cardinal von Rossum, head of Propaganda, made a tour through Scandinavia and later devoted books in Dutch and German to the needs of the 'Northern Mission Fields'. The Catholic Bishops in Stockholm, A. Bitter and J. Müller had a small and scattered flock of some 5000 in the whole of Sweden to look after; sometimes they tended to be irritated by what they experienced in Sweden, where the public, Christian and agnostic alike, no matter how divided on other issues, determinedly closed the ranks in a definitive stand against the supposedly Machiavellian machinations of the Vatican. Söderblom himself particularly in the first years of the nineteen-twenties, made moves to counteract what he sensed as unwarranted Roman Catholic pressure.[1] Doing so, he felt that he opposed a harsh system, devoid of Spirit and life.

Yet, Söderblom's attitude to the Roman Catholic Church was a complex one. This is a subject for a special study which cannot be undertaken here in its entirety. It should be recalled that it was Söderblom who in 1920, in the face of determined opposition, had insisted that Rome should be invited to the conferences of his Life and Work movement. His hand was strengthened in this stand by Davidson of Canterbury, and his struggle with the problem of the Church's unity made him insist increasingly that the unity of the Church must include Rome.

It was in that spirit that on the last day of his Stockholm Conference he made his oft-quoted reference to St. Peter's absence from Stockholm. St. Paul and St. John were there; 'the third apostle,

---

[1] The little French medium school, St. Botvid's at Saltsjöbaden, initiated in 1919 (it continued until 1923), was one such measure. The idea was to provide a French-speaking school, with Protestant teachers, for girls of the nobility and families in higher income brackets.

Peter, the spokesman of the disciples still tarries'. There was sad regret in those words; yet there was hope also, 'against hope', that the three would not thus remain divided.

Söderblom was to find that 'Stockholm' was a problem to Rome, perhaps even a challenge. Two highly competent Roman Catholic studies appeared, one in French, in 1927, and the other in German, in 1929, and Söderblom made well considered comments on both. The authors were first-class theologians and churchmen. Professor Charles Journet of Fribourg (born 1891, created Cardinal in 1965) had followed the development of French-speaking Protestant theology and felt that this tended towards rationalism, an idea which he had developed in his *L'esprit du protestantisme en Suisse*, 1925. He challenged the Stockholm movement in his important book *L'Union des Eglises et le christianisme pratique* (1927)[2]. Armed with his expert knowledge of the scholastic fathers he analysed the texts and declarations of the ecumenical movement and saw them as symptoms of dangerous tendencies, closely related to modern philosophical ideas. This is how he sums up the Protestant problem and that of the modern world: 'After the theological dilemma of grace or nature, and after the philosophical dilemma of spirit or body, came the social dilemma of the individual or the collective. Protestant theologians cannot get out of these without denying Luther. This dilemma as such has gone into *Emile* and the *Social Contract*. Stockholm could not resolve it and it is just about to tear the world apart' (p. 270). After his studies of French Protestantism he had a special ear for any spiritualistic tendencies in Protestant ecclesiology, and Söderblom in his answer, challenged on this point, was prepared to give Journet a lesson in Symbolics, which was however limited to a reference to the Augsburg Confession; this in fact claimed the visibility of the Church. Therefore, the accusation of spiritualism was unfounded, as Söderblom saw it. The Stockholm Conference, he claimed, had not underestimated doctrine, worship and the Church.

Max Pribilla, Jesuit, and co-editor of the influential *Stimmen der Zeit* (1874–1956), published his book *Um Kirchliche Einheit* in 1929 after the *Mortalium Animos*. It was a solid and competent piece of work. Pribilla had apparently made a very thorough study of the

---

[2] Söderblom's answer to Journet, in *Sv. Dagbladet*, February 19 and 21, 1928. Cf. Söderblom, *Christliche Einheit!* (1928). For a recent, generous study of the Journet–Söderblom debate, see L. M. Dewailly, En artikel av Nathan Söderblom, 1928, in *Lumen* (1967), pp. 141–168.

German texts from Stockholm.[3] Söderblom appreciated the positive note in much of what Pribilla said about Stockholm, and asked himself whether the learned father's intention was to explain away some of the negative aspects of the Encyclica.

Pribilla had studied his Söderblom and attempted to understand this *complexio oppositorum*, of apparent aversion against Rome and attraction to catholicity: 'the same man who does so unmistakably reject the tiara shows on every occasion of his solemn appearance a remarkable partiality for the mitre and the crozier'.[4] He tended to interpret Söderblom in terms of an Anglican eccesiology; and claimed that Söderblom had 'the Anglican branch-theory for which he coined the expression Evangelic Catholicity'.[5] Here Pribilla has not seen the difference between the Anglican position of comprehensiveness and that of Söderblom. Söderblom emphasized the tension between the three 'ways', or 'alternatives', of unity to which he referred. On Rome's absence from Stockholm, Pribilla wrote: 'It would be difficult for Söderblom to prove that there existed between Peter on the one hand and John and Paul on the other such doctrinal differences as between Stockholm and Rome'.[6]

Söderblom was impressed by Pribilla's study. His secretary, Paul Sandegren and Pribilla established real personal contact and friendship. Söderblom took the opportunity of Pribilla's criticism for an apologia of his own ecumenical work, in a study of a hundred pages, *Pater Max Pribilla und die ökumenische Erweckung*.[7]

But to Söderblom the most eloquent argument was not intellectual refutation, but action and love. It could show in unguarded moments. One reflex can be seen in a paragraph of a letter to Dr. Kapler, the German leader. In 1928, just after the publication of the *Mortalium Animos*, Söderblom discussed with Kapler which town to choose for the ecumenical conference to be held in Germany the fol-

---

[3] Deissmann's edition of the Stockholm proceedings was Pribilla's main document. In his case, a prophecy of Deissmann's in a letter to Söderblom had obviously proved true. When Deissmann's book appeared he asked his publishers, Furche, to present a copy through Nuntius Pacelli to the Pope. Pacelli informed Furche that the Vatican could manage without this publication. Deissman's healthy reaction in his letter to Söderblom deserves to be quoted. 'A sign of the times! But, most probably also one more buyer of the book, as the Vatican Library can hardly do without it.' Deissmann, December 30, 1926, to Söderblom.
[4] Pribilla, op. cit., p. 116.
[5] Pribilla, in *Stimmen der Zeit*, 1932, p. 303.
[6] Pribilla ibid., p. 128.
[7] In *Kyrkohist. Årsskrift*, 1931, pp. 1–99.

lowing year. He had two considerations. First, a place with an Evangelical cathedral; second: 'Because in the end we want peace and concord with our Roman Catholic brethren, it would be good, perhaps, to meet in a town where the Roman Catholics are numerous and where they themselves can and must remove their prejudices.'[8]

Lausanne, 1927

To Söderblom it was natural to compare Stockholm, 1925 and Lausanne, 1927. For one thing there was a great similarity of membership in both conferences. The two leaders, Brent and Söderblom, made important contributions to both; Brent had been a very loyal champion of the ideals of 'Life and Work'. Söderblom had been elected as one of the four vice presidents of Faith and Order, and at Lausanne he was made convener of the important Section VII which dealt with the Unity of Christendom and the Relation thereunto of Existing Churches. At Lausanne he could recognize all his co-workers in the ecumenical family, now engaged in 'that greatest Seminar in Symbolics which the world has ever seen'.[9]

On the other hand, there were differences between Söderblom's programme of Evangelical Catholicity and some of the dominant ideas in the Faith and Order movement. These differences were accentuated by Söderblom's own attitude in that from the outset he took for granted that Faith and Order represented that 'institutionalism' of the 'body', against which he emphasized his own 'spiritual' approach. Lausanne 1927 pointed up this misunderstanding and tension; on the other hand, one must listen carefully to the Lausanne documents in order to appreciate where the real tension lay.

Urgency was Söderblom's note for his Life and Work endeavour. Mankind that had just emerged from a World War could not wait. The Church, in order to fulfil its duty to suffering mankind, could not put off its involvement until some distant period in some unknown future.

Faith and Order seemed to be another proposition altogether. In the nature of things, the difficult theological problems which had to be faced here demanded patient deliberation over broad principles, for long periods of time. This difference in pace and temper had

---

[8] Söderblom, November 8, 1928, to H. Kapler.
[9] Söderblom 'Marginal Comments on Lausanne', *Sv. Teol. Kvartalskr.*, 1927, p. 336.

constituted the essence of Söderblom's answer to Bishop Anderson at the Uppsala meeting in 1919. This was the reason why the two movements must carry on along different lines, even though the ultimate goal was the same.

This interpretation of the difference between the two movements was accepted by most Church leaders,by Brent, Gardiner and other officers of the Faith and Order movement, engaged in the preparations of the World Conference, the date of which was set for 1927. To this end, it was felt that the Agenda of that conference should be kept flexible. Lausanne should be a 'conference for its own sake, without any suggestion of coming to an agreement or attempting to do so'. Ralph W. Brown, Gardiner's successor as secretary of the movement, agreed that the programme be as wide and as flexible as possible. He knew that that was what people wanted. 'They are fed up with ready-made solutions. So am I.'[10]

In preparation for the conference, a Subjects Committee was appointed, with a Bishop from distant Bombay as convener. Through him, to the surprise of almost everybody, a new dynamic was introduced into the calm and leisurely atmosphere. Palmer, as must perhaps be pointed out, was of course not just any 'overseas bishop'. He held a central position in the Anglican communion. More than anybody else he had been responsible for the Lambeth Appeal of 1920, and in Asia he was emerging as the theologian of the scheme of Church unity in South India. For Bishop Palmer would not accept the idea that the movement should leave the reunion issue alone. That view, he said with a note of urgency which seemed to herald Bishop Azariah's great and well-known utterance at Lausanne, 'may be true and important to America, but no-one would go on with the World Conference if it were true of the whole world. . . . In India the desire for corporate unity is urgent'.[1]

Palmer's view influenced the planning and the agenda of Lausanne to a much higher degree than is commonly realized. Through him, and his dynamic team of South India Churchmen, the scope of the Lausanne Conference was greatly modified. It could not be helped that there was also, because of this, a certain amount of confusion about the purpose of the Conference; and this explains something of the drama at Lausanne. In a conference where Western leaders thought in terms of long-range and slow-moving delibera-

---

[10] Faith and Order Secretariat. Memorandum prepared by Bishop E. J. Palmer, June 30, 1925.
[1] Ibid.

tions, this pressure from the Church in Asia admitted a new current of vibrant urgency. Yet in retrospect, the Asian Church was not satisfied with Lausanne. 'Lausanne was a conference of old men representing the old churches of the West.'[2]

Söderblom found himself in the limelight of the drama at Lausanne and this illuminated a problem of what one could call 'apparent *versus* actual issues' at Lausanne and in the ecumenical movement in general in the nineteen-twenties. To some, the tension at Lausanne appeared to be one of Catholics vs. Evangelicals; to others, Ecclesiastical Isolationism vs. a demand for Intercommunion as a manifestation of spiritual unity. Söderblom himself added his interpretation. Thinking in terms of his antinomy soul-body, he felt that the real issue, the dividing line at Lausanne,was 'between faith *and* order, however startling this may sound'.[3]

In the perspective of later developments, it is possible that the *actual* issue, at that very first world conference on Faith and Order, lay deeper than that. It was the problem of understanding, of the means of communication and of a common language, between traditions so long divided from, and unknown to one another. It was also a question of loyalties. Some of the members of the Conference discovered that the very confrontation with other traditions brought a new awareness of the riches in their own ecclesiastical heritage. Yet, as the ecumenical meeting with others made vivid the sense of confessional loyalty, there was also the question whether ultimate loyalty was with tradition and confession or with Christ.

In an earlier context we pointed out that in the preparations for Stockholm, 1925, Söderblom felt he had to give special attention to what was called 'the European points of view'. The nineteen-twenties constituted an early attempt at ecumenical encounter. The majority of delegates to the conferences at Stockholm and at Lausanne, 1927, met for the first time with representatives of other Churches, speaking other languages, and had to adjust themselves accordingly.

Söderblom, himself multilingual and enjoying this faculty, felt that some of his best and most valued friends in the North and in Central Europe, were hampered and tongue-tied because of this problem of language. With Söderblom this concern for language formed one element in his characteristic concept of 'Evangelical Catholicity'. His concept was of a wider and more elastic unity of

---

[2] Tubbs, *Lausanne and S. Indian Unity Proposals* (1928), p. 4.
[3] Söderblom, 'Marginal Comments on Lausanne'.

the Church, a unity which definitely and deliberately was not uniform. Within this framework he wanted to provide room for a variety of distinctive and linguistic expressions. Bishop Ostenfeld regarded him as protagonist for the interests of the smaller nations: Söderblom had of course stressed his concern for them throughout his tenure of office.

He was thus somewhat wary of a tendency towards Anglo-American preponderance in the debates, and this conditioned his standpoint.

He discussed this problem with the Swedish delegation at Lausanne. Including such names as Aulén, Brilioth, Nygren, all young men between thirty-five and fifty years old, this delegation was not, perhaps, without distinction. Particularly through Anders Nygren there was a natural affinity with the Lutheran groups from other countries, not least the German-speaking theologians who, as was the case with Nygren, now for the first time appeared on the ecumenical scene.[4]

Together with Bishop Headlam, Söderblom had to speak on the theme of Section VII. While Sections I–VI dealt with fundamental themes of Christian Faith and ecclesiastical order, Section VII focussed on the practical issue, how to visualize the unity of Christendom and the relation thereunto of existing Churches. In his Bampton lectures, *The Doctrine of the Church and Christian Reunion,* 1920, Headlam had drawn what was virtually a blue-print of the building for the following two decades. He had greatly contributed to Lambeth, 1920, and now at Lausanne he summed up some of his conclusions: a unity of faith, in the sacraments and in the ministry. But, he underlined, as and while the Church was divided, all existing orders were in some measure irregular, and the future united Church which he visualized, had to allow for the greatest possible diversity, for freedom and toleration.

Söderblom's address on that same occasion was not perhaps one of his most notable ecumenical pronouncements. His lecture, like other addresses, had been circulated well beforehand, but Söderblom felt that the better to present the Lutheran view, he had to make a last minute effort and prepare a new version. In that big gathering the difference between the printed text and the *viva voce* address

---

[4] The Swedish group also included some of Söderblom's faithful lieutenants in his daily work: H. Neander with his invaluable Orthodox contacts; H. Bildt, Söderblom's envoy friend from Cairo; Paul Sandegren of South India; and Major Sjöstedt.

was confusing. His address, a variation on his theme 'institution and Spirit' included an attempt to prove, or illustrate, the claims for the succession of the Swedish episcopacy, 'a stronger and more faithful continuity with the institutions of the Church of the Middle Ages than any other non-Roman section of Western Christendom'.[5]

With this illustration, clothed in terms which were altogether consonant with the main thesis of his own ecclesiology, he reiterated arguments from his programmatic writings of 1915. His ecclesiological vision, international as it was in scope and universal in intent, was nonetheless anchored in the concrete Swedish province, 'our peculiar situation and doctrine in the Church of Sweden'.[6] This was not without its charm, but just as obviously, at Lausanne, it had its limitations. For while some of his listeners were concerned with an urgent request for advice for shaping the United Church of the future, and were impatient that Lausanne seemed unready to any such advice, Söderblom seemed pre-occupied with the past tense—AD 1531 and 1571 in distant Sweden; an example, perhaps, of the proverbial traditionalism of the national Churches in Europe.

There was a paradox, or a touch of irony perhaps, in Söderblom's position at Lausanne, for while 'Stockholm' spelt urgency and immediacy, here at Lausanne he struck a different note.

In his own way, Söderblom at Lausanne came to feel that, as first steps to that far distant goal set by Faith and Order, two things were urgently needed, and he insisted on both. Perhaps there was a tension between them, but not in Söderblom's view. As he insisted on both intercommunion *and* on the formation of confessional groupings, he was convinced that they supported each other.

He compared Lausanne and Stockholm, and thought of the Communion Service at his own Stockholm Conference. To a very large extent, that act of worship had been made possible through his own ecumenical activity, his own 'Faith and Order' activity over many years. The situation at Lausanne was different. In commenting on the situation, Söderblom said:

In Stockholm we did not hesitate. We did not ask anybody. Should not the children of God have a right also in action around the Table of the Lord, to prophesy about that United Church, even if the Churches as such had a long way to go to the goal? Holy Communion in the Engelbrekt Church in Stockholm, August 23, 1925, became the high spot to date of the ecumenical movement.[7]

---

[5] H. N. Bate, *Lausanne, 1927,* p. 328.
[6] Ibid., p. 330.
[7] Söderblom, Marginal Comments on Lausanne, op. cit., pp. 373–374.

At Lausanne, as guests of the Evangelical National Church of Canton Vaud, they should take part in the local communion service. He added that many Lutherans, particularly from Scandinavia, communicated in that Reformed service of Holy Communion but he also registered some of the Churches that did not see fit to take part.

He told Lausanne:

That unity of faith which we experience deeply also here, ... must be realised in worship and Church order. There is little use to speculate about the forms of a United Church before we have attained the *conditio sine qua non* for such unity, I mean fellowship at the Lord's Table.[8]

His other effort, the formation of a Lutheran confessional group at Lausanne, with a particular declaration as to the understanding of the decisions of the conference, appeared to be concerned with confessional interests, and Söderblom himself felt that he represented this concern. He explained his initiative in this way. As he noticed the reactions of his Swedish colleagues and those of other continentals, he found that in and through the confrontation with different traditions, they discovered 'their deep and essential fellowship as Evangelical–Lutheran Christians'. The divided mind about the purpose of the Conference had its effect on the German and Scandinavian members. To them the original concept of the Conference, as suggested by Brent, Brown, and others, with its more provisional character, would have been congenial. Siegmund-Schultze of Germany, in his interpretation of the Lausanne Conference, spoke in criticism of 'the whip which at any cost wanted results'.[9] This was how he felt the effect of Palmer's firm grip and determination to steer the Conference to certain, definite practical results for the solution of urgent reunion problems in the world.

This, Söderblom felt, was driving a theological conference too quickly. Faith and Order problems had to be allowed more time and consideration. Together with others he made the move of calling together the Lutherans at Lausanne. This group prepared a separate Lutheran declaration which was announced to the Conference. It included the following:

As Evangelical Lutherans we feel it to be our sacred duty to labour for the unity of the Church in faith and hope and, especially in this day of dire need, in serving love to mankind. Of course, according to our Con-

---

[8] H. N. Bate, *Lausanne*, p. 322.
[9] *Die Eiche*, 1927, p. 379.

fessions it is not necessary to the unity of the Church that human traditions, rites or ceremonies, should be everywhere alike, but this unity consists in agreement concerning the doctrine of the Gospel and the administration of the sacraments.

To give accurate expression to the existing spiritual unity is, of course,
possible only in the direction pointed out by the Ecumenical Creeds. But
we question whether it is possible, and comports with the dignity of this
Conference and is worthy of Christendom, to announce at once as finalities
the formulations here made on fundamental principles of faith and order.

It is therefore our judgement that the Conference should in its public
proclamation strongly express the great significance of this gathering, that
deep spiritual unity which we recognize with gratitude to God, the serious
will to unity which prevails, and the value and necessity of thorough and
fraternal discussion in continuance of the labours here begun.

Accordingly no final vote should be taken on the propositions formulated here. They should be added to the proclamation as material for
further consideration.[1]

As we have already mentioned, it can be argued that Söderblom
was in fact pleading here not so much for separate confessional action, as for an opportunity for the non-English speaking group to
express its view.

This Lutheran intervention, which in the perspective of history
may be regarded as possibly the first embryo of confessional groupings in the organized ecumenical movement, led to a chain-reac-
tion in the conference. The leaders of the conference handled, or
sidestepped, the situation with great skill. Bishop Palmer, more eager
to make the conference a success than to insist for the time being on
his own particular approach, drew up a preamble for the Conference
resolutions, and he had Lutheran advice for his formula. With a
peculiarly Palmerian touch, the Churches were required 'to find the
truth as it is in God's mind' and to realize that the resolutions were
'subject-matter for the consideration of our respective churches'.[2]

In a setting the ethos of which was to a large extent determined
by Anglo-American procedure, Söderblom was concerned with pro-
viding Continental Christianity with an opportunity to be heard.
In a Swedish article he commented on his move in this manner:

To numerous Westerners, especially to one or other among the American
Episcopalians, these claims of Evangelical Lutheranism to be heard, was

---

[1] H. N. Bate, *Lausanne*, 1927, p. 373.
[2] H. N. Bate, op. cit., pp. 375-376. The Lutheran intervention led to similar statements from the Orthodox Church, and other churches and societies.

probably news, a surprise which may have caused a, as I hope, transient, disaffection.

Söderblom discussed the problem with Yngve Brilioth, his son-in-law, who analysed the situation in a rather trenchant manner:

The preponderance of the English language and of American parliamentary procedure made it sometimes rather difficult for those who did not speak English to get a real hearing. Oh, those discussions of procedure, in which Americans delight! These are, I think, mainly the facts behind the Lutheran declaration ...

In his Swedish comment, Brilioth quotes the episcopal convener of his group who would treat the humblest interventions in an unofficial group discussion with a solemn: 'Do you put that as a motion?'[3] Scandinavians and Continentals, in their simplicity, were not yet used to this rarefied atmosphere. In the nineteen-twenties they were still in primary classes of ecumenical education.

There was a complex set of reasons behind this seemingly confessional initiative on Söderblom's part, possibly not all of these as confessional as they might appear, but it must be noted that at Lausanne also, Söderblom the ecumenist made that Lutheran emphasis which in 1923 had taken the Federal Council in New York by surprise, and which, at that same time, contributed to establishing his position in Germany.

At the same time Söderblom obviously represented a tendency of his own in the Lutheran world, a tendency which some of the leaders of the Lutheran World Convention found difficult to understand or accept; he was all the more gratified by the understanding which some of the Danish bishops, particularly Ostenfeld and Ammundsen, showed for his standpoint.[4]

The separate Lutheran statement was read to the conference on the morning of August 17. That same day, Söderblom as convener of Section VII, presented the report on the Unity of Christendom

---

[3] Brilioth's contribution to E. S. Wood's book, *Lausanne 1927*, pp. 157–158. Brilioth's name does not appear in this connexion, but he has later stated that this 'Lutheran' view was his own. Cf. Brilioth, in *Sv. Teol. Kvartalskrift*, 1928, p. 298–299.

[4] In preparation for the Lutheran World Convention, Copenhagen 1929, some of the organizers wished to have Söderblom's name excluded from the programme. Bishop Ostenfeld threatened that he would go on a visitation tour to Greenland if Söderblom was not accepted. In the end Söderblom did attend the Copenhagen Convention, but greatly handicapped by ill-health. Interview, P. Sandegren.

and the Relation thereto of Existing Churches. It consisted of four parts, of which Söderblom himself felt particularly responsible for the first on Fellowship in Life and Work, including Talbot's famous formula, and the fourth on Completed Fellowship. Number two on Fellowship in Faith and Order, written, as it seems, by Dr. D'Arcy, Archbishop of Armagh, consisted of a somewhat modified 'Lambeth Quadrilateral', the modification being the insistence on liberty of interpretation. Number three had suggestions as to co-operation of Christians in each place, or 'in the same community'.

Söderblom knew that Palmer wanted the conference to visualize the Church of the Future, 'to draw a picture of the united Church'. This, he felt, he was not prepared to attempt. 'We abstained from drawing the outlines of the future Church, and instead tackled reality. We made our work more difficult by dealing with the actual task at hand', he said. A detailed drawing would confine the Churches to certain preconceived structures, but what if they preferred their own 'home customs', Söderblom asked. He went on: 'Certain illusions were crushed at Lausanne'.

Whatever the reason may have been, there was determined opposition to the resolution of Section VII from a vocal Anglo-Catholic minority. Bishop Gore struck the note and the others persisted. Bishops Manning and Morehouse took the line, according to which, in their Church review, *The Living Church,* this was a 'Pan-Protestant report', prepared by 'the Protestant element under the leadership of the Archbishop of Uppsala'.

Morehouse suggested that his Anglo-Catholic argument provoked 'the immediate feeling of rage' among the great 'Protestant majority in the house'.[5] Söderblom did not take this criticism with the light touch which he often managed to apply, in fact he was irritated by this particular opposition. His letters and articles contain reactions to this episode which we do not need to repeat here.

When a new draft was presented two days later, at the plenary session, Söderblom had already left. His departure was widely noticed, and various comments were made. As to his departure, Söderblom had in fact, as early as May 17, in a letter to Garvie, stated that he would have to leave Lausanne on August 15.[6] We hardly

---

[5] *Living Church,* Sept. 10, 1927.
[6] Söderblom, May 17, 1927, to Dr. Garvie, in parcel 'Faith and Order, Preparatory to Lausanne, 1927', Garvie papers, New College Archives, London. As far as we know there has been no earlier reference to this fact of the Söderblom letter to Garvie.

need to add that Garvie was not of course just any ordinary member at Lausanne, but he was, in Bishop Brent's words, 'Captain Garvie who brought the ship of the conference safely into port'.[7] This was an episode, but not without its effect on Söderblom, for it made him emphasize even more than before, a 'spiritual' approach over against an 'institutional'. It made him that more radical in his emphasis on the Spirit, just as his attitude on Peace had in the same period become more radical.

In concluding his Marginal Notes on Lausanne, he felt that the meeting had corroborated his view: 'In the Spirit I have seen a glimpse of the United Church, a distant goal from which Christendom cannot turn away, and which it may not neglect without thereby denying its Christian faith.'

Integrating the Ecumenical Movements!

In 1928, after the Faith and Order Conference at Lausanne, and the World Missionary meeting at Jerusalem, Söderblom was again prepared to review the whole ecumenical landscape. The various movements were gaining a certain momentum, but there were also dangers of overlapping and competition. At Berne, in 1926, Söderblom had together with his co-workers tried to define anew the relationship between his own movement and the World Alliance.

Some people may have had reason to feel that Söderblom himself had his share in these complications. About 1920, he had tended to draw the lines very sharply between his own organization and the others, in order to provide ground for the newcomer, his own Life and Work movement, and a platform for the particular concerns which only this agency seemed to consider. In May 1928 Söderblom had however prepared a blue print of an integration of these movements. He decided to address a letter on the whole problem to Archbishop Germanos. Germanos was the chairman that year of the Stockholm Continuation Committee. Moreover, as the great Orthodox spokesman in the ecumenical movement, he had a special standing and authority. Söderblom's letter reads:[1]

---

[7] Bishop Brent's words in H. N. Bate, *Lausanne 1927*, p. 441.
[1] We know the letter from a copy to the General Secretary of the Life and Work movement, H. Atkinson. Söderblom, May 14, 1928, to Atkinson: 'I write at the same time the following words to our President this year.' Hitherto we have sought in vain for reactions to this letter from Söderblom.

In reading the different documents after Stockholm in Lausanne and after Mortalium Animos, one question comes on me again and again. The really ecumenical initiative for a new epoch of cooperation and unity in the Church and in Christendom came from the Ecumenical Patriarchate in Constantinople, 1920, that is certainly from you [Archbishop Germanos]. Would not the time be ripe now for you to propose such a federation or league of Churches? You have the kernel in the Continuation Committee over which you preside yourself. Besides we have the World Alliance, the International Missionary Council, which has become, I am glad to say, eager to have also the Orthodox Church represented. Further, there is the Continuation Committee of Faith and Order. Can you not propose to the Executive Committee on Life and Work to invite a few men to come together and propose lines and rules for such a federation? In several cases, as with regard to yourself, the same man represents his Church in two or three or even in some cases in all four of those strivings and organizations for cooperation and unity. Such a federation would of course be most clearly distinguished from a real Church Unity, a reunited Church, an organic Unity, but as you said at Lausanne, and as you have explained on different occasions, federation is the first step and a necessary step. If such a committee could be entrusted in Prague with proposing and outlining the scheme of an Ecumenical Church Federation, it is not excluded that the Ecumenical Patriarchate of Constantinople and Christendom can celebrate in 1930 the pastoral letter of 1920 on a league of Churches, with the formation of such a Koinonia.

  2: Would it be wise to have, besides the representative or representatives of each Nation in our Continuation Committee on Life and Work, a Committee in each country, and in each denomination or national section of a denomination, for studying and advancing the sacred cause of Life and Work? We are contemplating here in Sweden the plan of enlarging the existing Swedish Committee of the World Alliance for the promotion of the program of Life and Work. Would it not be wise to recommend the creation of such commissions and to recommend to them the propagation and the study of the Message of Stockholm? It is a pity that that message was not in the hands of the members of the Jerusalem Conference, since the Jerusalem Conference was also fully aware of the necessity for the Christian Church to take up seriously the religious and moral problems involved in the industrial and social situation.

  3: Nothing more momentous has happened after Stockholm and Life and Work than the most gladdening idea of the Jerusalem Meeting of the International Missionary Council to create an Institute for Industrial and Social Research, especially for non-Christian lands. This is a corroboration of our decision in Stockholm. But it would be a too Protestant overlapping to have two such social institutes. The question came up late in Jerusalem, and Mr Sandegren and yourself and others mentioned of course our Institute at Geneva. It is of course absolutely necessary to

combine both, which will make both stronger. Would it not be wise to
invite a few persons from the Jerusalem Meeting to the Meeting of the
Executive Committee on Life and Work in Prague? – – –

Besides those, of course Mr. Oldham and the Bishop of Manchester,
vice President in Jerusalem, would be most valuable. Would it not be
wise to contemplate a joint Committee from Life and Work and the International Missionary Council for an enlarged Institute? Because the social industrial problems are just about the same everywhere in the world,
and can not be divided among two Christian social institutes.

This letter is of great interest. It was directed to Germanos, and
Söderblom hoped to have this plan of his presented by the Orthodox
leader. Germanos had no axe to grind nor any particular vested
interest in any of the mentioned movements. For Germanos to take
the initiative for this important move might be a stimulus towards
increased involvement of the Orthodox in the total ecumenical endeavour, and this had always been a main concern with Söderblom.
He mentioned the encyclical Mortalium Animos, which had just
been published, and Söderblom was preparing to refute it. Having
been branded there as one of the 'Pan-christiani' Söderblom may
have regarded it as all the more necessary to underline the role of
the Orthodox in the ecumenical movement. Apart from these considerations, there was a characteristic personal trait in Söderblom's
action to engage others, and even to fall back on the words of others:
we recall that such had been the case with his well known quotations
from Bishop Talbot and Dr. Kapler.

In its broad outlines this plan of Söderblom's, foreshadowing as
early as 1928 an integrated World Council was a great document, a
testament bequeathed by the ailing leader to the whole of the ecumenical movement.

'Ultimately, life, work, faith and order are expressions of an existing spiritual unity and ... each requires the other for its complete
fruition.'

This was his conclusion as at the end of 1928 he gave further
thought to his grand plan of an overall ecumenical integration. On
February 1st, 1929, he was prepared to send a more detailed scheme
to the Ecumenical Institute in Geneva, addressed to Dr. Adolf Keller. We quote the relevant parts of it in full as it reflects Söderblom's
wide vision of the ecumenical family; one notices that he reiterated
his own idea from 1919–20 of special consideration of the traditional
offices in the Church.

How shall such a free Commission of the Churches be organized? It is self-evident that it should not have the power to commit the respective Churches to anything without an independent decision in each case by each Church.

The history of the Church gives the idea of combining certain eminent trusted positions in the Church with personalities chosen ad hoc. It is also desirable that such a joint commission or council should not have too many members.

Should not the following services and appointments in the Church of God be represented as such?

1: For the *Orthodox* Church in the first place: The Ecumenical Patriarch of Constantinople or his deputy.

2: The Orthodox Church has three chief groups, the Greek Church, represented by the Ecumenical Patriarch, then the Balkan peoples and the by far greatest section of the Orthodox Church, the Orthodox Church of Russia. In the second place a representative of, not Greek, Orthodox Christianity in the *Balkan,* eventually the Patriarchs (primates) of Bucarest, Sofia, Belgrad in turn.

3: The Patriarch of Russia or his deputy.

4: The President of the Federal Council of the Churches of Christ in *America* or his deputy.

5: Another Churchman from *U.S.A.,* representing some large and important group, e.g. Methodism or Baptism or some other denomination not represented by the President of the Federal Council or his deputy.

6: For the *Anglican* Communion the *Archbishop of Canterbury* or his deputy.

7: In view of the importance and widespread membership of the *Anglican* communion one might contemplate another representative of Anglicanism, the *Archbishop of York* or another in Great Britain, Ireland, in the Episcopal Church of U.S.A. or in the East.

8: *The President* des Evangelischen Kirchenausschusses in *Germany* or his deputy.

9: Evangelic Lutheranism being the most numerous communion in the West after the Roman Catholic Church, it will be necessary to have also a representative of *Evangelic Lutheranism* in Germany, e.g. the Bishop of Saxony (Saxony being the largest Evangelic Lutheran Church in Germany) or another German Churchman elected in due manner.

10: *The Northern Church in Europe,* Denmark, Iceland, Norway, Sweden, Finland, Esthonia, Latvia, some 18–19 millions represented either by one Churchman elected by the primates of these countries, or the Bishops of Själland, Oslo, Upsala, Åbo, Reval and Latvia or their deputies in turn.

11: To represent Evangelic *Latin* Christianity le Président de la Fédération des Eglises Protéstantes de France with four substitutes:

a: A Churchman from French Switzerland, b: The Moderator of the

Waldensians, c: a representative of Belgian Protestantism and d: of Protestants in Spain and Portugal.

12: Evangelic Christendom of *Slave* nationalities from Poland, Czechoslovakia, Russia, Serbia etc. either alternating or elected in some way, (See Continuation Committee in Life and Work.)

13: The President of the Hervormde Kerk in *Holland* or his deputy alternating with the President of the Church Federation or his deputy in *Switzerland.*

14: A representative of *Hungarian* Protestantism e.g. the Evangelic Bishop of Budapest, the reformed Bishop of Budapest, and the Curator of the Helvetic Hungarian Church in Roumania in turn.

Those groups, 11, 13 and 14, represent a baptized membership and a population several times inferior to groups 1, 2, 3, 4, 5, 6, 7, 8, 9, 10. But it is important to have also those smaller groups directly represented in such a joint Commission.

15: A representative from Evangelic Christendom in the *far East,* China, Corea, Japan.

16: A representative from *India.*

Then there ought to be one General secretary from America, at present Dr. Atkinson, and another from Europe, perhaps from the largest Evangelic Church Federation in Europe, that is in Germany, Dr. Erich Stange.

That joint Commission or Ecumenical Council should then act on the following lines with the eventual consent of those organizations, and divide the personel and the tasks in clear and due manner.

A. The World Alliance: for Church and International peace.

B. The Life and Work: for the application of Christian ethics on social, economic and other problems.

C. The Diakonia, that is the Internationale Verband für Innere Mission und Diakonie.

D. The inter-church Relief work, admirably organized and led by Dr. Keller.

E. If, according to the wish expressed several times by the Preparatory Committee on Faith and Order, also that movement brought into existence by the Protestant Episcopal Church in America ought to be in any way organically enlistened in this joint Commission of the Churches it should of course have an independent position and role of its own.

a: There is no doubt anywhere about the fact that cooperation (federation) and the One United Church are too different things to be kept clearly separate from each other.

b: There seems also to be a fairly universal agreement on the persuasion uttered by the Encyclical of the Ecumenical Patriarchate of 1920, by the entire Orthodox delegation at Lausanne and by others, that Federation is a necessary and useful preparatory step towards Reunion.

With these far-reaching proposals, Söderblom had helped to suggest the foundation for the important reconstruction of the Continuation Committee at the Chêxbres meeting, September, 1930. A permanent body was now formed, under the name of the Universal Christian Council for Life and Work, most often referred to as the Ecumenical Council. It was built of five sections, of which the fifth was new and identical with the sphere of the Younger Churches. The co-operation of Söderblom with Paul Sandegren, himself for many years missionary in South India, and the insistence of Sandegren on this extension, had been of particular importance for the change. To Söderblom, the meeting at Chêxbres became his last contact with his brethren in the international ecumenical fellowship. As he celebrated Holy Communion in the little village church of Chêxbres, assisted by his great friend in the Oikumene, Wilfred Monod, he could not but be aware of the eschatological perspective of the Common Meal.

The Primate of Sweden

After 1925, Söderblom's position in the Swedish Church and in Swedish society was markedly different from what it had been a decade earlier. When, at the time of his appointment to Uppsala, certain Church papers and reviews expressed dismay, Anna Söderblom was shaken and seemed to take the adverse criticism seriously. But the Archbishop quieted her. 'Don't worry, in ten years time nobody will regret this'. He was right. After 1925, his unique position in the Swedish nation was established.

The attitudes to his contemporary, Hjalmar Branting, the Socialist Prime Minister had gone through a similar change: first rejection and eventually, in E. Wigforss's words, 'a measure of pride at the country's representative in international deliberations'.[1] The same applied to Söderblom. Stockholm 1925, and Söderblom's role in the ecumenical movement contributed to this new and general appreciation which he met. The press had a decisive influence here. He had always handled the press with care and generosity, and the journalists responded in kind. As he spoke in 1928 on 'the apostolate of the Press' and declared that if Tertullian had been alive today, he would have been a journalist, he won many of these influential men and women for himself. In Sweden, *Svenska Dagbladet* in particular supported him. A woman, Märta Lindquist, known as *Quelqu'une,* devoted a great part of her time and talent to an interpretation of the Archbishop's comings and goings.

---

[1] E. Wigforss, *Ur mina minnen 1964,* p. 247.

In the influential *Dagens Nyheter,* Ivar Norberg, an old research student of Söderblom's, of the History of Religions, handled Church matters; he had an unlimited admiration for his teacher and friend, and never failed to say so. In Eric Rinman's *Stockholms–Tidningen,* Söderblom as Archbishop had a particularly devoted and faithful supporter. Rinman was himself a historian of the Harald Hjärne school, and his values and attitudes were closely related to those of Söderblom.

A remarkable measure of Söderblom's ever increasing influence in Sweden was the way in which Arthur Engberg, editor of *Social Demokraten,* from having been a resolute opponent became an admirer. We saw how in 1919–1920, Engberg and Söderblom were engaged in a tough struggle over the Church–State relationship. Engberg became impressed by Söderblom's work for peace and Church unity. Of all the obituaries published after Söderblom's death, Engberg's in *Social-demokraten* (July 13, 1931) was possibly the most eloquent, and certainly the most moving.

But even the press was not unanimous in its praise. The greatest journalist of them all, Torgny Segerstedt, turned the shafts of his biting irony against the ecumenical endeavours of the Archbishop. The psychology of this relationship is difficult to understand and there are, in Sweden, a number of alternative interpretations of Segerstedt's attitude to Söderblom: a) Segerstedt, the Liberal politician connected with patrician Gothenburg, disdainful of the Labour-sympathising archbishop, or b) a difficult relationship of two ex-professors of Religionsgeschichte, each scorning the other for having forsaken his first love for the Church or the press, *or* again c) Segerstedt having abandoned his Christian faith and become an agnostic, bound by a complex feeling of love-hatred for the Archbishop; and finally of course, d) the *right* explanation, not yet revealed! Segerstedt had heard a rumour that Söderblom had been mentioned as a suitable candidate for the Nobel Peace Prize. This proved, Segerstedt said, not without a certain degree of condescension, to what an extent people's imagination had been stirred by the fact that the Church, too, just like socialists, lawyers or seamen, could organise an international conference. But, he declared, this admiration was hollow, for Stockholm 1925 was silent about 'the life nerve of Christianity, its faith': What importance have economic and social factors as compared with the question of eternal salvation and eternal damnation'?[2]

---

[2] T. Segerstedt, *Händelser och Människor* (1926), p. 112.

Different interpretations can be placed on Segerstedt's statement, but it impressed both his own Liberals, who liked to believe that the Church belonged once and for all to a past which had been left behind, and some of the diehard church people in Western Sweden to whom Söderblom was a Liberal in a bishop's cope.

In the Swedish Church the year 1925 marked the end of an epoch in that Bishop G. Billing of Lund passed away. Söderblom had always referred to him as 'the Patriarch of the North'. In the Bishops' Meeting and the Kyrkomöte, Söderblom was now incontestably the leader; too rapid in his movements perhaps, himself to be referred to as a 'patriarch', but despite this, the leader. Söderblom's role in his Church could best be interpreted in terms of 'innovation'. In order to show this in detail we would need to know more about the place of the Church in Swedish society 1919–1939, in the years of transition from 'poor' Sweden to 'welfare' Sweden. This is a study in itself which we have not been able to undertake here. Suffice it to say that undoubtedly one innovation performed by Söderblom was to open up the new international perspective for the Church. It is difficult to define to what extent this new dimension was part of a general internationalization of Scandinavia at the time and in what degree this was due to the vision and example of the ecumenical Archbishop. It is, however, safe to state in general terms that a new generation of Swedish Churchmen emerged, clergy and laymen alike, with a new awareness of the international responsibility of the Church, and this was largely Söderblom's doing. That he had opponents among the die-hards does not alter this general statement of fact.

At the Kyrkomöte in 1929 an important proposal, called 'the Bishops' motion' was presented and signed by virtually all the bishops. This was a move towards a greater measure of freedom for the Church. The motion was written by Bishop Einar Billing (together with Edv. Rodhe and S. Stadener). But Billing felt that he was commissioned by Söderblom, and that he had the enthusiastic support of the Archbishop. The very fact of this move on the part of the Bishops was a demonstration of a new assurance and perhaps even of a measure of self-esteem on the part of the Swedish Church. It was welcomed with particular interest by the Swedish Free Churches and furthered the rapprochement between them and the Church of Sweden. In his last years Söderblom increasingly emphasized the importance of these contacts.

'The Living God'

At home, as Pro-chancellor of Uppsala University, Söderblom was potentially in a position of some influence and in spite of all else that engaged him he found time and energy to use it. Both as Pro-chancellor and as Archbishop, he felt it to be his duty to revive the tradition of international scholarly congresses of study and research. As Prochancellor, and particularly when he had to act for two successive Chancellors who for one reason or another could not act, he had also a good deal of general administrative oversight to exercise. Fortunately he was well served by an old friend, O. Croneborg, the Secretary of the Chancellor. Most of the time Söderblom followed Croneborg's advice, scrawling an appreciative 'Excellent!' in the margin of the secretary's memos. There were complicated matters to settle. There was the case of a chair in Psychiatry: The Royal Medical Board had nominated Docent X, but the majority of the Consistory had voted for Y., the competitor. Croneborg put up the latter name to Söderblom, who concurred with a sigh and a laconic: 'Regrettably inevitable, but crazy. Thus, *quand même, Y!, N. Sm.*' And on other occasion, again in a Medical faculty, a professor had announced a junior post before Government had given any decision as to the necessary grants, and Croneborg the civil servant objected. 'Turn a blind eye', Söderblom wrote in the margin.[1]

At a time in Swedish culture when the historical ties between Archbishop and University were about to be severed, this great Prochancellor was above all anxious to defend the University's right of self-determination.[1a] It was not surprising that when in 1927 Söderblom's friend from the Paris years, Christian Eriksson, was commissioned by the University to make a sculpture of the founder of the Uppsala University, Jacob Ulfsson (d. 1521) he should borrow Söderblom's traits for the founder's face.

In the larger field of scholarship and research, and particularly in his own part of it, the History of Religions, he saw himself as the appointed guardian of a whole academic inheritance from pre-War Europe. In 1926 he wrote to a number of European scholars of the History of Religions and approached Professor Martin P.

---

[1] F. Croneborg papers. UUB.
[1a] F. Croneborg, in *Djursholms Tidning*, July 17, 1931.

Nilsson, the well-known classics scholar in Lund, with a view to commissioning Nilsson to arrange for a Congress at Lund. Söderblom and Nilsson co-operated over the preparations for this Congress which met at Lund in 1929.[2] Söderblom was resolved to attend the Congress himself and even played with the idea that he was going to give a lecture on Olof Rudbeck's *Atland*. This was a learned seventeenth-century work, in four heavy tomes, claiming that Sweden was identical with Plato's Atlantis and the Isles of the Blest, from which all culture emanated! Söderblom was of course far from sharing old Rudbeck's fantastic claims; but he was fascinated by the brilliance of the learned Swedish author's presentation of his case. —This was part of the interest which, in the last few years of his life Söderblom could devote to early Scandinavian history, to St. Ansgar at Björkö and St. Olaf in Nidaros, and, in the last resort, to the origins of his own ancestors, tracing them back to the graves of the Iron Age. With this concern the ageing Söderblom turned to a theme which had gripped him, when as a young scholar of twenty-two he had written his very first studies, on St. Ansgar and St. Staffan.—The Congress at Lund was held, but met without Söderblom. His doctor would not allow him to attend.

Söderblom's own standpoint is evident, too, in his attitude to the attempts at a union of the religions. Of course, he held, and maintained, a generous view of the world religions. Lecturing on Luther's universal significance he would broaden the view so as to state that 'one day, the fundamental religious texts of India, China, and Japan will become as many Old Testaments for the one New Testament of mankind'.[2a] Yet, he drew a line. Two of his friends, one a German professor of this History of Religions and the other, the American General Secretary of his own Life and Work Movement were engaged in promoting union movements, enlisting the combined forces of the world religions, for the cause of peace. Rudolf Otto formed his Religiöser Menschheitsbund in 1921; Henry Atkinson used his position and influence in the richly endowed Church Peace Union for a series of conferences with very similar programmes. There were similarities between these two movements; a number of people involved in Life and Work were engaged in the one or the other of these efforts. Nevertheless there were tensions between the two; essentially because of a certain incompatibility between the

---

[2] See M. P. Nilsson papers, University Library, Lund.
[2a] Söderblom, Från Upsala till Rock Island (1924), p. 107.

American and the Continental approach: thus reminding Söderblom of similar tensions within his own movement. Both Otto and Atkinson, from their various standpoints took it for granted that Söderblom was going to join and give moral support to their respective endeavours. But Söderblom could not be drawn. While he gave Neander his blessing when he was to attend Atkinson's World Religions for Peace Conference at Geneva in 1930, he could not contemplate attending himself. He wrote to Neander: 'You must go, but I wish to die as a Lutheran.'[3] Similarly he was critical of Otto's numerous ideas, because they struck him as too syncretistic for his taste; an added reason was Otto's emphasis on what he called 'World Union of Protestantism': this approach could never attract Söderblom.

Söderblom's position in the Swedish Academy must be mentioned here however briefly. This is Sweden's most exclusive and select academy dating from 1786, and limited to eighteen members. As is well-known, this Academy is entrusted with distributing the Nobel Prize for Literature. A member of the Academy is referred to as 'one of the Eighteen' [in the Swedish Academy]. Authors, scholars, prominent civil servants are elected. Until the Second World War, the Academy would include one or two clergy. Bishop Gottfrid Billing of Lund was a Member, and so was professor W. Rudin of Uppsala (d. 1921). It is a measure of Söderblom's standing that he was elected to the Academy in 1921, succeeding Rudin. This was an honour which gave him great satisfaction. He made every effort to be present at the Thursday sessions of the Academy in Stockholm. He met there some of his most beloved friends, particularly E. A. Karlfeldt, poet and the Permanent Secretary to the Academy. While the Academy's deliberations are confidential, we make bold to say that it was most probably Söderblom who promoted Bergson's candidature for the Prize in 1928. He had corresponded with Bergson since 1909 in the hope of securing him for the Olaus Petri Lectureship at Uppsala; and when the prize was to be distributed the Academy had asked Söderblom to give the address on its behalf. He dictated his speech, looking forward to the great occasion. But it was not to be. Health considerations, firmly underlined by Anna herself, prevented him from going. Instead of the glitter and stir he had the uninspiring alternative of hearing, through the crackling headphones of a crystal set, some other voice welcoming Bergson.

---

[3] H. Neander, *Med Nathan Söderblom* (1932), p. 126.

He gave much of his remaining strength in the last years to the preparation of his Gifford Lectures. This is of course one of the most famous lectureships in the world of scholarship. Since its foundation in 1888, only one other non-Anglo-Saxon had been invited to this series. This was C. P. Tiele who in 1896 and 1898, the years when Söderblom knew him best, lectured on Elements of the Science of Religion, published under that title in two volumes (Edinburgh) 1897 and 1899. The fact that Tiele appeared in this connexion must have made the invitation particularly attractive to Söderblom when it came to him in 1928. Having edited Tiele's *Kompendium der Religionsgeschichte* in a number of new editions, he thus could follow up Tiele's work in still another way. He shared with Harald Bildt one other consideration; he wrote in September 1929:

'If it is the will of the Most-High, I would like to add to *La Vie Future* ... and *Das Werden des Gottesglaubens,* another scholarly work, an original study in English, *Basal Forms of Personal Religion*—the fruit of life-long reserach.'[4]

A French volume, a classic in German, and then, at the end of life, one in English! This was *une honnête ambition* and, as such, very human. He intended to give two series of lectures in 1931 and 1932 in two volumes; had not Tiele done this in his day, more than a generation earlier? An immense amount of material was collected for his book and he could of course to a large extent fall back upon earlier studies of his own, mostly from his creative research period 1907–1914.[5] Parts of his chapters on Buddhism, the chapters on Socrates, on the Old Testament and the final chapter on the Continued Revelation belong to this category.

For his chapter on the Religion of Incarnation he could use the address he had prepared for the Jerusalem International Missionary Conference, 1928. He had not been able to attend that conference, but the lecture was published in the *International Review of Missions*, 1928, and now together with extracts from his Lent book of 1928, presented in a new way.

The Scottish audience welcomed the Swedish archbishop and scholar with great expectations. Sometimes, in those days, the lectures tended to be somewhat specialised. Sir James Irvine is quoted

[4] Söderblom, September 19, 1929, to H. Bildt; Ebildslätt Papers.
[5] Dr. F. Holmström has made a detailed study of Söderblom's use of his earlier writings for *The Living God. Sv. Teol. Kvartalskrift*, 1937.

as writing to Söderblom's friend, Bishop Hensley Henson on his experience as a listener in St. Andrews.

Indeed, the idea has grown up that the Lecturship is a kind of Nobel Prize. ... Hence it comes that to dwindling and mystified audiences, men have lectured on the dreariest of philosophies, on obscene savage rites, or on the mathematical conception of the Universe. ... We have heard more about the philosophy of Plotinus than of the teaching of Jesus Christ.[6]

There was some Plotinus in Söderblom too, of course, and indeed his chapter on Socrates belongs to the most interesting and enduring sections of his book, the result of his intense and original study of Socrates in the period 1907–1910. In 1967 we met a mayor in a Scottish town, who hearing Söderblom's name, referred to his study of the Greek philosopher as the best he had ever come across.

But the message of Söderblom's Gifford Lectures was to be found in his conclusion on 'Continued Revelation'. There he summed up his experience and his thinking:

Indeed, to-day, after the miserable and gigantic breakdown of our Western Commonwealth and European politics, courage is needed to maintain, *quand même,* in spite of the bankruptcy of European statesmanship and the general unrest and actual or menacing economic disorder and distress, the confidence that history is in God's hands and that it has a goal, surpassing human understanding. God's Revelation is not finished—it continues.

To the task of Christian thought it belongs little by little to make history understood in a religious sense, that is, to make men learn to see in the whole of history, in a prophetic way, God's miracle, his revelation. For that purpose are required, first and last, a scholarly penetration of the leading ideas of Scripture, then a broad and deep study of history, also clear and comprehensive thought, well versed in the progress of human thinking, and a truly scientific frame of mind, ever ready to modify and correct conceptions and views, however dear, in deference to better information. But it is essential that such a Christian thinker on history should place himself within the glowing beams of light that issue forth from God's mercy in Christ.[7]

His last words in the book were a promise to provide an interpretation of the idea of saints as carriers of that continued revelation. He felt there was a need for it:

---

[6] H. Hensley Henson, *Retrospect II,* pp. 302–303.
[7] Söderblom, *The Living God* (1932), pp. 377–378.

But the idea of saints is too great a thing and too much neglected in Evangelic–Catholic Christendom to be handled here only at the end ... Here, I give only my definition: a saint is he who reveals God's might. Saints are such as show clearly and plainly in their lives and deeds and in their very being that God lives.[8]

The ten lectures at Edinburgh delivered between May 19 and June 8, 1931 were a great success. They were called *Basal Forms of Personal Religion;* this was as close to Tiele's title, *Elements of the Science of Religion,* as he cared to go. But he was naturally not satisfied with this title for the printed book. His very last thoughts were devoted to this problem. The dying Nathan Söderblom found his title, *'The Living God',* on July 12, 1931, his last day; he confided to his wife and children that he had just decided on the title, and he went on: 'There is a living God. I can prove it by the History of Religions.'

This was, indeed, what all his Religionsgeschichte had aimed at throughout the years. In 1910 he had summed up his book *Religionsproblemet* in the same formula, 'The Living God'. At that time, a 'life mysticism' which did not admit the reality of Christian revelation was a target of his criticism. Against that alternative he placed in his book the assurance he had from the Bible and from the Swedish historian Geijer. 'Life' had been his theme throughout the years and 'Life' was the theme once again, even to the dying ... 'life in its essence is nothing less than the will of the Living God, who wills us truly alive'.[9] This had been his faith at the outset. This too was his key to Life Beyond.

---

[8] Ibid., p. 386.

[9] Söderblom, *Religionsproblemet* (1910), p. 442.

Some important dates

1866 Born 15 January, in the manse of Trönö, Hälsingland, as second son of Jonas Söderblom, curate, and Sophia, daughter of Dr. Laurentius R. Blume

1873 Hudiksvall Grammar School

1881 Confirmed at Bjuråker, by his father

1883 Matriculated at High School, Hudiksvall. First sermon, at Hälsingtuna, Midsummer Day. Immatriculated Uppsala University, September 19

1886 B.A. (Cand. Phil.) in Latin, Greek, Semitic and Nordic Languages, Philosophy and Geology

1887 Joined 'Allmänna Sången' choir

1888–93 Editor, *Meddelanden fr. Studentmissionsföreningen*

1890 Visit to United States, end of May through August

1890 First Curator, Gästrike-Hälsinge Nation. Elected member, O.D. Choir.

1891 YMCA conference Amsterdam

1892–93 President, Uppsala Student corps

1893 Ordained Priest, by Bishop Gottfrid Billing

1894 Pastor, Paris and Calais. Married Anna Forsell (b. 1870, d. 1955)

1897 Religionsvetenskapliga Kongressen, Stockholm, September

1898 *The Sermon on the Mount*

1901 Defended doctoral thesis at the Sorbonne, *La vie future d'après le Mazdéisme,* transl. by B. Quirielle

1901–14 Professor in Theological Encyclopedia and Theological Prenotions, Uppsala University
Prebendary, Holy Trinity, Uppsala

1903 *Religion of Revelation.* Tiele's *Compendium,* 3rd ed.

1905 Restauration of Holy Trinity Church, Uppsala

1908 Olaus Petri Foundation established
Serious attack of intestinal ulcer
(to Karlsbad); Oxford August–October

1910 *Religionsproblemet*

1911 To Rome, Athens, Constantinople

1912 Professor, History of Religion, Leipzig University, while retaining his Uppsala chair

1913 Church of the Revelation, Saltsjöbaden

1914 Archbishop of Uppsala, appointed May 20, consecrated November 8.
Pastoral Charge; Peace Appeal; Origin of Belief in God
Pro-Chancellor, Uppsala University

1915 His first *Kyrkomöte*. First invitation for a World Alliance Conference,
Uppsala
(H. Neander to Germany and Russia)

1916 Visitations, in Diocese, to 40 congregations

1917 Nordic Church Conference, Uppsala; Reformation Jubilee; Luther
lectures. (Johs Kolmodin to Constantinople)

1918 Attempts at international Christian conference, Uppsala

1918–19 Olaus Petri Found. series on Ecumenical Problems

1919 Faith & Order delegation to Uppsala. World Alliance conference at
Oud Wassenaar, Holland. *Humour and Melancholy in Luther*

1919–21 Relief work for Germany and Austria

1920 First conference of Life and Work, Geneva, August. Vice President,
Faith & Order movement
Episcopal consecration Uppsala, with Anglican participation, and
with Greek Orthodox Metropolitan

1921 Consecration, Reval (Tallinn)
Peterborough: Life and Work: Chairman European section. Polish
Church conference, Uppsala. Member, Swedish Academy

1922 World Alliance, Copenhagen. Life and Work, Hälsingborg
Consecrations, Riga. Visitations to Swedish-speaking congregations,
Estonians Islands
First serious heart attack (Dec. 1922–March 1923 seriously ill: to
Nauheim)

1923 Swedish Bishops' protest over Ruhr
To the United States, September through December. *Christian Fellowship*

1924 Copec, Birmingham
Hainstein, Germany. *From Uppsala to Rock Island*

1925 The Universal Christian Conference on Life and Work, Stockholm
(and Uppsala) 19–30 August
Nicea Jubilee, London

1926 Evangelism week, in the diocese
Sermon, League of Nations, Geneva. Life & Work conference at
Berne. First radio sermon. Donellan Lectures, Dublin (on Luther)

1927 Lausanne Conf. Faith & Order
Diocesan Priests' meeting. Uppsala University 450 years jubilee. *Passion of Christ*

1928 World Alliance conf. Prague
Hon. Chairman, European section Life and Work. Task as President
of same handed over to Dr. Kapler
Consecration, Modra (Slovakia). Visit to Dorpat

1929 The Swedish Bishops' "Proposition" on Church and State. Burge Lectures, King's College, on 'The Church and Peace'

1930 Life & Work conf. Chêxbres. Nobel Prize for Peace

1931 Gifford Lectures, Edinburgh (publ. posthumously as *The Living God,* 1932); *Pater Max Pribilla u. die ökumenische Erweckung*
Youth Conference; Planning Evangelist campaign for the diocese
Died at Uppsala July 12. Funeral, July 18. Grave below High Altar, Uppsala Cathedral

Design and inscription (Luke 17:10) on tombstone.

Index